DOWN IN THE DUMPS

Duke University Press   *Durham and London*   2008

DOWN IN THE DUMPS

PLACE, MODERNITY, AMERICAN DEPRESSION

Jani Scandura

© 2008 Duke University Press
All rights reserved
Printed in the United States of
America on acid-free paper ∞
Designed by Amy Ruth Buchanan
Typeset in Minion, Matrix, and
Futura by BW&A Books, Inc.
Library of Congress Cataloging-in-
Publication Data appear on the last
printed page of this book.

Duke University Press gratefully
acknowledges the support of the
University of Minnesota, which
provided funds toward the
production of this book.

IN MEMORY OF CLARE AND LUCY

TO ZACH

IN SPACE YOU CAN BE ANOTHER PERSON.

—SUSAN SONTAG

Contents

IMAGES xi

ACKNOWLEDGMENTS xv

INTRODUCTION A GEOGRAPHY OF DEPRESSION 1

1 **RENO** THE DIVORCE FACTORY 30

2 **KEY WEST** THE NATION AND THE CORPSE 70

3 **HARLEM** BLUE-PENCILED PLACE 122

4 **HOLLYWOOD(LAND)** WAX, FIRE, INSOMNIA 186

AFTERWORD THE PRISON AND THE PENTAGON 234

NOTES 247

WORKS CITED 285

INDEX 303

Images

Breadline at the FDR Memorial, Washington, D.C. xx
Unpublished cover of the *New Yorker*, March 4, 1933. Peter Arno 13
"In the Dumps—a profitable pastime," circa 1930s 15
Still from *My Man Godfrey* (Universal 1936) 15
Author's notes on English edition of Walter Benjamin's
  The Arcades Project (1999). 16–17
Map of Reno in *Fortune*, April 1934 30
Cartoon in *Vanity Fair*, August 1, 1931 33
Postcard for *The Women* (MGM 1939) 34
"Hooray! I'm a free woman!" Postcard 36
Reno Arch (1931). Postcard 38
Reno Arch (1937). Postcard 38
Reno Arch (1950). Postcard 38
Reno Arch (1964). Postcard 38
Reno Arch (1986). Architectural drawing 38
Four views of the Riverside Hotel (1862, 1872, 1920, 1946). Postcard 40
Riverside Hotel (1994) 40
Website for The Riverside Artist Lofts (2004) 40
"The Divorce Factory." Cartoon reprinted from
  The Reno Divorce Racket, 1931 44
"Mrs. Massie on way to Reno." ACME Newspictures photo,
  January 10, 1934 47
Entrance to the Stockade, circa 1940 47
"Just Married." Postcard, circa 1930s 52
Mary and Little Mary reading. Still from *The Women* (MGM 1939) 53
C Street, Virginia City, 1940 55
Transcript of *Baker v. Baker*, case no. 38,192 58
Cover of the *Reno Divorce Racket*, 1931 60
"The Cure." Postcard, 1930s 63

"Express to Reno." Postcard, 1913 65

Still from *The Women* (MGM 1939) 67

Demolition of the Mapes Hotel, January 2000 68

FERA clean-up. Cartoon, 1930s, by A. Dornbrush 70

"Key West To Get New Birth." Special edition of the
    Florida Keys Sun, July 1934 73

"Abandoned cigar factory. Key West, Florida." January 1938 75

FERA advertisement for tourism. December 15, 1934 77

Spaniards Landing at Cayo Hueso. WPA mural
    by William Hoffmann 79

FERA reconstruction of Key West. WPA mural
    by William Hoffmann 79

"Havana—the Paris of the Western Hemisphere." Postcard, 1931 81

Page from the August 20, 1933, edition of the Cuban
    magazine *Carteles* 82

"Over-the-Seas-Railroad to Key West." Stereoscopic print, 1926 83

Wreck of relief train at Marathon Key after 1935 hurricane 83

The Southernmost Point, 1995 84

The Key West Aquarium, 1935 87

Fishing trip (1930s) with Ernest Hemingway in Waldo Peirce's
    Key West scrapbook 91

Studio by Loren MacIver, 1939 94

Manuscript page of Elizabeth Bishop's story "Mercedes Hospital" 97

Bahama Village from Duval Street, 1995 102

Jungletown by Loren MacIver, 1939 102

Von Cosel and onlookers 104

The corpse of Elena Milagro Hoyos at the Dean-Lopez
    Funeral Home 106

Dead relief worker. Photo, Hemingway Collection 109

Elizabeth Bishop's typescript and notes on
    "Grandmother's Glass Eye" 113

Arm found in the belly of a shark. Detail from Waldo Peirce's
    Key West scrapbook 119

The Seven Mile Bridge and the remains of the Overseas Highway,
    Key West, 2005 120

Map of Harlem, 1953, signed by Langston Hughes 122

Exhibition Catalogue from Jacob Lawrence's "Harlem" exhibit,
    May 1943 124
Research notes by Jacob Lawrence for The Life of John Brown
    series, 1941. 126
Exhibition at Downtown Gallery, 1941, of Jacob Lawrence's
    The Migration of the Negro series 126
This is Harlem by Jacob Lawrence 128
Poster for the New York City WPA Federal Art Project, 1938 128
Lenox Lounge, Malcolm X Boulevard, Harlem, 2005 130
Arna Bontemps and Langston Hughes, circa 1948 132
"Signs in the window of a Marcus Garvey club" in Harlem, 1943 133
Press release for *Fire!!*, 1926 137
Draft of "Harlem/Good Morning, Daddy" by Langston Hughes 139
"New York's Harlem has its Housing Problems." Photo, 1946 142
Langston Hughes and Wallace Thurman, circa 1934 147
Langston Hughes and Dorothy West traveling to the
    Soviet Union, 1932 147
Dorothy West and Helene Johnson, circa 1920s 147
Manuscript page from Bruce Nugent's unpublished novel
    "Gentleman Jigger" 152
"Luxurious Condos" in Harlem, 2005 154
The Gumby Book Studio. Page of the L. S. Alexander Gumby
    Scrapbooks 156
Correspondence on the Gumby Book Studio in the Gumby
    Scrapbooks 160
Untitled (f.x. profumo) by Ray Johnson 161
Newspaper clipping on "The Collyer Hoard" 164
Collyer Brothers Park, Harlem, 2005 164
Pages 1–2 of Carl Van Vechten's Scrapbook III 167
Newspaper clippings on 1935 Harlem riot in the Gumby
    Scrapbooks 170
Technician taking an X ray in a Harlem clinic, 1930s 174
Family portrait of W. E. B. and Nina Gomer Du Bois and
    their son, Burghardt, circa 1897 175
Page of Wallace Thurman's draft of "Male X" 178
"Death Writes a Book." Cartoon by Chase in the Gumby Scrapbooks 181

Last known photo of Zora Neale Hurston, 1950s..................182

Helene Johnson reading to her daughter, 1940s..................184

Malcolm X Boulevard, New York City, February 2005..................185

"A Map of Hollywood." Cartoon, 1930s..................186

Hollywoodland poster, 1924..................188

Temple at Babylon. Still from D. W. Griffith's *Intolerance* (1916)..................190

Babylon set *Intolerance* (1916) amid Los Angeles bungalows..................190

Kodak Theatre, Los Angeles, 2005..................190

"Hollywood Reproduces the Riviera" in *Life* magazine,
    January 2, 1939..................192

Jean Harlow at Grauman's Chinese Theater, 1933..................196

Image from Bill Morrison's film, *The Mesmerist* (2003, 1926)..................197

Lyle Wheeler, his assistant, and the miniature of Atlanta for
    Gone With the Wind (1939)..................201

Still from *The Mystery of the Wax Museum* (1933)..................205

Fire at Warner Brothers (1952)..................214

Hollywood Brown Derby, circa 1930s..................216

Hollywood Brown Derby, 2005..................216

Temple in *The King of Kings* (1926)..................218

Jungle in *King Kong* (1933)..................218

The Burning of Atlanta in *Gone With the Wind* (1939)..................219

"French Street." MGM standing set, 1939..................220

Stand-ins for Cary Grant and Katharine Hepburn. Still from
    Bringing Up Baby (1938)..................222

Still from *The Wizard of Oz* (1939)..................226

"Girl on the Street. Hollywood, Calif." Photo, 1942..................229

Nipomo Dunes, 1990s..................233

San Francisco Ferry Terminal, circa 2000..................234

Alcatraz, outside view, circa 1930s..................236

Clothing factory on Alcatraz, circa 1930s..................237

War Department Building. *Popular Mechanics*, 1943..................239

Lunchtime in the Pentagon Building courtyard, April 17, 1943..........242

Old airplane hangars on the site of the Pentagon, 1941..................243

Acknowledgments

LIKE EVERY GENERATION THAT PRECEDED US, WE HAVE BEEN ENDOWED WITH A WEAK MESSIANIC POWER, A POWER TO WHICH THE PAST HAS A CLAIM. THAT CLAIM CANNOT BE SETTLED CHEAPLY.
—**WALTER BENJAMIN**, "THESES ON THE PHILOSOPHY OF HISTORY"

When you work on a book for many years, your debts run deep. For this project, costly in both time and money, it is especially true. I have been supported by a number of institutions along the way. I completed the book while an assistant professor at the University of Minnesota, variously supported by funding from the Department of English, the College of Liberal Arts, and the Graduate School, which provided me with two generous Grants-in-Aid, summer research funding, a semester leave, and a production grant. The McKnight Foundation also funded my research for two summers. The College of Liberal Arts, the Humanities Institute, and the Institutes for Global Studies funded the Space & Place Research Collective, which provided me with an intellectual forum that was essential to the completion of this project. Parts of this book were also completed on a postdoctoral fellowship in the humanities at Stanford University and, in the final production stages, at the Centre for Research in the Arts, Social Sciences, and Humanities (CRASSH) at the University of Cambridge. At the University of Michigan, where this project found its genesis, I was supported by grants from the Rackham School of Graduate Studies, the Mellon Foundation, the University of Michigan Department of English, the John F. Kennedy Library, the Hemingway Society, and the Center for the Education of Women. A portion of the chapter on Reno was published in *Modernism, Inc.: Body Memory, Capital* (New York UP, 2001), which I coedited with Michael Thurston; and a version of a section of the Hollywood chapter was published as "Cinematic Insomnia" in *New Formations* (Summer 2004). Early drafts of this book were presented as lectures at many venues, including the English Institute at Harvard University; the Modern Language Association conference; the American Studies Association conference; the Modernist Studies Association conference; the American Association of Geographers; and the British Society for Historical Geographers.

Many, many curators and librarians, some of whom have now moved on to other jobs, advised me, assisted me in digging up materials, and were generally indispensable. I would particularly like to thank Robert Parks at the Franklin D. Roosevelt Presidential Library; Lee Mortensen, Eric Moody, Lee P. Brumbaugh, and Phillip I. Earl at the Nevada Historical Society in Reno; Susan Searcy, Jacquelyn Sundstrand, and Kathryn Totton in Special Collections at the University of Nevada, Reno; Patricia Burdick, Special Collections Librarian, Miller Library, Colby College; Silvia Inwood at the Detroit Institute of Art; Alan Goodrich, Susan Wrynn, Megan Floyd Desnoyers, and, especially, Stephen Plotkin at the Ernest Hemingway Collection at the John F. Kennedy Library; Dean Rogers and Nancy MacKechnie at Vassar College Libraries Special Collections; Tom Hambright at the Monroe County Public Library in Key West; Norman Aberle at the East Martello Museum in Key West; Bob Cerkleski at the Key West Aquarium; Clayton L. Lopez at the Key West Neighborhood Improvement Association, Monroe County Public Health Unit; Michael Knes at the Detroit Public Library; Sandra Levinson, Director of Cuban Art Space and Executive Director of the Center for Cuban Studies in New York; Steven C. Thomas, Curator of Collections, UCR/ California Museum of Photography; Tara C. Craig, Emily Holmes, and Jean Ashton at the Rare Book & Manuscript Library, Butler Library, Columbia University; Patricia Willis, Nancy Kuhl, and Taran Schindler at the Beinecke Rare Book and Manuscript Library, Yale University; Danielle Kovacs at the W. E. B. Du Bois Library, University of Massachusetts Amherst; Amy Densford at the Hirshhorn Museum and Sculpture Garden, Smithsonian Institution; Diana Lachatanere, Mary F. Yearwood, and the other curators at the Schomburg Center for Research in Black Culture, The New York Public Library; Flo Turcotte, Special Collections, George A. Smathers Libraries, University of Florida; Wendy Hurlock Baker at the Archives of American Art, Smithsonian Institution; Cornelia Tishmacher at Richard L. Feigen & Co for providing materials and rights relating to Ray Johnson; Bruce Kellner for providing the rights to Carl Van Vechten's work; Thomas H. Wirth for providing materials and rights to work by Richard Bruce Nugent; Kathleen Collins at the New York Transit Museum Archives; Lauren Buisson, UCLA Arts Library Special Collections, Young Research Library; Jeff Rankin of the Public Service Division, Department of Special Collections, University Research Library, University of California, Los Angeles; Ned Comstock at the Cinema-Television Library, Edward L. Doheny Jr. Memorial Library, University of Southern California; Kristine Krueger, Faye Thompson, Linda Harris Mehr, and the other curators at the Margaret Herrick Library at the Academy of Motion Pictures; David Coleman, Linda Briscoe Meyers, and Steve Wilson at the Harry Ransom Humanities Research Center, University of Texas at Austin; Anthony L'Abbate, Stills Archivist, Motion Picture Department, George Eastman House; Marc Wannamaker at the Bison Archives; Bruce Torrence at hollywoodphotos.com; Mary Ilario and Holly Reed from the National Archives and Records Administration; Jacalyn R. Blume from the Schlesinger Library, Radcliffe Institute for Advanced Studies, Harvard University; Marcia Pancake, Matt Bowers, and Anh Na Brodie at the University of Minnesota libraries; Victoria Fox at Farrar, Straus and Giroux for securing rights to publish materials by Elizabeth Bishop; Wendy Thompson from Art Space, Inc.; the curators at the Wisconsin Center for Film and Theater Research, Wisconsin Historical Society, Madison; Michael Stier at Condé Nast; Dennis O. Palmore and Kurt Beals at New Directions Press; the James Laughlin family for providing materials related to Elizabeth Bishop; Dorothy Davis for providing permission to reprint an image by Griffith Davis; and Harold Ober Associates for providing permission to use manuscripts by Langston Hughes.

Several people, some of whom have since passed away, shared their lives, stories, and opinions with me including, Stetson Kennedy, Jimmy Dean, the Delaney family, and Eveillo and Mimi Cabot. I also am grateful to the photographers who searched their archives or took new photos at my request for this book: Stephen Bay, Tim Dunn, Frank Jermann, Terrah Johnson, Christy Transier Jonas, Mike Long, Michael O'Brien, Rob O'Neal, Lynn Radeka, Jeff Spicer, and my brother Joe Scandura, who trekked up to Harlem one cold winter day, his wife and new baby in tow. At various stages and in various guises, scholars, artists, and otherwise engaged individuals gave me helpful advice or provided useful input, including Molly Arrighi, Ed Baker, Dana Barton, Michael Bérubé, Erin Carlston, Mario Coyola, Jim Dawes, Tim Edensor, Laurel Erickson, Linda Groat, Beth Haas, June Howard, Mary Jacobus, Lemuel Johnson, Ludmilla Jordanova, David Levenstein, Jean Leverich, Sandra Levinson, Eric Lott, Janet Lyon, Scott McCracken, Mitchell Morris, Bill Morrison, David Nicholls, Erin O'Connor, Don Pease, Mike Reynolds, Bruce Robbins, Charles Rosenberg, Marlon Ross, Steve Soper, Karla Taylor, Rei Terada, Michael Thurston, Athena Vrettos, and the anonymous readers for Duke University Press. Elizabeth Allen, Lauren Berlant, Bill Brown, Russ Castronova, Alvia Golden, Cary Nelson, Eliza Richards, Carroll Smith-Rosenberg, and Leah R. Rosenberg deserve special recognition for their prodigious generosity over many years and in ways that I could not possibly have deserved. At Duke University Press, Anitra Sumaya Grisales was tireless in helping me get the manuscript and images ready for production. I would also like to thank the rest of the staff at Duke and especially Amy Ruth Buchanan and Mark Mastromarino for their work on this book. My editor, Ken Wissoker, was patient, wise, and generous; he believed in the project from the start and understood what I was trying to do. Simon Gikandi, Marjorie Levinson, Patsy Yaeger, and Geoff Eley have served as critics, advisors, and friends over the years in ways too numerous to count; there are few pages in this book upon which I cannot discern their marks.

At Minnesota, I have benefited from the insights of engaging and thoughtful colleagues, especially Bruce Braun, Dan Brewer, Juliette Cherbuliez, Lisa Disch, Vinay Gidwani, Muisi Krosi, Elaine Tyler May, Anca Parvulescu, Tom Pepper, Ajay Skaria, the members of the intercollegiate Americanist reading group at Macalester College, and, especially, Sonja Kuftinec, Karen Till, Margaret Werry, and the members of the Space & Place Research Collective. I am also grateful for the careful prodding and creative insights of my many students over the years, especially those who participated in my graduate seminars on The City, Depressive Modernity, and Modern Decay. Anca Parvulescu, Rebecca Scherr, Christina Schmid, Karen Steigman, Laura Zebhur, and Sara Cohen served as research assistants on this project. I owe them all tremendous thanks, especially to Christina, who in a Herculean six weeks helped clear the majority of rights to this project and acquired many of the images. I am also thankful to the staff of the Department of English and, in particular, to Pamela Leszinski and Rose Hendrickson for all their help in the final months of production. Colleagues in English who provided a supportive and rich intellectual environment in which to navigate the treacherous waters of junior faculty life, include Tom Augst, Sioban Craig, Pat Crain, Lois Cucullu, Maria Damon, Michael Hancher, Qadri Ismail, John Mowitt, Paula Rabinowitz, Rita Raley, Marty Roth, and Charlie Sugnet. Tom, Lois, Qadri, Pat, Paula, John, and Maria offered significant input on my writing over the years. And it is no exaggeration to say that to Paula, Pat, John, and Michael, especially, I owe my current livelihood.

Pam Kruger, David Rosensweig, Emily and Annie; Eric Hamilton and Linda Radosovitch; Maria Nordone; Wendy and Keir Dougall; Bruce Sandys; Leah Rosenberg; and Ellen-Marie Whelan housed me during my travels to Boston, New York, Washington, D.C., Kingston, and Los Angeles for periods that were longer and more frequent than even good friendship requires. Jim and Helena Dodds helped with childcare on many, many occasions when I needed to write. Pat Noonan Wagner, Aminata Diakité, Ibrahim, and Sek quite simply made writing possible. Au-delà de ce que je pourrais exprimer, je suis reconnaissante à la famille Viale, en particulier Lucien, Anita, Michèle, Stéphan, et Maïté, qui nous ont aidé pendant notre sejour en France. Lori, Larry, Sam, Danie, and Kevin Bendesky; Jeanne Scandura; Jules, Michael, Sam, and Eli Catania; Joe, Agnès, Ella, and Margaux Scandura; Joe and Alice Scandura; and Alex are whom I came home to, when I needed a home, and provided a backdrop for everything I do. For many reasons, this book would not have come into existence in quite this way without J. Scott Dodds, who was particularly crucial in the crunch time at the end. Nor could this book exist in its present form without the benefit of many, many long conversations and exchanges with Karen Till, who taught me more about the natures of space, place, and memory than any person I have known; any erudition I possess on the nature of geography I owe to her—any limitations have resulted from times I didn't listen well. Susan Rosenbaum read every version of every chapter of this book, from its earliest inception. My intellectual debt to her is perhaps largest of all.

This book was inspired by the stories of my grandmothers—Clare Baker and Lucy Scandura—inspired by what they told me, and what they could not tell. It is dedicated to their memory and to my son, Zach, my baby, my love, who was born just as I was beginning to see the arch of an ending to this book—and who opened my eyes to worlds well beyond its scope.

Introduction

A GEOGRAPHY OF DEPRESSION

METHOD OF THIS PROJECT: LITERARY MONTAGE.
I NEEDN'T SAY ANYTHING. MERELY SHOW. I SHALL
PURLOIN NO VALUABLES, APPROPRIATE NO INGENIOUS
FORMULATIONS. BUT THE RAGS, THE REFUSE—THESE I WILL
NOT INVENTORY BUT ALLOW, IN THE ONLY WAY POSSIBLE,
TO COME INTO THEIR OWN: BY MAKING USE OF THEM.
—**WALTER BENJAMIN**, *THE ARCADES PROJECT*

RESEARCH IS FORMALIZED CURIOSITY. IT IS POKING AND
PRYING WITH PURPOSE.
—**ZORA NEALE HURSTON**, *DUST TRACKS ON A ROAD*

THE DUMP IS FULL
OF IMAGES.
—**WALLACE STEVENS**, "THE MAN ON THE DUMP"

prelude: "the significance of insignificance"

← Breadline at the FDR Memorial, Washington, D.C. © Michael O'Brien Photography.

New Yorkers called it The Hill, a soubriquet that somehow softened the awful irony of its name: Fresh Kills. Overshadowed by Ground Zero (The Pile), it eventually rose above it, so high that if you stood at The Hill's edge you couldn't see the shoreline it bordered or the skyscrapers that still lit the city beyond. For over half a century, Fresh Kills had been the depository for most of New York City's trash—150 million cubic yards of solid waste spread out over 2,200 acres on the western shore of Staten Island.[1] In recent years, it was an eyesore to the New Yorkers who'd thought about it and a frustration for environmentalists who wanted to reclaim the wetlands that lay beneath it. So in March 2001, amidst much fanfare, Mayor Rudolph Giuliani closed it down.

Six months later, Fresh Kills opened once again. It was there that the remains of the World Trade Center were brought and sorted: 107,000 truckloads carrying 1.62 million tons of rubble that contained, among other things, 4,100 body parts, 1,350 crushed vehicles, clumps of human hair, the engine from one of the hijacked planes, dozens of Gap bags and Fossil wristwatches, chicken bones from restaurants, silver police shields, Blue Cross/Blue Shield insurance cards, leather shoes, firefighters' boots, diamond engagement rings, American Express cards, corporate IDs, sets of keys, fragments of keyboards, broken photographs, charred photo slides, baseball memorabilia, stuffed animals, and a few battered but intact Rodin sculptures.[2]

Fresh Kills became "the other graveyard,"[3] a growing mound that stood in contrast to the gaping hole across the water in Manhattan—though what was to be buried there was ashes, the remains of remains that could not be identified. Certainly, fierce efforts were made to distinguish the sorting task from the garbage processing that had occurred in the landfill just months before. Eighteen inches of polyurethane and asphalt fill were laid over the decades of refuse to protect investigators from methane gas and to minimize the stench.[4] A small village was built, complete with trailers, a mess hall, huge sorting machines, and two donated palm trees. As the Police Department's chief of detectives, William Allee, insisted to a *New York Times* journalist, "These truckloads of destruction are not just being brought here and dumped in a big hole. There is a process. There is a protocol."[5]

For a while it seemed as if the obsessive investigation of the minutiae of debris, which was collected, classified, preserved, disposed of, or dispersed, might minimize the blow. People found comfort in matter, in the production of traces that seemed to allegorize both the inexplicable loss and the fragmentation of the American psyche itself. Discussions about memorial exhibits abounded. By then, Fresh Kills had become an archive, revealing the close interdependence archives always have with dumps and dumps with archives. Curators from museums and libraries passed through and laid claim to some of what was found, as did medical examiners, federal inspectors, World Trade Center survivors, and relatives of people killed in the attack. Things like a credit card or corporate ID that had seemed without much significance before they were identified suddenly were rich with narrative potential. People told stories about how those who had possessed the objects might have died. Burns, rips, and fissures endowed the lowliest of fragments—from objects that were boring, ordinary, mass-produced—with the status of sacred relics.[6] Fragments of glass, bags of dust, canceled checks were gathered from the site to be preserved in private collections.[7]

It became clearer at that point how much history has to do with death, grief, and the fantasies of mourning; how much history is itself a substitute for the ineffable, for that which exceeds discourse and cannot be articulated; and how dependent historical narrative is upon serendipity, materiality, melancholia. There are pitfalls to endowing an actual, lived, and living place with the status of allegory, though that is, in part, how history gets produced. If the Twin Towers had been built as monuments to the grandeur and self-righteousness of progressive modernity (for it was progressive modernity and America's recurrent determination to embody it that were threatened in the attack), Fresh Kills seemed an allegory for modernity's less spectacular depressive twin, a modernity that moves neither forward nor backward, but idles, trembling, face-to-face with the fallout of progress.[8]

In truth, of course, Fresh Kills must be seen as an allegory for both progressive and depressive modernities. Many recuperated the place and cleanup process through narratives of self-congratulatory exceptionalism: such a task of dismantling and sorting had never been undertaken before.[9] The Twin Towers were similarly endowed with a double-edged role. They were built, remember, on landfill, thus suggesting both the spectacular heights to which garbage may be raised and the less popular vision of Capital built upon the foundations of its own refuse.

It therefore should have been expected: In March 2002, while debates raged about how lower Manhattan would be redesigned and the World Trade Center memorialized, while the medical examiner was still running DNA tests on fragments of hair and bone, New York City's new mayor, Michael Bloomberg, was faced with a garbage crisis. He reopened Fresh Kills as a dump.[10]

DOWN IN THE DUMPS

This is a book about dumps and depression. It is also about history and place and, even more so, about how Americans make place and are placed, and how they memorialize and memorialized their own history through place, making and remaking a past and its relationship to the present. That this brings us to American Depression is not accidental. If the American Revolution and the Enlightenment discourse that spawned it might be said to have been an inaugural moment (if not the inaugural moment) of modernity, and if America itself might be seen as modernity's poster child or even allegory,[11] then *Depression* must be seen as a central term in late modernity, a depressive modernity, a modernity that does not follow the forward thrust of mania, speed, and progress, but of depression, idling, and refuse—a modernity that is not so much a wasteland, as it is, in the words of Bessie Smith's song, "down in the dumps."[12] This book is itself a dump of sorts. It is narrated through unlikely associations and odd juxtapositions, conversation, and remembrance; it is chock-full of scraps—the refused and refusing matters, memories, subjectivities, and aesthetic forms of a modernity depressed.

When I refer to American Depression and to depressive modernity, then, I mean something broader than a historical moment of economic collapse. The temporal frame of this project lies at the borders of the U.S. governmental and business depression of 1928 to 1941. Often it traverses those limits, however, and, more often, it throws them out altogether. Moreover, the archives and arguments with which I am concerned are more allegorical and performative than empirical, although I rely heavily on materials that are connected to a specific moment or material site. *Depression* derives etymologically from the past participle of the Latin *deprimere* (to press down, dig deep, or plant deeply in the ground); it thus associates an affective state with spatial action. Because it also suggests "being brought down in status or fortune,"[13] even more than melancholia, depression associates psychological ill health with the attainment or loss of capital.

This was not always so. In the nineteenth-century United States, the term "depression" was generally used with a modifier, such as "economic"; "melancholia" was the term of choice for "blue devil" moods. After the 1929 stock market crash, however, "depression" came to refer simultaneously (and without antecedent) to psychological ill health and financial collapse in American clinical and popular discourse. The so-called Great Depression was marked both by economic and mass psychological depression. In 1933, a New York Home Relief Bureau supervisor described victims of the Depression as "sick, mentally and physically."[14] The following year, a Federal Emergency Relief Administration (FERA) investigator in New York reported that "'almost every one of her clients had 'talked of suicide at one time or another.'"[15] Suicide rates in the United States were higher throughout the 1930s than in the decade before or at anytime since.[16] The blurring of affect with economics that became visible in the Great Depression gestures toward larger transformations in the ways that Americans, and possibly modern subjects more generally, conceived of themselves and remembered and narrated modern experience. Indeed, the Depression might best be seen as a metonym for an ongoing ontological crisis within modern U.S. culture, a crisis that must be returned to over and over again in different guises and in different writings.[17]

It can be argued, for instance, that underlying much of the passivity with which many Americans initially acquiesced to the curtailing of civil rights, the inevitable news of corporate racketeering, and the single-minded neo-imperialist aggression of a deeply conservative and controversially elected government, the George W. Bush administration, was a deep-seated and recurrent collective national depression. I am not talking about the posttraumatic stress suffered by New York children after the collapse of the Twin Towers, or the squeamishness felt by many Americans when they returned to air travel, or even to the more deeply personal anguish experienced by those who were sent to fight in Iraq, or who had family in Baghdad or elsewhere in the Middle East, or even to the grief of those who were rounded up by the Immigration and Naturalization Service (INS) on some vague visa violation or kept without legal recourse in American prison camps. I am instead referring to a more enduring affective component of Americanism that exposes itself at those moments when the axioms of American culture and progressive modernity itself—capitalism, democracy, individualism, secularism, utopianism—are not so much brought under siege as put into question.[18] Always such moments are haunted by the specter of depression and the Depression, which is both a sign and symptom of what American national culture has never—and can never—fully work through.[19]

Depressive modernity is modernity in place. This is not to suggest that it is a strictly spatialized modernity or that it might be seen as the binary opposite of a temporalized or progressive modernity.[20] Nor can it be said to be a wholly discursive concept; it contains within it visceral, experiential, and affective residues. In the pages that follow, I produce texts out of places of refuse, dumps if you will—Reno, Key West, Harlem, Hollywood. But while place can be produced and read like a text, it is not itself a text.[21] Instead, I see place as a constellation of relations that resonates with what Henri Bergson, in his 1896 work *Matière et Mémoire* (*Matter and Memory*), calls *durée*. *Durée*, translated imprecisely as "duration," is usually read as a temporalizing move, albeit one that conceives of a mobile and multiplicitous time.[22] But Bergson's *durée* actually strives for an existence that is antidualistic, a "lived reality" that is "halfway between" homogeneous space and time, movement and fixity, "thing" and "representation."[23] It is upon this Bergson that Walter Benjamin draws when he lays out what he conceives of as a new theory

plan of work

1. Abstract
Down in the Dumps: Place, Modernity and the American Depression
During the Depression, the U.S. government and other powerful social and elite institutions used narratives of place to construct a cohesive model of Americanism. At the same time, competing practices of representation transformed portraits of abstract American space into highly particularized places whose very existence subverted monumental constructions of Progressive modernity and American national identity. This project focuses on four of these places—Reno, Key West, Harlem, and Hollywood—all of which served as depositories of individuals, objects, and narratives that refused or were refused by Progressive fictions of American identity. Each place tells a crucial story about a depressed America that reflects on the wreckage left in the wake of Progress and reveals how dominant narratives, such as Roosevelt's New Deal, attempted to incorporate the mess and repress difference. And each place exposes the transgressive logic through which refused Americans asserted themselves. Using the methods and resources of literary and architectural theory, cultural criticism, and extensive archival materials, *Down in the Dumps* uncovers a place-centered *vernacular modernism* that intersects high modernisms with mass culture and the products and experiences of everyday life.

2. Present Status of Knowledge
This project engages with a number of critical debates:[1]

a. Concerns about the relationship between modernity and space.
In recent years, theories of place and space have become prominent topics of discussion. The bulk of theoretical work, however, has focused on postmodern spatiality. Spatial modernism, marked by International Style, has been considered atopic or placeless. Consequently, the social, psychic, and aesthetic implications of a modernist notion of place seem at first counterintuitive. Indeed, most literary critics implicitly follow Fredric Jameson's assertion that space is the defining concern of postmodern rather than modern consciousness, which was dominated by temporal considerations. An increasing number of critics, such as David Harvey (*The Condition of Postmodernity: An Enquiry into the Origins of Cultural Change*, 1990), Peter Osborne (*The Politics of Time: Modernity and Avant-Garde*, 1995), and Henri Lefebvre (*The Production of Space*, 1991), have begun to question the complex relationship between modernity and space. Osborne points out, for instance, that it is in the repressed spatial premises of the concept of modernity that its political logic is to be found. Nonetheless, questions about spatial modernism remain underinvestigated—and politically fraught.

Focusing on 1930s American culture, *Down in the Dumps* investigates the material and ideological dynamics of place as a site for opposition as well as oppression. In doing so, I uncover what I call a depressive modernity, a modernity concerned not with Progress and speed, but with what Walter Benjamin calls the "wreckage of progress," the refuse that is left in its wake.

b. Revisions in cultural geography and theories of place.

My assumptions about place draw on an exciting new body of work by cultural geographers and architectural theorists. The new geographies of Edward Soja, Neil Smith, Doreen Massey, and Michael Keith and Steve Pile hypothesize "a different sense of place . . . no longer passive, no longer fixed, no longer undialectical . . . but, still, in a very real sense about location and locatedness." So far, however, these new geographies have tended to focus on contemporary culture and have difficulty "thinking backward" to the conflicted historical legacy of modernity. The influence of poststructuralist thinking has encouraged some geographers to think about space and place as text or as textlike (see, for instance, T. Barnes and J. Duncan, eds., *Writing Worlds: Discourse, Text and Metaphor in the Representation of Landscape*, 1991; J. Duncan, *The City as Text: The Politics of Landscape Interpretation in the Kandyan Kingdom*, 1990; D. Cosgrove and S. Daniels, eds. *The Iconography of Landscape: Essays on the Symbolic Representation, Design and Use of Past Environments*, 1989). This approach is still being hotly debated in geography circles. However, the stakes of the debate generally rely on a less nuanced interpretation of textuality, metaphor, and poststructuralist thought than has been the tendency in literary studies. In addition, the questions geographers ask are often somewhat removed from literary critics' concerns about language and aesthetics. In an effort to respond to these gaps, *Down in the Dumps* proposes a historically, materially, and aesthetically contingent theory of place. Rather than exploring representations of space in fiction or poetry, as some literary critics are doing, this project takes such diverse discourses as literature, cinema, architecture, fine art, advertisements, and cartoons as a collective and dynamically unfictive agency through which place is performed and produced.

c. Revisionist modernism and criticism of 1930s American culture.

My work also engages in contemporary literary debates about 1930s modernism. Revisionist criticism on 1930s American culture and modernism has tended in two directions: It either focuses exclusively on the labor movements and writings of radical intellectuals of the period, or it is primarily concerned with international High Modernism in an attempt to revise it. Alan M. Wald's *The Revolutionary Imagination* (1983), *The New York Intellectuals* (1986), and *Writing from the Left* (1994) situate 1930s labor writing within the larger discourse of literary modernism. Paula Rabinowitz's *Labor and*

Desire: Women's Revolutionary Fiction in Depression America (1991) theorizes the relationship of women's literary production during the 1930s to constructions of class subjectivity. Cary Nelson's *Repression and Recovery: Modern American Poetry and the Politics of Cultural Memory, 1910–1945* (1989) and Walter Kalaidjian's *American Culture between the Wars: Revisionary Modernism and Postmodern Critique* (1993) use a cultural studies approach to consider the relationship between High Modernist aesthetics, mass culture, and literary radicalism during the Depression. Shari Benstock's *Women of the Left Bank* (1987), Bonnie Kime Scott's *Refiguring Modernism: Women of 1928* (1995), Joseph A. Boone's *Libidinal Currents: Sexuality and the Shaping of Modernism* (1998), Rita Felski's *The Gender of Modernity* (1995), and Erin G. Carlston's *Thinking Fascism: Sapphic Modernism and Fascist Modernity* (1998) reframe critical assumptions about High Modernist aesthetics by engaging with theories of gender and sexuality and foregrounding works by marginalized or forgotten writers. Other critics, such as Houston A. Baker Jr. (*Modernism and the Harlem Renaissance*, 1987), Ann Douglas (*Terrible Honesty: Mongrel Manhattan in the 1920s*, 1995), Walter Benn Michaels (*Our America: Nativism, Modernism, and Pluralism*, 1995), Michael North (*The Dialect of Modernism: Race, Language, and Twentieth-Century Literature*, 1994) and George Hutchinson (*The Harlem Renaissance in Black and White*, 1995), emphasize the American context of modernism, particularly with regard to questions of race and ethnicity. But these writers focus largely, though not exclusively, on the period before the 1928 economic collapse.

Down in the Dumps resituates American modernism in the 1930s; and while it engages questions of labor, it focuses more largely on the place-inflected culture and aesthetics of everyday life. I argue that you can understand something about a writer's relationship to the ideologies embedded in a place through her aesthetics of representing it. The paradigm of place I employ allows me to set so-called High Modernist texts, such as those by Wallace Stevens, Ernest Hemingway, and Hart Crane, in conversation with the products of mass culture, the built environment, and political discourse as well as with unpublished or marginal works by writers such as Elizabeth Bishop, Mary McCarthy, Clare Boothe Luce, and Rudolph Fisher. Reading "refuse," I look both at those texts written by noncanonical writers and those texts that canonical writers themselves refused—their notebooks, scrapbooks, doodles, and excised passages from manuscripts. Deeply reliant on archival materials, *Down in the Dumps* is finally about the tension between archives and dumps. It is about that which we allow ourselves to remember—and that which we force ourselves to forget we ever knew. This is a narrative work as much as an analytical one. I employ multiple and fragmentary forms of prose narrative (journalism, autobiography, ethnography) in the conduct of analytical writing. The goal is to respond in my own labors to the critique I engage with textual materials. It is, then, a work deeply engaged with the postmodern as Jean-François

Lyotard defines it (*The Postmodern Condition: A Report on Knowledge*, 1985) for I am as concerned with examining the processes and methods of critical construction as I am with critical artifacts themselves. My hope is not merely to provide new ways of reading both canonical and underexamined modernist literary texts, but to begin to clarify a spatial genealogy of postmodernism.

3. Plan of Work

Each of the chapters of *Down in the Dumps* explores different narrative strategies for dealing with the multiple forms of refuse that were produced by—or became visible within—American culture during the 1930s. Part I examines the Reno divorce factory. Projecting a twisted Fordist industrialism onto a regendered American frontier, the Reno factory proposes to Reno-vate independent divorcées into ideal New Industrial Wives: heterosexual mothers who shop. Part II investigates the Afro-Anglo-Cuban bridge-space of a destitute Key West, annexed by the Federal Emergency Relief Administration and promoted as a microcosm of New Deal experimentation. Yet embedded in Key West's Caribbean aesthetic of discarded scraps, odd juxtapositions, and dismembered body parts is a renegade ideology of salvaging in which one survives and creates precisely from what others throw out. Part III considers the archiving of Renaissance Harlem in the 1930s through a complex discourse of remembrance, rewriting, and disassociation, what I call "writing in blue pencil." Part IV focuses on Hollywood, which Nathanael West called the "dump of dreams" to read the constructions of place, artifice, and identity embedded in representations of 1930s Hollywood architecture and set design.

A grant-in-aid will enable me to complete the research necessary to finish my book. To date, I have completed revised drafts of the first three chapters of the project. I still have substantial revisions to do on the Harlem chapter and need to conduct primary research for the Hollywood chapter. Because the project is concerned with narratives of place and is grounded in an analysis of unprocessed archival materials, it requires a significant amount of research time at libraries and in private collections in the cities I study.

4. Budget Justification

A grant-in-aid will enable me to spend one month in Los Angeles to gather archival and documentary materials during spring quarter, 1999, when I have a teaching release. I expect to use resources at the UCLA library special collections and film archives, the USC Cinema-Television Library, and the Margaret Herrick Library of the Motion Picture Academy of Arts & Sciences. I also will need to explore the city, and in particular visit a dig site in Guadalupe, where archeologists are excavating the massive buried set of Cecil B. DeMille's 1923 film *The Ten Commandments*. In addition, I plan to make shorter trips to New York City and Washington, D.C. In New York, I will visit the Motion Picture Film Stills Archive at the Museum of Modern Art to find film stills for the Hollywood and Reno chapters of the project. I will also make a return trip to the Schomburg Center for Research in Black Culture in order to use their periodicals and music collections, which will assist me in making revisions on my Harlem chapter. In Washington, I plan to make a return visit to the Library of Congress to look at WPA materials and to screen several rare films. Finally, I am applying for funds for a part-time research assistant (9 months, 25 percent time) to help me track down necessary out-of-print, rare, and obscure materials.

5. Word Count (Parts 1–4)
1. 183
2. 1,278
3. 366
4. 278

Budget

Personnel:
Research assistant: (9 months at 25 percent): $7,704

Trip to Los Angeles (4 weeks):
Flight to LAX: $478
Rental car (30 days, National compact car, includes U discount & taxes): $758
Food: $50 per diem x 30 days: $1,500
Lodging: one-month sublet approximately $1,200
Laundry: $30
Gas: $100
Xeroxing: $700
Parking: $100
Phone/Fax: $75
Postage: $100
Photo reprints: $200

New York trip (7 days):
Flight to NYC: $308
Lodging: $0
Food per diem (7 days @$50/day): $350
Taxis/Subway: $75
Xeroxing: $250
Photo reprints: $200
Phone/Fax: $30

Washington, D.C., trip (7–10 days):
Flight to DC: $311
Hotel: $126/day (according to US Gvt. per diem rate): $875
Food: $350
Taxis/metro: $75
Xeroxing: $100
Phone/Fax: $30

of history, his "dialectics at a standstill," but which might better be seen as a modern theory of place. For Benjamin, the Bergsonian image is set in dialectical motion as a "flash of awakened consciousness" in and within spacetime (*Zeitraum*).[24] "Where thinking comes to a standstill in a constellation saturated with tensions—there the dialectical image appears," Benjamin writes in an often-cited passage. "It is the caesura in the movement of thought."[25] The dialectical image appears, in other words, at the place of synthesis between time and space, where and when thinking exceeds—or imagines a possibility beyond—dualism. This, after all, is the promise of dialectics. Place, in other words, is not something. It is not an essence, but neither is it nothing.[26]

Depressive modernity, as a modernity in and of place, therefore, does not refer to a separate strain or oppositional modernity; instead, it might best be seen as *modernity at a standstill*. Neither spatially nor temporally fixed nor homogeneous, it is the lived and symbolic reality of a modernity that idles; like an idling car, like a video on still, it moves neither forward nor backward, but shimmers in place.

MEMORIES OF THE NEW

A story, then, about place: In a June 1934 fireside chat, Franklin Delano Roosevelt casually announces that during the summer, while he is away from Washington, D.C., "a long-needed renovation of and addition to our White House office building is to be started." What seems to be an incidental aside turns out to be the central concern of his talk—and the means through which he introduces his controversial Second New Deal. "If I were to listen to the arguments of some prophets of calamity who are talking these days," he declares,

> I should hesitate to make the alterations. I should fear while I am away for a few weeks the architects might build some strange new Gothic tower or a factory building or perhaps a replica of the Kremlin or of the Potsdam Palace. But I have no such fears. The architects and builders are men of common sense and of artistic American tastes. They know that the principles of harmony and of necessity itself require that the building of the new structure shall blend with the essential lines of the old. It is this combination of the old and the new that marks orderly peaceful progress—not only in building buildings, but in building government itself.
>
> Our new structure is a part of and a fulfillment of the old.[27]

Roosevelt shrewdly addresses the fears of potential foes on all sides of the political spectrum: This new-old renovation that constituted the introduction of the more radical second New Deal would neither reinstate a premodern, pre-Republican feudalism, nor introduce Soviet Socialism into the mix, nor impose the impersonal functionalism of a Fordist assembly line, nor create a haven for proletarian unrest. Though he does not speculate as to how the renovation will look, Roosevelt proposes an aesthetic and historical model in which the "essential" foundations of the past may be preserved and blended with new and innovative forms. He suggests, in other words, that only the unessential, the waste, the unnecessary will be stripped away from the previous structure while it is dismantled to make room for new decoration. What will be unbuilt is superfluous. What will be added is simply an updated version of the same pragmatic American form. In employing the passive voice (the reconstruction "is to be started"), Roosevelt makes the process of renovation seem autogenetic. In other words, Roosevelt is asking Americans to accept the changes in government he proposes and to do so by proxy.[28] He thereby transforms his story from an allegory of progress-as-change to an allegory of progress-as-trust, and ultimately to an allegory of progressive history itself, a model at odds with the very populism he had espoused earlier in his presidency.[29]

This anecdote is important for three reasons, none of which has much to do with Roosevelt himself or with the particularities of his political policies.[30] First, the anecdote is an example of how spatial metaphor is invariably found as part of the discursive arsenal of modern performances of social power.[31] Michel Foucault notes this when he remarks that, "endeavoring to . . . decipher discourse through the use of spatial, strategic metaphors enables one to grasp precisely the points at which discourses are transformed in, through and on the basis of relations of power," and, even more so, by his late admission that geography and geographical metaphor produced the condition of possibility for his own critique of power and knowledge.[32] Second, the anecdote demonstrates in a fairly obvious way how prominently place—its deployment and remaking—figured and figures in Depression discourse and cultural praxis. From the Hoovervilles that allegorized the Hoover administration's failed efforts to resurrect the economy, to the Tennessee Valley Authority project that legitimated New Deal intervention, to the Works Progress Administration (WPA) guidebook project that literally mapped America and paved the way for the novel and affordable adventure of domestic automobile tourism, the discursive, material, and affective making and remaking of place were at the center of the cultural imaginary of America in Depression. Third, and less obviously, the passage alludes to the role that refuse and its management played in negotiating the failure of capitalism as a national ideal. It is, after all, both the mess of renovation and those materials that will be lost in the transformation that Roosevelt asks Americans to ignore.

Refuse is never a stable category, as Michael Thompson points out.[33] What is refused may be recuperated into existent systems of value, even as a symptom of what has gone wrong.[34] More radically, refuse might be seen as the borderline for what is culturally and psychologically possible to see. Dietmar Schmidt, for instance, argues that "the existence of refuse is dependent upon the recognition of a symbolic order, to which refuse does not belong."[35]

Defining refuse as "matter out of place,"[36] Schmidt draws on Jacques Lacan's distinction between the symbolic, "what is missing from its place," and the real, which "is always in its place; it carries it glued to its heel."[37] "It is unnecessary to indicate where refuse is out of place as it applies to any place—even to the site of its final disposal when left to its own devices," he concludes. "Refuse is 'out of place' in the most radical sense: it has no purpose anywhere."[38]

For Lacan, however, place cannot be said to be "purposeful"; it is instead always a placeholder for the play of signification. "It is evident ('a little too self-evident')," Lacan writes in his seminar on Edgar Allan Poe's story "The Purloined Letter," "that between letter and place exist relations for which no French word has quite the extension of the English adjective odd. Bizarre, by which Baudelaire regularly translates it, is only approximate. Let us say that these relations are . . . *singuliers*, for they are the ones maintained with place by the signifier."[39] Poe's story is about a missing letter, a letter that is placed in plain view but that cannot be found by the police who are charged with its recovery because it has been disguised, crumpled, and torn, and is therefore outside the order in which they operate. And the seminar, which includes Lacan's telling adaptation of James Joyce's homophone "A letter, a litter," is one of the psychoanalyst's most famous. The letter *is* litter for Lacan, in the sense that it is outside the symbolic order. But so too is litter the letter because it reveals the symbolic order's shadowy outlines as well.

Unpublished cover of the *New Yorker*, March 4, 1933. Peter Arno. Courtesy of the *New Yorker*. Reprinted by Permission. All Rights Reserved Galbraith/ *Vanity Fair* © 1931 Condé Nast Publications, Inc. Photo courtesy of the Franklin D. Roosevelt Library, Hyde Park, New York.

Nonetheless, refuse cannot be readily mapped onto Lacan's concepts of the symbolic or the real; rather it marks the borderland where the two overlap. Certainly, to be "out of place" presupposes the formation of the symbolic and modern subjectivity and may even be said to mark its contours. After all, the concept of refuse is a modern invention in the West that entered European and American discourse only somewhere between the eighteenth and nineteenth centuries, just as the modern subject came into being.[40] Yet, neither refuse nor place can fully be subsumed into or explained by a symbolic system—although charting the boundaries of the symbolic order is what is most explicitly at stake in a study of refuse and part of what is negotiated through place making more generally.

Roosevelt, in other words, is making no incidental gesture in his use of an allegory about office renovation. By making reference to refuse (his old office materials), he gestures to the contours of the symbolic order in which he operates and to his own role as patriarch. But he also produces refuse, constructing the parameters of what must remain unsignifiable; and in doing so

A GEOGRAPHY OF DEPRESSION **13**

"In the Dumps—a profitable pastime."
Photo by Acme, 1935–46. No. 249453. Farm Security Administration and Office of War Information Collection (LC-USZ62-75084, Library of Congress).

Still from *My Man Godfrey* (Universal 1936).
Courtesy of Cinema-Television Library, Edward L. Doheny Jr. Memorial Library, University of Southern California.

(pages 16–17) Author's notes on pages 456–57 of the English edition of Walter Benjamin's *The Arcades Project* (Harvard University Press 1999).

he seems to rechart the boundaries of the symbolic. His political genius revealed itself in his first campaign in his suggestion that refuse (even of the human sort) could not be easily erased. For most Americans, the Depression shattered a national imaginary—perpetuated by big industry—that was grounded in progressive narratives of history and culture. It was as if Benjamin's famous angel of history had momentarily faltered and, for an instant, was not being pushed "backwards into the future" to watch the wreckage of progress "hurled in front of its feet."[41] The angel hovered in the present, wounded and surrounded by trash. Roosevelt gave people a way of making sense of the wreckage they saw, yet couched it in a comfortable, still progressive rhetoric of rehabilitation and renovation. Early in his presidency, for instance, he introduced as an archetype of the times the category of the Forgotten Man, a species of human wreckage who inhabited dump sites and other marginal spaces. Simply in being remembered the Forgotten Man seemed rescued. In fact, declared Roosevelt, the Forgotten Man "at the bottom of the economic pyramid" was himself a building block, the foundation upon which lay his plans to rehabilitate "these unhappy times."[42]

In introducing his second New Deal, however, Roosevelt pays homage not to the forgotten and insignificant, but to the grand narratives of compensatory restoration and rehabilitation that were inherent in early twentieth-century historic preservation projects and that became increasingly visible during the 1930s.[43] Such projects, largely funded by industrial capitalists, set out to confirm "the inevitableness of the path from past to present as they reaffirmed the superiority of capitalism, progress, and the American way of life."[44] Of these, the John D. Rockefeller–financed rehabilitation and restoration of Colonial Williamsburg, begun in 1928, is perhaps the preeminent example. Touted as "an endeavor to restore accurately to preserve for all time the most significant portions of an historic and important city of America's colonial period,"[45] it constructed a spatial and historical narrative that did not include slave quarters or other distasteful reminders either of the distant past or the recent present. In describing the rehabilitation, Hildegarde Hawthorne concedes that "before reconstruction, destruction was necessary. The hideous shops, the bungalows and cottages and school houses, the modern excrescences on many an old house, bay windows, sleeping porches, verandahs, the telegraph poles. . . . such litter [was] . . . swept away."[46] The largely working-class African American and white inhabitants of 1930s Williamsburg were removed along with the rest of the trash.[47] In short, the social and material sanitization of the freshly painted place erased the "wreckage" of progress, while declaring such erasure progressive.

At the same time, however, the project claimed to restore absolute authenticity to the place. The Colonial Williamsburg project's Department of Research declared, for example, that "root, branch, leaf and flower, all would be true to the period, and whenever possible, no matter what the pains required,

N

[On the Theory of Knowledge, Theory of Progress]

> Times are more interesting than people.
> —Honoré de Balzac, *Critique littéraire,* Introduction by Louis Lumet (Paris, 1912), p. 103 [Guy de la Ponneraye, *Histoire de l'Amiral Coligny*]

> The reform of consciousness consists *solely* in . . . the awakening of the world from its dream about itself.
> —Karl Marx, *Der historische Materialismus: Die Frühschriften* (Leipzig ⟨1932⟩), vol. 1, p. 226 (letter from Marx to Ruge; Kreuznach, September 1843)[1]

In the fields with which we are concerned, knowledge comes only in lightning flashes. The text is the long roll of thunder that follows. [N1,1]

Comparison of other people's attempts to the undertaking of a sea voyage in which the ships are drawn off course by the magnetic North Pole. Discover *this* North Pole. What for others are deviations are, for me, the data which determine my course.—On the differentials of time (which, for others, disturb the main lines of the inquiry), I base my reckoning. [N1,2]

Say something about the method of composition itself: how everything one is thinking at a specific moment in time must at all costs be incorporated into the project then at hand. Assume that the intensity of the project is thereby attested, or that one's thoughts, from the very beginning, bear this project within them as their telos. So it is with the present portion of the work, which aims to characterize and to preserve the intervals of reflection, the distances lying between the most essential parts of this work, which are turned most intensively to the outside. [N1,3]

To cultivate fields where, until now, only madness has reigned. Forge ahead with the whetted axe of reason, looking neither right nor left so as not to succumb to the horror that beckons from deep in the primeval forest. Every ground must at some point have been made arable by reason, must have been cleared of the

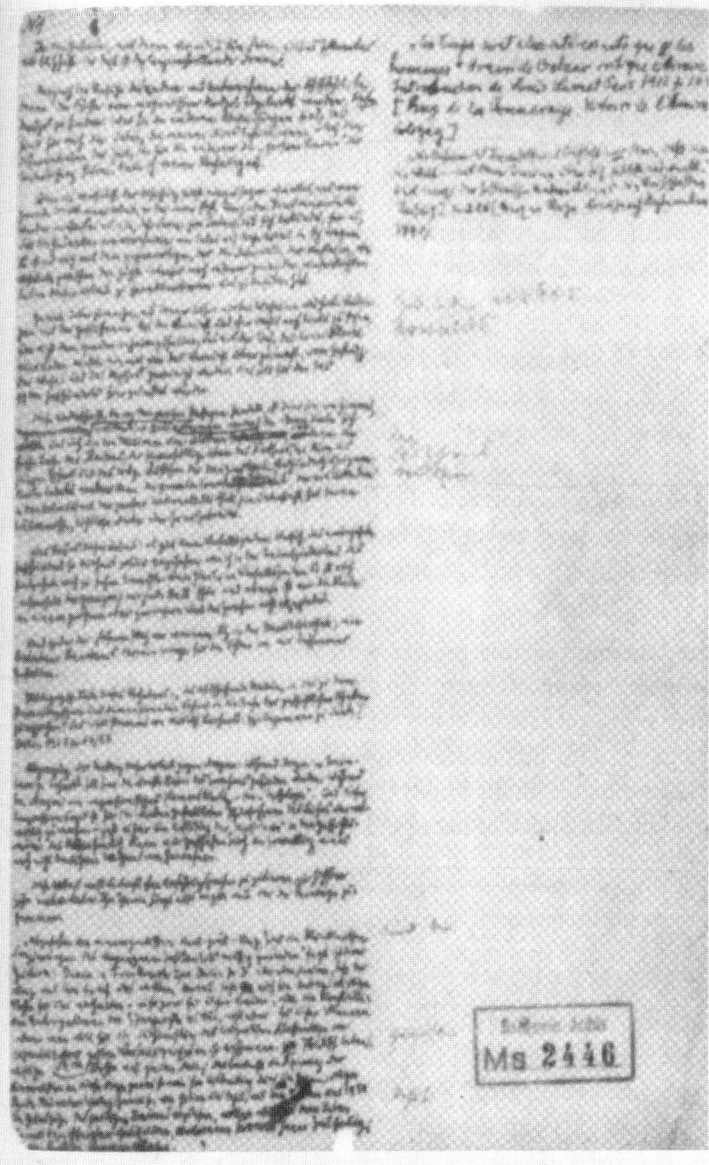

A page of Benjamin's manuscript, showing the beginning of
Convolute N.

undergrowth of delusion and myth. This is to be accomplished here for the
terrain of the nineteenth century. [N1,4]

These notes devoted to the Paris arcades were begun under an open sky of
cloudless blue that arched above the foliage; and yet—owing to the millions of
leaves that were visited by the fresh breeze of diligence, the stertorous breath of
the researcher, the storm of youthful zeal, and the idle wind of curiosity—they've
been covered with the dust of centuries. For the painted sky of summer that looks

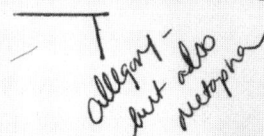

A BRIEF HISTORY OF TRASH

Rubbish was the curse of North American industrial culture during the late nineteenth and early twentieth centuries. The American concern with the urban refuse problem and the advance of the so-called municipal housecleaning movement had been ongoing since the 1880s.[1] According to Martin Melosi in *Garbage in the Cities*, the "dramatic rise in the automobile, chemical, and electrical industries during the 1920s" vastly increased the amount of trash produced in urban spaces and posed increasingly complex problems of how to dispose of it. Not unrealistically, the title character in John Dos Passos's 1927 play *The Garbage Man*, shrieks, "Don't you see that everywhere's littered with waste and garbage?"[2]

While writers in the 1920s, such as Dos Passos and, more famously, T. S. Eliot, used trash as a metaphor for the universal ruin of the modern subject, the Depression era complicated the discourse about trash and the dump. In *Chasing Dirt: The American Pursuit of Cleanliness*, Suellen Hoy argues that with the help of mass advertising, the culture of cleanliness was domesticated, taking root in the modern American home during the 1920s and 1930s.[3] (The kitchen garbage disposal, though not popularized until the 1950s, was a product of Depression-era waste management.)[4]

The period also saw the shift from an early twentieth-century concern for how to efficiently collect trash to an obsession with what to do with it once it was picked up. During the 1930s, the incinerator and garbage grinder replaced the open-air dump and were replaced at the close of the decade by the less expensive sanitary landfill. By the late 1920s, the popular press had begun to tout instances in which dump sites were remade into parks, golf courses, and other attractive sites. A 1927 article in *American City* proudly exonerated an early attempt at "sanitary fill," in which refuse and garbage were used to fill a sixty-foot gulch to street level, then covered by a thin layer of dirt and transformed into a park.[5] The famous Garbage Park in Sausalito, California, was, in one writer's words, "an effort to make garbage respectable." It disguised a sea dumping station with a luxurious garden in which the "fragrance of blossoms was induced to counteract the garbage stench."[6]

The manufactured makeover of the dump posited a kind of recuperative model of rubbish, a transformation in the mode of waste erasure from imperfect destruction to a more complex process of masking. The masking process extended to nationwide cleanup projects that were naively supposed to improve the American economic forecast (or at least to make it appear as if it were not so bad). A 1930 *Fortune* magazine article gently satirizes the efforts of the wives of the industrialists Henry Ford and John D. Rockefeller, Jr., who were "at the vanguard of a great army" that wanted to "pick up the country" as a way to increase mass consumption and, theoretically, improve the nation's prosperity. The article nostalgically marks the disposal of American rubbish as a sign of the passing of American vernacular culture into a new world order and a suggestion that America is "growing up."[7] Until the Depression, the *Fortune* writers attest, America had "recklessly like a child . . . [hurled] refuse out the window and [didn't] care how high piled the tin cans in the backyard."[8]

Defining junk as "ugliness and waste," the curious, absurd, and hideous that is relegated to "America's porches and backyards," and setting it in opposition to the products and processes of modern technology—the "new America, its skyscrapers, its airplanes, its dynamos"—the *Fortune* article collapses the system of rubbish and junk into the larger category of vernacular culture, while extricating modern technology and modes of production from its own product—trash—and occluding the relationship between capitalist production and product disposal. Moreover, it posits an opposition between the urbane and tasteful sites of High Modernist functionalism and International Style and the messy, vernacular spaces of American folk culture and everyday life. The writers proclaim, "Every garbage dump, every row of ramshackle houses lining the railroad tracks, is evidence of our boundless wealth. This is a space we do not need."[9]

Depression-era marketing techniques inaugurated a throwaway economy that reached its apex in the 1970s and 1980s. Stuart Ewen notes that the 1930s marketing philosophy of "progressive obsolescence," which drew on the advertising strategist Earnest Elmo Calkins's business philosophy of rapid, planned stylistic change, could be seen as a "sometimes desperate attempt to build markets in a shrinking economy."[10] The puritanical impetus toward thrift died hard among consumers, and the planned production of waste was not always readily accepted by the masses. The consumer "engineers" Roy Sheldon and Egmont Arens wrote in 1932, "Scratch a consumer and you find an opponent of consumptionism and a fear of the workings of progressive obsolescence."[11] If a plentitude of garbage and an expanse of material space marked the health of American industrial capitalism, the stoppage of trash production seemed to allegorize the failure of capitalism; it underscored the closing of the American frontier and imperialist excess, and marked an increasing shortage of American space. Capitalist America needed trash on display—but in a space that could be contained, ordered, and regulated, a space that could be distinguished and set at the margin of American industrial life.

For the unemployed and transient classes of Americans, however, trash became a commodity. Increasingly, during the 1930s, magazine articles proposed salvaging rubbish as a way to yield wealth. As one scrap collector commented in a 1937 article in the *Saturday Evening Post*, "'Junk' is merely another word for 'money' or cash."[12] The *Post* writer explains, "Rising prices have transmuted waste products, the junk, the scrap of an industrial civilization into a great essential world resource which is wanted very badly indeed."[13]

The industrialists' interest in cleaning up trash arose not from a desire to erase it, but from a desire to draw attention to the presence of trash on the American landscape. A plentitude of trash, it was thought, might suggest a burgeoning consumerism and the possibility that corporate prosperity could soon be at hand. The populist effort to make wealth from refuse was simultaneously a necessity and a sign of the American empire's demise.

For many of the more than one million homeless Americans, remaking refuse was a means of survival. "Here was need, and here lay old cellars, full of loose brick and odd metal work, with old foundation walls standing and now and then some stone steps," wrote Jeannette Griffith in a 1932 *Survey [Graphic]* essay about an encampment built on a dump. "In this setting I saw the drama of satisfying basic needs—food, shelter, clothing and companionship. Over a hundred men had already settled in. People in the vicinity, pals on the lot or dump carts on route to the disposal barges nearby had helped to provide a vast variety of the makin's [sic] of home."[14]

The essay follows with a series of photographs of the men on the vacant lot, making use of scraps to build shacks and burn fuel. The photos are titled "companionship," "shelter," "clothing," and portray the men in various domestic guises, chatting, sitting, and hanging up laundry amidst the rubbish. The recuperation of the dump as a domestic site both appeases the voyeuristic impulses of *Survey Graphic*'s socially progressive readers, who sympathize with the hardships of these "Forgotten Men," and makes them more accepting—and acquiescent about the little they have left. At the same time, the photographs ennoble the imagined perseverance of these Hooverville inhabitants, who maintain their dignity, modernity, and humanity by continuing to clean, wash laundry, and cook meals. Rather than feminizing the men who perform these tasks, domesticity is recoded to serve as a sign of their independence and resilience (read: masculinity) and demonstrates their ability to remake, even conquer, place.

The "domestication" of Depression-era dump sites such as this shifted that which was outside and at the margins of culture to the inside. As the places sanctioned to contain, control, recuperate, and destroy what was refused by the material and discursive systems of culture, Depression-era dumps took on a prominent role as sites in which to explore different strategies of cultural remaking. It was there that ideologies of belonging were negotiated.

Depression-era dumps were renovated, as was Colonial Williamsburg. They were sublimated and masked, as was Sausalito's Garbage Park. Or they were recuperated and transformed into commercialized self-parodies. The most potent example of this last phenomenon was played out in the 1936 screwball comedy *My Man Godfrey* (Universal Pictures), which narrates the simultaneous transformation of the Forgotten Man Godfrey Smith (William Powell) into a gentleman and the transient camp he inhabits in the opening sequence into a swank, neon-lit nightclub, aptly, if ironically, named, The Dump.

On one hand, the Depression-era dump enabled the "bourgeois spectator [to survey] and [classify] his own antithesis";[15] on the other, it revealed the fragility of social boundaries. After all, even the blue-blooded Godfrey could land on a dump. (Though, of course, he had the wherewithal, with a bit of help, to pull himself up by his bootstraps to self-made wealth.) Ultimately, though, the dump suggested that the divide between middle-class subjects and the working class or unemployed was so tenuous that it was no longer enough to artificially mark the divide. As the writers of the above-mentioned *Fortune* article point out, "Garbage, like most general nouns, is a relative term."

---

1. See Melosi, *Garbage in the Cities*, 3–20.
2. Dos Passos, *The Garbage Man*, 123.
3. Hoy, *Chasing Dirt*, 151–52.
4. The present-day concern with decreasing the amount of rubbish produced did not really come to the fore until the 1960s.
5. "Building a Park on a Garbage Dump," 175. See also Harmon, "Garbage Park, Oakland, a Successful Experiment in Esthetics."
6. "Abating the Garbage Nuisance," 18.
7. See Burchfield and Steiner, "Vanishing Backyards," 77. I am indebted to Miles Orvell for this citation and for his reading of "trash" in *The Real Thing*, 287–99.
8. Burchfield and Steiner, "Vanishing Backyards," 77.
9. Ibid., 78.
10. Ewen, *All Consuming Images*, 244. See also, Calkins, "The Beauty of The New Business Tool," 145.
11. Cited in Ewen, *All Consuming Images*, 244.
12. Atwood, "Out of the Scrap Heap," 97.
13. Ibid., 8.
14. Griffith, "Dug-outs and Settle-ins," 381.
15. See Stallybrass and White, *The Politics and Poetics of Transgression*, 128.

actual eighteenth-century material itself must be found and bought." Nonetheless, like the Oval Office, Colonial Williamsburg would be modernized. For "even though the new Williamsburg was to be the old Williamsburg," the designers decided, it was also to be "thoroughly modern in its lighting, sanitation and heat." To preserve the appearance of historical authenticity, therefore, modern-day necessities would be buried underground (as were the telegraph and telephone wires), wrapped in colonial-era reproductions (the street lamps were copies of older lanterns), or otherwise disguised ("the post-boxes [were] sunk into walls or into a jog of the fences where they offer[ed] merely a discreet slit for your letters").[48]

Colonial Williamsburg, Incorporated, the company that held title to the properties, produced a modernist precursor of Disneyland that was heralded as authentic by denying its own modernity. Williamsburg, it was decided, "stands curiously out of time," fixed "somewhere in the past . . . because there is nothing pushing it into the present."[49] Colonial Williamsburg did not propose to be a representation of reality, but reality itself—a reality that the present imagined ought to have been. Yet these attempts to fix Williamsburg as place through a self-conscious erasure of the material tensions and transformations of space over time and the insistence on an absolute separation between the past and the present necessarily fail. Like the renovation of the Oval Office as it functions in Roosevelt's allegory, the making of Colonial Williamsburg reveals that the only way an ideal present might be seen as a seamless "part of and a fulfillment of" the past is if that past were first reimagined as itself fixed in place and thereby coherent, homogeneous, classifiable, preserved. As Michael Shanks, David Platt, and William L. Rathje remark, the "site's original inhabitants would have been totally mystified by such behavior. They were accustomed to throwing garbage on the street."[50]

"THE FORGETTERY"

This book stages an encounter with the past through its dumps, but it is not attempting an act of salvage, a term that takes on a greater significance in the section on Key West.[51] Nor is it simply an effort to "read history from the dustbin," or to speak for "those people, acts, and events that are casually left out of history or forcefully excluded from it."[52] For it also looks at the mechanisms through which refuse is managed, manipulated, and defined. The recuperative mechanisms at play in the chapters that follow—Reno-vation in Reno, salvaging in Key West, remembrance in Harlem, incineration in Hollywood—are all destined to fail, but the ways in which they fail are quite distinct. Since refuse constitutes a borderline for signification, tracing its boundaries produces a kind of map (imperfect though it is) of the Depression symbolic. Some of those boundaries are to be expected—those, for instance, that fluctuate with changing conceptions of gender, sexuality, race, citizenship, consumption, production, and representation. Others are less readily visible—the negotiations between memory and forgetting, for instance, or emotion and embodiment, or language, being, and death. There are, of course, boundaries of which I am unaware. And since I cannot see what is unseeable or say what is unsayable, I have left space for readers to meander, feel, and make connections on their own. While this book is not without argument, what it argues explicitly is not its most important part. One's own immediate and visceral experience in reading is important here. For what is at stake is not just a concept, *depressive modernity*, or an object of study, *refuse*, but a method.

After all, using refuse as an object of inquiry is nothing new. Nineteenth-century discoveries of accidental or lost remains and refuse came to shape the nascent disciplines of historiography, archeology, and anthropology.[53] In 1857, for instance, the German historian Johann Gustav Droysen attempted to understand history by developing "a theory of remains" that gauged the "truth content of documents and materials according to how much they resist[ed] being recognized as historical signs."[54] That is, according to Cornelia Vismann, he distinguished between materials that had been intentionally preserved for posterity and those "more truthful" fragments that had been accidentally or unconsciously preserved from the past. By calling these remnants or "remains" (*Überreste*) rather than refuse (*Abfall*), Vismann argues, Droysen emphasizes "the connection between the past and the present"; remains become "latent historical sources that can only become manifest for historians via a procedure that decontextualizes them from the present and recontextualizes them in the past—a procedure that Droysen calls 'recognition of true place.' The historian of remains becomes an analyst who has to track the misplacements and the displacements of those locations."[55] In other words, Droysen uses the remnant as the means through which to return things to place, that is, to transform refuse into artifact by resituating it within the boundaries of the symbolic order—to archive it, to give it a name.

Fourteen years later, in 1871, another German scholar, Rudolph Virchow, stumbled upon century-old food waste (oyster shells, "mussels of considerable size," and "many deer, pig, chicken, and goose bones") during the excavation of a Berlin building site and developed what Dietmar Schmidt calls "refuse archeology."[56] The bones and kitchen waste that Virchow found are "remains" in Droysen's sense in that they serve to link the present back to the past and allowed the archeologist to surmise dietary habits and commercial exchange from the previous century. Nonetheless, as Schmidt points out, Virchow uses the term "refuse" (*Abfall*) to describe his findings. In doing so, Virchow emphasizes that the importance of the shells and bones lies in what we might call their *refuse*-value; they are not accidental leftovers, but had been purposefully rejected. They *had never had* value in the past; it is only in the present that they attain one. Following Vismann above, then, we might say that Virchow is less interested in uncovering or recovering his fragments in the present in order to return them to their "true" place in the past than he is in understanding their process of being doubly displaced—both in the present and the past. In either century, oysters had no business turning up in the middle of Berlin. That said, the term "refuse archeology" is a bit of a redundancy; as Shanks, Platt, and Rathje observe, "Garbage: 99 percent of what most archeologists dig up, record, and analyze in obsessive detail is what past peoples threw away as worthless."[57] And yet for both Virchow and Droysen, whether called remains or refuse, their findings are invested with a kind of auratic relationship to the past; they become fetishistically endowed with an ability to stitch together the hyphen between space and time.

My interest in refuse in this book, then, lies in staging the methodological struggle that accompanies the investigation of that which is refused and that which remains. How can one use refuse without at the moment of inquiry—by virtue of inquiry—immediately transform refuse into object, even fetish?[58] It is because of this question that the specter of Walter Benjamin, modern philosophy's most famous trash picker, haunts this project. His work is of interest not because he collected or exposes the debris of progressive history, but because he struggles to "make use" of the refuse he finds. "But the rags, the refuse," he writes in *The Arcades Project*, "these I will not inventory but allow, in the only way possible, to come into their own: by making use of them."[59] For Benjamin, remaining within that struggle—*idling* at a standstill—is the answer. But this is easier to suggest than perform. "For the true critic," he writes in a 1931 fragment, "the actual judgment is the ultimate step—something that comes with a struggle after everything else, never the basis of his activities. In the ideal case, he forgets to pass judgment."[60] *Down in the Dumps* was written in part as an effort to understand the depth of Benjamin's struggle, the discourse within which it was produced, and to explore what it means to radically forget, not something but the drive to judgment itself.

"A letter, a litter."[61] The more interesting wordplay in Lacan's reading of Poe's "A Purloined Letter" is not the famous letter-litter homophone he borrows untranslated from Joyce, but the one that is rarely addressed: The less overt and yet not insignificant punning he performs between litter and the literal. "It can literally be said that something is missing from its place only of what can change it: the symbolic," Lacan writes. In other words, it matters that the letter (and letters) are litter—and, as important, that they can be spoken of "literally." Like *letter* and *litter*, *litter* and *literal* are *faux amis*—they sound similar but do not have a common etymology. *Letter* and *literal* do. *Literal* comes from the Latin *littera* (or *litera*) for "a letter." It is an expression of exactitude and precision that means "according to" or "following the letter" of verbal expression. *Litter*, on the other hand, derives from the Latin *lectus*, Old French *litiere*, and modern French *lit*, which means couch, bed, or birthplace (as in a pig's litter); it is only in the eighteenth century, with the advent of modernity, that *litter* takes on its current connotation as refuse, "odds and ends, fragments and leavings lying about, rubbish; a state of confusion or untidiness; a disorderly accumulation of things lying about." Thus, while the precision and erudition of the letter seem directly opposed to the earthy disorder of litter, it nonetheless contains litter within it.

The literal, in fact, might be said to be the litter that the letter refuses. To read literally is to read to the letter. But, in Lacan's terms, since "the letter is not anywhere—it lacks a place," to read literally, to the letter, is to read not for what is "missing from its place" (the symbolic), but for what lacks a place, what is or has been radically refused. To do this seems an impossible task, for it requires a kind of forgetting, or a least a return to a moment that precedes one's interpellation into the symbolic order.[62]

Reading literally is thought to be the most naive of interpretive practices, the least well informed, and one for which professors, myself included, notoriously take first-year students to task.[63] Yet what if reading literally could amount to something like a method, a method that is experiential and childlike, not so much resistant to the symbolic order as unsure of its parameters and dependent upon an active forgetting of the system of relations that produce place? Again and again in the introductory chapter of his "prehistory" of American modernism, *A Sense of Things: The Object Matter of American Literature*, Bill Brown evokes the literal when talking about things.[64] He writes, "The very idea of ideas in things—literalized by the child's search [in Baudelaire, Toni Morrison, and his own writing]—is repeatedly revealed as a fantasy doomed to exposure."[65] Later, after making reference to Martin Heidegger, Lacan, and Gaston Bachelard's writings on things, he observes, "Taken literally, the belief that there are ideas in things amounts to granting them an interiority and, thus, something like the structure of subjectivity . . . it amounts to asserting a kind of fetishism, but one that is part of the modernist's effort to arrest commodity-fetishism-as-usual."[66] And later still, citing Benjamin's account of opening a chest of drawers as a child in search of a pair of socks hidden therein, Brown asks, "How is it . . . that such a fantasy—of ideas in things—sustains one version of what we name American modernism? . . . The answer, of course, is that this literalization of [William Carlos] Williams's creed ["no ideas but in things"] violates his own poetic practice of rendering things—'a red wheel/ barrow'—in their opacity, not their transparency."[67] Brown's recourse to the literal when he writes of children's experiences of things calls to mind both a child's naive quest to find something ineffable—an essence, a soul, a subject—in things and the childlike quality of literalizing.

What would a literal reading look like? Or, to put it in more familiar terms, what would it mean to read a cigar as just a cigar? (And no, Freud never said that—but what if he had?) Why is that prospect both so comforting and nearly impossible to imagine? What happens, for instance, when one attempts, as I do in these pages, to reanimate the tension between live and dead metaphor, between living and dead things? Certainly, attention must be paid to the senses, to one's visceral, and emotional response. And so too does it seem important to consider conditions of material production, paying particular attention to the way matter is defined. But it also requires a kind of willed defamiliarization with the object and with an a priori reliance on the dualisms of subject and object, outside and inside, thought and experience.

The literal as I use it should therefore not be confused with what Jennifer Ashton, in a critique of Marjorie Perloff and Michael Fried, identifies as the "literalist" art object, those poems, paintings, and sculptures that foreground the material form of a poem and invite the spectator or reader to "participate in the process of construction."[68] Ashton writes that while Perloff's literalism "appears to have corrected one New Critical mistake—that of equating objecthood with autonomy—it has simply reinstated the more foundational one—that of equating experience with interpretation."[69] Making a sharp distinction between reading-as-experience and critical interpretation, Ashton argues that as a result of its peculiar demands on its audience, the literalist art object ceases to be an "object of understanding," becoming instead "an object of experience."[70] She observes, finally, "The critical practice that literalist texts require would have to amount to something like field work—compiling all the experiences that readers have of them."[71] For Ashton, in other words, the problem with the literalist artwork is that it calls upon one to perform the childlike practice of reading literally. By contrast, the drive to "look for ideas in things" that Brown alludes to, and which I suggest underlies literal reading, is extra-experiential, fostered by a desire to glimpse at the shoreline of the prelinguistic imaginary and the symbolic, and of the symbolic and that which resists signification, the real. In other words, a literal reading is a *littoral* reading.[72] That is, it takes place at the coastline, "upon or adjacent to the shore." Elizabeth Bishop's surrealist story, "The Sea and Its Shore," describes such a reader, a trash picker who collects and reads the random writings he finds on scraps of paper he removes each night from the beach. The trash picker, Edwin Boomer, "read constantly" and lived "the most literary life possible,"[73] by which Bishop means struggling to make meaning of the words while experiencing print and paper as material facts. Boomer, for instance, uses the paper as insulation from the cold and hammers scraps of paper on his walls; he remarks on the smell of different prints, notes the thickness, wetness, creases and color of paper, and observes the ways that newspaper changes when damp, sunburned, or stretched.[74] His approach to reading, his "literary" approach, then, is a holistic one that assumes no absolute opposition between the material qualities of paper and the content that is printed upon it. But if this mode of reading, what we might call a *hypermaterialism*, seems random, "without discernable goal," like the papers floating in the wind that Boomer describes, it also is subject to serial categorizations. He asks how much a fragment connects to his own life, for example, or how much it puzzles him. He

on the nature of experience (or what i might have said)

So you also should know that this project was conceived in depression. In the black hole of a summer. In a summer of loss. At the time, I admonished myself for being too much inside myself and struggled to recognize the objects I passed. There. A cloud hung overhead. There. A yellow car sped down the street. There. A cat shrieked. The attempt to see and sense my surroundings seemed futile, so persuasive was my psyche's centripetal pull. The cloud, the car, the cat disintegrated as soon as they appeared. My vision failed at the periphery. Time slowed. It was clear to me, even then, that depression severs any hyphenation between time and space. The inward focus and obsessive dwelling on the self that marks depression may only be a mask for the processing of loss that cannot be articulated, but it is an elaborate mask indeed—and one that cannot easily be lifted. Unable to accept the loss of a loved object and confronted by the failure of language to compensate for that loss, the depressive, according to Julia Kristeva, withdraws, taking "refuge to the point of inaction (pretending to be dead) or even suicide."[1] Depression, in other words, implies imprisoning, enclosure coupled with the existential fear that there is no way out. To be depressed, for Kristeva, is to live captive in a stagnant place, a void where one cannot be, cannot leave, cannot speak. Meaning shatters. Trapped inside, withdrawn, the depressed person experiences a spatial, temporal, and symptomatic death, finding protection only outside of the animate world of language as an Other. A Corpse.

And yet. There is something liberating about that otherness, about becoming a "thing"—and seeing from the inside of things—that has always been facilitative of writing. It is only later, of course, once you have returned from the void, that you realize it. By then you live haunted by its specter, ever fearful of its return. But you know, without having the words to describe it, what it is to momentarily leave subjectivity behind and glimpse, ever so briefly, the painful birth of one's making.[2]

---

1. Kristeva, *Black Sun*, 10.
2. Melanie Klein argues, for instance, that the ego is formed through the adoption of the "depressive position" in infancy. See, in particular, Klein's 1935 essay, "A Contribution to the Psychogenesis of Manic-Depressive States," 262–89.

struggles. For "the more papers he picked up and the more he read, the less he felt he understood," but also the more he reads, the more everything—even the sand—begins to look like a printed page; that is everything becomes legible, text. The goal to his collecting and reading, however, lies beyond the accrual of knowledge or content. He hesitates. Reading forestalls burning, the destruction of paper that he must inevitably perform. After all, "burning paper was his occupation, by which he made his living, but over and above that, he could not allow his pockets to become too full, or his house to become littered."[75] The trash-picker at the littoral makes his living by litter, but he too is threatened by overabundance, by the littering of his house (*lit*?), which is a "shelter, but not for living in, for thinking in," that is, a thinly veiled metaphor for the subject, for that thing that thinks.[76] Boomer hesitates. And it is in this moment of hesitation before burning that literal reading emerges. Such a practice, then, entails the suspension, however momentary, of the idealist dualisms between idea and object, matter and mind, intellect and emotion. A literal reading practice neither presupposes formal or figurative qualities in the things it encounters nor upholds a dualistic distinction between analytical and affective or experiential response. Instead, it is constituted by the struggle to read at a standstill.

ORIGINS

This book struggles with standstill. I consciously reveal the false starts and elisions, the offhand remarks and intense conversations, the costs, passions, and fatigue that shape but are effaced in the labor of writing. Full of half-told stories and unfinished sentences, amateur photos and newspaper headlines, it imagines the writer both as a collector and frustrated actor who wants to perform all the roles as well as produce and direct.

Things do, at times, get out of hand. This book, it has to be said, is cluttered. How else could one stage the story of dumps? It sides more with Bishop's embrace of "loose ends" than with the modernism of Wallace Stevens's tightly crafted poetics. In method, this book resists the process of refusal that is inherent to writing. If the reading practice this book lays out is literal, the logic through which it proceeds is associational or, rather, dissociational, the implications of which will become clearer in the Harlem section. This is another way of saying that it has an affinity for a certain theoretical strain of modernism whose European trajectory follows from Pierre Janet to Henri Bergson to Walter Benjamin (and, more recently, to Gilles Deleuze).

Today, when one speaks of dissociation, it generally is to refer to the complex that has become known as multiple personality disorder, in which "subpersonalities" or "parallel memories" function alongside one another within a single subject.[77] However, dissociationism, developed in the nineteenth century by the French hypnotist Janet, meant much more. Janet has received some attention of late as the "nearly forgotten founder of the analytic tradition in psychology" and arguably as the methodological father (though their contemporary) of Josef Breuer and Freud.[78] But Janet's model of dissociationism must be read within a broader context of nineteenth-century intellectual debates, since his method was developed as an explicit attack on the British Associationist psychologists, who then dominated European and American discussions about the mind and memory. The Associationists' model of memory relied on the theory that associations were made between discrete ideas or images that combined into more complex thought. Drawing on a Newtonian physical model, they saw ideas as something like atoms.[79] Janet agreed that memory was produced through the connections made between different ideas and images; but he rejected the atomic model of the Associationists, suggesting instead that each aggregation of ideas and images was in some sense unique, "with its own personality or shaping characteristics."[80] For Janet, according to John Ryan Haule, the "guiding image for this was the phenomenon of multiple personality."[81] Haule and others have traced the trajectory of Janet's legacy and interest in multiple personalities to Jung. But dissociationism's more mobile notion of the image impacted Bergson and, later, Benjamin in quite a different way.[82]

Bergson was in lifelong conversation with Janet, with whom he had been a student in the philosophy section at L'École Normale Supérieure. It is within that context that we might read Bergson's rail against the British Associationist psychologists in *Matter and Memory*, of whom he writes, "Having stiffened individual memory-images into ready-made things,"[83] they substitute for the "continuity of becoming, which is the living reality, a discontinuous multiplicity of elements, inert and juxtaposed."[84] The Associationists ask the wrong question, Bergson argues: "What we really need to discover is how a choice is effected among an infinite number of recollections which all resemble in some way the present perception, and why only one of them—this rather than that—emerges into the light of consciousness."[85] "Association," he declares, "is not the primary fact: dissociation is what we begin with."[86] Bergson's critique of what Deleuze calls "false problems" consists in part "in showing that there is not less, but more in the idea of nonbeing than being, in disorder than order, in the possible than the real."[87] Bergson argues, for instance, that "in the idea of disorder there is already the idea of order, plus its negation, plus the motive for negation."[88] Following this trajectory of thought, we might conversely say that there is "more in refuse" than in signification, because refuse contains within it the idea of signification, plus its refusal, plus the motive for its refusal; and more in depression than progress, for similar reasons.

It is with an eye to allowing for the mobile logic of dissociation that I do not always make explicit the connections between the images, metaphors, and allegorical figures that turn up over and over again in the following pages, in different contexts and in historical moments and material sites. Places blur into one another: Harlem shows up in Hollywood; Hollywood in Reno; and Reno in Harlem; Key West and Alcatraz, in the afterword, share the same nickname, "the Rock." What follow, then, are not case studies, but sketches. They are not representative or exhaustive. They provide not answers so much as questions. This book is a travelogue, scrapbook, journal, conversation. Reno. Key West. Harlem. Hollywood. The sections and selections that follow might be read as itineraries, field notes, performances, aphorisms, dissociations.

In the beginning, there was an exhortation: "Say something about the method of composition itself: how everything one is thinking at a specific moment in time must at all costs be incorporated into the project then at hand. Assume that the intensity of the project is thereby attested, or that one's thoughts, from the very beginning, bear this project within them as their telos. So it is with the present portion of the work, which aims to characterize and to preserve the intervals of reflection, the distances lying between the most essential parts of this work, which are turned most intensively to the outside."[89] It is no matter that this exhortation wasn't mine. Because it was in the middle that this book began. With me (I am a middle child). With Reno (which was, for a time, a middle chapter).[90] With Benjamin, whose own unfinished work about a middle century (the nineteenth) took up his middle years. During the time it has taken me to write this book—more years than I care to count, though I can—it has transformed, morphing as my own intellectual engagements, knowledge, and personal commitments and experiences changed and deepened. Loss was certainly part of it—loss of people, of intellectual innocence, and, at times, of optimism. And it is marked as well by a sense of loss at what writing, particularly academic writing, leaves out: The warmth of the stove in Descartes's small, empty room before he dismissed sensation. The ache of my fingers after typing all day. The scratch of starched hotel sheets. The dust on my shoes from walking miles on dry streets. The startling recognition of my dead grandmother's eyes inside those of an interview subject. The longing, always, for the comforts of a bed, a cat, and, later, a child at home.

"DEBRIS"

> Do the faces and the words come back to you;
> Do all the things the drinking and the talk once more blotted
>   out come back to you now,
> With the bitter cigarettes in the morning air?[91]

July 2004 Minneapolis

RENO

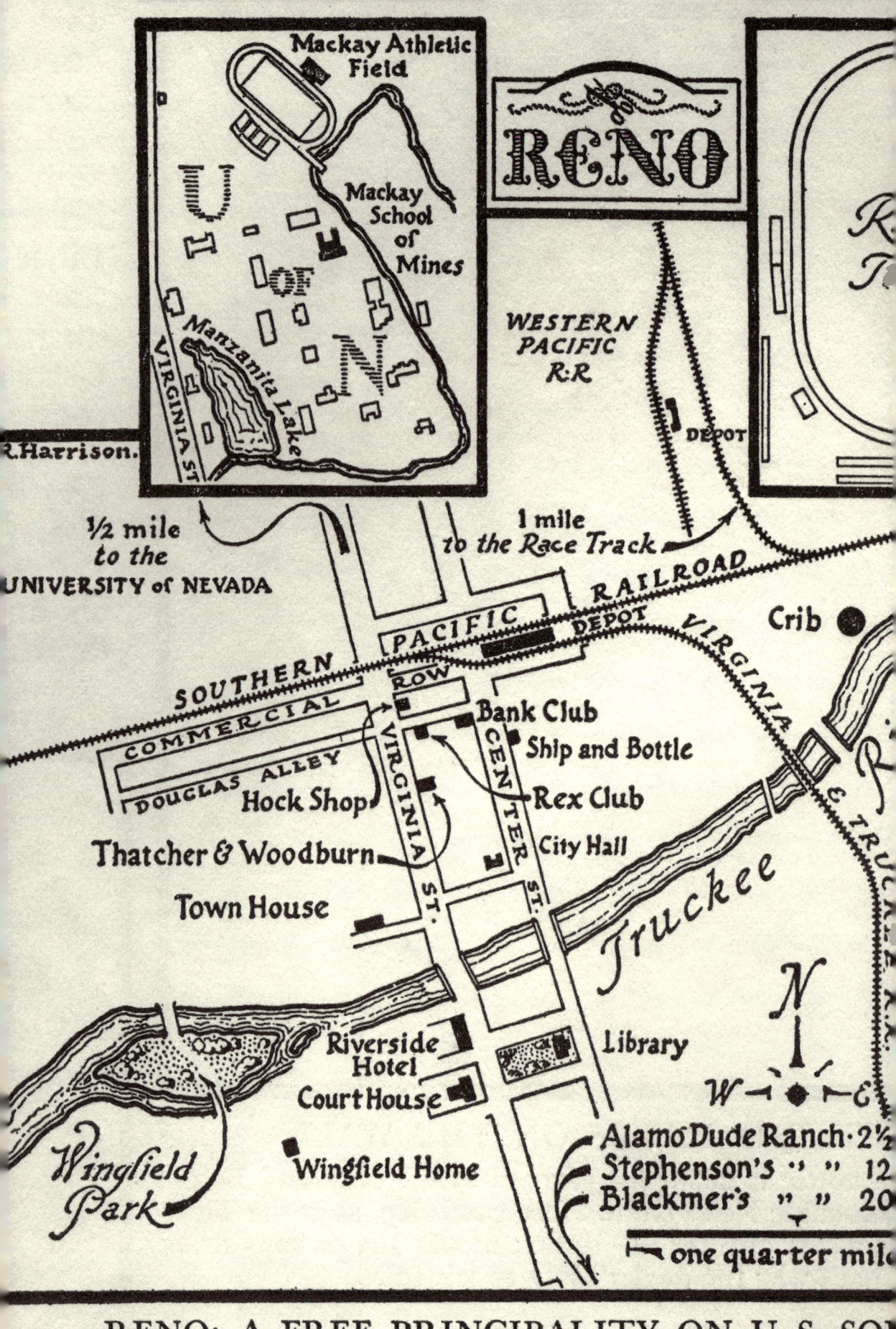

Mackay Athletic Field
Mackay School of Mines
U of N
Manzanita Lake
Virginia St.
R. Harrison.

½ mile to the UNIVERSITY OF NEVADA

1 mile to the Race Track

WESTERN PACIFIC R.R.
DEPOT

SOUTHERN PACIFIC RAILROAD DEPOT

COMMERCIAL ROW
DOUGLAS ALLEY
Hock Shop
Thatcher & Woodburn
Town House
VIRGINIA ST.
CENTER ST.
Bank Club
Ship and Bottle
Rex Club
City Hall

Crib

VIRGINIA & TRUCKEE R.R.

Truckee R.

Riverside Hotel
Court House
Wingfield Park
Wingfield Home
Library

N
W — E

Alamo Dude Ranch · 2½
Stephenson's " " 12
Blackmer's " " 20

one quarter mile

RENO: A FREE PRINCIPALITY ON U.S. SO[IL]

1

Reno

THE DIVORCE FACTORY

AND MY MIND WHIRLED WITH FORGOTTEN STORIES OF MALE SERVANTS SUMMONED TO WASH THE MISTRESS'S BACK; CHAUFFEURS SHARING THE MASTERS' WIVES; PULLMAN PORTERS INVITED INTO THE DRAWING ROOM OF RICH WIVES HEADED FOR RENO.
—**RALPH ELLISON**, *INVISIBLE MAN*

IT IS A PLACE. IT STICKS.
—**SHERWOOD ANDERSON**,
"SO THIS IS RENO"

PART 1. THE WASTE OF PROGRESS

← Map of Reno in *Fortune*, April 1934.

Divorcées always arrived in Reno by train. They boarded the Twentieth Century at Grand Central in New York City, switched in Chicago to the Overland Limited, and three days later stepped out of their Pullman cars at the Reno Union Pacific Station, where fatherly divorce attorneys gathered them up "like great sheep dogs, shepherding their lambs."[1] Reno was the 1930s Mecca of the controversial "quickie" divorce, easy to be had on almost any grounds as long as one stayed in the state for six weeks.[2]

That is how the story goes.[3] And this is another story, a story that rereads those narratives of Depression-era Reno, a bricolage of a story that builds a text of the place. Reno is a wasteland, as we shall see, but it is a wasteland that subverts any pretensions to the universalized space that T. S. Eliot proposed.[4] Reno is a peculiarly American wasteland, a wasteland of the feminine, of divorcées and prostitutes, of private reminiscences and mass-produced tales. It is a nonelegiac wasteland that reveals the grotesque machinery of modernity in crisis and relies on the economically and ideologically beneficial mass production of trash. This is a story, then, about Reno and gender, but it is also a story about modern place.

For statistically, despite all the brouhaha, Reno divorces never amounted to much. During the seven years following Mary Pickford's much-publicized 1920 Reno breakup with Owen Moore, Nevada courts granted about 1,000 divorces a year.[5] In 1927, Nevada reduced its nineteenth-century residency requirement from six months to three months and increased its annual divorce count to 2,500. Three years later, in 1931, the year gambling was legalized, Nevada lowered its residency requirement to six weeks, again doubling its rate of divorce "production." But in 1931, when an unprecedented 5,260 people got their decrees in Reno, divorces there still constituted less than 3 percent of divorces nationwide.[6] Nonetheless, to most Americans, Reno *meant* divorce—as well as a number of other illicit vices. A 1933 article in the pulp magazine *True Detective* gushed, "Whatever you want—wine, women, or song—gambling, prostitution, marriage or divorce—Reno has it. And it's legal. Reno's motto is: You can't do wrong—we'll legalize it!"[7]

Divorce and its by-products proved a lucrative industry.[8] The Reno residency period was carefully designed to guarantee that divorcées would pay several months' rent and purchase a multitude of other necessary and luxury services during their stay. In his 1942 history of Nevada, Richard G. Lillard remarks that for the roughly eighteen thousand inhabitants in Reno in 1932, there were thirteen women's clothiers, twenty-three beauty parlors, forty-three doctors, and sixty-two restaurants.[9] A 1934 *Fortune* magazine article estimated that divorce brought in approximately $3 to $4 million in income to Reno and that individual divorce seekers spent an average of $1,500

The departure for Reno

▪ For now, alas, not secretly nor under cover, but openly, with all sense of shame put aside, now by word, again by writing, by theatrical productions of every kind, by romantic fiction, by amorous and frivolous novels, by cinematographs portraying in vivid scene, addresses broadcast by radio-telephony, in short, by all the inventions of modern science, the sanctity of marriage is being trampled upon and derided . . . POPE PIUS XI. From the ENCYCLICAL ON MARRIAGE

Cartoon by Galbraith in *Vanity Fair*, August 1, 1931. © 1931 Galbraith/*Vanity Fair* © 1931 Condé Nast Publications, Inc.

during a six-week stay (although the writers suggest that exceptionally frugal women could get by on as little as $225).[10]

Famous for attracting movie stars and socialites,[11] Reno also became the temporary home of the divorcing literati. Over the years, Sherwood Anderson, Kay Boyle, C. L. R. James, Clare Boothe (Luce), Mary McCarthy, Arthur Miller, Katherine Anne Porter, and the wives of Eugene O'Neil, Sinclair Lewis, Orson Welles, and Waldo Frank all came to Reno to get their decrees. By the 1930s, questing to Reno seemed almost inevitable in the lives of modern middle-class women—at least according to the plethora of Reno narratives that flooded popular culture. In the year following the 1931 change in Nevada residency laws, at least eight novels about Reno divorces were published.¹² In fact, many of the period's most popular writers of romance and detective fiction, including Faith Baldwin, Earl Derr Bigger, and Leslie Ford, penned Reno divorce novels. Hollywood followed suit, not only with a smattering of Reno references and a plenitude of divorce films (what Stanley Cavell calls the 1930s "films of remarriage"),¹³ but also with films in which the Reno divorce quest occupied center screen. MGM's star-studded 1939 film adaptation of Boothe's satirical play *The Women* is simply the most expensive and best known of a fairly rich genre of motion pictures.¹⁴ Yet it is this film that sums up the prevailing popular sentiment about middle-class marriage when thrice-married Countess DeLave (Mary Boland) laments, "No matter what you pick [your husbands] for where does it get you?" "On the train to Reno," the soon-to-be-divorced Mary (Norma Shearer) and Miriam (Paulette Goddard) answer in refrain.

That a railroad quest set Reno production in motion seemed to underscore the ideological import of the destination—and of this means of getting there. "Railroads were the referent, and progress the sign, as spatial movement became so wedded to the concept of historical movement that these could no longer be distinguished," writes Susan Buck-Morss in her reading of Walter Benjamin.¹⁵ If Marx, perhaps optimistically, used the locomotive as a metaphor for revolutionary progress, Benjamin suggested instead that "perhaps revolutions are the reaching of humanity traveling in this train for the

Postcard for *The Women* (MGM 1939). Author's collection.

emergency brake."[16] Social revolution, Benjamin implies, necessitates a slowing down or stopping of modernist progress. (At the very least, a price must be paid to race through time en route to Somewhere.)

In contrast to monumentalist narratives of competitive capitalism and imperialism, those allegorized by the train, Benjamin insisted on focusing on the "small, discarded objects," the waste products of progressive narratives of history. The dialectical relationship between allegories of trains and those of trash seems abundantly clear. Not only do trains produce trash, the waste and refuse of fuel, machinery, and bodies in transit, but trash itself implies movement, history, and labor. Trash is the exhausted material of "no worth or value," the abject defilement that "is jettisoned from the symbolic system[s]" of modernity.[17] It is the mess that spews forth from historical gaps, which narratives of progress have thrown out, ridden over, stitched between, glossed. And it defines its own mode of production. "To trash," according to the 1911 *Century Dictionary*, is to "walk or run with exertion, to fatigue, to labor a point"; while "to be trashed" is to be worn out, "bungled, spoiled; ill-treated or injured; run down" and, implicitly, to have had a past when one was new, healthy, cherished, and whole.[18]

It is therefore telling that the Divorcée Special to Reno was a train filled with trash, the rejected partners and families who refused—or were refused by—the impositions of American progressive modernity. Nor is it surprising that 1930s Reno was largely narrated by trash—the pulp novels, sensation magazines, cartoons, and B-films that collectively made up the formulaic rubbish that was hungrily devoured by the voracious American masses.[19] Aptly, the train station at Reno materially performed the metaphoric intersection between progressive narratives of modernity and those "small, discarded objects" left in their wake. Reno flaunted its trash at the tracks. "Reno throws its worst face directly at the station," wrote Max Miller in his 1941 cultural history on the city, and it "appears to take pleasure in doing so, appears to take pleasure in indicating a turmoil of shack-stores, cheap saloons, a burleycue of gambling houses, even a tattoo shop, tough alleys—and a blur of constant excitement."[20] By legalizing gambling as a way for divorcées to pass time during their enforced residency, Reno relied on an economy that simultaneously enforced and alleviated the boredom of waiting, literally wasting or discarding time, which, according to Benjamin, is another by-product of modern life.[21]

Certainly, divorce, particularly a Reno divorce, can be considered a product of modernity as well as its sign. It seemed to redo and renew the institution of marriage. "But you will divorce, *nicht wahr*?" Susan Hale's German friend asks her in *Half a Loaf*, Grace Hegger Lewis's roman à clef about her breakup with Sinclair Lewis. "It is so easy I am told in America in this place so funnily named Renoo. You have also the word 'renew'? Renoo, renew—the same thing?"[22] Divorce itself seemed to modernize Reno. In John Ham-

Postcard.
Courtesy of Special Collections Department. University of Nevada, Reno, Library.

lin's 1931 novel *The Whirlpool of Reno*, stodgy Minnie Brooks exclaims, "Why Reno is a real up-to-date town now, thanks to our divorcees." A fellow permanent resident, Jane, snaps back the plaint of many critics of modernity in its Depression-era guise: "A shame we're not as we used to be.... Far better to be provincial and pure than up-to-date and corrupted."[23]

covering tracks

Landing in Reno one October night in 1994, I saunter blindly past the airport slot machines, rent a silver Cavalier, and drive to Circus Circus, a gigantic, cut-rate casino decorated with a neon clown-faced facade that dominates Virginia Street. Almost no one takes the train to Reno anymore; few of the unhappily wed need travel here for their decrees. (Still, the tradition holds somewhat. The next day, in the midst of all the takeout wedding chapels, I spot a small brick office with window signs that proclaim, "Divorce Made Easy. Papers while you wait").

I am not a divorcée. I am not a gambler either, at least not of the monetary sort, and while there are many gamblers here, there are few of the high rollers who frequent Las Vegas, Reno's twin city to the south. It feels incongruous to do archive research here amidst the neon and polyester crowd, a crowd that loses you in its girth and anonymity. Still, everyone seems familiar, as if you'd seen them on a rerun of *Roseanne*: white, overweight, middle-aged, lower middle-class. It is not the Reno I have imagined for so many months. Yet it does possess the dim-lit tackiness coincident with tourism brochures. The next day, a woman at the Reno tourist bureau marks a street map to point out landmarks of Old Reno, a Reno of seventy years ago, a Reno of modern times.

The Art Deco facade of the El Cortez hotel, one of the few Depression-era hotels still in use, is majestic. But inside, the dingy, smoky lobby seems out of touch, passé, even seedy. On the wall of the bar next door, past rows of the omnipresent slot machines, are pictures of the Old Days, of women gambling and cowboys riding in the rodeo. That afternoon, I drive past the mansions that overlook Riverside Drive. Autumn leaves glow red, bronze, and brown against the late-afternoon sun, and the houses, formerly owned by Nevada governors, gamblers, and racketeers, are a bit imperial, if in cases somewhat run-down. Beneath them, by the Truckee River in Wingfield Park, three teenage boys toss around a basketball in the fading light.

I haven't yet found what I am looking for. Embedded in my own Reno quest is the search for a private saga in a public tale, a missing piece of my family narrative that has been unwritten from our history. Once, over dinner, my mother divulged all she knew of a family secret: Long before he met my grandmother, my grandfather had married a woman who "ran around," then ran off and killed herself in New Orleans. There were obvious gaps in this outdated Victorian narrative. Several years later, I discovered where my grandfather's first wife ran off to—not to New Orleans, at least not at first, but to Reno. To get a divorce.

RENO-VATING THE PAST

It has been argued that modernity reduces "culture to the language of production."[24] In these terms, it might be said that Reno spoke a rather complicated tongue. The wordplay and puns popularly used to narrate the spaces and symbols of Reno during its heyday construct meaning by simultaneously building and unbuilding themselves. A few of these "high-comedy localisms" as defined by Lillard in his 1942 history of Nevada:

> taking the cure (putting in six weeks' residence), Alimony Park (the city plaza opposite the county courthouse), Bridge of Sighs (the Virginia Street bridge over the Truckee River),[25] pouring a divorcee on the train (seeing her off after the decree), wash day (Monday, sometimes Tuesday, too, when default cases come up), the Separator (the courthouse),[26] divorcee (meaning either man or woman, from arrival in Nevada until actually divorced), Divorcee Special (the noon train from the East), Dresden (a relatively sexless woman who lives to be looked at), six weeks' sentence, the divorce business.[27]

The wordplay largely relies on making absurd connections between divorce and the built environment—buildings, legislation, and time schedules. A building has agency, a bridge has emotions, and a person awaiting her divorce decree is always feminine (a divorcée) and always already divorced.

Today, the overarching aesthetic of Reno is one of unbuilding and re-a b

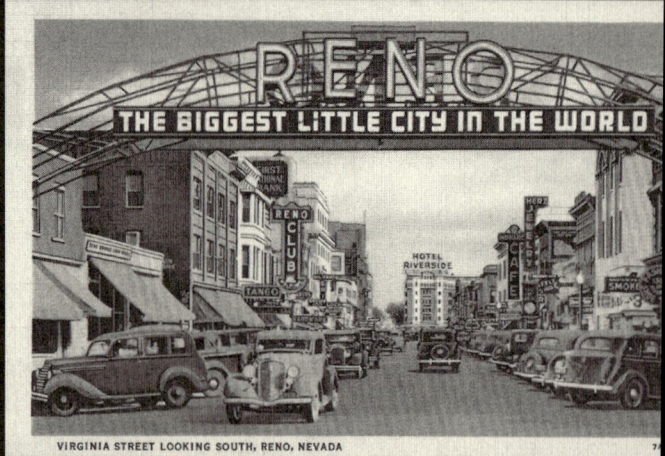

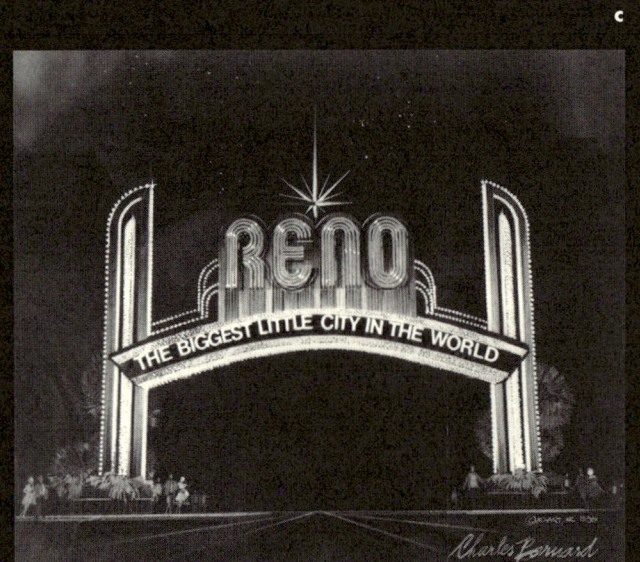

c

d

building monuments, of erasing the past while retaining its names.[28] The famed Reno arch, at the gateway to the casino district on Virginia Street, inscribes in gaudy neon Reno's self-proclaimed slogan, "The Biggest Little City in the World." The arch that crosses Virginia Street today was built during the 1970s, replacing an earlier neon version built in 1964, which replaced an electrically torched gateway constructed in 1938, which replaced the first arch, a bulb-lit wrought iron structure that was designed for the Nevada Transcontinental Exposition in 1927 that celebrated the completion of the Lincoln Highway and the New Victory Highway (U.S. Route 40).

The Riverside Hotel, which housed many of the wealthier divorcées in small apartments and adjoining suites, went through four complete reconstructions between 1872 and 1960, three of them between 1923 and 1951. The turreted Victorian hotel, built in 1872, burned to the ground in 1923. The lot was bought by the Reno financial luminary George Wingfield and reopened, rebuilt under the same name in 1927. At the height of the divorce boom in 1948, the architect of the 1927 structure, Frederic DeLongchamps, designed a massive renovation and expansion project that doubled the hotel in size and capacity. Yet by the mid-1990s, the Riverside stood in a liminal space. Asbestos-filled and too expensive to renovate, it was boarded up but not demolished, its plastic facade cracked and windows plastered with Do Not Enter signs. Throughout the 1990s, the building remained much the same, though eventually colorful signs emerged, which optimistically proclaimed the building's future transformation into an artists' cooperative. And, as these things happen in the odd liaison between artistic communities and gentrification, the Riverside Artist Lofts did finally open in October 2000.[29] They include subsidized apartments and workspaces for artists, a gallery, and "arts friendly" commercial spaces. "You have to pinch yourself every morning," the Artspace Website quotes a resident artist as saying.

The structure is symptomatic of Reno's present identity crisis. "Reno wants to be Las Vegas," a directory assistant operator tells me in a rather extended call for information. "But it's not." Defined by negation, Reno is a multivalent text that continually, cyclically builds and unbuilds itself. Its name stays the same, but the surface changes. Narratives about contemporary Reno consume and rebuild Reno's past, without renaming the present. In doing so, they simultaneously deny and affirm that an altered past ever was there, that historical change could ever occur. In Reno, urban renewal is obscured because the names of the built environment never seem to change. Present-day Reno seems a disposable place that seeks the illusion of durability, a place that is grounded in an aesthetic of change that reads itself as an aesthetic of permanence. The contemporary erasure of the discursive and material alterations of modern Reno's built monuments seems to eradicate the grotesque sideshow of labor and waste, as befits a place that foregrounds consumption."[30] Yet, 1930s Reno did not flaunt the "front stage of mass con-

a. Reno Arch (1931).
Postcard.
Courtesy of the Nevada Historical Society.

b. Reno Arch (1937).
Postcard.
Author's collection.

c. Reno Arch (1950).
Postcard.
Courtesy of the Nevada Historical Society.

d. Reno Arch (1964).
Postcard.
Courtesy of the Nevada Historical Society.

e. Reno Arch (1986).
Architectural drawing.
Courtesy of the Nevada Historical Society.

RIVERSIDE HOTEL 1862 to 1946

The Riverside Artist Lofts

THREE MONTHS IN RENO
Designed by noted Nevada architect Frederic J. DeLongchamps, the Riverside Hotel is an impressive six-story red brick edifice in the Late Gothic Revival style. It was built in 1926 to provide temporary living quarters for out-of-state visitors seeking to take advantage of Nevada's liberal residency requirement — three months — for obtaining a divorce. With the advent of no-fault divorce laws in the 1970s, it went into decline; in 1987, one year after being named to the National Register of Historic Places, the Riverside closed its doors.

A NEW HOME FOR ARTISTS
The Riverside occupies a picturesque site on the south bank of the Truckee River in the vibrant Reno Redevelopment District, a burgeoning arts and entertainment area. Downtown Reno is just across the river; the Washoe County Courthouse is next door. Upper-floor residents enjoy panoramic views of downtown Reno, the Truckee, and, in the distance, the Sierra Nevada mountains.

In transforming the 61,320-square-foot building into an affordable live/work development, a $7.8 million project, Artspace converted the upper five floors into 35 units containing one, two, or three bedrooms and ranging in size from 780 to 1,300 square feet. All units have large, open floor plans and large windows that admit abundant natural light — ideal environments for artists.

Part of the ground floor is occupied by Sierra Arts, the Reno-based arts group that served as Artspace's local partner on the project; Sierra Arts' space includes a gallery in which Riverside residents and other artists can exhibit their work. The rest of the ground floor is designated for arts-friendly commercial uses at market rates.

'YOU HAVE TO PINCH YOURSELF'
The opening of the Riverside Artist Lofts in October 2000 was big news. Some artists actually camped out in front of Sierra Arts' office the night before it began accepting applications. After the Riverside opened, the Reno Gazette-Journal described its new occupants as "some of downtown Reno's luckiest residents." The artists themselves agreed. "I love it," said one. "It's great. You have to pinch yourself every morning."

17 South Virginia • Reno, Nevada 89501 • Opened 2000

Artspace

sumption" in which "extraction, production, distribution, waste and pollution [were relegated] to a hidden backstage."[31] Modernist Reno reveled in making waste. Projecting a model of regulated, assembly-line production onto communities of women who were discarded from socially sanctioned American society, then transforming these transported East Coast women in the post-frontier West, Reno relied on a refuse economy that negotiates between two of the fictional monuments of American progressive modernity: Fordist industrial Americanism and imperialist frontier Americanization. If, as Benjamin suggests, every monument to progress leaves in its wake the refuse of archival fragments, pulp fiction, and other less institutionally sanctioned forms of narrative trash, then the critic who undergoes a quest to reread modernity's monumental fictions must wade through this waste, must gather signs, symbols, and clues, and piece them together as text and performance of modern place.

a. Four views of the Riverside Hotel (1862, 1872, 1920, 1946). Postcard.
Courtesy of the Nevada Historical Society.

b. Riverside Hotel (1994).
Photo slide by author.

c. Website for The Riverside Artist Lofts.
Courtesy of Artspace Projects, Inc.

part 2. the gender factory

My first day at the Nevada Historical Society archives, I am sick. I tell myself halfheartedly that I must be regurgitating the indulgences of intellectual gluttony. More likely, it's the minishrimp. Three days at Circus Circus are enough. Too much red gilt carpet and smoke lingering in my hotel room. I move down the street and over a bridge to the University Inn, a hybrid hotel and dormitory across the street from the University of Nevada, Reno campus.

Each day from then on, I sign in at the entrance of the archives and strip down, removing anything that might leave a permanent mark, an unwanted trace of my search. I browse carefully, fingers dry, through endless stacks of magazines, postcards, and folders of newspaper clippings, typing my findings onto a laptop computer or scratching them in pencil onto a yellow legal pad.

One day, among the case files and photos and torn Christmas cards in the papers of the famed Reno judge George Bartlett, I find the following scrap: From the then future playwright Clare Brokaw (Boothe Luce) to Judge Bartlett, July 15, 1929:

> Judgie it is two months since I left Nevada with a divorce decree in my hand, and in my heart a conviction that events have not born out (you could have told me this!) that the major decree would settle all my problems, all the major ones, at least. Alas! I find that a decree is very much like a peace-treaty which ends a state of war, but leaves the countries in an infinitely more precarious and delicate psoition [sic] of reconstructions and readjustment. At first you are wildly glad that it is over, and you are inflated with a feeling of victory and power, but then, as you survey the little ruins and desolation

around you, you are overwhelmed with remorse that it ever had to be. Then you resolutely turn your face to the future, resolving all sorts of intelligent things, and start in painfully, a little wearily to reconstruct your life anew."[32]

"MASS CULTURE AS WOMAN"

Rising divorce rates after the Great War were attributed to all the supposed pollutants of modern-day life, including "the movement for women's rights" and the "entry of women into industry" as well as a myriad of causes such as "low mentality," "nerves," "yellow journalism," "jazz," "the Ford car," and "irreligion."[33] Alfred Cahen's influential 1932 study statistically derived "four important factors" that he believed were the cause of increasing divorce rates: the rise in economic production; the growth of cities; the increase in women wage earners; and the declining birthrate.[34] In Cahen's logic the rupture of the patriarchal family system became a toxic by-product of modern industrialism and urbanization. Divorce was construed as a problem of laboring women who had been seduced by the products and processes of modernity and had thereby become less dependent on men.

Still, the possibility that domestic life could be remodeled to function on modern paradigms became a utopian as well as an ominous prospect for social theorists—and was a premise already put into practice by Henry Ford, who made no secret of attempting to intervene in the private life of his workers.[35] If Fordism seemed to be gender-neutral because it distinguished between concrete tasks rather than individual workers, then the logical outgrowth of its practice would be to "take to pieces" the machinery of the patriarchal family and the stay-at-home wife. In practice, however, Fordism relied on a logic in which gender superseded task differentiation, in which workers first were distinguished through gender-appropriate jobs. As Peter Wollen remarks in his analysis of Antonio Gramsci's writings on Fordism, "the workforce of a factory . . . is itself 'like a machine which cannot, without considerable loss, be taken to pieces too often and renewed with single parts.' The wife waiting at home becomes another such permanent machine part."[36]

The gender-appropriateness of women's employment was a point of contention during the Depression, when the economic hardship of the 1930s forced an increasing percentage of married women into wage labor. By 1940, 35 percent of all wage-earning women were married, as opposed to 28.5 percent a decade earlier.[37] Moreover, the proportion of unemployed women, while significant, was generally lower than that of men, especially in states that relied on heavy industries such as mining, metal work, and building.[38] This disproportion caused a backlash against women workers, according to Alice Kessler-Harris, who quotes Norman Cousins's 1939 solution to unemployment: "There are approximately 10,000,000 people out of work in the

United States today . . . there are also 10,000,000 or more women, married and single, who are job holders. Simply fire the women, who shouldn't be working anyway, and hire the men. Presto! No unemployment. No Relief rolls. No depression."[39]

Some industries had done just that. Section 213 of the 1932 Federal Economy Act legislated that married employees (usually women) should be fired first in the event of a personnel reduction if their spouses (usually men) also held federal government jobs. Public school systems both refused to hire and often fired women teachers. Railroads and other transportation industries were barred to married women. Unions refused women admission. Until 1939, legislatures in twenty-six states were reviewing bills to ban married women from state employment.[40]

Representations of Depression-era Reno addressed these controversies head-on. For the Reno economy quite literally projected a Fordist ideology onto the public regulation of private life and in doing so revealed its ruptures. The legal assembly line of the Reno "divorce mill,"[41] as it was popularly called, relied on the specialized labor of interchangeable lawyers, defendants, and prosecutors to mass-produce trials that were grounded on identical evidence (a vague assertion of cruelty and desertion); from prosecutors with identical residency status (exactly six weeks' continuous residency and the declared intention to make Nevada a permanent home); affirmed by identical witness testimonies (landlords who swore "I saw her every day for six weeks"); which resulted in identical judgments (a divorce decree).[42]

Reno divorcées were metaphorized as factory workers. In *Half a Loaf*, Susan Hale comments that in moving to Reno she "had bound herself to a definite six months' job."[43] And like assembly-line work, the routine of getting "Reno-vated" is so monotonous a labor for divorcées that an "asterisks" or "a line of stars" would be quite adequate to cover the narratives of the "empty five months and twenty-nine days in the lives of many of the women Susan met."[44] If divorcées were workers, however, they also were processed like so much raw material in an industrial mill. The tenets of Nevada's residency laws made all of Reno's temporary citizens not just "created equal," but interchangeable like industrial parts. In *Half a Loaf*, Susan's lawyer reminds her of the generic testimony she is to give in court: "Don't forget to say 'yes' when you are asked if you intend to make Reno your permanent residence."[45] Before her divorce trial, Sheila Randolph's Reno attorney, in Charles Parmer's 1932 novel *After Divorce?* reminds her, "Just remember—answer as I coached you."[46]

Fordism always unbuilds while building, renovating means of construction to build ever more identical products faster, more cheaply than ever before, to make, as Terry Smith argues in *Making the Modern: Industry, Art and Design in America*, "nothing original, but everything new."[47] Reno divorce legislation, as organizing structure, transformed itself simply by shortening the residency requirement allowed in the state, thereby offsetting threatened

"The Divorce Factory." 1931 cartoon reprinted from the *New York World-Telegram* in *The Reno Divorce Racket*. Courtesy of the Nevada Historical Society.

competition for divorce from Arkansas, Florida, the Virgin Islands, and Mexico. But while standardized divorce production became increasingly time-efficient in Reno, the product, like the Model T, didn't change. Nor did the power dynamics of the Reno factory's patriarchal management structure—the lawyers, judges, politicians, and police—ever substantially alter.

The Reno factory relied on a strictly gendered economy. Although historically about two-fifths of Reno divorces were obtained by men, in Reno narratives divorcées are almost always portrayed as women alone. Upon arrival in Reno, writes Lewis in *Half a Loaf*, divorcées soon began "casting about for male society. There wasn't any."[48] Of course, there were men in Reno, those cowboys, gamblers, miners, and divorce lawyers who constituted the largely male permanent population of Reno. Local men bucked for money and power within the system; each change in legislation seemed to promise the arrival of more prospective divorcées and a bundle in easy income for the residents of Reno. The August 17, 1933, entry in the attorney Clel Georgetta's diary suggests just how central divorce had become to the Reno economy:

> Today I have in my office 11 active unfinished divorce cases and 6 other cases—17 cases in all. But then, Clel, calm yourself, that is only a drop in the ocean compared with Judge Souters [sic] practice. Today he has 52 unfinished divorce cases—$250 each and a few contests at from $750 on up. At least $13000—in sight WOW! Came to my office in the evening.[49]

By 1932, Reno employed 127 lawyers compared to the 44 in Ogden, Utah, a town that had over twice Reno's population at the time.[50] Litigation revenue averaged $250 in lawyers' fees plus $40 in court costs per client for an uncontested divorce and could run well into the thousands of dollars for contested cases or when large settlements were being negotiated.[51] In Dorothy Walworth Carman's 1932 novel *Reno Fever*, Elisabeth Wane reflects, "The law had been carefully administered to bring money to the town. Every broken life means so many dollars."[52] "We are all caught in the legal machinery of marriage and divorce," comments Nairn in Carman's novel before she does herself in.[53]

44 RENO

factory life

An inquiry from William D. Shew, Attorney at Law, Hartford, Conn. to George A. Bartlett, Esq. Reno, Nevada, April 3, 1943:

> I have been consulted in the last few days by three girls, all of whom are factory workers in Hartford, relative to the possibilities of securing Reno divorces. I believe they are live prospects and are held back solely by the question of finances and what I would like to find out are two things. First, if two or three of these girls came out, just what could you see your way clear to secure their divorces for? Let me know, including costs. Secondly, they desire to know whether there is a reasonable possibility of their securing work of any kind while they are in Reno. It could either be factory work or even restaurant work, just so long as some of their living expenses were paid.

Reply from George A. Bartlett to William D. Shew, April 8, 1943:

> It is difficult, of course, without discussing with clients so as to know the amount of labor that might be involved with their particular case, to fix fees in advance but with people who have to work for a living, as the girls you refer to must, I usually, after discussing conditions with them, fix a very moderate fee, depending, of course, upon their capacity to pay, either at the close of the case or later on; rarely, however, charging above $150 and sometimes cutting that to $100 or less. The costs of Court approximate $53. inclusive of both sides; defendants' appearance fee, I think I can arrange to have done for $25. each.
>
> There is a reasonable possibility of securing work, but of course I cannot guarantee it. It would be more apt to be a restaurant or housework, as we have no factory enterprises here; however, please be assured I will do my best to secure work for them and fix fees according to capacity to pay.[54]

SEX AND STANDARDIZATION

The new methods of work required by the "planned economy" of Fordist Americanism were "inseparable from a specific mode of living and of thinking and feeling life," according to Gramsci. Therefore, they necessitated the production of a new type of worker and a new type of man—a man whose sexual instinct had been "suitably regulated" and "rationalized."[55] Gramsci points out, however, that American attempts at rationalizing the sexual instinct had backfired, producing "unhealthy 'feministic' deviations," sexually liberated upper-class divorcées who had achieved economic independence through favorable divorce settlements.[56] Although this group never constituted more than a tiny percentage of American women who divorced, it came to represent the norm.

Gramsci harps on the divorcée as an emergent American class and the modern counterpart of the European "parasitic" noble classes. Even the male industrialist does not seem to warrant such wrath. While the male industrialist labors, Gramsci writes,

> [his wife and daughters] . . . travel; they are continually crossing the ocean to Europe. . . . (It is worth recalling that ship's captains in the United States have been deprived of their right to celebrate marriage on board ship, since so many couples get married on leaving Europe and divorced again before disembarking in America.) Prostitution in a real sense is spreading, in a form barely disguised by fragile legal formulae.[57]

For women, temporal, spatial, economic, or marital displacement becomes prostitution, the *real* thing, according to Gramsci, which regulated prostitution presumably is not. While he declares that "the new industrialism wants monogamy," he simultaneously warns against the "abolishment of organized, legal prostitution." Divorce becomes even less respectable than regulated prostitution, which in Reno was a socially sanctioned gendered division of labor.[58]

During the 1920s and 1930s, Reno housed the last legal red light district in the United States.[59] The most notorious (or at least famous) of the Reno houses was the Stockade, opened in 1923 and overseen by the city government until 1942, when the federal War Department shut it down permanently.[60] Legally relegated to the sidelines of the city—250 feet from any public thoroughfare—and thereby erased from the dominant spatial narrative of the city, the Stockade was not so much a brothel as a workstation for as many as eighty "self-employed" prostitutes who paid the management company that ran the red light district $1.50 for meals and $2.00 to $2.50 to rent a "crib," a small, two-room apartment, for one of three eight-hour shifts.[61] The women reaped whatever profits were to be had in that time, at an average $2.00 per trick and $20 to $40 in eight hours.[62]

The Reno city government received taxes on the land and building and bankrolled patrolmen at $250 per month to protect the entrance to the district. Prostitutes were required to register their off-hour addresses with the police, were fingerprinted, checked through the FBI for criminal records, and submitted to a weekly medical examination by a city health officer for gonorrhea and a monthly exam for syphilis.[63] "A block of business offices, that was the stockade," muses the hairdresser Dorothy Boswin in Baldwin's 1940 collection *Temporary Address: Reno*: "The girls didn't live there. They worked there. No respectable woman got to see the fence and the terrain it shut off from the rest of town, there on the left bank of the Truckee."[64] To be transgressive in this scenario, then, was not to be a prostitute, but to be unprofessional, to be unregistered and unexamined or to perform sexual services outside of sanctioned spatial or temporal boundaries.

The Stockade was an unimpressive structure made up of two low brick buildings that faced onto a tree-covered courtyard that was blocked on one end by a high wooden fence and on the other by a dancehall called the Pastime Club. "From the outside [the Stockade] looked like the rear of a movie set, makeshift and unfinished," wrote Lillard in 1942:

> A few weak bare electric lights hung above an unpaved parking lot in front. Inside, the "Stockade" or "Bull Pen," was a long, narrow, slightly bent lane between two low continuous red-brick buildings. . . . The lane was a promenade for male visitors. It was shaded by small trees. In the daytime it looked tawdry. Illuminated at night by more bare electric lights, strung on wires, it gave the purely visual effect of a livestock pavilion at a country fair or of a debutante's garden party with booths and concessions. At no time during the night or day did it seem glamorous or enticingly sinful. It was only banal.⁶⁵

In its banality, the Stockade performs the tension between narrative and materiality that is constitutive of place making. Lillard suggests that the brothel is legible as a material site—for it could be anywhere and anything—only as a result of the stories told about it. Narrative, then, is what produces place out of site and suggests the means through which singularity might coincide with the interminable sameness that drives the Reno factory. In paralleling cattle pavilions, country fair booths, and a debutantes' receiving line with a

"Mrs. Massie on way to Reno." Photo from ACME Newspictures, Inc. January 10, 1934. *New York World-Telegram* and the *Sun* Newspaper Photograph Collection (Library of Congress, Prints and Photographs Division) LC-USZ62-134364.

Entrance to the Stockade. Photo courtesy of the Nevada Historical Society.

THE DIVORCE FACTORY 47

house of prostitution, however, Lillard makes it clear that narrative is itself subject to the constraints of genre and reception. Women are all produce and similarly produced, he suggests; they are all prostitutes, all debutantes, all commodities-on-display. What distinguishes one from the other is the way that generic stories are distinctly read.

For some, as I suggested earlier, the threat of modern marketing and mass production was that they might erase the visible external markers of social distinction that used to delineate the good girls from the bad. "Since the jazz age gave cosmetology and 'sex appeal' to all women," writes Lillard, "prostitutes have lost their monopoly on traditional means of allure."[66] Walking around town on their off-hours, prostitutes look like "any working girls." He claims, "Only seeing a Nevada woman in a house of prostitution indicates her means of livelihood."[67] Reno old-timer Piute Pete tells *True Detective* reporter Con Ryan, "Here in Reno the Bull pen gals got just one complaint the amateurs, the divorcees and debutantes, cut into their business too much. 'Tain't accordin' to union rules, but I guess they ain't nothin' the local gals can do about it."[68]

Indistinguishable from prostitutes, divorcées become prostitutes. *Real* prostitutes. And prostitutes become, well, something else. "The women who come out here ... to divorce their husbands, their second husbands sometimes, or their third, or fourth, the women with other men waiting for them, the women out to get all they can, what makes 'em better than the stockade girls?" the Reno rancher Kenny plaintively asks Dorothy Boswin in *Temporary Address: Reno*. "They start out even. . . . I suppose it's legal either way."[69] In fact, Kenny comments that he has more respect for "those girls in the stockade" than for Reno divorcées. After all, the unofficial, but supposedly authentic, cause of all Reno marital breakups was sexual incompatibility.[70] "Consciously or unconsciously, my dear young ladies, sex dissatisfaction is at the bottom of every divorce," Nairn's Reno lawyer tells her and Elisabeth Wane in *Reno Fever*.[71]

Yet if modern marriage relies on an economy of sex, what distinguishes even doting wives from prostitutes? Hale, in *Half a Loaf*, complains of Reno's "social disorder" in which, "the garage assistant may be the best golfer at the country club, where you play roulette beside the woman who shampoos your hair, where you gossip with the hotel chambermaid who is also getting a divorce."[72] Reno might give the illusion of obliterating class boundaries because the temporary residents are most obviously and collectively categorized as divorcées, but within Reno class markers are not wholly erased. "You are of the elite, Mrs. Randolph," Sheila's Reno lawyer tells her in *After Divorce?* "Your set either goes to a dude ranch in the hills, takes a bungalow, or else a suite at the Riverside Hotel; I chose the bungalow for you; a bit more privacy, don't you think? . . . The remainder—of our clients . . . take furnished apartments in town, or else go to boarding-houses, where rabbit stew is the *pièce de résistance*. Rabbit stew and the odor of cabbage."[73] Immersed in the confusingly crass ubiquity of mass production and modern social mores, women cannot be distinguished through the usual means. Without the signatures of husbands, all modern women seem to look and behave exactly alike. Only the spatial and legislative context in which a woman is housed might signify her social place.

a joke (part 1)

From the *Nevada Review Monthly*, May 1928:

> A San Francisco couple had decided that they were no longer compatable (*sic*) and were making plans for their little girl and the lady of the family to spend 3 months in Reno. One evening before the departure of the wife and daughter the better half said to the husband: "What have you been telling our little girl about Reno, I just heard her saying her prayers and she said, 'Good-bye God, we are going to Reno.'"
>
> "That's queer," answered the husband, "I will listen to her tomorrow night and see what she says then, as I have not been telling her any tales about Reno."
>
> The next evening after listening to the daughter say her prayers, the husband said to the wife: "You must have been wrong, for she only said, 'Good! By God we are going to Reno.'"[74]

SEX AND SPACE

In *Making the Modern*, Smith analyzes the spatial implications of industrial Fordism. The mobile assembly line in Ford's Highland Park factory becomes, he argues,

> a frame in space—across which one's task slides. In other parts of the factory, the stand vanishes to become a similar frame upon which the worker's task appears to be performed, then again and again. And the task is now much reduced from a gathering together, however regulated, to a passing touch, utterly controlled.[75]

Smith points out that the assembly line regulates space both by limiting the area in which workers can perform their tasks (workstations are close together, even toilets are close to the line) and by regulating their movement within that limited space. Touch itself is regulated so that too lingering a contact on the parts passing through the line upsets the machinery. If we consider how Fordism gets projected metaphorically onto sexual and domestic relationships (not insignificantly by Ford himself), this suggestion has several interesting consequences: Movements and touch that do not strictly enhance productivity or, perhaps, reproductivity become not simply superfluous but unallowable. They threaten to slow the whole system down.

Regulated prostitution, therefore, fits a Fordist scenario well. It has no superfluous moves, systematically reproducing a model of sex that is ritualized and regulated to enhance the temporal and spatial flow of male semen. A man must thrust his penis efficiently, with the rhythmic and regulated movement of a robot performing a limited task within a limited time. (Women, who are distressingly inconsistent when it comes to their sexual response, don't easily conform to such a systematic approach.) In fact, when procreative reproduction is not desired regulated prostitution actually offers a preferred method of satisfying male sexual need. Prostitution sets a time limit on touch. The more clients a prostitute services during her eight-hour shift, the more money she makes. If a Stockade prostitute makes forty dollars during her eight-hour shift, that means she must see twenty men at twenty to twenty-five minutes per trick. Such a model of sexuality does not enforce male monogamy, as Gramsci would like, except where procreation is concerned. Instead, it relies on a logic of heterosexual promiscuity that requires workers to participate in production (if not reproduction) by identically tightening an infinite series of women's screws. The conveyor belt of the Fordist assembly line ensures that as soon as a worker finishes each task, an interchangeable object on which to labor identically must appear. Indeed, the object will appear whether the worker has accomplished the last task or not.

But who is the worker in such a scenario? The prostitute or the client? And who then is labored upon? Prostitutes in traditional Marxist analysis are considered to be not workers, but commodities that symbolize man-to-man exchange.[76] Yet the Reno Stockade's internal, tree-covered courtyard with its rows of open-doored cribs that reveal women-as-commodities does not so much represent a "livestock pavilion" as a skylit shopping arcade or, more explicitly, a department store that sells sex/women as mass-produced goods. "Business it was," writes Lillard, "more above board and honest than many a transaction in department stores."[77] Following Benjamin, Buck-Morss points out, however, that, given agency, the prostitute becomes a dialectical figure:

> Whereas every trace of the wage laborer who produced the commodity is extinguished when it is torn out of context by its exhibition on display, in the prostitute, both moments remain visible. As a dialectical image, she "synthesizes" the form of the commodity and its content: She is "commodity and seller in one."[78]

In Reno, a legalized prostitute reveals this dialectic only within the confines of the Stockade, where she is commodity, laborer, and seller. Outside of that context the dialectic is erased. As a woman in Reno, she is still a commodity, but she loses the ability to sell herself. More important, because the prostitute seems unsellable outside of the Stockade, she ceases to reveal the sellability of all women in Reno, ceases to reveal how Reno's economy is dependent upon women's bodies and stories being bought and sold.

a joke (part 2)

From the Reno lawyer Clel Georgetta's diary, Monday, September 11, 1933:

> This A.M. I ran off Frank L____'s (New York) divorce case. The courtroom was full. He testified his wife drank and gave wild parties. I asked him if she ever did anything that embarrassed him. He said yes. So I asked him to re late to the Court a specific incident. He said that one night, while living in an apt. house the wife was staging a party. The landlord put his head in the dumbwaiter shaft and called upstairs to be quiet. The wife walked over and dumped a pail of garbage down on the landlord's head. He came up and put them out of the apt. that night. Frank said, Well, yes I was embarrassed. The whole court room broke out in a roar, even the Judge laughed and continued to laugh for some time.

NEW INDUSTRIAL WIVES

A narrative collapse between prostitutes and divorcées serves to obscure the specificity of Reno's divorce machinery, a machinery that is particularly modern both in what threatens it (single, financially independent, and productive women) and what sustains it (refused or refusing married and marrying women, geographic and social displacement, economic viability). Despite the titillating narratives that construct it, the Reno divorce mill is largely a social renovation machine. It takes the raw material of women who have been overly modernized and transforms them to fit the old frame. The past integrity of these raw materials (as married women) is incidental to the process that dismantles and refashions them into what Gramsci called a "new feminine personality," a woman who is "independent of men," *individual men*, but not of patriarchy itself. Renovation of women as raw materials, or *Reno-vation*, actually puts modern women back in their (traditional) place. Remade and refeminized, Reno-vated into remarriage and traditional roles, divorcées become ironic New Women, a far cry from their feminist predecessors, though perhaps not from Victorian wives. As the Reno local Minnie Borne points out in *Whirlpool of Reno*, "Free and easy as all get out in their talk; smokin' cigarettes, drinkin' cocktails, wearin' as few clothes as law'n order'll let 'em; but under their pretty skins [young divorcées are] prezactly the same as we used to be, now ain't they?"[79]

To be Reno-vated is not simply to get divorced, in other words, but to be quickly married again. While on a Reno dude ranch waiting for a di-

Postcard.
Courtesy of Special Collections, University of Nevada, Reno, Library.

vorce, Sylvia Fowler (Rosalind Russell), in MGM's *The Women*, reads from a newspaper clip about her husband's future wife: "Miriam 'Vanities' Aaron is now being *Reno-vated*. Three guesses Mrs. Howard Fowler who she's going to marry." The film opens with a telling tracking shot that follows a young woman through the rooms of Sydney's, the Taylorized beauty salon in which beauticians perform specialized functions, undoing society women through manicures, permanents, massages, and exercise instruction. The clients pass from room to room becoming increasingly monstrous and contorted until they exit the salon, finally remade but looking the same as when they entered. In this context, divorce becomes another normalizing gender process—along with grooming and fashion. A 1930s *Good Housekeeping* article goes so far as to conclude that "marriage can profit from divorce."[80]

The Reno-vation process is, in fact, a necessity. What would one do with these feminine products otherwise? Products gain value only through exchange, thus making the symbolic leap to commodities. In the Reno divorce mill a married woman enters as raw material; if remarried, she gains value, for she allows, as Luce Irigaray, Gayle Rubin, and others suggest, a homosocial exchange between men.[81] The johns who buy sex can offer prostitutes potential moral reform by Reno-vating their bed partners into feminine New Industrial Wives. "Many [Reno] prostitutes wished to get married and settle down," claims Lillard. "Some married local men, raised families and circulated in community life without meeting prejudice."[82] The Reno-vated wife, therefore, is the same with a difference. She is also "new and improved," making Reno-vation less akin to traditional Fordism than to the 1930s marketing philosophy of progressive obsolescence, in which products are consciously manufactured to become quickly outmoded, initiating their faster, more regular replacement. Progressive obsolescence made Ford's eschewal of style, what Stuart Ewen calls "Ford's puritanical commitment to 'homeliness,'" outmoded and a thing of the past.[83]

Still, in all cases, semen seems the ultimate Reno-vator. And children become the preferred products of the New Industrial domestic machine. The production of Reno-vated wives ensures reproduction as a means through which to increase the populace of consumers. In *Reno Fever*, Elisabeth wonders if a divorced woman with children was in a better way, for "at least she had something to show for the years. And yet, a child was always a link with the past. She could never make a fresh beginning."[84] Certainly, *The Women* relies on a progressive narrative that directs women to a life of dependent motherhood. Peggy Day (Joan Fontaine) is reunited with her husband only when she phones him from Reno to tell him there is a baby on the way. Edith Potter (Phyllis Povah), the only married New Yorker who does not get divorced in the film, is a regular reproduction machine. While her companions wait out their six weeks at a Reno dude ranch, she gives birth to her eighth child.

In contrast to Edith Potter's healthy brood, the child of the overdressed and "over-sexed" Delia in *Reno Fever* is disastrously "pale and meager." He has the

> undersized, second-rate look of an unwanted child. He kissed his mother timidly on the cheek. Delia treated him with that condescension which women, who make a career of sex, use for their children—by-products of the main industry. No, Delia was not a perfect animal because she could not reproduce healthy young. A stock breeder would have shot her.[85]

Mary and Little Mary reading. Still from *The Women* (MGM 1939). Courtesy of the Academy of Motion Picture Arts and Sciences.

In Reno, independent, sexual, career women become prostitutes or livestock, transforming their own children into trash. They are, in fact, worthy of little more than social and bodily erasure. Women's sexuality and sexual pleasure, therefore, must be subordinated to the tasks of running a home. In his 1943 pamphlet *Roads to Reno*, a contemporary evangelist, U. E. Harding, advised young wives, for example, that "cooking, cleaning and keeping yourself up" would prevent the need for Reno-vation.[86] Homes were rebuilt during the 1920s and 1930s on the philosophy that housework could be rationalized according to the principles of scientific management. "For women, the [home-]machine was to become a treadmill," argues Judy Wajcman. "The kitchen, now designed for a servantless family, was a compact fitted kitchen with room for one worker, the housewife. Neither its small size nor its location, sealed off from the rest of the house, were conducive to the sharing of kitchen duties."[87] Le Corbusier's utopian plan of a mass-produced "House Machine," which provided the impetus for such designs, was imagined as "healthy (and morally so too) and beautiful in the same way that the working tools and instruments which accompany our existence are beautiful."[88] As Ford himself hoped, rationalized living had become morally upright.

Reno becomes, finally, not a divorce mill, but "a regular matrimonial exchange. The air reeks of it."[89] And divorce is, in fact, only an odorous byproduct, pollution, blown off during a production process that transforms modern women into New Industrial Wives.[90] If women leave Reno without the prospect of remarriage and recommodification, the noxious stench of divorce tends to cling. Like their transgressive Victorian mothers, Reno women who refuse to remarry, refuse Reno-vation, refuse to become New (Industrial) Wives become disruptive by-products and must be discarded as pollution, rubbish, societal trash.

Being refused, according to Adele Leyton in *Whirlpool of Reno*, transforms one into refuse. She surmises, "It was to get away from this depressing, horrid sensation of being cast off, alone in the world, that threw these women into the reckless whirlpool of Reno's divorce colony."[91] Adele née Addie Brooks avoids this fate by paying for plastic surgery with her stock market winnings to lose and forget "her hideously twisted nose."[92] She returns remade to Reno, posing as a seductive divorcée, Adele Leyton, and claims that without such reconstruction she had only two choices: "Suicide or a nunnery—I couldn't decide which."[93] Refashioning her body and identity even before she puts herself on the Reno assembly line, Adele profits from Reno-vation, ultimately marrying a rich rancher without having to first go through a divorce. Yet un-Reno-vated women who refuse remarriage, domesticity, and reproductive bliss go crazy (like Sheila in Latifa Johnson's novel *Sheila Goes to Reno*), are abandoned after having abortions (like Dee in *Whirlpool of Reno*), take lethal doses of pills (like Nairn in *Reno Fever*), or, like Delia, preferably, are shot.

C Street, Virginia City, 1940. Photograph by Arthur Rothstein.
Courtesy of Library of Congress, Prints and Photographs Division, FSA-OWI Collection, Reproduction Number LC-USF34-029808-D DLC.

part 3. "the desert of the real"

The courthouse and archives are closed on Sundays, so I drive down Virginia Street out into the desert to pick through the remnants of the Comstock era.[94] And when I arrive at Virginia City, directed by billboards that promise endless treasures in the town, I have to remind myself that this is the real thing—a frontier town built in the silver mining days and abandoned (or almost) by the turn of the century. It's just gussied up and freshly painted, commercialized—it was so even back in the 1930s—to look both less and more real than it is.[95] It gives you that queasy feeling you get in Colonial Williamsburg; you recognize it because you've seen copies of it in Disneyland and in the sets of movie westerns.

Down on C Street in Virginia City, kids pan for gold and tourists stick coins in old-time slot machines. A fourteen-year-old belts out a country and western ballad in a casino not far from the opera house where Jenny Lind sang so many years before. Across the street is a museum of Mark Twain memorabilia. It fits to remember him by the name he invented for himself; it is all manufactured authenticity, this clutter you pay two dol-

THE DIVORCE FACTORY 55

lars at the door to walk through. It is the last day of the tourist season; tomorrow the town shuts down for the winter, and I feel lucky I made it to the last tour of a silver tycoon's B Street mansion in order to inspect the cracks in the walls created by (choose one) an earthquake or a mining blast a century ago. On the outskirts, the hills are scarred by miles and miles of underground mining tunnels. This is desert. Ochre and purple mountains are etched against the sky, and for a moment I forget about the crowds clamoring for fudge and frozen yogurt and a souvenir to remind them of something that never was.

I am never alone in Reno, even though I came out here alone. The repairman who fixed my hotel window left a few sprigs of flowers on the table by my bed with a note asking me out for coffee. I drove to Virginia City instead. The front desk clerk at the hotel saw me running in the evenings out by the tidy botanical gardens, past the barren Civil War cemetery fenced off behind a wire grate. He told me he felt a connection from the three words of greeting we shared. And I think, Reno is no longer used to women alone. Maybe, despite all those divorcées' claims, it never really was.

PRODUCING THE WEST

If violent reconstruction underlies many Reno narratives it is perhaps because embedded in the divorce colony is a legacy of imperialist frontier conquest. Unquestionably, Reno is narratively overdetermined by its spatial position in the American West, on the edge of the ruins of the Comstock Silver Mines. A 1939 pamphlet that largely focuses on Reno names Nevada the country's "last Frontier." Nevada becomes a place where a divorcée might "go Reno" by buying western riding togs.[96] Trend-conscious divorcées played cowboy (and *with* cowboys) on sometimes austere, sometimes luxurious dude ranches, taking full advantage of their stay in the not-so-Wild West.

When considered in this context, Frederick Jackson Turner's omnipresent and controversial 1893 thesis on the role of frontier expansion in constructing "the American, this new man" becomes curiously significant.[97] For Turner, the imagined frontier was both a "consolidating *agent*" that promoted the formation of a "composite nationality" and a *process* of encountering, settling, and traveling through "free space" in search of ever more novel places and experiences. The frontier as process was repetitive, according to Turner, requiring the individuated participation of "three classes of men"—pioneers, farmers, and entrepreneurial capitalists—who rolled one after the other "like the waves of the ocean" or, one might suggest, like parts on an assembly line.[98] Turner's evolutionary model posits the transformation of the frontier as an allegory for an American experience, one that has been perpetually repeated and is reproducible. Turner's American was an able-bodied individual who combined the peculiarly macho traits of "coarseness and strength," "acuteness and inquisitiveness" with a "practical, inventive turn of mind," a "masterful [though inartistic] grasp of material things," a "restless, nervous energy," a "dominant individualism," and "buoyancy and exuberance."[99] The deeper into the supposedly barren and primitive frontier the pioneer traveled the more American (read: masculine) he became.[100] Thorough Americanization seemed to erase even traces of his European (read: feminine) side.[101]

For Depression-era Americans, the conflation of migration and Americanization was not so ideologically simple. If freedom and mobility were constitutive of what Turner imagined as the American character, they also seemed responsible for divorce. "Modern freedom, the doctrine of Self Expression, the throwing off of restraints of a moral nature—all these factors give rise to the divorce evil," claims Harding.[102] Reno encouraged migration, providing *temporary* citizenship to individuals who quested West for the sole purpose of obtaining a divorce. By 1953, an estimated three million tourists visited Reno annually; transient residents outnumbered permanent residents by a ratio of one hundred to one.[103] However, whether Reno migration could be considered American was a subject of some debate. On one hand, the Reno divorce became a symbol of an inherent ideological conflict of American legal doctrine, which attempts to construct a cohesive nation out of united, but individually sovereign, states.[104] Advocates of individual state sovereignty, who argued that the U.S. Constitution requires that a legal judgment of one state be given "full faith and credit" in another, were forced into the awkward position of defending Reno divorces.[105] Opponents of divorce were forced to defend increasingly consolidated federal power over states' individual rights by attempting to legislate the National Uniform Divorce and Marriage laws that would effectively stop the Reno divorce industry in its tracks.[106]

On the other hand, a Reno divorce seemed to protect American women from un-American men. In Rupert Hughes's 1931 novel *No One Man*, a Reno judge grants "Nep" Newbold her divorce after hearing that her husband had "socked" her in the jaw; the judge wanted "to prove that Joe Sturgis [the husband] was the exception who proved the rule about American men never being rude to women."[107] Reno legend has it that the infamous Judge Moran once refused to grant a divorce because of insufficient evidence but changed his mind when he discovered that the plaintiff's husband was English. In Moran's opinion, Englishmen "niver [sic] knew how to treat a woman."[108]

case no. 38,192: divorce american-style

The native New Yorker Dorothy Butler divorced my English grandfather, Douglas A. Baker, on November 27, 1931, at 4:07 P.M. Judge B. F. Curler presided. When I later searched for Curler's files to see if I could uncover some record of the letters or notes exchanged before the divorce, I learned that time?

A. My husband told me at that time that he no longer cared for me and absolutely refused to support me.

Q. Did you give him any cause to leave you?

A. No, sir.

Q. Now, you have also alleged that for more than one year last past before the filing of this complaint, as a second cause of action, that since November, 1926, he neglected and refused to provide you with the common necessities of life. Is that true?

A. Yes, sir.

Q. And could he have provided you with clothing, food, and shelter if he had wanted to?

A. Yes, sir.

Q. Was he an able-bodied man?

A. Yes.

Q. And was he at that time?

A. Yes, sir.

THE COURT: I think that is sufficient, Mr. Raffetto.

MR. RAFFETTO: I believe that is all. You may cross-examine.

CROSS-EXAMINATION

BY MR. BURROWS: Q. Are you familiar with your husband's handwriting?

A. Yes.

Q. Have you often seen him write?

A. Yes, sir.

Q. I show you a paper which purports to be a power of attorney and ask you if that is the signature on that they were not accessible. The judge's private files had been destroyed or, at least, had not yet been donated anywhere. Dorothy was represented by Fiore Raffetto, Esq. of Frame and Raffetto. My grandfather wasn't present but was represented by John W. Burrows, Esq. Both attorneys were prominent in Reno. Their names appear on countless court documents. And when the microfilm coughed up a transcript of the trial it showed that the proceedings went through without a hitch.

My grandfather must have given in. Court records show that Dorothy's earlier complaint, which alleged nonsupport and willful desertion (both summary assertions), was rejected. On November 10 came this response: "Denies each and every allegation set forth and contained in paragraph V, of said complaint. WHEREFORE:—Defendant prays that plaintiff take nothing by her complaint."

No explanation. Nothing else was filed. In the end, the record stated that Douglas deserted Dorothy. She testified in court, "My husband told me . . . that he no longer cared for me and absolutely refused to support me." Dorothy got her decree.

Transcript of *Baker v. Baker*, case no. 38,192 in the Second Judicial District Court of the State of Nevada, County of Washoe. Filed November 27, 1931, at 4:07 P.M. Image by Ahn Na.

PUTTING WOMEN IN THEIR PLACE

The "Reno controversy" raised questions about what it meant for Americans to be defined by how (and where) they moved and what such movement implied.[109] Most women in Reno were narrated as migrants and transitory citizens who were decidedly displaced even as they simultaneously were placed through their spatial allegiances. Consider, for example, the cluster of nicknames that labeled the Reno brothel: A stockade is the holding pen in a prison; a bull pen is the cell in which prisoners are detained until they enter court; and a crib is an enclosed stall, chamber, or bed; a lockup or thieves' den; a "solidly built floating foundation or support."[110] Each of the terms describing the structure that marks Reno prostitutes refers both to its enclosed nature and to the transience of those it contains: It is a holding pen or waiting room; its foundation floats. Moreover, as I suggested earlier, being a legal Reno prostitute seemed a fluid social state since prostitutes could be Renovated into appropriate wives.

Likewise, the so-called floating population of Reno divorce seekers, Reno's "foster children" as one writer dubs them, live in a liminal state.[111] They are transient but fully viable citizens of Nevada. They belong both to Reno and, presumably, to the homes they have left. It is crucial to remember that for the bulk of their stays in Nevada, the heroines of Reno narratives, although referred to as divorcées, are not yet divorced. Such liminality has its benefits, according to Mary McCarthy in *The Company She Keeps*, who writes that *potential* Reno divorcées are accorded a state that is "deeply pleasurable in somewhat the same way that being an engaged girl had been."[112] It is, in

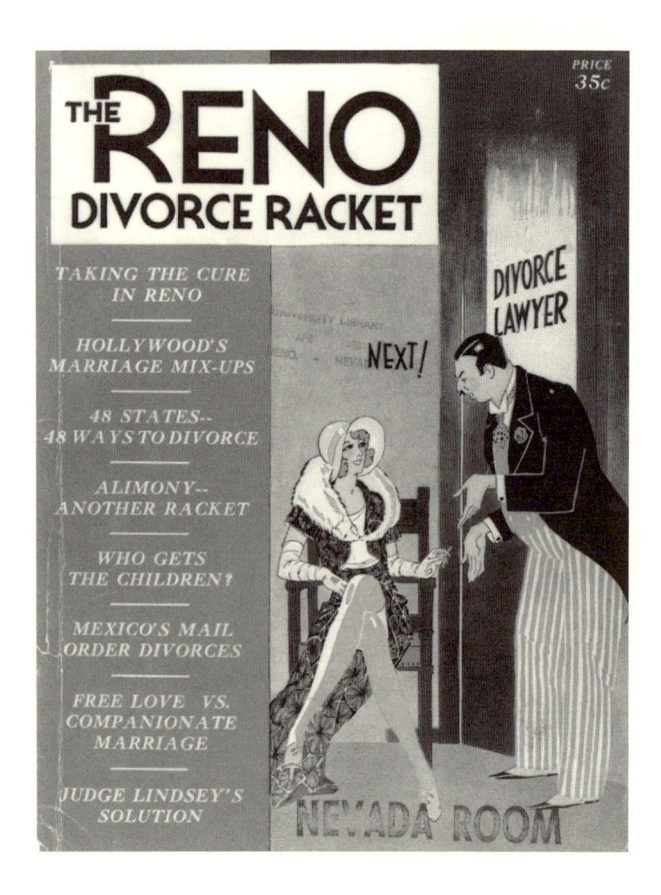

1931 cover of the *Reno Divorce Racket*.
Courtesy of the Nevada Historical Society.

other words, the potentiality of these divorcées-to-be that makes their position so discursively resonant. They are unfinished, uncompleted. They stand in the midst of a process of building an institution (divorce) that relies on a simultaneous unbuilding and rebuilding of institutions that already stand (marriage, citizenship, gendered roles of production, renovation, reproduction, and consumption). In McCarthy's terms, this unfinished state is pleasurable in its power to play the game either way, in its potential not to be narrated, finalized, closed. Still, for divorcées the pleasures of liminality are temporary at best. Most Reno narratives end with the divorcée remarrying and returning back East in the same social position as when she left.

Therefore, despite the general claim that "Reno is an experiment in letting people do what they please," in "severing the shackles" of marriage, it is not surprising that a metaphor of imprisonment underlies narratives of Reno divorce and prostitution.[113] If stockades, bull pens, and cribs connote temporary dwellings, they are also places of constraint. Regulated prostitutes, though called self-employed, can solicit only during eight-hour shifts while under city surveillance in hidden districts on the back streets of town. Reno city publicity boasted of its tight city surveillance, its police force of one hundred officers—more than twice the number usually needed in cities of comparable size in other parts of the country.[114] By making prostitution legal, Reno officials effectively transformed mobile streetwalkers into stagnant ladies in waiting. Potential clients had to solicit these ladies, seeking out prostitutes who were bound inside one place.

And if, as tourists, divorcées seem to be freed from the social surveillance that oversees permanent dwellers, freedom for all of these women is illusory. The supposed "Richmond wife" entitles her 1930 exposé of Reno for the *Richmond Times Dispatch* "Serving Sentence in the Divorce Colony." Susan, in *Half a Loaf*, laments, "She had money, she had two strong legs, but she was a helpless prisoner. How did the other women stand it?" The last time she gets on a "tee-rain" to go "adventuring," it is not with Tim, her writer-husband, the fellow "old bum" with whom she traveled to "places, my dolly, places and places."[115] Her last quest is to Reno, alone, to live "on death row" in unchosen exile.[116] Elisabeth Wane in *Reno Fever* complains, "It's like a jail sentence. A week is nothing back home, but a week is a lot in jail."[117] A photo caption in the 1931 publication *The Reno Divorce Racket* suggests that in one case the metaphor was literalized: "The upper windows of this famous house in Reno are pointed out to visitors, for here, the tale goes, was the room where a prominent man kept his wife prisoner during their famous divorce trial in Reno. The three upper windows were covered with steel mesh."[118]

Federal law already scripted mobile women as transgressive and sexually promiscuous. The Mann Act of 1910 prohibited the transportation of women across state lines for potentially sexual purposes with anyone other than a spouse. In supposedly preventing the hypothesis of "white slavery," the act presupposed all unmarried women to be potential prostitutes and all unregulated movement illicit.[119] Reno's divorcées, like its prostitutes, were legislatively and spatially trapped. Divorcées were required to check in with a witness-in-residence each day of their required six-week stay in the state and forbidden from crossing state lines during their residency. As citizens, divorce seekers were subject to the jurisdiction of their legal home (Reno), although they were prevented by their short residency from actively participating in defining its laws.

As a metaphor, then, the Reno prison is ironically apt. Reno is reliant on a carceral economy in which the work of gender regulation is the primary labor performed. In comparing the nineteenth-century prison to the pre-Fordist industrial mill, Michel Foucault argues that "the prison is like a machine whose convict-workers are both the cogs and the products. If, in the final analysis, the work of the prison has an economic effect, it is by producing individuals mechanized according to the general norms of an industrial society."[120] The prisoners of the Reno divorce mill become its laborers as well as its detainees, its products and cogs. Reno-vating women become their own makers, disciplining themselves in Foucaultian fashion to adopt, perform, and internalize the gendered norms of New Industrial culture. And like the assembly line laborers at Ford's factory, women are automated in this model. They are stripped of the authority or ability to alter the end products, themselves, or even to alter the speed with which they (these newly remade women) are reproduced.

on consumption

At the archive, I meet a geographer who is mapping the divorce economy onto the city planning maps of 1930s Reno. We share croissants and citations at a casino coffee shop. She visits Reno often, she tells me, and gambles while she is here. Late that night, I wait outside a restaurant inside Harrold's Club, sipping an Absolut and tonic. I thrust two quarters in a slot

machine, rejecting the more complicated gambling fare. A bunch of cherries. A bar. A banana. Days later, low on cash, I spend the night cross-legged on my floral hotel bed munching Kentucky Fried Chicken, drinking Diet Pepsi, filing photocopies of archival postcards in blue "U of N" folders. I put on an Aveda mud "masque," paint my toenails a Lancôme red, and read a Charlie Chan "Reno" novel while *Frasier* blathers on the TV. And outside of my window, the neon blinks in the blackness like tree lights on the day after Christmas, like Christmas lights wasted on crack.

THE CURE FACTORY

In 1926, two Reno businessmen, H. H. Scheeline and W. E. Barnard, commissioned the Riverside Hotel's architect Frederic DeLongchamps to design a strangely hybrid building in the center of Reno. Both a medical office building and a chic shopping arcade, the construction, according to a 1927 advertising brochure, was intended to abet consumers in Reno and the surrounding area who might "require the services of the very ablest Dentists and Physicians, and who would shop at stores carrying the latest and best in everything."[121] The arcade proposed to be a microcosm of Manhattan, the megametropolis of the East. It was "a replica of Fifth Avenue at its best," and the "familiar names" of Fifth Avenue shops sold goods imported from places that sold to New York.[122] Surgeons, internists, urologists, and ophthalmologists advertised in the supplement alongside the dress, gift, jewelry, and beauty shops.

Located at 130 North Virginia Street, near the now-demolished Mapes Hotel, the hybrid office building and shopping arcade was just "three steps" from "flop houses, swinging-door saloons,"[123] underscoring spatially the complex interrelationships between the metropolis and the frontier—and among consumption, curing, and conquest. The pamphlet gushes: "The Medico-Dental Building is in the very heart of the City of Reno, which in turn is in the very heart of an Empire that is destined for a new and unparalleled era of progress and prosperity."

The connection between curing and consumption already had a well-charted history in the West. During the early twentieth century, Theodore Roosevelt's prescription for "the Strenuous Life" promised to counter the ill effects brought on by living in the "sick society" of urban America.[124] Roosevelt sought a sanitized national body composed of individuals who "lead clean, vigorous, healthy lives."[125] A "West Cure"—which consisted of a few weeks' camping and hiking in the western wilderness—often was prescribed as a cleansing mechanism. Droves of middle-class male "brain-workers" suffering from the ills of neurasthenia, "over-civilization"—and potential femininity—took temporary trips to remasculinize and re-Americanize themselves in unsettled conservation parks in the West.[126]

Reno regendered this trope. The popular press, which published accounts of prospective divorcées who went to Nevada to be Reno-vated at the divorce mill, also joked that divorcées quested West to "take the Cure." Divorce, that symptom of modernity, was metaphorized as an illness in many Reno narratives: "We were all brought up to believe that divorce is horrible. So we watch ourselves to see how we're living through it, just as we watch ourselves when we're sick," remarks Millicent to Elisabeth Wane in *Reno Fever*, a novel whose title makes the connection explicit.[127] Elisabeth earlier noted that she told others of her divorce "warily as news of cancer."[128] The hypothetical Patsy, who narrated her Reno quest for the *Richmond Times Dispatch*, summed up the Reno of 1930 as a symptom of the American modernist problem of transitioning from a pioneer mentality to a modern, urban one.[129] And Julia Johnsen had made the point more succinctly in her 1925 introduction to *Selected Articles on Marriage and Divorce*, arguing that since "divorce is a symptom and not a cause of ills in the social body, efforts should be made to improve conditions at the source."

A 1915 Washoe County Medical Society pamphlet advertised Reno, with its high altitude, dry air, and moderate temperatures, as an ideal location for individuals suffering from "chronic diseases of the heart";[130] but by the 1930s, Reno had made a business out of healing more metaphoric heartache. Reno was variously described as a "hospital for hopeless marriages"[131] or for the "victims of apartment house quarrels, for the victims of city nerves, for the victims of what Bill said to Jane and what Jane hurried and told Julia and what Julia told to Johnny,"[132] a "Clinic like the Mayo Clinic,"[133] and a hybrid "Cure factory."[134]

If the "Frontier" immersion of Roosevelt's "Strenuous Life" cured individuals from the effects of contemporary urbanization, then the Reno cure might heal American women from the infection of modern life. But Reno as cure ironically repositioned marriage, not divorce, in the disease-bearing position. Moreover, if the West cured by masculinizing overly modernized subjects, the Reno cure became yet more problematic. For rather than gaining behavioral freedom, cured Reno women simply lost control of their shapes. "Without shame," Susan Hale notes in *Half a Loaf*, Reno divorcées "would pull out a persistently offending black hair from a white chin, and discuss

"The Cure." 1930s postcard.
Courtesy of Special Collections, University of Nevada, Reno Library.

the methods of a chiropractor who had special thumps for reducing the hips."[135]

In time, these bearded, big-hipped women became veritable androgynes. Their supposed attempts to walk like a man and look like a woman are subverted: as they slim down and masculinize their hips, they sprout unwanted facial hair. In short, Reno divorcées don't risk losing their gender identity, but rather the identifiers of biological sex. What is immutable, then, is not behavior or embodiment, but the equation between behavior and sex. For example, a 1930s cartoon in *Pic* shows a young, voluptuous, hyperfeminine divorcée leaving the Reno courthouse accompanied by her lawyer. "Boy," she exclaims, "I feel like a new man!"[136] Clearly, the cartoon satirizes the economy of marriage produced in Reno, in which men rather than women become progressively obsolescent, and where modern women periodically need to exchange a new man for the old. In doing so, it mocks the authority of modern women who seem to participate in the "traffic in men"; after all, to initiate a transaction in which men become the sign of exchange is to overturn the authority of patriarchal family relations.[137] However, the potential political import of this kind of resignification is immediately squashed when the cartoon is taken more literally. A woman so well endowed could no more feel like a man than she could look like one. Certainly, she is kidding herself. And that is the point.

Underlying all this gender blurring is the fear not that women will turn into men, but that the masculinity inherent in all women might become visible, flaunted, exposed. Those black facial hairs are horrific not because women possess them, but because they flaunt them without shame. In the end, if women temporary residents are cured in Reno, then the disease from which they seem to be freed is not marriage, but masculinity or at least the attempt to adopt—and expose—some of its traits.

If Reno threatens to make women men, for divorcing men it has the opposite effect. "Normal men don't usually come out here [to Reno]. They send their wives. They're too much tied up in business," explains a world-weary Gretchen to two new Reno arrivals in *Reno Fever*.[138] Millicent replies, "I'd rather go around with a native rather than a male colonist. They are all so queer."[139] Men who divorce in Reno are largely portrayed as effeminate (especially in contrast to cowboys or even dude "wranglers") and perhaps homosexual. At the very least, men in this feminine community threaten to become queer, losing their wives to predatory lesbians. In *Reno Fever*, "the hero of [Gretchen's] crowd was Edgar Ray, who had come out [there] for a divorce because his wife was seduced by a woman."[140]

In fact, the threat of queer desire underwrites most Reno narratives.[141] In *Reno Fever*, "somehow the thought that she would love Nairn forever [comforts] Elisabeth's heart."[142] And Nairn responds likewise, saying to Elisabeth, "Promise me one thing, Elisabeth. No matter what man is in your life—no

1913 postcard.
Author's collection.

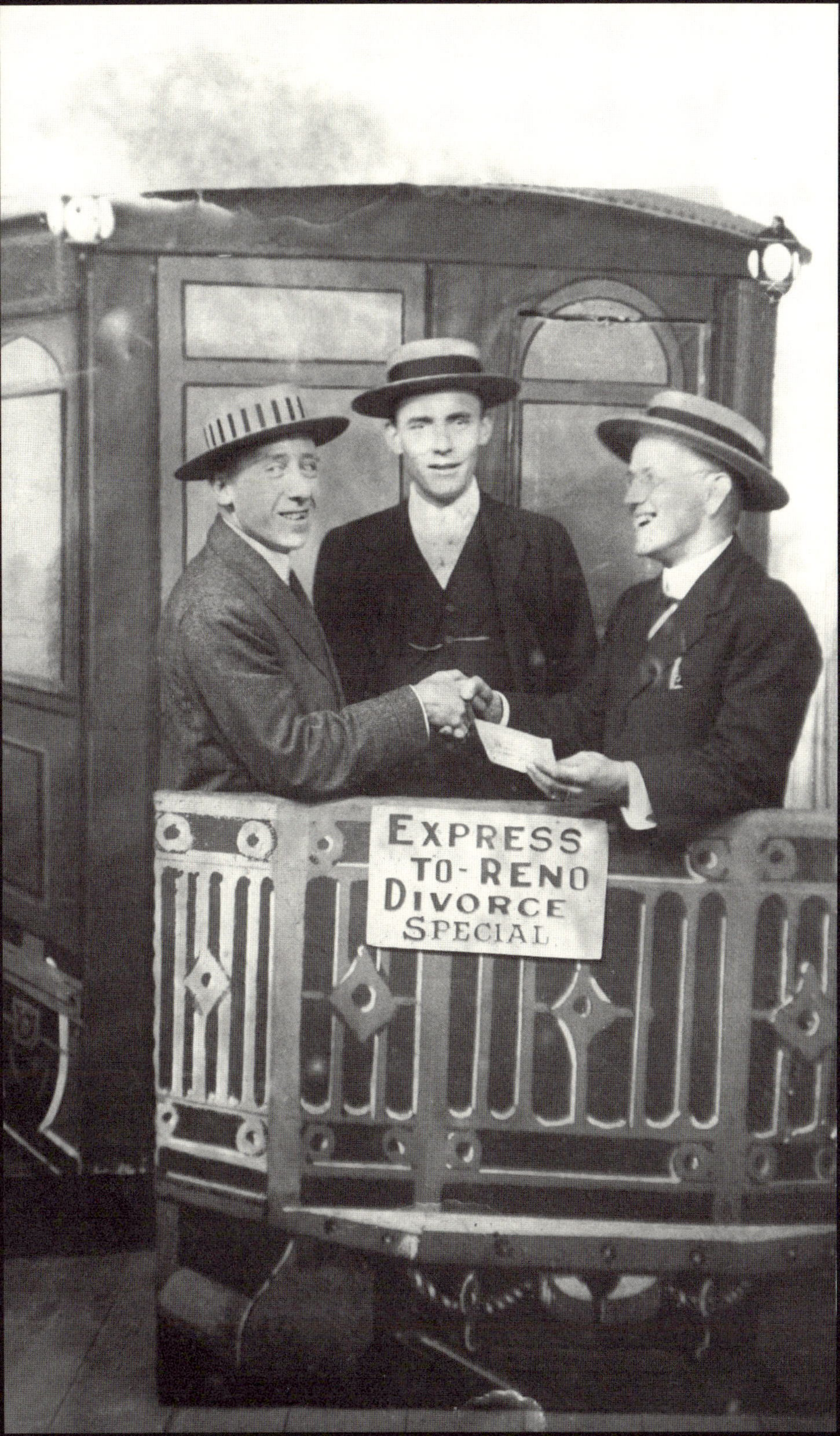
EXPRESS
TO-RENO
DIVORCE
SPECIAL

matter what happens—we'll spend our last Reno night together." To which Elisabeth replies, "There won't be any man. Nairn, I love you."[143] Nairn and Elisabeth's romance is cut short by Nairn's suicide. Potential lesbian desire (like all female sexual desire outside of marriage) is not simply subdued, but made deadly.[144]

Modern marriage that produces lesbians and androgynes becomes the noxious culprit for which divorce is the cure. And ultimately, Reno divorcées are cured by becoming rediseased. To catch "Reno-itis" is to participate in a constant circulation of Reno gossip, that "drivel about love and marriage."[145] The virulent "Reno Fever," to which all are exposed as they are being Reno-vated, transforms women into enthusiastic consumers of material goods. A Reno clerk tells Elisabeth, "[Divorcées] all buy clothes just before they go home. It's a fever that gets hold of them. We store clerks all notice it."[146] The Latin *sanare*, to cure, means also to rehabilitate or restore. The German term for renovation, *Sanierung*, is etymologically linked to it.[147] So, finally, to be Reno-vated means not just to remarry, but to be restored or cured by becoming what Ellen Wiley Todd calls a 1930s "revised New Woman," a woman who shops.[148]

This function gives an answer to Gramsci's conundrum when he noted that while the American frontier (or pioneer) spirit enabled Americans to embrace Fordism more wholly than Europeans, it also was responsible for the modern "moral gap" found among American divorced and divorcing women, those "luxury mammals" who threatened to idly consume. Female consumerism is precisely the goal.[149] Fordism is predicated not simply on a division of labor, but on the creation of a laborer who buys what she builds.[150] Consumption, that modern ailment which makes good girls bad, becomes both gender disease and gender cure. Reno-vation becomes the process of producing a self-surveying and self-regulating consumer.[151]

It now makes sense why MGM's *The Women* is really about shopping—in salons and restaurants, at perfume counters and fashion shows. Though the women traipse out to a dude ranch in Reno, the train they take actually sends them *back* to New York and the patriarchy and products they have left. "Mary, listen to the wheels, don't they seem to be saying something," asks the saccharine-sweet Peggy Day (Joan Fontaine) who shares a Pullman sleeping berth with Mary Haines. "Don't they seem to be saying, 'Go back. Go back. Go back.'" The camera closes in and fixes on a close-up of the two women, who cuddle cheek to cheek. A moment passes. Mary breaks away and declares to Peggy, "Go back to him."

The train Peggy hears directs her away from the possibility of a supportive (and potentially self-contained) female community in a Reno ranch that the film depicts as being far from department stores. Indeed, Peggy's train doesn't slow in a reach for Benjamin's "emergency break" of revolution but actually moves in reverse. Peggy's train goes back to a world in which nar-

Still from *The Women* (MGM 1939). Courtesy of the Academy of Motion Picture Arts and Sciences.

ratives of progress are devoid of independent modern women; middle-class women join forces only to preserve the middle-class family from women who labor, and women need only reproduce.[152] Inevitably, all the women do go back finally Reno-vated to the East, where they remarry the same or new, but interchangeable, husbands and become mothers and Reno-vated shoppers of mass-produced goods.

Their most important purchase, however, is Reno itself—and their remade selves are its advertisements. If the West is a masculinizing space, then the Reno divorce factory is not so much a feminine place—or even a feminizing place—as a woman, a so-called "gay blond little haven of freedom."[153] Reno comes to allegorize both the feminization of place generally and the degraded and eroticized production of the modern tourist site which sells its notoriety as a commodity.[154] For if the story of 1930s Reno is a story about how gender is produced, remade, practiced, and situated, it is also, not coincidentally, a story about the performative compulsion of making modern place. Place, both gendered and as gender, is made through imitation, to paraphrase Judith Butler, an imitation for which there is no original and which "may be said to exceed any definitive narrativization."[155] Thus, Reno,

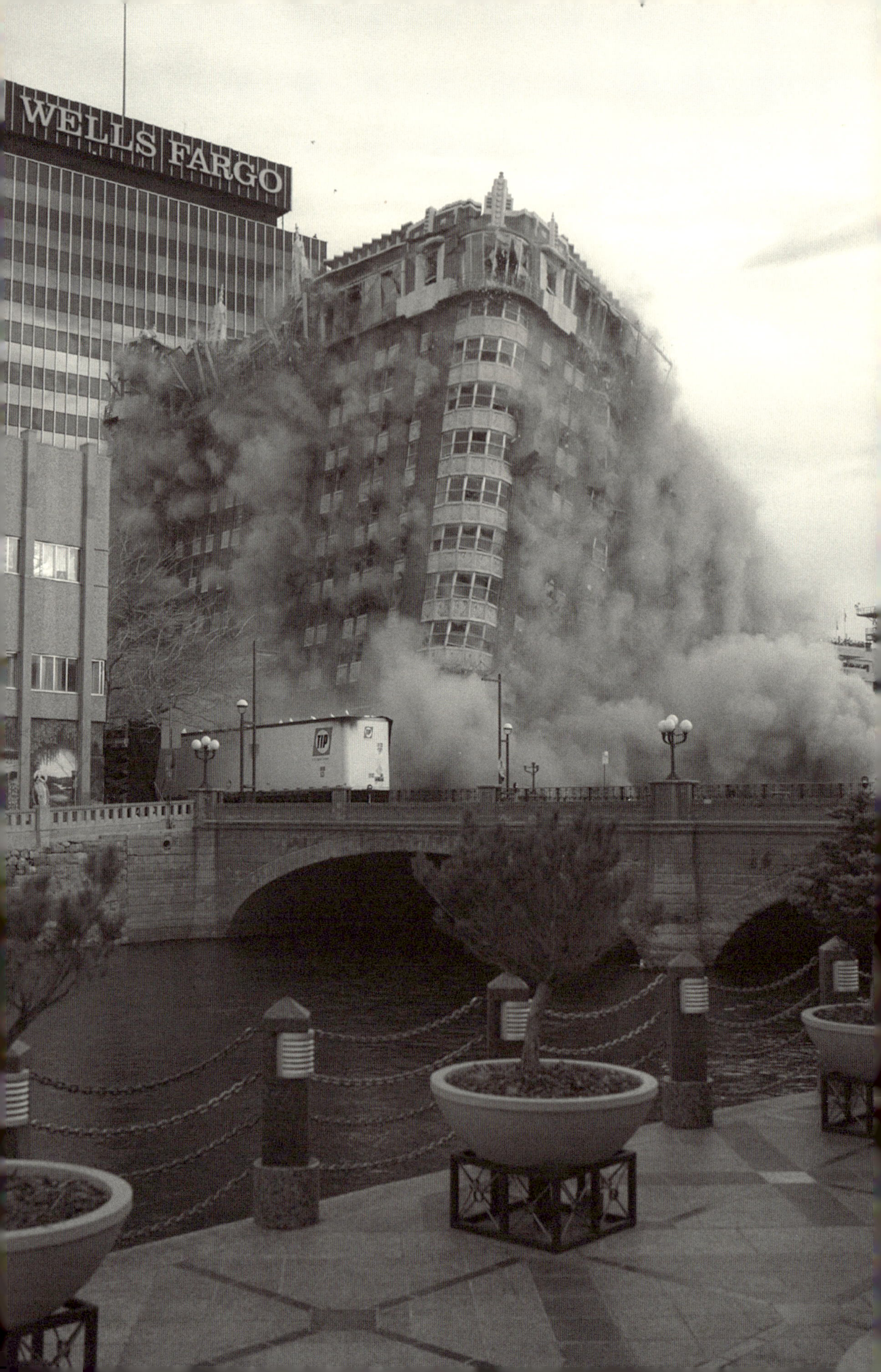
WELLS FARGO
TIP

amnesiac, though ever in flux, exposes the irreducibility of the performative itself. We know it when we see it. But when we see it, it's not there. Reno, as place, is produced both retroactively and in advance through the repetition, approximation, and improvisation of the detritus of generic tropes, in the iteration of recognizable aesthetic, narrative, and material forms, and in the commodification and codification of those iterations. As a divorce colony, "Reno was losing its old identity, but it was making money. Reno was a prostitute," surmises Elisabeth in *Reno Fever*. "Well, weren't most places?"[156]

DANGER: do not enter

Toward the end of my Reno stay, I seek out the apartment that Dorothy Butler Baker declared was her permanent home. She had rented a room on Island Avenue in a house just steps away from the door of the famed Riverside Hotel and around the corner from the courthouse where her divorce case was heard. That is the last trace she left. The house had been demolished sometime in the 1950s—at least according to alterations in the city fire and insurance maps. When I finally find it a construction site stands in its place, guarded by a high wooden fence and sign that forebodes, No Trespassing: KEEP OUT. I peer through the cracks in the fence at a debris-filled dirt pit. Even now, it seems to swallow up the traces of my ancestral past. Even now, it seems to spit the gap out whole.[157]

Demolition of the Mapes Hotel, January 2000.
© Jeff Spicer 2000.

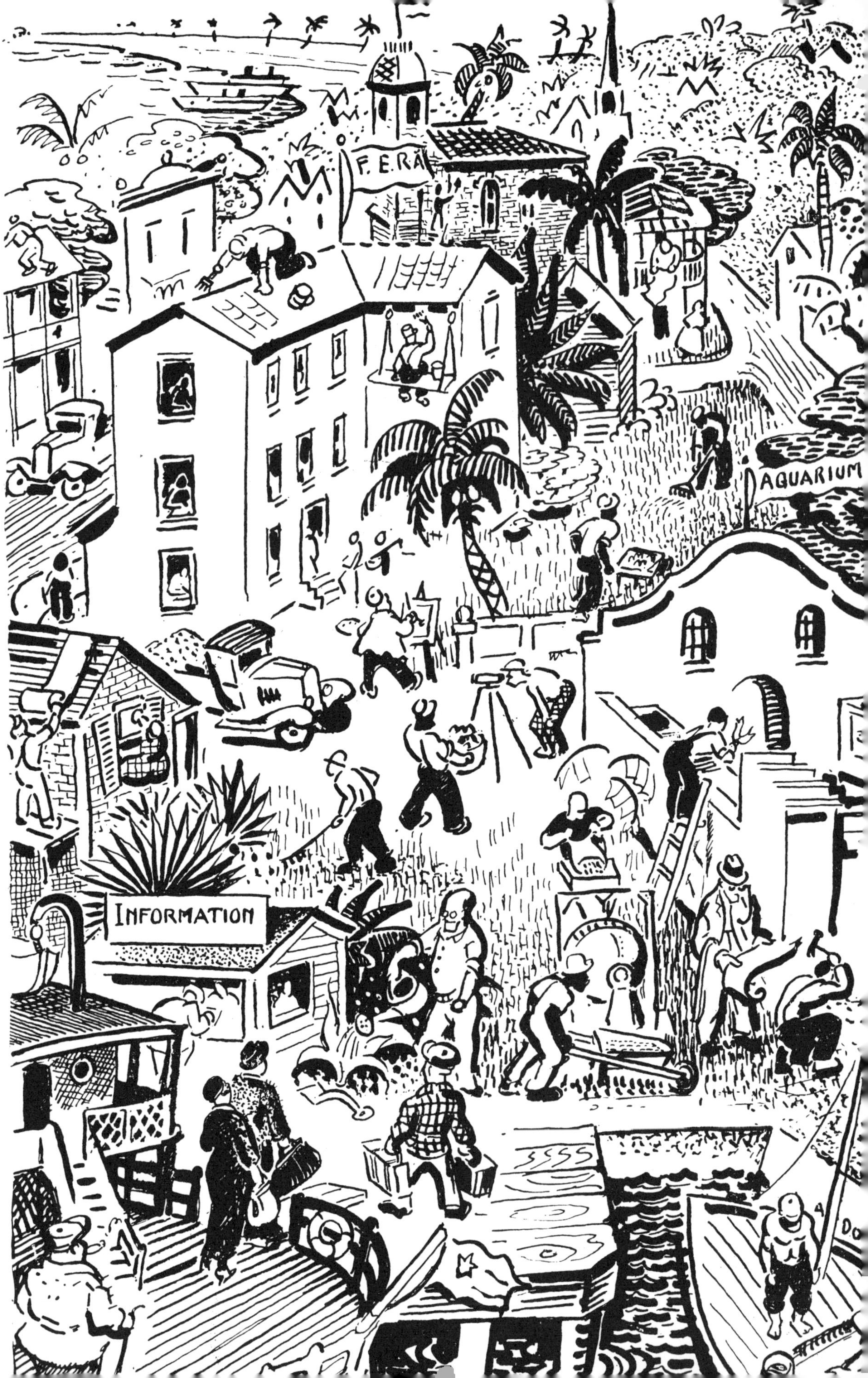
F.E.R.A.
AQUARIUM
INFORMATION

② Key West

THE NATION AND THE CORPSE

KEY WEST HAS BEEN DEAD FOR 15 YEARS.
THE FUNERAL PROCESSION HAS JUST
BEEN HELD UP, WAITING FOR SOMEONE

PART 1. "THE THIRTIES HAD COME IN LIKE A HURRICANE"

← FERA cleanup. 1930s cartoon by A. Dornbrush.
Courtesy of Wright Langley Archives, Inc.

"Key West To Get New Birth." Special edition of the *Florida Keys Sun*, July 1934.
Courtesy of Wright Langley Archives, Inc.

When the 1935 hurricane hit the Florida Keys on September 2, it missed Key West entirely.[1] The place got wrecked anyway. By mangling the Overseas Railroad, which ran from Key Largo to Key West, the storm severed the link between the island and the Florida mainland. It thereby squelched the year-old effort by the Florida Federal Emergency Relief Administration (FERA) to transform Key West into the Bermuda of Florida, to transform it, in other words, from Wasteland into Paradise—a place that was to be decidedly part of the American nation, like Bermuda was of Great Britain, but still romantically distinct from it.

Just over one year earlier, on July 2, 1934, the Key West government had been faced with a problem: an estimated 75 to 80 percent of the island's population of fourteen thousand were on federal relief rolls. The city declared itself bankrupt and turned Key West over to state and, ultimately, federal control. The New Deal government's Key West project was headed by a controversial lawyer named Julius Stone, whom Robert Frost dubbed "the Rehabilitator," describing him as "a rich young man in shorts with hairy legs."[2] A Roosevelt protégé, Stone understood the importance of symbolic gesture, even in what he wore. He strutted around the island in Bermuda shorts, the favored garb of British imperialists, and thereby symbolically in addition to fiscally asserted the dominance of Anglo-American hegemony over the hybridized, Anglo-Afro-Cuban island culture already in place. "Now shorts aren't new to Florida," wrote Arthur M. Duke in the *Orlando Reporter Star*. "Any Englishman entering a warm country breaks out into shorts just as naturally as an 8-year-old breaks out with measles, under proper conditions."[3]

Stone sought to revise the American population's view of the island-city—and, more important, to bring it into its consciousness in the first place. Under his direction, FERA produced Key West as a test site and laboratory for the "unique experiment" of New Deal Progressivism.[4] Responding to FERA publicity notices, newspapers adopted the scientific discourse of medicine, of bodily death and revival, to describe the happenings in Key West. "Key West Gives Up the Ghost and Asks State and U.S. to Take Charge of Its Affairs," announced the *Jacksonville Journal* in July 1934. "Key West will get treatment from 'Dr. FERA,'" declared other Florida newspapers at the time. "Key West the Town That Died Is Battling Grimly for New Life,"[5] ventured the *Washington Post* in April 1935. Within a year of the FERA takeover, newspapers announced that Key West had come back to life: "Uncle Sam Revives Dead Town" and "Key West, Broke and Asleep, Is Resurrected from Civic Grave by Government Aid" and "Bankrupt Key West Alive Again."[6]

FERA's economic prescription called for a mix of sanitization and renovation, to cure through cleaning—and commodification. Because of the city's financial destitution, garbage, not disposed of for the eighteen months pre-

EXTRA   Rehabilitation Special!   **EXTRA**

FLORIDA KEYS SUN

DEDICATED TO CITIZENSHIP AND PROGRESS IN THE CITY OF KEY WEST • IN MONROE COUNTY • ALONG THE KEYS

VOL. V—NO. 32   KEY WEST, FLORIDA, JULY 6, 1934   PRICE FIVE CENTS

Key West To Get New Birth

Complete Transformation of the Island Into Beautiful Tourist Paradise Planned by FERA

CITY AND COUNTY TO BE OPERATED BY THE GOVERNOR

Commissioners and Council Transfer Authority To State Executive.

In order to give Governor Dave Sholtz and the FERA a free hand in developing the extensive rehabilitation program planned for Key West, the county commissioners and city councilmen, turning over all their rights, powers and authority to the Governor to use as he sees fit. Resolutions embodying this transfer of power were unanimously passed by the commissioners and councilmen at special sessions held Monday, and forwarded on the afternoon train to the Governor in Tallahassee.

Under these resolutions these two boards practically become "rubber stamps" for the rehabilitation administration. The two boards have assured the Governor and Julius F. Stone, Jr., FERA administrator for Florida, that they are in hearty accord with the plans proposed and will co-operate to the fullest extent.

In outlining their plans Sunday, however, the rehabilitation official made it very plain that they will expect such co-operation, but that in the event the local boards fail to perform as requested the measures they ask for will be put into operation in spite of local opposition, explaining that in carrying out the extensive program they must have a free hand in developing, improving and beautifying the city. The resolution adopted by the county commissioners, which is essentially the same as the one passed by city council, was as follows:

"Whereas, The major portion of the population of Monroe county is unemployed and there is considerable financial distress, property owners are unable to pay state, county and municipal taxes and the County of Monroe and City of Key West are unable to pay their employes and other operating expenses, and by reason of lack of finances, both the county and city are unable to carry on the functions of government, leaving the population in a dependent and distressed condition, and

"Whereas, About one half the pulsation is on the Federal Relief roll, and the normal assistance given to the people of Monroe county under the present system is inadequate and affords

(Continued on page 8)

CITY OBSERVES HOLIDAY IN OLD FASHIONED WAY

Parade, Horse Race, Boat Races Feature Kappa Pi Y Program.

Thousands of Key Westerns enjoyed the Fourth of July at the Athletic Club house and beach as the guests of the Kappa Pi Y Club yesterday. The celebration was one of the most successful staged in Key West for many years.

The day's entertainment was launched with a parade which moved forward promptly at 10:30 a. m., from in front of the Naval Station. In the line of march were Chief of Police Ivan Elwood and Captain of Police Everett Rivas on horseback. They were followed by city and county officials in automobiles. Members of the Kappa Pi Y Club, bearing a large American flag, were next in line. The American Legion drum and bugle corps, sailors and Marines from the destroyers Perry and Zane, Boy Scouts, fire department, a float from the Pythian Sisters, and automobiles bearing members of the Improved Order of Red Men and other fraternal organizations were also in the line of march.

A pleasing entertainment on the day's program was the exhibition drill given by the Legion drum and bugle corps.

Ygnacio Carboneli won the city tennis championship, defeating Peter Varela, defending champion, 5-7, 6-3, 6-4.

The horse Star, with its owner, Gilbert Weech, in the saddle, won the horse race by a neck. Lightning, with Juan Madole astride, was closing in at the finish and was a close second.

Dr. W. P. Kemp's outboard motor, Black Diamond, was being pressed by the Cecelia, with Leo Haskins at the wheel, until that boat experienced engine trouble and Dr. Kemp pushed his craft on to win easily.

James Noble's boat, Buddy, had little opposition in the free for all race.

Over a mile course in as pretty a sailboat race as ever was witnessed in Key West, Junior Potters, piloted his Skip to a well deserved victory. The George Futz, with Futz at the helm, was second and The Spark Plug, with Captain Richmond Roberts at the rudder, finished third.

Miss Elizaebth Niles won first prize in the bathing beauty contest in which a score of pretty

(Continued on page 3)

June Temperatures Were Above Normal

To most Key Westers, the month of June seemed unusually hot, but the official weather reports for the month show that the average daily temperatures were only .6 of one degree above the normal 81.9 for June. But June was a hot month, the temperature reaching the unusually high altitude of 90 on the longest day of the year. The lowest point recorded was 72, two days later.

But, as usual, things could have been worse, or hotter; and no doubt would have been had the sun been making its usual record. As it was Old Sol made only one perfect score during the month, and scored 90 or better on only four other days. That held the heat records down a lot.

There were only six clear days in June; thirteen partly cloudy; eleven cloudy and ten on which there was precipitation.

Rainfall for the month amounted to 2.84 inches, which was 1.40 inches short of the normal for June.

Prevailing winds for the month were from the southeast, with a total movement of 6,874 miles, or an average hourly velocity of 9.5 miles an hour, which again proves that Key West has nearly always boast a breeze, no matter how hot it may be.

Assessment Rolls Total $4,140,000

Monroe county's tax assessment roll presented to the county commissioners Monday by J. Otto Kirchheiner totaled $4,140,000 and is subject to change by the county commissioners who are now receiving complaints against the assessments.

The book as compiled by Mr. Kirchheiner shows a reduction of $160,000 under last year's book, which was more than a million dollars less than the year previous.

The intangible property reaches $303,990.

"Charley, dear," said young Mrs. Torkins, "do you believe in going according to the will of the majority?"

"Of course. Everybody does."

"Then why doesn't the umpire try to make his decisions that way oftener?"

County Commissioners and City Council Turn Government Over To Governor and FERA For Complete Rehabilitation Plan.

By O. L. JAY

The complete transformation of the island of Key West into a beautiful and artistic tourists' paradise, and the construction of all the necessities, attractions and entertainment features that go to make up a modern tourist resort, is to be undertaken at an early date, according to an announcement made by Governor Dave Sholtz from Tallahassee on Thursday.

When these improvements are completed it is stated that Key West will probably be the most beautiful spot in America. To bring this about the Monroe county commissioners and the Key West council have practically abrogated their offices, turning the county and city governments over to the Governor to administer as he sees fit. The Governor, in turn, will turn the Key West rehabilitation project over to Julius F. Stone, Jr., FERA administrator for the state of Florida.

Formal resolutions asking Governor Sholtz to take over the county and city governments, transferring to him all the rights, powers and authority of the commissioners and councilmen, were adopted by the two boards at special sessions held Monday afternoon and forwarded to Tallahassee on the afternoon train.

For the purpose of launching the movement to transform Key West from a "has-been" city into a beautiful paradise, where literally "every prospect pleases," Governor Sholtz and Mr. Stone spent several hours here last Sunday, when they conferred with the commissioners, councilmen, other officials and interested business and professional men, giving only a brief outline of what they have in mind for the rehabilitation of the city and county.

Under the terms of the resolutions asking the Governor to take over the governments, the state executive is given complete control of the city and county governmental affairs. His word, when spoken through Mr. Stone, the FERA administrator, will be final and will carry the same force as if it were the combined pronouncement of the commissioners and council.

This rehabilitation project, according to those behind the movement, is in the nature of an experiment in rehabilitation on a large scale. Key West has been selected for the scene of this great project because of its natural beauty, its strategic location, unexcelled climate and its isolation, which makes it free of all influences that would tend to retard the work in hand. Another consideration, too, is the fact that this city, once the metropolis of Florida, known throughout the world as a manufacturing, fishing, sponging, Army and Navy center, has met with one reverse after another, until most of its citizens have either moved away or have lost practically all their former financial prestige.

Governor Sholtz and Mr. Stone, while here Sunday, did not have sufficient time to enter into a detailed discussion of all the plans they have in store for Key West, but they did mention several projects they have under consideration, which will afford unlimited labor for all of Key West's vast army of unemployed.

Among the projects mentioned was the construction of shuttle trains to be used in transporting automobiles across

(Continued on page 2)

ceding the FERA takeover, had filled Key West's streets and vacant lots. So when "the city sat up to take its first dose of medicine" from "Dr. FERA," as the Tampa *Daily Times* proclaimed, the first order of business was to tidy things up. Bolstered by the FERA motto, "Help to Those Who Help Themselves," Key Westers worked on a volunteer basis to clean up trash and debris around the city, plaster and paint houses, plant flowers, build sewer lines to replace existing cisterns, reconstruct the $175,000 navy submarine base into a yacht basin, build a public aquarium and cabanas on Rest Beach, and create an art gallery that specialized in Key West art. Of the $326,099 in funds allocated to the Key West WPA project, $8,748 were used to demolish old houses, $29,924 to control mosquitoes, and $16,148 to collect and dispose of garbage. The local newspaper, the *Key West Citizen*, urged residents to use "proper garbage cans" with metal covers and publicized a contest for a slogan to be placed on trash receptacles. FERA set up training schools to prepare maids whose job it would be to maintain clean domestic spaces for the expected onslaught of middle-class tourists.

The garbage cleanup also extended to moral lines. One of the first steps FERA took toward rehabilitation was to ban the multiple forms of gambling —bolito, Cuba, selo, and the like—from the island. "Evidently the man who is virtually acting as a receiver for the City and County is not a believer in the theory that a community can gamble itself out of debt and into prosperity," wrote a cynical journalist for the *Tampa Daily Times*.[7] With a nod to Key West's large Cuban population, the WPA issued a bilingual brochure, "Hospitality Hints for the Key West Resident/Avisos de Hospitalidad para el Residente de Cayo Hueso."[8] It included such behavioral guidelines as (no. 3) "Storekeepers should display their wares in an orderly fashion"; (no. 4) "All persons dealing with visitors should keep their persons neat and trim"; and (no. 6) "Keep Key West as quiet as possible. Your auto horn need seldom be used. If your car makes a racket, repair it."

Six months after his arrival, Stone proclaimed Dr. FERA's prescription of cleaning and commodification a cure: "We have cleaned up the city, collecting 50,000 cubic yards of trash. We have cleared and cleaned some 200 vacant lots, and have made a dozen parks. We have carride [*sic*] on a campaign of demolition and renovation to make homes of relief clients habitable."[9] By the first anniversary of the FERA takeover, Key West had hosted thirty-eight thousand visitors, the best tourist season on record. That number constituted a 46 percent increase in the number of tourists, an 86 percent increase in hotel registrations, and a 150 percent increase in rooming house guests.[10]

The FERA project can be seen as an attempt to sterilize the processes of death and decay that were so omnipresent in the Depression economy and thereby to distinguish the ruins of the past from the wreckage of the present upon which progress must inevitably turn its back. Connecting decomposing flesh with putrefying buildings, the architect Bernard Tschumi argues

"Abandoned cigar factory. Key West, Florida." FSA photograph by Arthur Rothstein, January 1938.
Courtesy of the Monroe County Public Library.

that the modernist anguish about death relates to the "phase of decomposition," the grotesque and visible process of decay, and not to respectable "dry white ruins," petrified skeletons, and preserved (read: rebuilt) historical sites.[11] FERA's efforts at sanitization can be seen as an effort to sterilize history, to demonstrate that the violence and immediacy of "corrupted flesh" is safely buried and a thing of the past. Thus, by December 1937, Nina Wilcox Putnam could observe in *Collier's* that "Key West has a completeness which is remarkable for any American city. There are no ragged edges.... There are no raw outskirts. It's just *there*—unique, a perfect unit."[12]

scavenging

Key West is everywhere. Scattered. Relics of the place are carefully preserved in the temperature-controlled rooms of archives at Vassar, Columbia, Yale, and the John F. Kennedy Library in Boston. So journeying back to 1930s Key West first requires traveling elsewhere—a long summer tour through the special collections of the academy elite. Imagine it. The scrapbooks, the notebooks, the marked-up manuscripts, bad sketches, and let-

ters, steamer tickets and bills. You find things you are not supposed to see, or at least to pretend to ignore if you do. Things that are misdated, misordered, disintegrating. So much stuff. But in Key West it is worse because it dawns on you finally that the disorder, the mismanaged fragments, the half-baked scraps of speech are really, actually, precisely the point.

THE ISLE OF BONES

The metaphors of death and revival that pervade discourse about the FERA renovation of Key West are intriguing both because they anthropomorphize or animate a place, and because they mark a construction of life and death that is particular to a capitalist modernity. Sentience becomes dependent upon economic viability, upon the affluence of a place's population—however that wealth is gained. Key West "is a very, very dead place because it has died several times," wrote Frost in a letter of December 1934:

> It died as a resort of pirates, then as a house of smugglers and wreckers, then as a cigar manufactory (the Cubans moved over here to get inside the tariff wall), then as a winter resort boomtown. Franklin D himself has taken it personally in hand to give it one more life to lose. FERA is all over the place. This town has been nationalized to rescue it from its own speculative excesses.[13]

In Frost's view, the island, self-destructively addicted to passionate "excesses," seemed to have died of consumption—the disease, according to Susan Sontag, of "repressed sensuality," of "excessive passion," of "dematerialization."[14] It is a disease whereby one might be overcome by liquids or liquidation, as island commerce might be, drowning in the thing that keeps one afloat.

Ironically, the so-called Dr. FERA suggested that Key West wasn't consumptive enough. In fact, it posited economic disease as one of *under*-consumption. Stone tried to enhance his public relations maneuvers in Key West by promoting the place as a colony for artists and writers. The isolation, inexpense, balmy weather, and good fishing of the island already had made it attractive to writers, artists, and intellectuals who did not receive or were not in need of WPA grants. In addition to Frost, Ernest Hemingway, John Dos Passos, Josephine Herbst, Elizabeth Bishop, Archibald MacLeish, Wallace Stevens, Mike Strater, Waldo Peirce, John Dewey, and later Tennessee Williams and Charles Olson, all spent time on the island. Langston Hughes passed through Key West en route to Cuba. Hart Crane paid homage to the place. Following the FERA takeover, however, WPA grants also brought to Key West artists such as Loren MacIver, Richard Jansen, Avery Johnson, W. Townsend Morgan, William Hoffman, Walton Blodget, and writers such as the poet Lloyd Frankenberg and the journalist Stetson Kennedy. In promoting and financing a population of artists, Stone ensured that cultural rep-

FERA advertisement for tourism from December 15, 1934, issue of the *New York Journal*. Courtesy of the Monroe County Public Library.

resentations of Key West abounded. But while these writers, artists, and intellectuals brought Key West to American cultural consciousness, more often than not they represented the place in a way Stone might not have desired. "What they're trying to do is starve you Conchs out of here so they can burn down the shacks and put up apartments and make this a tourist town," warns Harry Morgan in Ernest Hemingway's Key West novel, *To Have and Have Not*.[15] FERA only partly succeeds.

The debates about whether Key West was too consumptive—or not consumptive enough—mirrored debates that were being had on a larger scale across the nation during the 1930s. Rita Barnard argues, for instance, that the 1930s marked a transition in American culture from a focus on a problematic of production to one of consumption.[16] Certainly, increased consumption was promoted by many during the 1930s as a cure for the ills of economic depression. At its base, the FERA renovation of Key West relied on promoting tourism as a way to increase consumption in the place, a method that transformed Key West into a commodity that sold itself, and by extension sold a construction of a conjoined America, a healthy America, an America free of rifts.

The discourse of disease and embodiment that prevailed in representation of Key West was found as well in discussions about the nation in depression. That America was sick was not in question in the decade following the stock market crash. In the United States between 1929 and 1941, discourse narrating the effects of economic depression portrayed them as both abstract or statistical and visceral, as an "empty feeling in the stomach."[17] Herbert Hoover proposed a model of citizen self-reliance in December 1930, arguing that "economic depression cannot be cured by legislative action or executive pronouncement. Economic wounds must be healed by the action of the cells of the economic body—the producers and consumers themselves."[18] A decade later, in his 1939 popular history of Depression America, *Since Yesterday*, Frederick Lewis Allen surmised, "The sickness of the economic system was infinitely complicated and little understood."[19] Cities, wrecked by unemployment and in economic catastrophe, were described through allusions to injury and pain: "The enormous organism of Detroit is now seen, for all its Middle Western vigor, to have become atrophied," reported Edmund Wilson in a 1931 essay on the hard-hit auto industry. "It is clogged with dead tissue now and its life is bleeding away."[20]

Yet the medicinal metaphors that described Key West also allude to the island's complex history, a history of cyclical death and reanimation, a messy history of bodies dismembered and disinterred. The Anglicanization of the island's Spanish name, Cayo Hueso, the isle of bones, encrypts in English a violent past of Spanish conquest and of warring Native American tribes before that. Legend has it that Spaniards, upon reaching Key West, discovered the bleached remains of hundreds of skeletons, the remains of a treacherous battle between islanders in which few survived.[21] While this history was reconstructed as a myth of origin by FERA, the impact of Key West's later history of piracy and salvage, a history dependent upon the recovery of wreckage, was more difficult for FERA to sanitize.

The highly legislated practice of wrecking and salvage, which entailed scavenging cargoes from ships that crashed on the Florida reefs, had made Key West the richest city in the United States during the nineteenth century.[22] Embedded in this scavenger economy is the recognition that lost objects, even refuse, have value—and that one can live off others' loss. The parallel shaping mythology of Caribbean piracy (often connected to and confused with wrecking) suggests that one might create loss for one's own gain, that the boundaries between the self and the other, between loss and acquisition, are most productive when blurred.

Key West's mythology of piracy embodies an alternative myth of the building of America, a narrative that embraces revolt and revolution, that reveals the violence buried in all narratives of nation building, a narrative of dismemberment, disinterment, and mixture (*mestizaje*) rather than cohesion, cleanliness, and Manifest Destiny. Antonio Benítez-Rojo suggests that the "mythification of piracy" prevalent in Caribbean texts should be seen as "an attempt to authenticate through narration itself . . . an entire field of allusion, scarcely explored in literary criticism, which speaks of sacking and kidnapping, of burning and booty, of buried treasure and secret maps." The violent underpinnings of these traditions, according to Benítez-Rojo, "make up a system of differences" specific to Caribbean "Peoples of the Sea," which links piracy with maroon uprisings and runaway slaves.[23]

B. R. Burg's study on "sodomy and the pirate tradition" evaluates the queer and androgynous underpinnings of seventeenth-century Caribbean pirate culture.[24] And Marcus Rediker argues that the eighteenth-century sea workers' struggle against the authority of their captains and the nations that bred them, made most manifest in pirates, is prescient of the broader political struggle of the American Revolution and, more so, of industrial workers who "continued the fight for democracy and freedom" against factory masters in latter-day labor disputes.[25] Rediker destabilizes what he calls the "romantic notion" of the sea, which he links allegorically to the American romance with the frontier.

Spaniards Landing at Cayo Hueso. WPA mural at Key West High School (now Glynn R. Archer Elementary School) by William Hoffmann. Photograph by Rob O'Neal, *Key West Citizen*, 2005.

FERA reconstruction of Key West. WPA mural at Key West High School (now Glynn R. Archer Elementary School) by William Hoffmann. Photograph by Rob O'Neal, *Key West Citizen*, 2005.

THE NATION AND THE CORPSE 79

Forged through violence and alterity, Key West becomes an outlaw site that embraces the in-between spaces of racial heterogeneity, androgyny, and labor rebellion. Within this context, FERA's annexation of the place warrants closer scrutiny. One might suggest, for instance, that FERA's takeover of Key West was itself an act of salvaging. In fact, it lacked and even squelched the political legacy of rebellion embedded in Key West's Caribbean history. An investigation of FERA-controlled Key West exposes the ideologies that shaped the tiny test site and reveals some of those that underpinned the New Deal cultural project as a whole.

In the May 1935 issue of *Harper's* magazine, Elmer Davis points out that Key West

> was the New Deal in miniature—high intentions and bold beginnings, hampered and bedeviled by the need of respecting vested interests and laggard public opinion, by the ease of compromise and the difficulty of cutting Gordian knots; by the unhappy American tendency to regard a thing announced in the newspapers as a thing done. . . . One almost felt that it was all history in miniature, an apologue of the aspirations and the shortcomings of man.[26]

For Davis, Key West's FERA-controlled renovation was an "apologue" or allegory of Depression-era America. If this is precisely how FERA hoped Americans would read Key West, Davis exposes the slippage embedded in such a proposal. Within the span of several paragraphs, Davis posits Key West both as the "New Deal in miniature," as an allegory of the American nation itself, and as an interstitial site, "neither Florida nor Cuba, neither American nor Caribbean." Moreover, he extends his allegory from the particular to the general, from New Deal history to *all* history, suggesting that the struggles surrounding Key West's reconstruction might be seen as symptomatic of the universal desires and "shortcomings" of humanity itself.

The paradox of FERA-controlled Key West, which Davis inadvertently reveals, lies at the heart of American self-construction during the 1930s. How could Key West represent the nation "in miniature" and be "neither American nor Caribbean"? Moreover, how could Key West be "neither Florida nor Cuba" and still be part of the nation? By extension, how could America be represented as unified, if all those diverse elements didn't congeal into one? "To miniaturize is to conceal," writes Sontag;[27] and part of what the reconstruction of Key West concealed was U.S. imperial aggression. As the southernmost point of the continental United States, Key West was situated a mere ninety miles from Cuba, closer to Havana than to Miami. And Cuba, in 1934, was consumed by revolution. Between 1933 and 1935, more than one hundred revolutionary strikes—bombings, assassinations, sabotage—occurred in Cuba.[28] In July 1933, one year before FERA arrived in Key West, a military coup overthrew the corrupt Gerardo Machado government and installed Carlos Manuel de Céspedes as president. Within a month Céspedes was ousted in a revolt lead by Fulgencio Batista, who helped establish a provisional government lead by the leftist Ramón Grau San Martín.[29] Bolstered by the slogan "Cuba for the Cubans," Grau's revolutionary "government of 100 days" sought major labor reform and repudiated the 1903 Platt Amendment, which had authorized U.S. authority over Cuba following the Spanish-Cuban-American War. Alarmed that the United States might lose its economic and military foothold in Cuba, the interventionist U.S. ambassador Sumner Welles "deliberately characterized the new government in terms calculated to promote suspicion and provoke opposition in Washington."[30] Pressured by the United States, Batista switched allegiances and, in January 1934, established the Mendieta-Batista government, which was supported by the American government.[31] As payoff, the Platt Amendment was abrogated that year. By turning itself over to FERA, Key West enabled the isolationist U.S. government to reclaim the Caribbean, "Americanizing" its own island possession, while monitoring a post-Platt Cuba. Although the United States had remained officially uninvolved in the Cuban crisis, by the mid-1930s twenty-nine warships patrolled the waters between Key West and Cuba.[32]

"Havana—the Paris of the Western Hemisphere." Postcard, 1931. Author's collection.

FERA's Key West takeover domesticated the "disembodied imperialism" that Amy Kaplan argues is paradigmatic of modern American expansion: The American Empire maintains "total control, disentangled from direct political annexation" through networks of international markets linked to the states through "gateway" or bridge colonies like Hawaii, the Philippines, and Cuba.[33] Key West became a colony within, a colony that denied the engulfment of imperialism of the state to the federal government, of the Caribbean to the United States. By erasing the material signifiers of Key West's troubled and rebellious Caribbean history, FERA seemed to reassert the authority of a sanitized Anglo-American patriarchy that might be extended to the whole, heterogeneous United States. The federal "annexation" of Key West became a crucial move for a government that hoped to suppress disruptive narratives of cultural pluralism and rebellion, in favor of those that imagined a unified, even-tempered, and homogeneous nation.

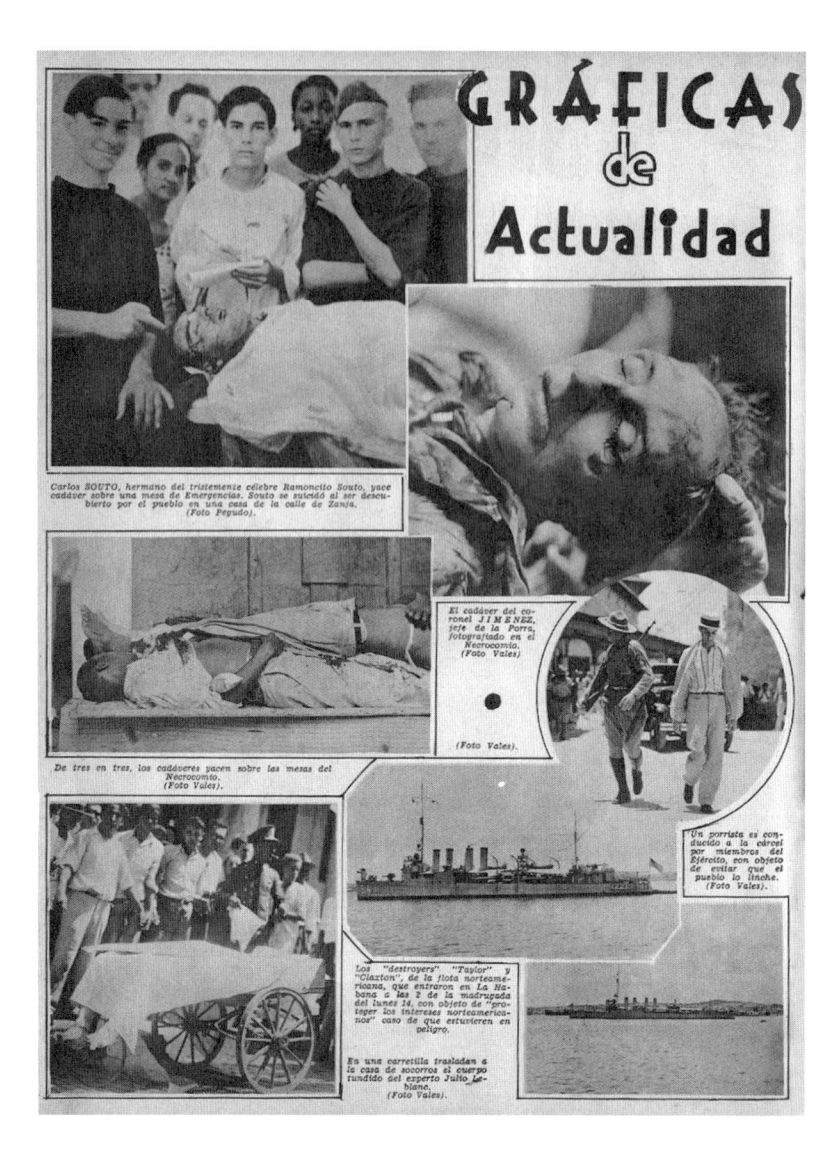

Page from the August 20, 1933, edition of the Cuban magazine *Carteles*.
Author's collection.

"The Triumph of Flagler's Vision— Over-the-Seas-Railroad to Key West, Florida." Stereoscopic print, 1926.
Keystone-Mast Collection [26802], UCR/California Museum of Photography, University of California at Riverside.

Wreck of relief train at Marathon Key after 1935 hurricane.
Photo No. EH 8174P in the John F. Kennedy Library.

So when the hurricane hit on Labor Day in 1935, it destroyed more than the railroad and shoreline highway to Key West, more than the hundreds of WPA-employed veterans who were drowned trying to build the bridges that would materially attach Key West to the United States, more than the train cars that were washed away in the rescue attempt. Key West already had been described as a forgotten city, a stranded town: the destruction of the Overseas Railroad made complete the material—and metaphoric—dismemberment of Key West from the American nation.

The train, which served in Reno as an allegory for progress and civilization, was confronted by the hurricane, the material embodiment of the capriciousness of nature. And yet, the hurricane, like nature itself, is a discursive

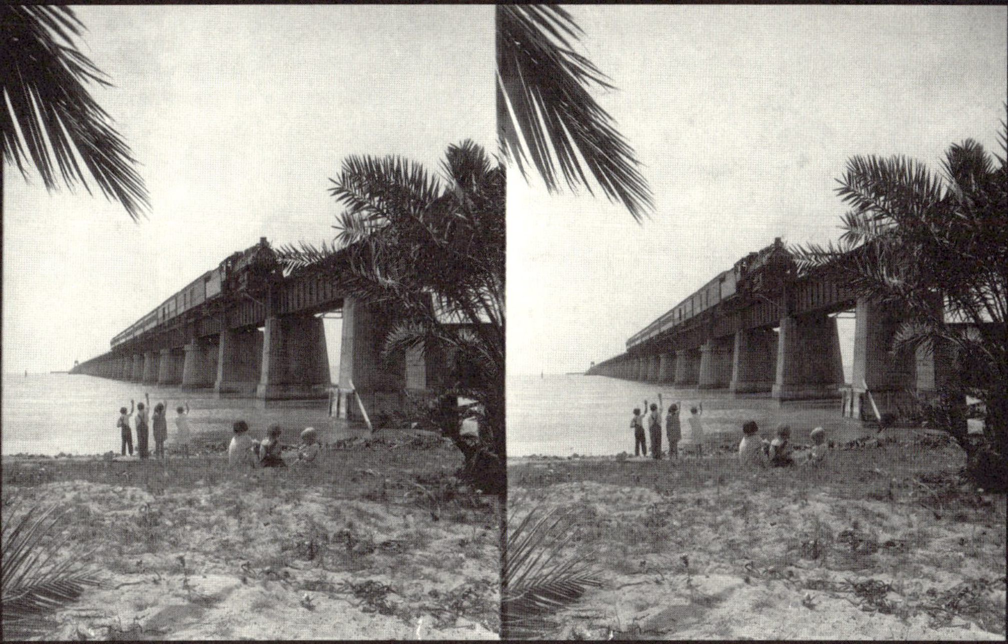

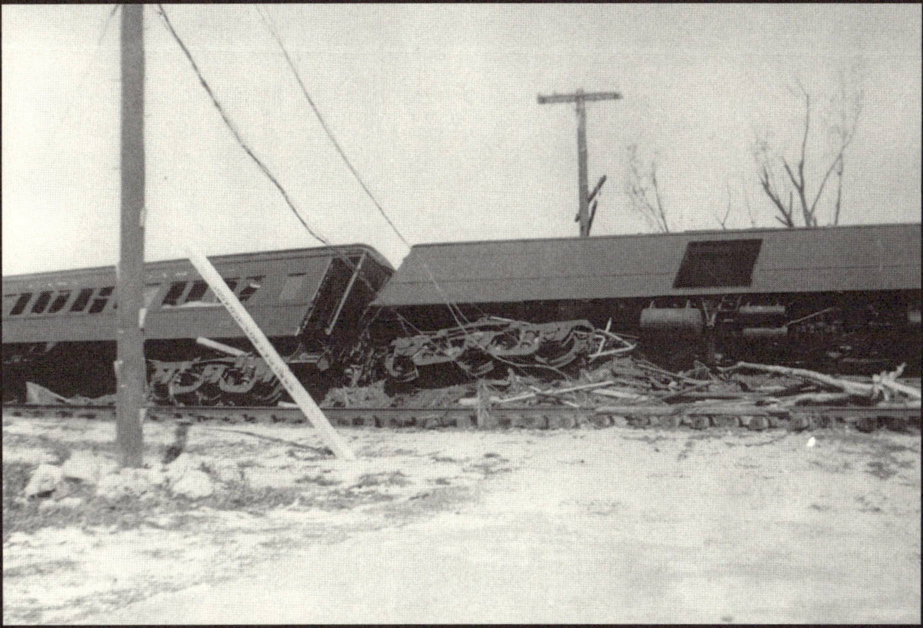

force—serving as well, for some in Key West, as an allegory for what Marshall Berman calls the modernist *maelstrom* of "perpetual disintegration and renewal"[34] or what Walter Benjamin names the "storm . . . we call progress." It is this storm that "irresistibly propels" Benjamin's famous angel of history backward into the future to watch, impotently, that single catastrophe piling "wreckage upon wreckage" and hurling it "in front of his feet." Benjamin argues that his angel of history "would like to stay, awaken the dead, and make whole what has been smashed."[35] It cannot.

Refusing to accept its impotence in the face of this wreckage, denying its role in stirring it up, the American government reimagined Key West as a place where wreckage might be salvaged, where the dead might reawaken, where smashed fragments might reassemble and speak. But Key West had built itself by acknowledging wreckage, by embracing dead things, tossed fragments and scraps. It is precisely this quality that the American government, in the guise of FERA, tried to knit together and erase. So when the hurricane broke, it exposed a gap in New Deal rhetoric, a gap in the nationalist rhetoric of progressive modernity. It lay bare, for a moment, the wreckage that progress had wrought.

part 2. a geography of drift

When I arrive in Key West, it is August, the height of hurricane season. It is so hot, melting really, that I shower in cold water for three days before I realize that the water heater in the tiny efficiency I rent doesn't work. Eight hundred dollars for two weeks in one room where the air conditioner works only sporadically. At off-season rates. Each night on the news I hear word of Hurricane Felix blowing off the west coast of Africa,

The Southernmost Point, 1995.
Author's photo.

crossing the ocean to Bermuda, to Florida, to the American continent. (It never hits the Keys but races across Pensacola in the northern tip of Florida, a city that is even harder hit by a hurricane the following month.)

Visually, Key West is a disappointment. The streets are splattered with drunken, tanned cruise ship tourists who cluster around brightly painted wooden shacks that promise to take them elsewhere—on glass-bottom boats out to the Atlantic, on snorkeling expeditions through the reefs, or on sailing trips to the old prison on the Tortugas. The edge of the island, Mile Zero of Route 1, is the self-proclaimed edge of the continent. And although the sea rubs up against the land on all sides, the island feels peninsular. Attached. Biking along Roosevelt Boulevard, you can pass through Stock Island, the next island over, before you realize you have left Key West. Swimming beaches are hard to come by. Small, rocky, and infrequent. And yet. The sea is so warm, so blue, the air so liquid, that it seems as if land, sea, and sky melt into each other. Key West is a beginning and end where space itself disappears.

One day, while a gale is blowing from the northeast, I meet Jimmy Dean. ("It's really James Dean," he tells me. "But you know . . ." I ask him if he has heard of the sausage guy. "It's like that either way," he agrees.) Jimmy Dean is a Conch, descended from Anglo-Saxons who had immigrated from the Bahamas in the nineteenth century.[36] He's a mortician at the Dean-Lopez Funeral Home, like many in his family before him. His small living room is cluttered with large handblown glass bottles that ripple like water. "They're valuable now," he says of his collection of demijohns, explaining that rumrunners used them to smuggle liquor during Prohibition. He shows me photographs he won't reveal to the curators at the public library. The smugglers' families, he explains, might not want to be reminded of their past. And outside, the island drips. The streets, flooded with rain, slide into the sea. Forms evaporate. They congeal.

WAVE MOTION

Key West is a tiny island, two miles wide and four miles long. Regulated spatially by the tides, its material boundaries are constantly in flux, making the place seem ever at risk of disappearing altogether. Elizabeth Bishop describes Key West as a "weightless mangrove island,"[37] populated by "perishable"[38] unpainted houses that are "air-color, almost."[39] It is a place where "the buildings faint/The tin roofs break/into a sweat."[40] For Bishop, the islands of the "keys float lightly like rolls of green dust."[41] And Florida itself seems weightless, if somewhat filthy, for it too "floats in brackish water."[42] Susan McCabe points out that Bishop's Florida poem "with its mostly long lines with interrupting shorter ones, is itself a 'sagging coastline.'" It performs typographically the geography it describes.[43]

Fluid, hybrid, without solid boundaries, Key West embodies a spatial "principle of drift," which Douglas Darden argues is embedded in theories of quantum mechanics that make molecular structure uncertain, entropic. Within Darden's description of built spaces lies the possibility of a geography "where nothing is fixed and where we can neither touch bottom nor support ourselves on the surface," that is "filled at best with only conditional and slippery meanings," that "aestheticizes the circumstantial and interruptive," the gap, the between-space of mixture and chance.[44]

Given the context of Key West's slippery geography, the small concrete building that houses the Key West Tropical Aquarium is an intriguing choice for the island's first FERA-funded tourist attraction. Today, it is just another of the quirky sites in the kitsch cove that has become Mallory Square. Here, in the most densely packed part of Key West, tourists clamor to munch on conch fritters and Key lime pie and to board the Conch Train that tours the island like an open-air motorized caterpillar. Here, every evening at sunset, tourists pack onto the pier to watch jugglers, buy T-shirts, and occasionally glance at the sky. Here, jewelry stores sell "Real Spanish Doubloons" salvaged from shipwrecks encased in gold as necklaces and earrings. Here, the aquarium, despite the life-size plaster seaman standing near the entrance, looks a bit too archaic and quaint for its surroundings. A roof, built in the 1950s, encloses the building so that it seems a tiny dark cave—a slightly weathered dollhouse version of the more familiar mammoth structures built of glass and concrete in Monterey and Boston.

The brainchild of Robert O. Van Deusen, the director of Philadelphia's Fairmont Park Aquarium, the Key West Tropical Aquarium was to be the first open-air aquarium in the nation, a modern structure that epitomized Key West's embrace of twentieth-century technology while flaunting the riches of its natural habitat.[45] (There were only four aquariums open to the public in the United States during the early 1930s.) But with 70 percent of the $30,000 in funds allotted to the project consumed by labor costs, the project soon ran out of financing. In March 1934, the half-built building was left abandoned. Using FERA's volunteer labor force, the project was taken up again in September and completed that winter. A self-congratulatory administration touted its completion as one of their first "tourist-centered" achievements.

The small, modified Spanish-style concrete building was admittedly odd in design. Only 126 feet long and 50 feet wide, it had been built on a sinkhole on the north end of Whitehead Street that had been called Guava Grove for the trees planted there. Two long walls were lined with tanks, and at the center of the enclosure were two oblong pools and a center fountain; the rear wall extended out to the bay and into decks, and crawls were built to house larger species, such as sharks and turtles.[46] The aquarium stood like an enclosed garden, open to the sky. Simultaneously manufactured and natural,

The Key West Aquarium, 1935. Courtesy of the Monroe County Public Library.

located on land that geologically the sea threatened to reclaim, the aquarium blurred the boundary between inside and outside, between the built and natural worlds, between the island and the sea in which it floated. It domesticated marine life that was already at home and manifested materially ideological and spatial permeability, the drift endemic to Key West. The structure controlled and ordered that permeability, made it visible, banal, instructive, and entertaining.

The aquarium was the sea domesticated, made placid and miniature; it reasserted the spatial dominance of the island over the sea, which threatened the island with its high water table—even as it created its existence. Enclosed in its concrete skeleton, the aquarium, which seems solid and inert, embodies Key West, the so-called Rock, in its deceptive fluidity. It is a microcosm of the microcosm that was FERA-controlled Key West. It controls and contains the unruly glimpse of fluidity it proposes to sell.

the nature of fluids

A letter of March 20, 1940, to Arthur F. Bentley from the philosopher John Dewey in Key West, Florida:

> I wish I knew more physics. This damn individual-social business must be linked with the discrete-continuity. As far as I can get is that, no matter how extensive the field, observation is so centered that a certain discreteness or "nuclear" quality belongs to its material. While reasoning (discourse that is ordered) is like radiation or continuous wave motion.
>
> Maybe this is a crazy notion.[47]

THE SEA AND ITS SHORE

Perhaps it is Key West's lack of fixity that made it appeal to Hart Crane, who belatedly decided to change the title of his collection of Caribbean poems to "Key West: An Island Sheaf." There is little evidence that Crane spent anytime in Key West. In fact, letters suggest he began composing most of the poems included in the posthumously published collection during his stay on the Cuban Isle of Pines between May and October 1926. He continued to revise them until his suicide in 1932. Letters also reveal that Crane pondered several possible titles for the collection of Caribbean poems: "Grand Cayman," then, significantly, "The Hurricane." But when the poems were found arranged in a folder after his death, the title Crane had underlined on the cover was "Key West."

It is the subtitle that provides a clue to the imaginative site that Crane hoped to capture in his title. In its most literal form, "An Island Sheaf" seems self-explanatory. The collection is itself a sheaf, papers bound together materially and aesthetically to narrate the island, the palms, pirates, and "airplants" he describes. With Crane, however, one must also consider the double entendre, the pun, which Paul Giles astutely argues provides a key to Crane's aesthetic.[48] (The pun is itself linguistically fluid, simultaneously revealing that which it obscures.) Read through the lens of the pun, "An Island Sheaf" becomes an "Island Sheath," something that gloves the island like a foreskin. Crane's poetry is dialectical. In accentuating/obscuring the sheath, Crane draws attention to that which it covers—Key West itself. Significantly, there is no Key West poem listed in the contents table of the titled folder collection. But there is a Key West poem, a poem set aside in draft copy, enclosed at the back of a second, untitled folder that contains a series of other manuscripts. "Key West," then, is enclosed in a sheath of other poems, in a sheath of sheaves.[49] The poem itself finally exposes what Crane hides.

Crane's "Key West" resides outside of gender. It is a place where "skies impartial" "do not disown me/Nor claim me, either, by Adam's spine nor rib."

The ambiguous speaker can be either Key West or of Key West. The poem describes a speaker who finds the voice of androgyny through the ambiguity of the place. Or is it an androgynous Key West that is not only scripted, but speaks? In either case and, I would suggest, precisely in both, Key West allegorizes for Crane an escape from emplacement—and a fixed notion of place. At the time of his death, Crane was deeply concerned with the constraints of fixed identity placement. He declared in letters that he "was not homosexual," for he had fallen in love with Peggy Cowley. His declaration was not, however, an affirmation of heterosexuality—he still slept with men—but a rejection of the modernist compulsion for authentic self-placement and an embrace of the borderland of bisexuality.[50] Crane's suicidal leap from a steamer into the Atlantic Ocean between Cuba and Key West in 1932 performed (if self-destructively) his embrace of the interstices and his quest for an androgynous and fluid geography of identity.[51]

By contrast, Wallace Stevens is resistant to the androgyny he fears is inherent to the production of poetry, is inherent to Key West. He instead attempts to control the fluid spatiality of Key West, to construct some kind of "Idea of Order."[52] For Stevens, in his 1936 poem "Farewell to Florida," Key West does not float; instead it "sank downward under massive clouds." It is stagnant, built with "shadowless huts," "rust and bones," and "trees like bones."[53] Stevens imagines Key West not as androgynous, but as feminine, a dumping ground for the snake that has molted there and "left its skin upon the floor." The speaker declares that "Her mind will never speak to me again./I am free." While this line generally is assumed to refer to Stevens's poetic muse, it also refers to the space of poetry, which Stevens fearfully saw as feminine and, perhaps, homoerotic.[54] To leave Key West, then, liberates him from the alluring threat of a feminine/queer and, yes, artistic spatiality. The speaker writes, "I am free." Free of feminine impulses, of gender confusion, of the ambivalences of unlicensed desire.

The waves repeat in refrain the effort of the speaker's molting "Of this: that the snake has shed its skin upon/The floor." Key West becomes "the floor," the end, the bottom of America, and most important, the dumping ground of poetic imagination. Like Crane, Stevens employs the image of the sheath in this "shed" skin, but with more ambivalence about its gendered implications. Stevens's speaker must "shed its skin," leaving it in the feminized space of Key West, in order to return, remasculinized to the violent urban north. Indeed, it is only by making Key West unnaturally concrete, stagnant, and sinking, only by projecting that fluidity onto the urban, commercial north, where "the men are moving as the water moves," that Stevens's speaker can face his departure. And still, embedded in this action is the melancholic recognition that to leave Key West behind, to shed his feminine skin, is also to forego art.

Stevens tries to order, to contain Key West, to reject the fluidity of its boundaries. In an earlier poem, "Theory," Stevens's speaker perceives the importance of context and situatedness to identity, for "I am what is around me."[55] And in "The Idea of Order at Key West," he recognizes that poetry arises out of ambiguity, for "in ghostlier demarcations keener sounds."[56] Stevens's declaration of "the maker's rage to order words of the sea," in "The Idea of Order at Key West," finally becomes the poet's rage to order the materials he employs, to repress their violent histories, their origins "in ghostlier demarcations." For Stevens, to be vomited forth from the crypt of the sea means already to be lost.

things to see in key west

Hemingway's image is ubiquitous in Key West.[57] He grins from advertisements. On plaques outside buildings. In paintings and photographs in Duval Street bars. At Ripley's Believe It or Not Museum in the Old Strand theater. (They have acquired one of his high school yearbooks.) Aspiring look-alikes flood the town during Hemingway Days every July. Most are bearded, gray-haired, and overweight; the preferred image of the writer is as the overcooked salt of later years. (Perhaps it's simply that this representation of Hemingway, like that of the side-burned bloated Elvis, is easier to imitate since it already parodies itself.)

The Hemingway house on Whitehead Street is the biggest sightseeing attraction on the island. In 1934, FERA published a sightseeing guide to the island that marked the house as the eighteenth stop on the tour "between Johnson's Tropical Grove (number 17) and Lighthouse and Aviaries (number 19)."[58] (Hemingway responded to this honor by building a stone wall around his yard.)

The Hemingway house tour is at once serious and pure camp. (The male guide who shows me around wears black eyeliner.) Little in the house is authentic, a point the guides make no effort to deny. (I am especially suspect of the original Picasso sculpture of a cat, sitting upright on the bureau in the bedroom.) Live cats, supposedly authentic descendents of Hemingway's six-toed felines, lounge underfoot. They are named conspicuously after movie stars: Judy Garland, Marilyn Monroe, and Fred Astaire.

Outside by the saltwater pool, the guide points to a nickel embedded in the cement. He tells us a story: Knowing that Hemingway liked to swim, his second wife, Pauline Pfieffer, spent $20,000 building a saltwater pool while he was away in Spain helping the Republican cause. Upon returning, Hemingway supposedly asked what it had cost, threw a nickel in the wet cement, and said, "Here, now you can spend my last nickel!" I ask the guide later why he didn't point out that Hemingway had lived off Pauline's family money for most of his time in Key West and that, in fact, at the time he was in Spain he was having an affair with Martha Gelhorn, who would

1930s fishing trip with Ernest Hemingway, in Waldo Peirce's Key West Scrapbook. Courtesy of Special Collections, Miller Library, Colby College, Waterville, Maine.

"eric" of Sun also Rises
& it with Duff
next
& Spanga cap

become his next wife. The guide tells me that in a brief tour one can't say everything. Indeed. (Elizabeth Bishop once commented that Hemingway had pirated a story written by his wife Pauline "about the fellow who goes to salvage a wreck and sees the blond woman's floating hair through the porthole.")[59]

In a 1937 letter, Bishop writes, "Key West is nice, not because of all this sport and these he-men litterateurs, but just because it is so pretty, so inexpensive and full of such nice little old houses. It is NOT like Provincetown."[60] Yet the Hemingway house tour both reflects the infusion of queer culture in contemporary Key West, and reveals the ambiguity, the androgyny of Hemingway's texts, of Hemingway, of Key West itself.[61]

IDEAS OF ORDER

The relationship between place and representation is a slippery one. It certainly is not unilateral or causal. Nonetheless, we can understand something about an artist's relationship to the ideologies constituted by and of that place at a particular moment in time through the way she or he negotiates the aesthetics of representing it. If we consider Key West as enabling a poetics of the interstices, of fragmentation, of fluidity, as Crane suggests, then the place's attraction to certain writers and artists interested in alterior spaces makes a great deal more sense. Writing on Marianne Moore, Bishop notes in her Key West notebooks, "Miss M's method applied to 'interstitial situations'—oblique realities that give one pause that [glance] off a larger reality illuminating like light caught in a vessel—."[62] In Bishop's terms, the interstitial spatiality of Key West is a dialectical one that illuminates through obscuring, enclosing, covering up.

Consider, as well, the fragmentary, "patchwork quality" of Hemingway's Key West novel, *To Have and Have Not*. The novel has been dealt with harshly by critics. "Hemingway's new novel will strike many people as confused and some people as transitional," wrote Louis Kronenberger in the *Nation* in 1937. "It is a book with neither poise nor integration, and with shocking lapses from professional skill.... It is like writing a letter and then adding to it an appalling number of postscripts."[63] In the *Southern Review*, Delmore Schwartz complained that "'To Have and Have Not' is a stupid and foolish book, a disgrace to a good writer, a book which should never have been printed ... the conversation is repeatedly false, or rather falsetto, and the descriptive passages sometimes read like improvisations." Schwartz continues his rant for a good while, remarking finally, "And the progress of the story is as poorly constructed as it possibly could be by a writer who once said that writing is architecture and not interior decoration."[64]

Yet it is precisely the things these writers critique—the shifts in voice and genre, the fragmentary dialogue, the fluidity, one might say, androgyny, of its "falsetto" form—that make *To Have and Have Not* a Key West novel. "It is significant that the America of 'To Have and Have Not' is Key West," wrote Alfred Kazin in *New York Herald Tribune Books*, one of the few kind reviews of the novel. "For like the Paris of 1925, Key West is at once an outpost of a culture and its symbol." Kazin recuperates the novel—one might say salvages it—by remasculinizing it. Paradoxically, he does so by inadvertently situating it within a larger aesthetic framework of Key West art:

> It is by Key West that Hemingway went home, and it is Key West, apparently, that remains America in cross-section to him: the noisy, shabby, deeply moving rancor and tumult of all those human wrecks, the fishermen and the Cuban revolutionaries, the veterans and the alcoholics, the gilt-edged snobs and the hungry natives, the great white stretch of beach promising everything and leading nowhere.
>
> For this is a Hemingway who can get angry and snarl with his heart open. It means a novel thrown together with a fury that leaps from one page to another, a succession of styles instead of a chopped, frozen manner; it means that as he wrote the book he was forced to see his way through in terms of his own position, so that chapters are broken nervously, speeches are begun but never finished, characters enter from all sides and at all times.[65]

Like Bishop and Crane, like Waldo Peirce in his Key West scrapbooks and Loren MacIver in her Key West WPA paintings from 1939 and 1940, Hemingway employs an aesthetic so slippery that it spans the limits of visual and linguistic media. Such an aesthetic forges a link between finished forms that are themselves "constantly on the brink of disappearing" and those unfinished scraps—notebooks, manuscript excisions, scrapbooks, letters, and everyday gossip—that disappear in the ordered materialization of the artistic product.[66] In foregrounding the evanescence of these found objects, which evaporate at the moment they become embodied in text, these artists foreground the instability, the drift inherent in the production of modern literary and artistic texts and in those texts as finished products.

In MacIver's 1939 Key West painting *Studio*, for example, forms reveal themselves through gesture. Objects are never explicitly articulated, never wholly abstract. Miniature chairs, cups, potted plants, sketched in broken outlines, float weightlessly in a sea of grayish brown. Hyperattentive to objects, the painting reveals how objects dissipate in their own representation. In the lower left corner, brown rectangles fade into brown rectangles. They gesture toward unfinished canvases, multitudes of them, on which representation continually threatens to disappear. A faint white line, which bleeds persistently through the paint that covers it, exposes the constructedness of art that occludes its own production process and erases the mistake. But for MacIver, the mistakes, and the creative process they imply, are what make a

Loren MacIver, *Studio*, oil on canvas, 47 in. x 49 in., 1939. Gift of the Works Progress Administration, Federal Art Project. Photograph © 1965 The Detroit Institute of Arts.

representation art not mimesis. Far from being stable, material objects are possibilities that always threaten to dematerialize, to drift, to transform into something else.[67] *Studio* represents the fluid space of artistic production in Key West, blurring the boundaries between inside and outside, begging the viewer to question what it means to represent a place.

What I call a Key West aesthetic resonates both with surrealism and Caribbean art forms, conveying a politicized and *mestizo* modernism, a slippery, twilight modernism.[68] "The island starts to hum/like music in a dream," writes Bishop in her unfinished poem "Full Moon, Key West," thereby depicting a modernism that assumes that abject fragments and odd juxtapositions don't reveal themselves in our sleep, but rather lie unnoticed in our conscious everyday lives.[69]

Simon Gikandi argues that "the 'modernization' of African cultures in the Caribbean" engenders a conflicted literature of alterity among Caribbean writers that negotiates between new art forms and the legacy of colonial oppression embedded in them.[70] "An integrated discourse of the self is surely the ultimate or possibly utopian desire of Caribbean writing," Gikandi surmises, "but it can only be reached after the negotiation of a historically engendered split between the self and its world, between this self and the language it uses."[71] What evolves in Caribbean texts, according to Benítez-Rojo, is the *mestizo* rhythm of the "Peoples of the Sea," a rhythm that concentrates the dynamics of differences and rejects a logocentric notion of Progress that relies on the "biological, economic, and cultural whitening of Caribbean society." Benítez-Rojo explains:

> The Caribbean poem and novel not only projects for ironizing a set of values taken as universal; they are, also, projects that communicate their own turbulence, their own clash, and their own void, the swirling black hole of social violence produced by the encomienda and the plantation, that is, their otherness, their peripheral asymmetry with regard to the West. . . . Thus Caribbean literature cannot free itself totally of the multiethnic society upon which it floats, and it tells us of its fragmentation and instability.[72]

Gikandi's literature of alterity and Benítez-Rojo's fragmentary, *mestizo* model of Caribbean poetics might provide a great deal of insight into Key West aesthetics—except for one thing. Few of the writers and artists who represent Key West during the 1930s are Caribbean or are of African, Latino, or Native American ancestry. Indeed, the individuals we are discussing are largely white, Anglo, middle-class, educated U.S. citizens who came to Key West as adults. With the exception of the bilingual newspapers, few extant manuscripts and artworks depicting Depression-era Key West were created by native Key Westers.[73] Black, Conch, and to a lesser extent Cuban working-class lives reveal themselves largely through WPA oral histories, newspaper clippings, and other archival mishmash and through representations found in works by white middle-class writers and artists who were not from the place.[74]

Key West was attractive to many of these white, transplanted writers and artists because it enabled them to employ a Caribbean poetics of alterity as the means through which to disrupt the fantasy of happy cohesion advocated by the New Deal. But this was a complex negotiation. On one hand, these writers and artists disinterred, spoke, and represented the unnarrated stories of everyday Key Westers. At the same time, they imperfectly recognized their complicity in reinforcing the existent social order. A Key West aesthetic is an aesthetic of salvaging, a borrowed form that builds art from found objects and native wreckage. It recognizes that it has been dredged up from and speaks for the unnarrated stories at the depths of the sea.[75] It becomes a strategy used by these artists in an effort to bring what they see as foreign into the self, while simultaneously recognizing the other's autonomy.[76]

Bishop, for instance, foregrounds the autonomous histories of the materials that build artistic texts, those scraps, the refuse inherent in the creation process.[77] She begins her story "Mercedes Hospital" with an obituary clipped from the local newspaper. She writes, "One day in the summer of 1940 the following notice appears in the Key West *Citizen*: José Chacon Died Today." Then she includes the obituary in its entirety and the poem which followed it on the page. She pasted the actual newspaper clipping in the text of the original typewritten manuscript of the story. The story continues: "I find this brief account of the death of an old man in what is really just a poor house, the Casa del Pobre, very touching. And of course the poem is touching too, but it naturally does not occur to me to connect them."[78] The story, which is about her visit to Key West's Mercedes Hospital, a hospital for the poor, begs the reader to seek out that connection, but even more so, to connect fiction with historical documents, reportage. One cannot make meaning by interpreting only verbal language, she suggests, but need consider spatial language—where something lies on the page. Writing, for Bishop, is like constructing a collage, aligning disconsonant objects, making meaning through juxtaposition.[79]

Manuscript page of "Mercedes Hospital." Elizabeth Bishop Papers, Special Collections, Vassar College Libraries, Poughkeepsie, New York. Excerpts from unpublished writings of Elizabeth Bishop reprinted by permission of Farrar, Straus and Giroux, LLC, on behalf of the estate of Elizabeth Bishop. Copyright © 1999 by Alice Helen Methfessel.

an interruption

"So this guy Julius Stone thought that he owned Key West because they sent him from Washington," Eveillo Cabot, an eight-five-year-old former cigar maker tells me one day in Key West over tea and bread pudding.

"Well, he did," his wife, Mimi (Amelia), interjects.

"No, well, he didn't own Raul," Eveillo continues. "So, I'm there at the door at Raul's club like to greet [people].[80] I ask [this guy] what is your name? And he says, 'Julius Stone. I want to eat, I want a little gambling.' As soon as he says 'a little gambling' I think something's wrong here. So I went and I told the owner Raul Vasquez. I said there's this guy Julius Stone, he says he's a big shot from Key West, he owns Key West. Raul says, 'No, he don't own Key West. This is my property, he don't own this.' He was a hell of a Spaniard . . .

"Raul comes [outside] and [Stone] says, 'I'm Julius Stone.' And [Raul] says, 'And I'm Raul Vasquez. I'm the owner of this club.' [Stone] says, 'I want to eat. I want to do a little gambling.' [Raul] says, 'I don't mind [if] you come and eat and have a little gambling or whatever. But before you come in you've got to put on clothes. You're almost naked.' 'No,' [Stone]

MERCEDES HOSPITAL

One day last evening?
On April 17th, 1940, May the following notice in the newspaper:

JOSE CHACON DIED TODAY

BURIAL THIS AFTERNOON AT 5:30 O'CLOCK FROM FUNERAL CHAPEL

Jose Chacon, 84, died 3 o'clock this morning in the Mercedes Hospital. Funeral services will be held 5:30 p. m. today from the chapel of the Pritchard Funeral Home, Rev. G. Perez, of the Latin Methodist Church, officiating.

The deceased leaves but one survivor, a nephew, Jose Chacon.

And on the next day, April 18th, appeared the following poem:

FRIEND?
By L. S. NASH

How often you have called
 Someone a friend
And thought he would be
 Everything it meant?

While you were on top of the
  world,
 With money in your hands,
They flocked around everywhere,
 Even at your command.

says, 'these are my shorts.' And [Raul] says, 'And this is my club. And you're not coming in unless you go and dress yourself.'"

"Can you imagine that?" Mimi asks.[81]

SALVAGING POLITICS

The aesthetic strategy of salvaging does not lie in employing found objects for one's pleasure or undermining the opposition between high art and mass culture, as had been the case for much of the European avant-garde. It strives to uncover this refuse in order to remember forgotten moments of loss. Salvaging for 1930s Key West artists and writers becomes an aesthetic response to Crane's plaintive question in "O Carib Isle!," published in 1927. Confronted with "death's brittle crypt," Crane's speaker asks,

> And yet suppose
> I count these nacreous frames of tropic death
> brutal necklaces of shells around each grave
> Squared off so carefully (8–11).

The poem's speaker asks, in other words, what the revelation of the violent disorder buried in such tidy graves might convey. He questions a worldview that aestheticizes skeletons and shells as the sterile relics of history while erasing the materially specific incidences of violence and decay they simultaneously signify. The resonance of such an aesthetic approach with salvage ethnography is important to note. For any attempt at salvage is always a kind of piracy, both violent and fetishistic, like early ethnography itself. Moreover, it relies on a kind of appropriative mourning, a desire to preserve or fix in place that which has never been but is nonetheless lost.[82]

Within this framework, we might read the series of narrations of bodily death in *To Have and Have Not* as a kind of recovery mission for the profusion of anonymous corpses that were endemic to 1930s Cuba and Key West. Death, in Hemingway's novel, comes heavy-handedly through secreted acts of silencing that transform named characters into anonymous corpses. The rich, English-speaking Cuban Pancho has his face blown off by unnamed revolutionaries in the opening pages of the novel; Harry Morgan kills the smooth-talking Chinese Mr. Sing, who had paid him to smuggle twelve Chinese immigrants into the United States, by dislocating his arms, crushing his voice box, and choking him; and the four Cubans revolutionaries whom Harry helps escape after they rob a bank, shoot the lawyer Bee-lips, the FERA relief worker Albert, and finally Harry himself, who dies without disclosing the details of what happened to his assassins.

Significantly, there is only one anonymous corpse in the novel, described as the close-up photograph of an unnamed black man "with his throat cut clear across from ear to ear and then stitched up neat." The photograph warns Harry not to tell anyone about the Havana bloodbath narrated in the first pages of the novel; for the dead man holds "a card on his chest saying in Spanish: 'This is what we do to lenguas largas,'" that is, those with a *long tongue*, those who speak of the repression they see.[83] In a text that obsessively records the particular circumstances of bodily death, this corpse's material history is made doubly anonymous and doubly encrypted. Its death narrative becomes generic—narratable in captions—and in being made generic is translatable, removed from the specificity of its Spanish-Cuban context into a hybrid Spanish-English (or American) one. The transformation from subject into sign that is constitutive of all corpses recalls in this case as well the troubling translation of an African subject into commodity in the Caribbean slave economy—and in doing so reproduces that economy by producing the anonymous black corpse as a sign for all black bodies and for Cuban repression itself. The black corpse, in its anonymity, in its isolation, in its silence, thus comes to re-member the corrupt slave trade and colonialism in the Caribbean that gave birth to North American capitalism, a capitalism that during the Depression seemed to speak its own demise. The black corpse makes noise in its silence—of squelched maroon rebellions, of a nation built on the bones of black corpses. In declining to narrate the specific demise of this corpse, in retaining the body's anonymity, Hemingway can be read as being complicit in the societal repression he critiques. And yet, by preserving the anonymity of the black body, by treating that body as so much stuff, the text inadvertently alludes to enslavement as a problematic within Caribbean labor history that precedes the midcentury labor struggles that are embroiling Cuba and Key West—and indeed is encrypted within them.

If Hemingway only ambivalently disinters the politicized Caribbean mélange of histories, Stevens dismisses it altogether in "O Florida, Venereal Soil," as

> The dreadful sundry of this world,
> the Cuban, Polodowsky,
> The Mexican woman,
> The negro undertaker
> Killing the time between corpses.[84]

The Afro-Cuban poet Nicolás Guillén alludes to a similar "sundry" in his 1934 poem "West Indies, Ltd," in order to indict U.S. imperialism. If this sundry is "dreadful," he suggests, it is because Euro-American capitalism has both produced and exploited the color line:

> Aquí hay blancos y negros y chinos y mulatos.
> Desde luego, se trata de colores baratos,
> pues a través de tratos y contratos
> se han corrido los tintes y no hay un tono estable.
> (El que piense otra cosa que avance un paso y hable.)[85]

[Here there are whites and blacks and Chinese and mulattos.
Of course, we're talking about cheap colors,
since through deals and contracts
the shades have run together and there is no stable tone.
(He who thinks anything else, let him take one step forward
and speak.)][86]

Benítez-Rojo argues that Guillén's poem "goes beyond the strictly Cuban and connects with the discourse of resistance that flows within the pan-Caribbean plantation. . . . Cuba, for the first time, is linked by a poem to the sugar-producing order that has subjected the whole archipelago."[87] That archipelago is a *mestizo* one, with "no stable tone," for which narratives of the "sundry" of ancestral or racial origin and difference are subordinate to, indeed invalidated by, a collective Caribbean legacy of colonialism, slave labor, and indentured servitude.

Writers and artists who foreground Key West's Caribbean and especially Cuban heritage must confront the complex and gendered discourse of *mestizaje*, "Cuban color," and racial mixing that was alluded to by writers from José Marti to Guillén.[88] Like Guillén, Bishop recognizes in her poem "Florida" that "the state with the prettiest name" is also the place that squelches even as it cashes in on its African, Spanish, and Native American heritage.[89] Yet unlike Guillén, she suggests that racial division and segregation, the commercialized congregation of diffuse and disempowered "black specks/too far apart, and ugly whites; the poorest/postcard of itself," are themselves an inheritance of that legacy. Through the decayed images of "barnacled shells" and "skulls" of dead turtles, "the tide-looped strings of fading shells," Bishop searches for traces of violence encrypted in the objects she scavenges. From the biblical "Job's Tear" of native Arawak who were ravaged in the name of Christian conversion, to the "Chinese Alphabet" of those indentured Caribbean laborers from Asia, to the mulatto "parti-colored pectins" of Bahamian immigrants and Maroon, to the pioneer women's "gray rag of rotted calico" and the "buried Indian Princess's skirt," Bishop resurrects the multiple forgotten histories of American nation building through found objects and skeletons, the material traces of those whose histories were erased. In particular, she seeks out the feminine histories of "calico" and "skirts" that Cuban politics of *mestizaje* repress.

When Bishop figuratively uncovers the body of the black Bahamian woman servant in her poem "Cootchie," she exposes what Key West administrators had refused to recognize.[90] The drowned Cootchie is black, working class, a woman (and as a "cootchie" or cunt, every woman). She has died forgotten, drowned in an environment of white seas and "egg-white" skies: "black into white she went/below the surface of the coral-reef." But when Cootchie's corpse is discovered by the lighthouse attendants who seek someone else, they will "dismiss all as trivial," though "the sea desperate,/ will proffer wave after wave." For Bishop, the sea spews forth wreckage, even human wrecks that uncomfortably refuse to stay lost. As the material sign of a geography of drift, Bishop's sea seems to cry out for a language of salvaging, for the uncovering of lost objects and histories, for the salvaging of remains. And yet, the sea itself creates loss. To be "at sea" speaks simultaneously of the threat of aimlessness, of wandering, of fluidity—and of the concomitant loss and isolation, the marooning, such drift implies.

"Don't forget I did live in the south," writes Bishop in a letter of March 13, 1965, to her aunt Grace Bulmer Bowles. "My dear old laundress's (black) son was murdered by the Key West police because one of them wanted his wife. Everyone knew this and nothing was done about it. The laundress was given her son's body in a coffin, straight from jail. She said 'I looked at his arm Miss Elizabeth, it wasn't an arm anymore . . . ' etc. etc."[91] The arm that is no longer an arm is separate from the corpse; yet it also signifies the corpse, a body that is *unheimlich*, literally, un-placed, something that "ought to have remained hidden but has come to light."[92] It is here that language fails Bishop as she drifts into the placelessness of the unnarratable. The "etc.," those unnamed "odds and ends," become placeholders for that which cannot be said.[93]

part 3. "late air"

I came to Key West looking for brothels, the Square Roof in particular, on whose steps I spied a young Elizabeth Bishop in a photograph once taken there.[94] "Elizabeth, Louise [Crane], and some others thought it was fun to go there," said Martha Sauer, a painter who had befriended Bishop in Key West, in a March 16, 1989, interview. "They used to have a few drinks and sit around. I once went with some friends and Elizabeth, and I was never more uncomfortable in my life. It was slumming—there were these black prostitutes sitting around, and there was somebody playing the piano."[95]

I ride through Old Town on my ancient rental bike, past the white mansions on Whitehead Street, and turn right before reaching the Hemingway house into Bahama Village, the poor black section of town, what was once more problematically called Jungletown. No cruise ship tourists here, just locals, mostly of Bahamian and Haitian ancestry. Men sit together outside on the steps of small saltbox shacks painted in bright Caribbean colors. The Square Roof still stands on the corner of Emma and Petronia streets. Large and white, the two-tiered Bahama-style building houses a social services office on the ground floor.

I stop an older man, Charles, age seventy-three (he doesn't give me his last name), who is standing nearby and ask him about Key West brothels. "They had bars. The women drank water and the men drank liquors. It usually cost ten cents for a drink," he says, then gestures to the Square Roof

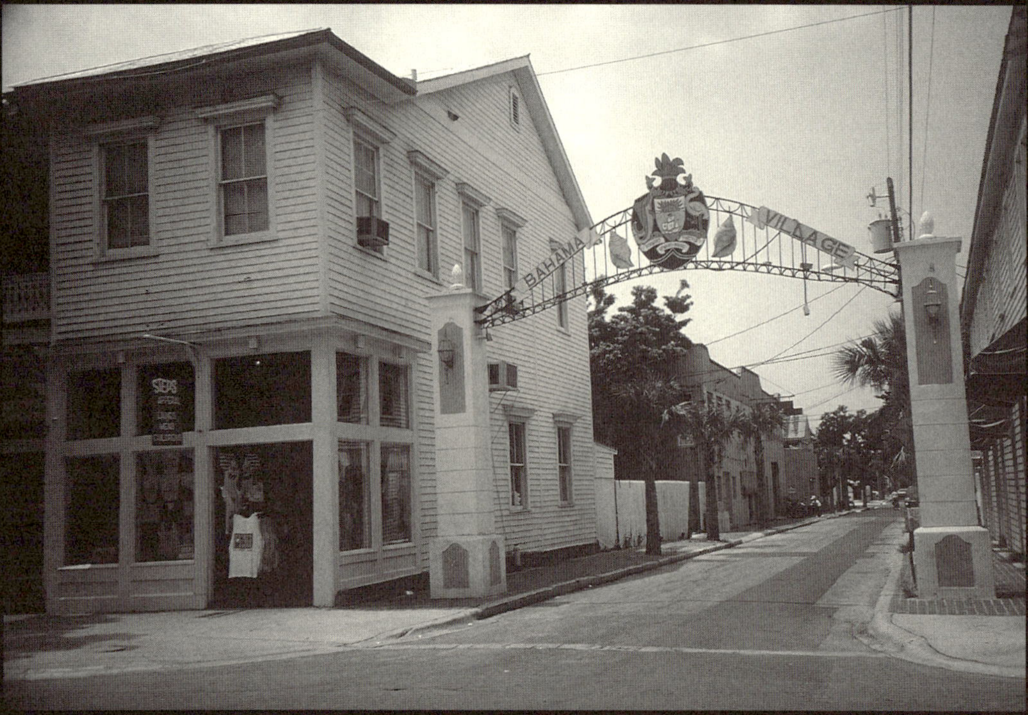
BAHAMA
VILLAGE

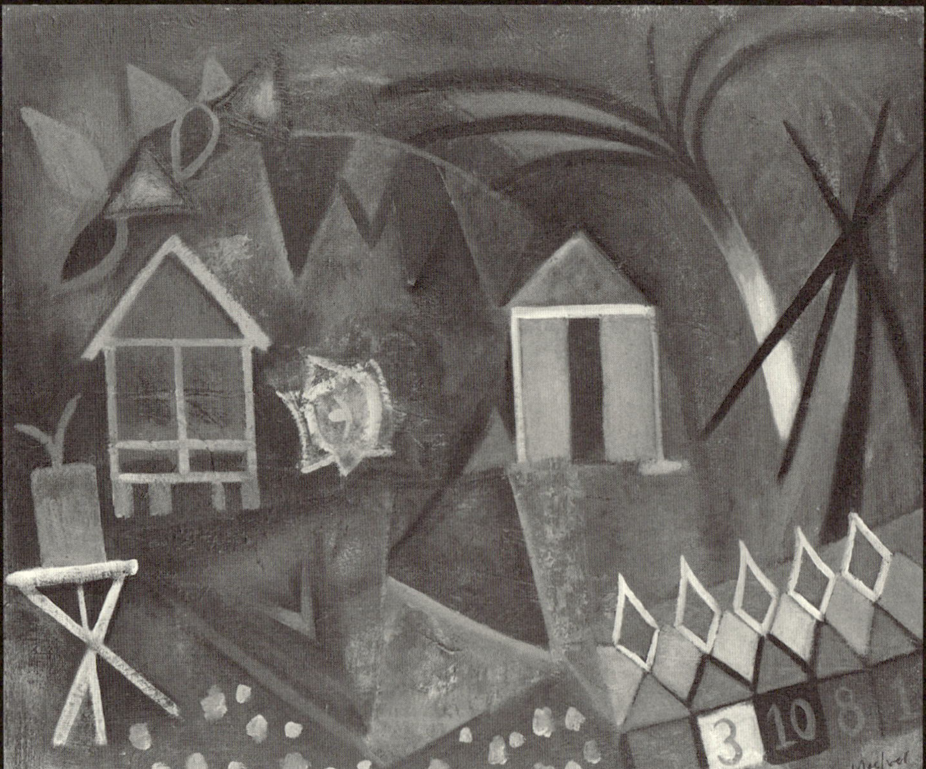
3 10

building. "A place like that could charge thirty or forty cents [for a drink]." I ask whether it is true that the prostitutes at the Square Roof were all black and the clients only white men. "They [the women] had good hair, like you," he replies elliptically and refers me to someone named Shine, who lives a few streets away. (I find out later that Kermit "Shine" Forbes had sparred with Hemingway back in the thirties—at least according to local legend.) Shine's tiny house is bedecked with objects—broken dolls, conch shells, tattered fishing nets. It looks like a souvenir shop gone awry. I knock. No one answers. The door to the house beside Shine's is swung open wide to let out the heat; inside a young woman is sweeping the floor, peering up periodically from her work, catching glimpses of the Spanish soap opera on television.

A few days later I speak to Francis Delaney, an eighty-five-year-old white man from an old Key West family.[96] He had been chief clerk of the WPA office and claims to have typed a draft of *To Have and Have Not*. ("Hemingway, he was a man's man," Delaney tells me, "But women liked him, because he was a woman's man.")

"We had a well-developed red light district.... The Square Roof was probably the biggest [of the houses]; they had twelve or fifteen girls," he continues. "I think they were tacitly approved of by the whole populace. The men had to have a place to go, and the women were content to have them in a place away from children.... I've never heard of a campaign [to get rid of them] originated by the women of Key West.... [The Square Roof] had a dance floor and a bar. A lot of men went down for recreation. It was high-class. Had a big business. We had a big party in there one day; it involved some of the most prominent men in Key West. When a new girl was brought to town, men would vie for the privilege of spending the night with her. Prices were usually two dollars and up. A new girl could bring in twenty-five dollars or something like that. The Square Roof usually charged three or four dollars for regular girls.... Black people had their own houses. A lot of white men would visit the black houses, but they couldn't have the black boys visit white houses."

Bahama Village from Duval Street, 1995.
Author's photograph.

Loren MacIver, *Jungletown*, oil on canvas, 1939.
Gift of John S. Newberry. Photograph © 1952 The Detroit Institute of Arts.

A KEY WEST ROMANCE

In 1940, a sixty-four-year-old German immigrant who called himself Carl Tanzler Von Cosel was arrested in Key West for having disinterred, embalmed, and slept for seven years beside the corpse of Elena Milagro Hoyos, a young, poor woman of Cuban heritage. He claimed that Hoyos was his bride. That she had been married to another man did not deter Von Cosel. Hoyos's husband had deserted her. And Von Cosel had kept a (sometimes annoying) vigil beside her as she lay dying of tuberculosis. Claiming he was a scientist, he offered her unconventional treatments for the disease—and showered her with presents. When Hoyos died at age nineteen in October 1931, Von Cosel paid for the funeral and her burial in the Key West cemetery.

A year after the girl's death, Von Cosel disinterred, reembalmed, and "rebedded" (at least purportedly) the corpse in a large concrete crypt he visited daily. He said he was fearful of water damage to the body. Two years later, responding to pleas he believed emanated from the coffin, Von Cosel disinterred the corpse once again. This time he did not return it. He brought the corpse home and spent the ensuing years coddling, disinfecting, and apparently sexually penetrating it. Von Cosel's odd bed partner was discovered and reclaimed by the courts seven years later. In the few days that followed, while the courts were deciding who had rights to the corpse, the waxen effigy was laid out in public view at the Dean-Lopez funeral home, where over six thousand people were said to have gawked at the sight. Eventually, Von Cosel was released on bond and never prosecuted because the statute of limitations had run out.

Von Cosel (in hat) and onlookers.
Photo courtesy of Wright Langley Archives, Inc.

Surprisingly, public opinion at the time was largely sympathetic to Von Cosel, who became a romantic cult figure of sorts. Newspapers and magazines nationwide were plastered with headlines such as "Immortal Kisses Were His Goal"[97] and "The Man Who Loved a Corpse: Incredible saga of a love that burned beyond the grave!"[98] In fact, only one contemporary newspaper, the ill-reputed *Miami Life*, offered a more lurid narrative. The article warned its readers that other newspapers, "especially the *Miami Herald*, have probably caused you to sympathize with the crackpot 'scientist.'" "You may even, like some, have hotly demanded that the old man be given back the 'body,' and that he somehow be allowed to live out his 'idyll' with it," the writer of the article admonishes. "If you feel aforesaid sympathy, MIAMI LIFE's advice to you is to avoid Key West. For there you'll be disillusioned, startled, disgusted by the real truth."[99] The "real truth," according to the newspaper, was that the mummified corpse-doll was a sex toy. "The old German had devoted most of his artistic attention to the breasts and re-created female organs," it states. "He had built up these parts of the 'body' to look as natural as possible. He had used a composition of gauze and wax and what-not; portions of this he had painted a rose-pink to make them more life-like!"

This sensationalized version of the story, which actually had basis in scientific evidence, never replaced the more romantic narrative. The curious and sympathetic flocked to the island. Von Cosel congratulated himself for boosting tourism. "Elena's body [laid out at the funeral home] . . . was the biggest sight-seeing attraction that Key West had ever known. No less than 6,850 people viewed the body," Von Cosel boasted in his retelling of the story in the pulp magazine *Fantastic Adventures*.[100] In fact, upon being released on bond, Von Cosel made a mini-industry of his newfound fame. He sold discarded objects as macabre souvenirs—bits of the bridal dress he had bought for Elena, photographs of her corpse, nails and screws from his "laboratory," and plaster of Paris deathmasks of her face. "For months on end this public interest set new records for traffic on the highways and on the toll-bridges leading to Key West," he wrote. "People began to tell me that I had 'put Key West on the map.'"[101]

Von Cosel's embrace of his role in publicizing Key West begins to makes sense only when one recalls the FERA rhetoric that constructed tourism as an antidote to Key West's own death. Key Westers had little interest in maintaining the less romanticized version of the Von Cosel narrative—certainly not one that might make Key West a place to avoid. Moreover, the sympathetic version of the Von Cosel narrative allows for the possibility of reanimation. Von Cosel professed that Hoyos had risen from the dead in July 1936; he claimed she spoke to him and sang songs. She even requested a new wedding gown. If a corpse consumed by consumption could rise from the dead—if only in the imagination—then couldn't the island itself?

In view of the discourse of death and reanimation that surrounded the FERA reconstruction, it becomes easier to understand why residents of Key West (and other Americans) became so intrigued with Von Cosel. In him they recognized a "good old doctor" who, if slightly bizarre in his attachment to the dead, truly seemed to believe that the dead might be raised back to life. In creating the "biggest sight-seeing attraction" in Key West, Von Cosel transformed Hoyos's mummified corpse into a commodity, and a literalization of the phantasmic quality of all commodity fetishes. In disinterring the corpse, Von Cosel exposed the secrets of the crypt while simultaneously reencrypting the woman. He preserved what he imagined her to be—transforming her corpse into its own copy, making it simultaneously the copy and the original, transforming himself into the creator of both. He wrote,

> I decided to make a plaster cast of her, so as to have a permanent and nonperishable record. In order to make certain and to be sure that one, at least, would turn out perfect, I made several casts. I discovered that the fine oiled silk which I had used to cover and protect her face, eyes, and hair, had fastened itself tightly to her skin. I left it so and painted over it with a thin solution of bees' wax and balsam. Being transparent, her eyebrows showed through delightfully. I did not dare to pull it off her beautiful face, as the plaster of Paris, when setting, had pressed it so tightly against the surface of the skin. She looked as beautiful as ever and

it looked like her own skin. It also proved an effective protection against ever-present insect pests and microbes.[102]

Von Cosel employs the language of salvage, as Stone's FERA machine did, to use that which has been discarded and buried, a corpse. But Von Cosel's attempts to sanitize the decay process, to artificially embellish the corpse, become a perverse literalization of the ideology embedded in the FERA cleanup of Key West.

The mummified corpse of Elena Hoyos reveals the precariousness of Key West's embrace of commodification, of its self-transformation into spectacle. For the corpse materially exposes what such a transformation must forget. The mummified corpse is disturbing not because it looks too lifelike, but because it no longer looks like it had been alive. (Most spectators claimed the corpse looked "like a doll.") A corpse that is removed from its crypt might be disturbing because it reveals the secrets of disease and decay; but the mummified corpse is even more unsettling because it reveals its own constructedness, a use value that is only display value, a sanitization that re-members the body's internal putrefaction, the festering of those "microbe-like structures" that Michel de Certeau suggests allegorize the miniature, quotidian structures of transgression in (and from) everyday life.[103]

Von Cosel's actions become conservative as well as preservative. In attempting to maintain the status quo, Von Cosel uncovers the corpse but does so to preserve and contain it, to obfuscate the potential disruption of visible fragmentation and decay. Visibility is the crucial factor here since it is the signs of putrefaction he seeks to arrest, not death itself. The public embrace of Von Cosel demonstrates how deeply rooted the desire for cohesion was in American culture at that time and shows to what lengths many Americans would go to preserve its imaginative structure. Key West threatened the nation with an analogous problem, the possibility that as microcosm it might become microbe—a transgressive force erupting from within the boundaries of the United States. Yet to indulge in such an analogy makes for an even untidier mess, for it produced the nation as a corpse—and those who sought to preserve the cohesion of the now-dead nation as something quite worse.[104] There was incentive, in other words, to protect Von Cosel's secret. The graphic details

The corpse of Elena Milagro Hoyos at the Dean-Lopez Funeral Home.
Photo courtesy of Wright Langley Archives, Inc.

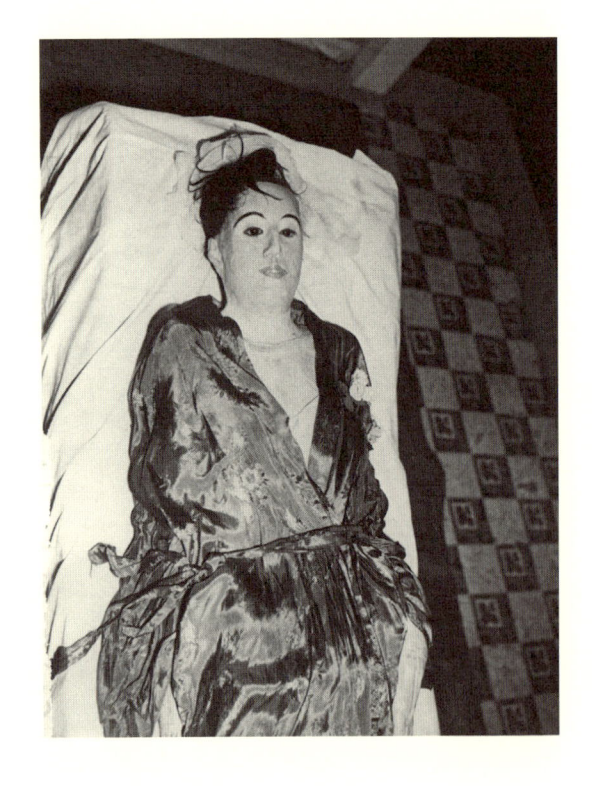

106 KEY WEST

of his necrophilia, which included evidence of sperm in the cotton-stuffed tube that served as the corpse's vagina, were not made public even to the courts by forensics experts until the early 1970s. After the trial, government-sanctioned authorities dismembered Hoyos's mummified corpse, then buried the fragments in a tiny box in an unmarked grave, the location of which was known only to three individuals, all of whom have since died without revealing the site.

Dismembered, encrypted in an unmarked grave, the corpse no longer exists in visible material form. And yet the crypt haunts. Visitors still come to Key West to imaginatively resurrect, not the woman, but Von Cosel's reconstructed, mummified corpse. As for Von Cosel, he did the authorities one better by exploding the crypt whose secrets he had revealed. If the corpse was to be buried, then so was its crypt. On the day Von Cosel left Key West forever, Hoyos's then-empty crypt was exploded with dynamite, shattering it once and for all into dust. And when Von Cosel's own rotting corpse was found weeks after he had died in 1952, next to him lay a waxen replica of the body of Hoyos he had crafted years before, the perfect replica of his replica —not the woman, but the corpse.

"killing the time between corpses . . ."

A typescript from the private papers of the WPA journalist Stetson Kennedy of his 1939 interview with the Key West cigar maker Norberto Diaz:[105]

> Every time I pass in front of the Cuban Club I think of Isleno. The other day, I was down to the beach and seen the palm tree where he was hung. It's funny, but that was the first coconut palm to die from the disease that's killing most all the palm trees on the island. I believe Isleno's *brujo* [ghost] is killing the palm trees, too. People say the whole island's cursed and that's why there is so much bad luck and people do not have enough to eat. . . . Isleno was a Spaniard from the Canary Islands . . . [He] began living with a brown—a mulatto girl. We called her Rosita Negra. They lived in a room right in back of [his] coffee shop. . . . Then one night—it was Christmas Eve [1921]—about twenty of the Ku Klux Klan came marching down from Duval Street, all dressed in white robes with hoods over their faces and carrying guns and torches. . . . [Isleno] put up an awful fight, but they tied him and dragged him to the beach, stripped him, and beat him 'till his kidneys burst. Isleno fought so hard he got free of the ropes and tore the masks off half a dozen of the men. He cursed them all, swore he'd be revenged and that they would all died horrible deaths. They beat him some more until he was unconscious, and then hung him up in a tree. He was left for dead but he came back to his senses and got loose from the rope somehow, and walked all the way back to his coffee shop. . . . He looked just like one of those red

cube streaks that has been diced up to make it tender.... About twelve o'clock Mr. Olstrom, a leader of the Klan and a very prominent man, was walking past the Cuban Club with his arms full of groceries he was taking home for Christmas dinner. When he stopped across the alley, Isleno came out, his pants all bloody in front, with a revolver in his hand. He shot Mr. Olstrom in the belly five times and [Olstrom] fell on the sidewalk begging Isleno not to shoot again.

"But Isleno stood there and put five more bullets in the gun and shot Mr. Olstrom five more times. Then he climbed up in the attic of a vacant house and barricaded himself in. The police and the sheriff and the deputies and the National Guard surrounded the place, but Isleno kept them back with his shooting.... The [military commander who was stationed there] came and promised Isleno protection. When Isleno surrendered, the sheriff promised the military man he would protect Isleno if he would turn him over to his custody. So the sheriff took Isleno upstairs in the jail where he beat him some more. After he was unconscious they grabbed him by the heels and dragged him down those iron steps, his head cracking like an egg on every step. They tied a rope around his neck and pulled his body through the streets behind an automobile and down to the beach. Isleno was already plenty dead, but they hung his body up in a palm tree where it stayed I don't know how long till the buzzards and smell got so bad they had to cut it down.

ABJECT GEOGRAPHIES

Key West finally can be seen to manifest the borderland geography of the abject. With regard to the spatiality of the abject, Julia Kristeva writes,

> The space that engrosses the deject [the one by whom the abject exists], the excluded, is never *one*, nor *homogeneous*, nor *totalizable*, but essentially divisible, foldable, and catastrophic. A devisor of territories, languages, works, the deject never stops demarcating his universe whose fluid confines—for they are constituted of a non-object, the abject—constantly question his solidity and impel him to start afresh.[106]

In Kristeva's terms, the recognition that space is fluid, that boundaries are not solid, causes the dejected to attempt to order space, to seek a fixed place, and thereby encrypt that which he seeks to reject. But the geography of abjection is a geography of drift. If the subject must define itself through its objects, then faced with the abject, the unnamable Other, the subject remains perpetually unmoored. Refusing to accept the slipperiness of the abject forces one to continually "start afresh" so that one can never define oneself as a subject, never stick to one place. In fact, this effort to control the abject—to erase the transition from living body to dust—sets in motion a maelstrom, the unstable cycle of disintegration and renewal, death and reanimation, repetition and repression, that is progressive modernity itself.

Key West drifts. And for this reason, a Key West aesthetic is a fractured aesthetic, one that undermines an absolute divide between subject and object. The literal presence of the abject can never be fully subsumed into the metaphoric forgetting endemic to representation. It is the literality of the abject that 1930s Key West refuses to forget.

And so we return to the hurricane. For the hurricane, even in inducing new destruction, also stirs up a legacy of past wrongs. Allegorizing the maelstrom and train wreck as a double problem of New Deal pacification, Hemingway writes in his impassioned essay "Who Murdered the Vets?"

> And the wind makes a noise like a locomotive passing, with a shriek on top of that, because the wind has a scream exactly as it has in books, and then the fill goes and the high wall of water rolls you over and over and

Hemingway collection photo of a dead relief worker after the 1935 hurricane.
Photo No. EH8180P in the John F. Kennedy Library, Boston.

THE NATION AND THE CORPSE 109

then, whatever it is, you get it and we find you now of no importance, stinking in the mangroves.[107]

Hemingway's hurricane speaks as a train, speaks a sound that mimics its allegorical significance, speaks with such material force that it engulfs those in its wake and leaves them dead, shattered, putrefying. Hemingway locates *To Have and Have Not* precisely after FERA's Key West invasion in July 1934 and before the September 1935 hurricane that kills most of the indigent World War I veterans that populate the text. The veterans are "the very top cream of the scum," whom first Hoover, then Roosevelt have tried to erase. "What's the next move?" one of the veterans asks Richard Gordon. "They've got to get rid of us."[108] This plaintive question seems to beg the obvious response that these vets—the refuse of modern capitalist society, a refuse that could potentially revolt—were "gotten rid of" when they were sent to work in the Florida Keys during hurricane months.[109]

The "Florida Keys in hurricane months" become a war zone, a "site of extreme danger" in which to destroy the wayward and rebellious, the potentially revolutionary factions of working-class men who displease "their superior officers" of the American government. The novel becomes a harsh critique of FERA's efforts to revivify Key West, becomes an attempt to expose the inside of Key West and the secrets it hides. For Hemingway, the train of progress is deceptive, a false train that is the maelstrom in disguise. It not only arrives too late, but in the East Coast Railway's situation becomes the vehicle that facilitates the insurgent veterans' demise.

Hemingway's class-bound view of the hurricane's destruction is limited, however, for it ignores the somewhat more complicated discourse of race and ethnicity in Key West. In "A Norther—Key West," Bishop evokes the colonial legacy of Shakespeare's Caliban to suggest that the threat of "the Tempest" has turned the sea into "lime-milk sherbet," a racialized melting pot in which whiteness becomes all that one sees. Protection from the maelstrom she envisions is not simply too late. It doesn't fit. The "little Negros," Hannibal and Herbert, cannot be protected by the "ancient winter coats" manufactured to clothe "an immense white child." For Bishop, New Deal efforts to protect Key West from the economic wreckage of modernity's maelstrom are built for the white working classes. They omit, even erase, the racialist elements of government aid. (During the December 1935 WPA workers' strikes in the Keys, for example, WPA administrators warned that the "charged atmosphere" might incite "race riots.")[110] As Key Westers prepare for a FERA-instituted carnival, Bishop notes, "While Negro children, who are not allowed,/Look on solemnly from among the crowd."[111] Critics have argued that the carnival embodies a maelstromlike order of chaos and levels social distinctions.[112] Bishop negates such an optimistic reading, suggesting instead that the carnival is segregated from the start.

Yet as an ethnographer might, Bishop romanticized the black Bahamian Key Westers. "I want to take a great many pictures of the wooden houses with their scrollwork verandahs, and the sweet little Negro children too," Bishop wrote to Marianne Moore in 1938. And then again, she continued, making the black Key Westers positively poetic: "The Negros have such soft voices and such beautifully tactful manners—I suppose it is farfetched, but their attitude keeps reminding me of the *tone* of George Herbert: 'Take the gentle path,' etc."[113] Their bodies seem extreme to Bishop; they seem to stretch almost out of control. Her "Negro cook" is "very tall, very black,"[114] the "Negro" who "buds" her rosebush is "old, old . . . with white hair and a large white mustache,"[115] a "Negro—mulatto, rather—carpenter" looks "Miltonic—epic at least—a 'chieftain type,' with an enormous head, . . . long bony features and deep-set eyes." And though the carpenter is the "smartest, most conscientious person" she talks to in Key West, Bishop notes that he absurdly "can't pronounce 'v,' and when I took him a bottle of Coca-Cola he said I was 'wery, wery kind.'"[116]

I mention these examples not to expose Bishop's racism, for she is aware of the dynamics of race in Key West in a way that almost no other Anglo-American writer is. Rather, Bishop's recognition of and complicity in the racialist discourse of Key West actually unmasks a subtext that is sublimated in most representations of Key West and in the folk mythology of the place itself. Many Key Westers attest, even today, especially today, that there is no racism in Key West—that actually there never was. They proudly proclaim that Key West was the only place south of the Mason-Dixon line that sympathized with the Union during the Civil War. This belief in racial harmony remains strong, even among black and Cuban Key Westers, despite the fact that the Ku Klux Klan remained active in the city throughout the 1920s and 1930s, despite the fact that WPA projects reinforced the inscription of racial segregation, despite the fact that African-descended Key Westers always have lived in a spatially segregated section of the city, called in the 1930s Niggertown in addition to Jungletown, though now as I mentioned, Bahama Village. By reasserting racial difference, Bishop constructs an alterior subject that, voyeuristically, she can scrutinize and narrate while revealing the racist crypt of segregation and inequality that Key West culture vehemently denies.

Both Hemingway and Bishop ignore the prominence of the hurricane in Caribbean writing as a symbol of counterrebellion. The speaker in the 1928 poem "Plena de menéalo" (Shaking it), by the *Negrisimo* writer Luis Palés Matos, cries out,

> Dale a la popa, mulata,
> proyecta en la eternidad
> ese tumbo de caderas
> que es ráfaga de huracán, y menéalo,

> de aquí payá, de ayá pacá,
> menéalo, menéalo,
> ¡para que rabie el Tío Sam!
>
> [Shake your butt, mulatta,
> project into eternity
> this beat of your hips
> that's the hurricane's gale, and shake it,
> back and forth, forth and back,
> shake it, shake it,
> to make Uncle Sam rage!]][117]

The poem posits the hurricane's percussive rhythm, "menéalo, menéalo," as a kind of talking drum that can bolster the overthrow of U.S. imperialism. Traces of the drumbeat are found even in Crane's poem "Hurricane," about an earlier storm he experienced on the Isle of Pines, now Cuba. Drawing on Afro-Cuban Santería culture, Crane "attempted to secure the grand rhythm of the hurricane" in his poem.[118] He mixes the pounding of the drumbeat of Yoruban Africa with the words of a Christian prayer: "Nor, Lord, may worm out-creep/Thy drum's gambade, its plunge abscond!"[119]

part 4. a re-vision

A page in Bishop's Key West Notebook II at Vassar College Library in Poughkeepsie, New York reads as follows:

Typescript and notes. Elizabeth Bishop Papers, Special Collections, Vassar College Libraries, Poughkeepsie, New York. Excerpts from unpublished writings of Elizabeth Bishop reprinted by permission of Farrar, Straus and Giroux, LLC, on behalf of the estate of Elizabeth Bishop. Copyright © 1999 by Alice Helen Methfessel.

> Off & on I have written at a poem called 'Grandmother's Glass Eye' which should be about the problem of writing poetry. The situation of my grandmother strikes me as rather like the situation of a poet: the difficulty of combining the real with the decidedly un-real; the natural with the unnatural; the curious effect a poem produces of being as normal as *sight* and yet as synthetic, as artifival [sic], as a *glass* eye.[120]

RE-MEMBERING KEY WEST

Seven months after the hurricane washed out the Florida East Coast Railroad to Key West, the federal Public Works Administration (PWA) loaned the Florida Overseas Road and Toll Bridge Commission $3,600,000. The commission paid $640,000 in salvage fees to the railroad receivers and converted the ruined viaducts and railway grades into an automobile highway.[121] The road ran over the washed-out tracks and filled in the gaps in the passageway between Key West and the mainland with a seven-mile bridge between Matecombe and No Name Key. For the first time, Key West was materially

4.

Never until the mankind making
Bird beast and flower
Fathering and all humbling darkness
Tells with silence the last light breaking
And the still hour
Is come of the sea tumbling in harness..."

Baudelaire: "Les soirs illumines par l'ardeur du charbon..."
where charbon is the telling word - surprising, accurate, dating the poem, yet making it real, yet making it mysterious -

Spontaneity - Marianne's marriage, N. Y. -
Herbert's EASTER

"RISE, heart; the Lord is risen."

Hopkins "Glory to be God for dappled things" -

* * * * *

My maternal grandmother had a glass eye. It fascinated me as a child, and the idea of it has fascinated me all my life. She was religious, in the Puritanical protestant sense and didn't believe in looking into mirrors very much. Quite often the glass eye looked heavenward, or off at an angle, while the real eye looked at you.

"Him whose happie birth
Taught me to live here so, that still one eye
Should aim and shoot at that which is on high."

~~I have always wanted to~~ [off & on I have wanted to] write a poem called "Grandmother's Glass Eye" which should be about the problem of writing poetry. The situation of my grandmother strikes me as rather like the situation of the poet: the difficulty of combining the real with the decidedly un-real; the natural with the unnatural; the curious effect a poem produces of being as ~~[illegible]~~ [normal] as sight and yet as synthetic, as artificial, as a glass eye.

(call the piece "Grandmother's Glass eye"???)

spontaneity occurs in a good attack [tight], a rapid line, rhythm -

Brazilian Poetry: I am reading B. P. I began naturally with the big poets & I started to work backward [to B. & Portuguese poetry]. I've found many good things, but I feel that I don't know the language well enough, or the body of poetry, to say anything about it at present would be an impertinence.

Quote letters + MVDM — last part -

attached to the nation, part of a spatially significant highway, U.S. Route 1, that ran 2,187 miles along the eastern seaboard through New York, Philadelphia, and Washington, D.C., from the northern tip of Maine to Key West.

In the wake of the 1935 hurricane, Key West had come to represent less a microcosm of the United States than its detached appendage. Key West has "such a beautiful cartographic presence the way it flies off the state like the arm of a spiral nebula," wrote Bishop in a 1939 letter to Moore. With the construction of the highway, opened in 1938, the FERA project quite literally re-membered the so-called forgotten city, materially reattaching the island to the continent. And the Seven Mile Bridge, which closed the gap, served as a prosthetic, a built link between two materially and discursively disparate bodies. The architect Mark Wigley writes,

> In a strange way, the body depends upon the foreign elements that transform it. It is reconstituted and propped up on the "supporting limbs" that extend it. Indeed it becomes a side effect of its extensions. The prosthesis reconstructs the body, transforming its limits, at once extending and convoluting its borders. The body itself becomes artifice.[122]

Key West became the graft, that which was added to "prop up" an American nation debilitated from Depression. At the same time, as Wigley suggests, Key West, as "foreign," created the nation to which it was attached. The body that needs a prosthetic recognizes its deficiency, recognizes that it is somehow not complete. Yet the Key West model is more complex than a prosthetic attachment of the natural with the mechanic, the graft of the foreign onto the self. In this figuration, the Overseas Highway, not Key West, becomes the prosthetic extension of the American nation. Key West is simply a reattached part of the national self.

A bridge is a confusing prosthetic, for it adjoins two separate bodies, making each borderless, making each the foreign element, each the Other's other (depending upon where one aligns). At the same time, it erases the distinction between self and Other. Both become part of a whole. Unlike salvaging, which necessitates recognizing the Other's otherness, even as it is brought into the self, the prosthetic fantasy underlying the FERA bridge is to reach out to the Other, incorporate it, and forget that the Other was ever not part of the self.

If FERA hoped to perpetuate a national narrative of cohesion through annexation, many Key West writers re-membered dismemberment and death in its grotesque materiality. In doing so, they reveal what is at stake in rejecting the dominance of the American continental nation over Key West, what is at stake in resisting the construction of the Overseas Highway Bridge. In his essay "Homage to Key West," Tennessee Williams remembers a curious dinner he had in 1941 with the owner of a Key West boardinghouse, Mrs. Black, and her daughter and son-in-law, Marion and Regis Vacarro. Williams writes,

> Regis Vaccaro had a glass eye, and one night at dinner, for no apparent reason, he scratched it out of its socket and hurled it at Mrs. Black. It landed in her soup plate. Being a true lady, she made no exhibition of dismay at this rather Bohemian gesture. She simply fished the glass eye out of her soup and gave it to [her daughter] Marion in a soup spoon with the casual remark, "I think that Regis lost something."[123]

Underscoring the significance of his anecdote by aligning his text with the subject of his narrative, Williams mimics Regis's symbolic amputation. He closes his homage with a raw-edged fragment: "Now please don't hurry down here: The island has finally run out of coral-rock extensions into the sea. Almost no one plays bridge and there is almost nothing at all to do but drink or swim or—."[124] In amputating his text, Williams makes explicit a connection between the event, his text, and the place, Key West, he describes. Moreover, he does so by drawing attention to the limits of representation and to the inadequacy of metonymy, in which the part can never stand in adequately for the whole. Whatever he writes can only simulate reality and, therefore, always occludes as much as it exposes. And when the simulation's artifice is disclosed—so too is its commercial nature. The glass eye lands in a soup plate to be consumed along with the noodles and stock.

At first, Williams seems to posit Regis as a renegade Vincent van Gogh, who not only cut off his own ear but, legend has it, sent the bloody appendage to his lover. It was that final action that Georges Bataille argues was van Gogh's actual transgression, expelling him from the narrative circle that collapses grotesque mutilation into the sacred sphere of self-sacrifice.[125] The rage allegorized by what Bataille calls that "monstrous ear in an envelope" transforms van Gogh from victim into villain and, rather than van Gogh's mutilated body, refigures the bloody appendage into an agent, the proprietor of loss.[126] Yet the incident Williams recounts is uncanny not because Regis gouges out his eye, but because in doing so he reveals that eye's artifice. The glass eye is an odd prosthetic. Unlike van Gogh's ear, or even an artificial leg or arm, a glass eye is not utilitarian. It functions simply as a complex illusion, a copy of the natural organ whose sole function is to appear to make whole.

Regis's action does not, like van Gogh's, signify the outrage of the grotesque part expelled from the body. It cannot for the eye is already gone. Instead, it discloses how the memory of violent dismemberment has been erased. In plucking out his artificial eye to violently reenact the material trauma of the natural organ, Regis refuses the artifice of representation, refuses to let the prosthetic stand in for the scar. He exposes the falsity of the prettified copy that produces the deception of wholeness and masks his original, irrecuperable loss.

The episode Williams describes is, therefore, both a narrative of loss and a fantasy of impossible return, a throwing away of the substitute object as a way of warding off the trauma of partial blindness. The episode allegorizes, therefore, the seeing-unseeing that constitutes trauma, in which one bears witness to an event that cannot be fully known as it occurs, but that reveals itself in the prosthetic return of recurrent dreams.[127] Within this context, the performance of Regis Vacarro's self-reenucleation becomes both transgressive and exceedingly pathetic. For Vacarro reenacts what Bataille calls "cannibal delicacy," the extreme seductiveness at the boundary of horror (or one might say, "the Horror") of the enucleated eye, which the white man (read: imperialist; read: the U.S. government; read: the white middle-class writers who narrate Key West) desires to bite into but never will, and from whom "the eyes of the cows, sheep, and pigs that he eats have always been hidden."[128] The disembodied eye cries out in its absence, "See that which you will not see, this eye you deny having already eaten." At base this is a problem of eating—or potential miseating—the incorporation or bringing into the body and in doing so revealing the object's Otherness, its artifice and externality.

Arthur Kroker and David Cook argue that the disembodied eye is "nothing less than a pure sign-system," a metaphor "of carceral power abstracted from corporeal existence" and a "perfect phantasmagoria, nothing in itself, a scandal of absence, it exists as an inscription of pure, symbolic exchange."[129] Yet this homage becomes, rather, a scandal of presence, and the anecdote Williams relays may be seen, finally, as a reenactment of the *terror* of territory, of acquisition and exchange, of what W. J. T. Mitchell calls the "enforcing of boundaries with violence and fear" that is "poetic geography."[130] Key West comes to signify not a "secular landscape" in Mitchell's terms, but a *specular* landscape; and Regis's dramatic toss into the soup bowl declares a mis-sighting of *site*. It becomes, then, a flagrant disincorporation, a refusal of the visual as a way of knowing and re-membering, and, more profoundly, a refusal to produce place out of *site*.

FERA hoped that the material and imaginative act of re-membering the forgotten city could become the normal order of things, an order that obsessively forgot that Key West was ever detached. As a whole, Key West might become part of the whole, a glass eye that melded into the constructed homogeneity of New Deal Americanism, occluding the blind socket it hid. Fusing the gaps it closed. "Aquí en Key West encontramos la fusión amistosa de estas dos culturas" [Here in Key West we find the amicable melding of two cultures], wrote Harold Ballou in the August 1939 issue of *Cayo Hueso*, the Key West Spanish language newspaper.[131] But the linguistic dissonance of translation belies the fusion of which it speaks. It reveals the cracks in the graft. For it speaks of an unequal fusion in which English—in which the continental United States—dominates the fragmentary Afro-Latino Caribbean.

It is significant, therefore, that in *To Have and Have Not*, Key West government officials search for ejected prosthetics, the artificial substitutes, not for lost bodies or body parts themselves. Mrs. Tracy cries out for her lost husband, Albert, but her voice is cut off as she falls in the "green water, the scream becoming a splash and a bubble."[132] She returns to the surface having lost her "plate," her false teeth, which, unlike the corpse of her husband, the Real Thing, the Coast Guard assures her they'll find. "We'll dive it up in the morning," the skipper of the Coast Guard cutter told her. "We'll get it all right."[133] Her body, silenced, will be remade to look whole.

But in an excised passage from the typescript of *To Have and Have Not*, Hemingway explains what happens to lost limbs, and in doing so, the politics that motivate his text.

> [A gap. (It is unfortunate.) "The Hemingway family is not currently granting permission to publish 'unpublished works or derivative material' and explicitly asks that neither the family nor their literary rights manager, Michael Katakis, be contacted directly about permissions. If there is a legitimate question about permission, Simon & Schuster will refer the enquiry to Mr. Katakis." So. Imagine a passage if you will. It's very good. Hemingway likens the increasing repression and graft in Cuba to the quantity of noise. A body thrown in the Gulf or tossed in a vacant lot serves as a warning. It makes noise. But when tyranny is complete, missing bodies are buried and destroyed quickly in lime. Buttons——or, say, a dismembered arm——no longer turn up in the bowels of a shark to be caught by fishermen. Corpses no longer rot in vacant lots to be picked at by buzzards. When tyranny is complete, there is no evidence. There is no noise.][134]

In this passage (the one that I, unfortunately, have excised here as well), the dismembered arm, found in the remains of the disemboweled shark becomes a sign of rebellion, a sign of a revolution not wholly squelched, a sign of an encrypted voice rising from its grave. Hemingway collapses the language of tyranny, of capital, into the language of the body. The amputated body part becomes a sign of secrecy, of corruption, of graft (his term), *and* its visibility. A graft is something—living tissue, capital or ill-gotten gains according to the *Oxford English Dictionary* that is "acquired through private or secret practices or corrupt agreement"—that is, "inserted in or incorporated with another thing to which it did not originally belong." But a graft is also a signifier for the heterogeneity of textuality itself. Jonathan Culler points out, "If, in Derrida's aphorism, 'toute thèse est une prothèse'—every thesis is an attached prosthesis—one must identify grafts and analyze what they produce."[135] For Hemingway, what the graft—the arm—produces is not visibility, but noise, that is, sound that is banished from the realm of language, music, intention.[136]

The ungrafted, exposed, dismembered arm in Hemingway's texts thus speaks the complex language of materiality. A "crying wound," it makes noise in its silence, reveals the threat of difference in a repressive, homogeneous society, the threat of being anything other than artifice, than a prosthetic illusion.[137] It also exposes Hemingway's own encryptment of the politics of his text. The above passage—this clue that re-members Hemingway's politics—has itself been cut out, silenced, erased. It is an excised passage in a text that has been itself mostly excised from the Hemingway canon. This excerpt then suggests Hemingway's own complicity in the complete tyranny that the novel anticipates. (A task taken up, perhaps inadvertently, by his heirs.) In a text that Hemingway hopes will make noise, he silences himself. The severed limb has been erased from the text.

Yet it is the narration of loss—not lost objects themselves—that is ultimately the novel's concern. Hemingway's absent text is figuratively reproduced in a conversation about the arm that the rumrunner Harry Morgan loses in traversing the waters between a tyrannical Cuba and FERA-run Key West. In the opening of part 3 of the novel, Bee-lips asks Harry how he lost his arm:

> "I didn't like the look of it so I cut it off," Harry told him.
> "You and who else cut it off?"
> "Me and a doctor cut it off, Harry said. He had been drinking a little and he was getting along with it. "I held still and he cut it off."[138]

Harry loses his arm after being spotted by the FERA hack Frederick Harrison, who is "one of the biggest men in the administration," a man who calls himself a doctor, "but not of medicine."[139] It is not enough, in other words, to suggest that FERA officials or even the Cubans who shot Harry are responsible for the loss of his arm. Harry is complicit in his own amputation. He held still as the doctor (Dr. FERA?) cut it off.

Bishop makes clear why this matters. In her Key West notebooks, she recalls a car accident of 1937 in which her friend Margaret Miller's arm was amputated at the elbow. She writes,

> The arm lay outstretched in the soft blown grass at the side of the road and spoke quietly to itself. At first all it could think of was the possibility of being quickly reunited to its body, without anymore time elapsing than was absolutely necessary.
> "Oh my poor body! Oh my poor body! I cann't [sic] bear to give you up. I wish! I wish!"
> Then it fell silent while a series of ideas that had never occurred to it before swept [rapidly] over it.[140]

Along the margin in minuscule writing Bishop scribbled, "So this is what it means to be really 'alone in the world!'" Barbara Page argues that this passage signifies the development of Bishop's poetics of "discontinuities, cultural incongruities and dilapidated things."[141] More significant, she reads the mood of the passage as being shaped by Bishop's own socially marginal experience

Detail from Waldo Peirce's Key West scrapbook. Arm found in the belly of a shark on a fishing trip with Ernest Hemingway near Dry Tortugas, 1930s. Courtesy of Special Collections, Miller Library, Colby College, Waterville, Maine.

as an orphan and lesbian: "And the comment from the margin of her own text, a graphic whisper, gives evidence of a heartbreaking effort to come to terms with a sense of immeasurable loss."[142] Page doesn't recognize, however, that it is precisely that loss, the arm's disassociation from the body's authority, that enables it to speak—and, more important, to think that "series of ideas that had never occurred to it." As both Bishop and Hemingway suggest, only detached in its grotesque materiality can the limb signify the potential for violent transgression, for heterogeneity, for revolt. Only detached can the severed arm find its voice. Re-membered, materially attached, the limb loses its power to speak.

J. Hillis Miller points out that Stevens's famous poem "The Idea of Order

The Seven Mile Bridge and the remains of the Overseas Highway, Key West.
© 2005 Christy Transier Jonas Photography.

at Key West" also employs a metaphoric amputation. "The sea," Miller writes, " . . . is like a multiple amputee fluttering the empty sleeves of a shirt with no arms to put in them."[143] However, in positing the sea as an amputee in search of the prosthetic voice of the poet, Stevens (again) is trying to have it both ways. He thus performs the slippery gesture of rejecting identity with Key West, yet refusing to wholly align himself with the New Deal–constructed U.S. nation. What happens to amputated body parts is less important to Stevens than the "constant cry" of the amputated body. In positing the sea, not the continent, as amputee, Stevens posits the Caribbean as a site of loss. At the same time, he positions it as Other, for its "cry" "was not ours although we understood."

Though sympathetic, even Hemingway and Bishop are pessimistic about their ability to speak for the forgotten Key West. In *To Have and Have Not*, Mrs. Tracy fails to speak for her husband's missing corpse.[144] And upon Harry's death, his widow, Marie, goes "dead inside." The last paragraphs of the novel narrate the inevitable burial of Key West's working classes, the Conchs, by rich "winter people," FERA, and military ships. The narrative moves outside to the external, material world of the upper classes who would make up Hemingway's readers and to the burgeoning tourist colony, where it was "a lovely, cool, sub-tropical winter day and the palm branches were sawing in the light north wind" and "winter people were laughing" and "on the horizon you could see a tanker . . . hugging the reef."[145]

Implicit in Bishop's and Hemingway's texts is the knowledge that while a body can survive dismembered, a dismembered limb disintegrates on its own. Harry Morgan's last words become a hopeless recognition of this fact: "No matter how a man alone ain't got no bloody fucking chance."[146] A man cannot survive all alone. But not on his own, he's erased. Key West allowed itself to be grafted onto the continental nation. By the time Williams wrote, in 1941, the illusion of wholeness was already set in place. But like Regis's glass eye, Key West re-membered its scar. It kept forever the suggestion that one day it might again break apart. In fact, Key West, as the Conch Republic, did secede from the nation for one day on April 23, 1982. It is a day that is celebrated each year.[147]

on loss

Day after day at Key West's Monroe County Library, I stand at the Xerox machine near the front door photocopying photographs, maps, and WPA pamphlets to be tallied and paid for by check in the evening. Regulars pass through the doors, drawn by the air conditioning and comfortable chairs. Everyday, no matter when I arrive, there is a white-bearded man perched in the reading lounge, scanning daily newspapers and back issues of *Time*. He wears a tank top, a sea captain's hat, and smells vaguely, I imagine, of sea salt and sweat. It is days before I realize that his arm has been cut off at the elbow.

One afternoon, a tiny dark-haired girl named Julie hands me a drawing and asks me to photocopy it for her. I do. She gives me another, asks me what I'm doing, and for an hour stands beside me, chatting, sorting my papers, telling me that she begins kindergarten next week. "They don't have beds there for naps," Julie discloses nervously. And when her father finds us much later, he apologizes on her behalf: "She likes women, always talks to them, at the grocery store, everywhere." I look at him curiously. "She doesn't have a mother," he explains. "I mean she does, but her mother is an addict, couldn't take care of her. So I'm her guardian now." And Julie, watching us talk, grabs him by the hand. "I thought you told me that we had to leave," she insists.

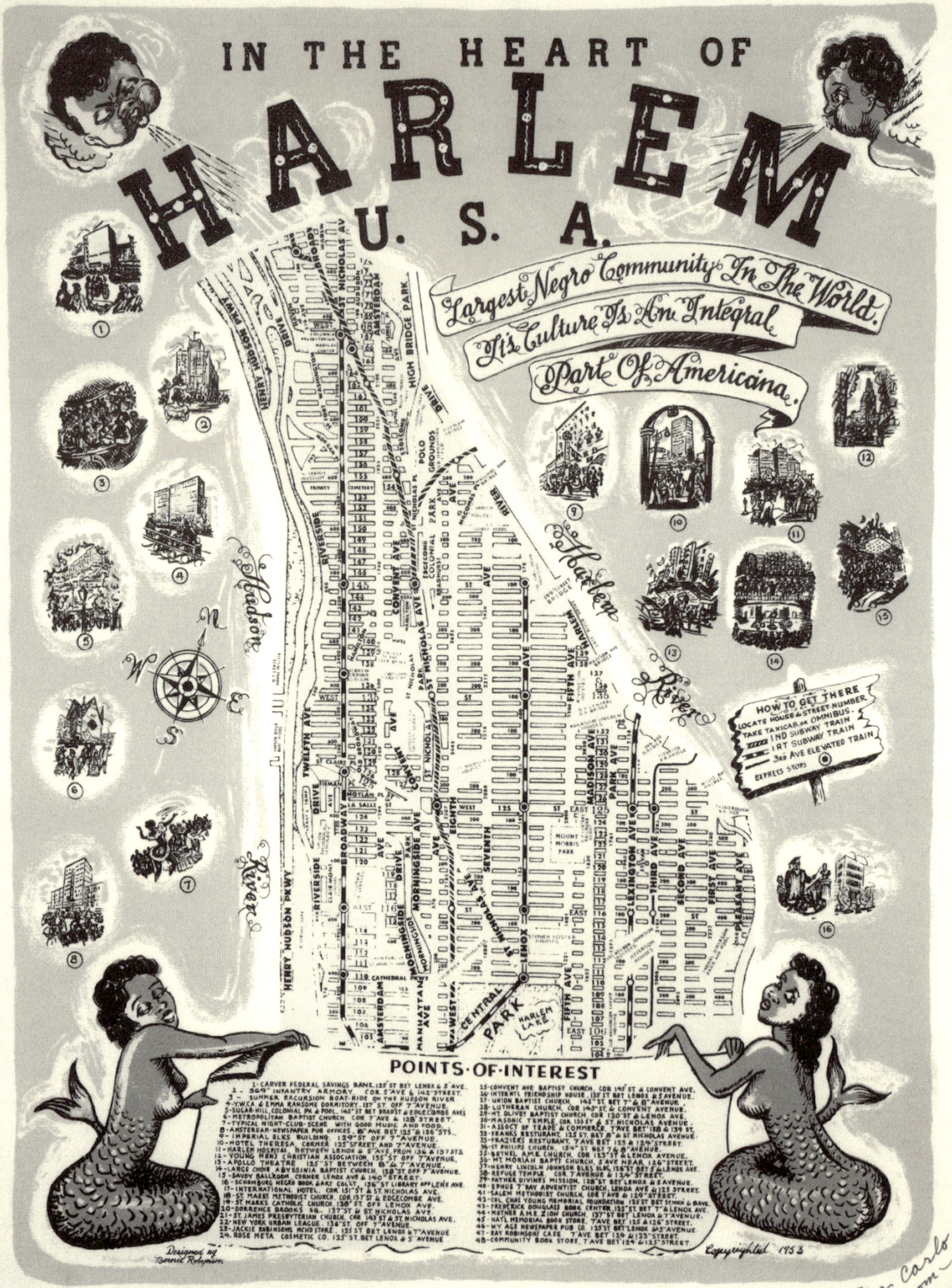

For Carlo from

3

Harlem

BLUE-PENCILED PLACE

FIRST SERIES. "HARLEM, LIKE A PICASSO PAINTING IN HIS CUBISTIC PERIOD"

Actually, the thirty small "Harlem" panels the young Jacob Lawrence painted between 1942 and 1943 are quite similar to the series paintings that had brought him public acclaim—and representation by the aptly named Downtown Art Gallery—in the late 1930s.[1] Like his historical and biographical series on the lives of Touissant L'Overture (1937), Frederick Douglass (1938), Harriet Tubman (1939), and John Brown (1941) and, most famously, like the sixty panels that narrated *The Migration of the Negro* (1940–41), the Harlem paintings were originally exhibited together. Like the earlier series, they were numbered; and they contained written captions.[2] And as he did in the series paintings, Lawrence painted his Harlem panels on brown paper or gessoed poster board using gouache or tempera in primary and secondary colors. Even now, the paintings are most often referred to as the "Harlem series." But in a 1979 letter, Lawrence makes a clear distinction when describing his early work: The Harlem paintings, he writes, "were not a series, but a theme."[3]

The distinction is a crucial one. If in the earlier paintings Lawrence was inspired by the new and growing collection of books on African American history and biography that he found in the stacks of the New York Public Library on 135th Street, or by his conversations with Charles Seifert, a book collector and self-taught intellectual who lectured on the subject at the library and at the Harlem YMCA, Lawrence's Harlem paintings found their formal inspiration in jazz.[4] Lawrence used color to paint sound. He wasn't alone in

← Signed 1953 map of Harlem.
By permission of Harold Ober Associates Incorporated. Langston Hughes Papers. Courtesy of Yale Collection of American Literature, the Beinecke Rare Book and Manuscript Library, Yale University.

Exhibition Catalogue from Jacob Lawrence's "Harlem" exhibit at Edith Halpert's Downtown Gallery, May 11 to 29, 1943.
Courtesy of Downtown Gallery Records, 1824–1974. Archives of American Art, Smithsonian Institution.

this venture, but unlike Stuart Davis, Romare Bearden, and Aaron Douglas, who also were inspired by jazz and the blues, Lawrence stretched sound compositionally across a number of interconnected paintings rather than composing his so-called "visual blues" within a single frame. His art is not metaphorical as much as mimetic; his paintings are not so much like music—as they aspire to be music.[5]

In jazz—and in any modern music—a series always implies relation and succession. Compositional elements are governed—"connected or joined"—by their relation to a common rule or law.[6] (The intellectual and formalist serial music of Arnold Schoenberg in the 1920s, for instance, was composed through permutations of the twelve-note scale.) Rule-bound and rule creating, the series has a deep affinity for language and, at times, for the properties of traditional historical narrative. A series progresses. In this sense, a series format is more conducive to the historicizing and narrative project of Lawrence's earlier works. The Migration paintings, for instance, were divided up when they were sold—but divided in such a way as to preserve a sense of narrative linearity:[7] The Museum of Modern Art in New York bought the even-numbered paintings. The Phillips Collection in Washington, D.C., bought the odd.

The Harlem paintings were different. While a viewer might read the painting captions of the Harlem group in a narrative progression as is appropriate for the series paintings, the relationships between the Harlem panels and the captions that narrate them are better seen as polyphonic and multidirectional. Lawrence's Harlem, produced in the year preceding Harlem's second riot in a decade, depicts a landscape seared by rent strikes, poverty, tenements, filth, alcohol, work, religion, disease, markets, pool halls, and class conflict that is as well, and not at all contradictorily, a place of reading, dance, and play. A painting announces, "This is Harlem," and the succeeding images serve as responses, coming from everywhere at once: "Most of the People Are Very Poor Rent Is High Food Is High," ... "They Live in Old and Dirty Tenement Houses," ... "They Live in Fire Traps," ... "Often Three Families Share One Toilet," ... "This is a Family that Lives in Harlem," ... and so on.

At its most rudimentary, a jazz theme is produced when a harmonized melody (for example, "my lovely valentine") or a series of harmonies ("This is Harlem") is followed by a succession of improvised variations based on, but distinct from, that first melody or series. In traditional jazz form the melody is repeated at the end of the piece. A theme, therefore, both contains the series and is its opposite; it is constituted not by serial regularity, but by irregularity and serendipity. Like the series, a theme implies both relation and succession, but its hallmarks are repetition, remaking, and return.

A jazz theme, in other words, is beholden to the image and to chance. Theme is derived from the Greek θέμα for "to put, set," to "place, lay down." To read Harlem as theme, therefore, is to place it—to make it place. In plac-

John Brown's long meditated plan ..... to fortify himself somewhere in the mountains of Virginia or Tennessee, and from that fastness, with his band of soldiers, sally out and emancipate slaves, seize hostages and levy contributions on the slaveholders.

" From F.B. Sanborn's *The Life and Letters of John Brown*"

ing Harlem as theme, Lawrence makes several assumptions: First, that place comes into being through a process of naming: This is Harlem (i.e., melody). Second, place is polyvocal and improvisational in form and emphasizes becoming rather than being (it requires improvisations on a named melody or harmonic series). And third, place making implies remembrance (the improvisations name the melody retrospectively as an originary moment). (But "the 'originary' is a move—like the clutch disengaging to get a stickshift car moving," Gayatri Chakravorty Spivak reminds us. "The originary is precisely not an origin.")[8] The relations between different components of a theme are always at least twofold; they refer not just to the improvisations that succeed or precede it, but always simultaneously to a common image, "This is Harlem," an image that is produced in and through its remaking, that is placed in being dis-placed, but that never disappears.

In the Harlem paintings, Lawrence positions the viewer looking down from above—"the rooftops seem to spread for miles"—pressed up against facades, and close-up in interior spaces, so that one seems to take in all views of Harlem at once. Harlem becomes the centerpiece of a contrapuntal arrangement in which individual scenes must be read not linearly or associatively, but dissociatively as relations that can continually be disordered and unmade. The ordering of the panels matters less, in other words, than the fact that each must be read in relation to the ones it follows and precedes and to the first panel, which declares its primacy, "This is Harlem," even while in doing so it destabilizes its own textual boundaries. The panels succeed as individual works, some are quite famous; and they were rarely (if ever) exhibited together after that first time. Unlike the Migration paintings, they were widely dispersed into private collections when sold.[9]

When you see one of the Harlem paintings now, so small and fragile on a big museum wall, it seems haunted by absence. *This is Harlem*, in particular, emphasizes the arbitrariness of its own spatial and narrative limits—objects and shapes are cut off in the middle. Lawrence implies that any suggestion that *This is Harlem* is necessarily incomplete. It is all Harlem, the painting suggests. It is not Harlem. Harlem, as theme, stretches beyond any strictly temporally, spatially, or even narratively bound notion of place. Situated within a historical moment yet reaching across time, Lawrence represents Harlem as simultaneously continuous and discontinuous; the paintings constitute the perpetual present and flux, the is, will be, and has been, that are constitutive of place making.

And Lawrence's Harlem is shadowed by death. Bodies splay across roofs and on streets. Crosses, found most famously in Lawrence's 1942 painting *Tombstones* show up over and over again like grave markers teetering atop churches, spliced through buildings, and pressed across the torsos of the figures he paints.[10] True, all places are deathscapes of a sort.[11] But death, in Lawrence's lively, colorful, crowded paintings, seems to ooze out of Harlem's

Research notes by Jacob Lawrence for his 1941 The Life of John Brown series.
Courtesy of Downtown Gallery Records, 1824–1974. Archives of American Art, Smithsonian Institution.

Downtown Gallery exhibition of Jacob Lawrence's The Migration series, New York, 1941.
Harmon Foundation. Courtesy of National Archives. Photo no. 200-HNE-9-8. Reproduction by As Man.

DANCE
BEAUTY-SHOPPE
LUNCH-ST
FUNERAL
HOME
BAR

HUNDREDS ARE RECEIVING
FREE
INSTRUCTION
DRAWING·PAINTING·WEAVING
LITHOGRAPHY·SCULPTURE·ETCHING
METAL CRAFT·PHOTOGRAPHY
COSTUME ILLUSTRATION
HARLEM COMMUNITY
ART CENTER
290 LENOX AVE·NEW YORK NY
FEDERAL ART PROJECT
WORKS PROGRESS ADMINISTRATION
235 EAST 42 STREET·NEW YORK NY

pores and constitute its frame. (The lower left corner of *This is Harlem*, for instance, is dominated by the words "Funeral Home" above the picture of a coffin, an image that provides a counterpoint to the "Bar," "Beauty Shoppe," and "Dance" hall that also frame the piece.) The paintings are exuberant, in the way that earlier Harlem works by, say, Archibald Motley are; but they also grieve.

Lawrence had learned to paint as a young man at the WPA-funded Harlem Community Arts Center, run by the former New Negro poet Gwendolyn Bennett; his talent was fostered in the late 1930s by those who were— by then—Harlem's old hats, the sculptor Augusta Savage and the muralist Charles Alston. And even though the 306 Group of artists who hung out at Alston's studio on 141st Street hit their stride in the midst of the Great Depression, and even though some of Harlem's greatest art was still to come, it is also clear that by the time Lawrence painted, Harlem—and its Renaissance—had already died.

take the A train

New York is home. But, in 1994 when I begin research, I know little of Harlem. I do not know, for instance, that Lenox Avenue has been renamed Malcolm X Boulevard. Neither, it seems, do some Harlem residents. "Where?" a woman asks me on the uptown bus when I give her my stop. "Oh, you mean Lenox . . . I've lived here all my life and never knew that's what it's called." The street sign, it turns out, is ambivalent too: "Malcolm X Boulevard (Lenox Avenue)." What history, it seems to ask, should you remember? The 1960s Civil Rights movement? The 1920s Renaissance? Black Power? The New Negro? Uplift? Activism? Politics? Art?

What past can it be possible to know? "Don't believe the propaganda," declares a 1939 brochure for visitors to Harlem by the Pathfinder Bureau (Price 10 cents):

> You are as safe in Harlem as in any place in New York if you behave yourself.
> You can get any information from any business, church or institution mentioned in this booklet. Any of these agencies can furnish rooms or guides that can be depended upon. If you fail to get what you want from these sources get in touch with us.
> YOU ARE SAFE IN HARLEM!
> This Bureau will furnish you a guide or information on application.
> Speakers furnished for all occasions if due notice is given.

Today, outsiders can visit Harlem without leaving the house. The number of Websites devoted to the place is plentiful and growing. And now that

This is Harlem by Jacob Lawrence
© 2006 The Estate of Gwendolyn Knight Lawrence/ Artists Rights Society (ARS), New York. Hirshhorn Museum and Sculpture Garden, Smithsonian Institution, Gift of Joseph H. Hirshhorn, 1966. Photograph by Lee Stalsworth.

"Hundreds are receiving free instruction: Drawing, painting, weaving, lithography, sculpture, etching, metal craft, photography, costume illustration [at] Harlem Community Art Center." Poster by Jerome Henry Rothstein for the New York City WPA Federal Art Project, February 9, 1938.
Library of Congress, Prints and Photographs Division, WPA Poster Collection, LC-USZC2-5383 DLC.

Lenox Lounge,
Malcolm X Boulevard,
Harlem, New York
City, N.Y., February
2005.
© Frank Jermann,
Germany / rAtgallery.com.

gay couples and buppies are renovating brownstones and former President Bill Clinton resides alongside Starbucks and Old Navy, local tourism has picked up again. The Website for New York Visions, Inc, which specializes in "diversity" tours, promises in English, Français, Español, Italiano, and Deutsch, "one stop shopping for your New York vacation." I click on The Landmark Tour ($100): "Bring your walking shoes and camera for this fun filled and informative morning in Harlem," the Website entices. "Take the A train to the Mecca of Black culture. Walk along wide tree lined boulevards and charming neighborhoods while learning about its people and history. Visit the prestigious Schomburg Center for Research in Black Culture and learn about the achievements of African Americans who made their mark on history. Enjoy shopping for souvenirs in Harlem's local boutiques. This walking tour of Harlem is sure to enchant you."

There is no denying my own voyeurism here, on people-packed sidewalks framed by brownstone and brick, in diners, on-line, and, yes, in archives as well. It is something I feel more acutely here, closest to home, than anywhere else. (One day on the steps of the 135th Street subway station, I take out my camera to photograph a crowd in the street. A man glares at me and snaps: "Take pictures of your own neighborhood.") Still, I spend weeks here on foot, in the subway—and sitting down at library tables, gently turning the delicate pages of the facsimile letters, typescripts, scrapbooks, and photos that produce the here that has been. Of course, as was true with Key West, these days *here* is scattered—across New York, New Haven, and Washington, at the Schomburg Center, Columbia and Yale. At Yale especially, you can't help but notice a certain cheekiness rubbing up against the desperate drive to preserve. Carl Van Vechten, Harlem's white insider-outsider who spent the last decades of his life assembling the James Weldon Johnson Collection for the Beinecke, contributed his own bawdy scrapbooks along with piles of more highbrow fare.

"WE WERE SO HAPPY, HAPPY I REMEMBER"

Harlem, it must be said, continued to die for quite some time.[12] For a young dancer talking in 1939 to Vivian Morris, who was collecting oral histories as part of the Federal Writer's Project, the end came early and was precise: November 1927, when "the Republicans swep' Harlem, Marcus Garvey bein' deported, an' our Queen a Happiness [the actress Florence Mills] died."[13] For Wallace Thurman by 1928 Harlem was already gone. In the play *Harlem*, which Thurman coauthored with William Jordan Rapp, Mother Williams sneers to her son, "City of Refuge! Dat's whad you wrote an' told us. Harlem is de city of refuge. Is yo' shure you don't mean City of Refuse? Dat's all dere is heah."[14] "Harlem is not in compared to Hollywood," Thurman writes to Langston Hughes from Santa Monica the following year. "Why not run out for the summer after the strenuous work of graduating is over. It is only $151 a round trip." (And Hughes makes his way west not long after that.) For Hughes, however, Harlem's ending changed several times. He remarks in his 1940 memoir, *The Big Sea*, that when the Harlem hostess and heiress A'Leila Walker dies during a party in August 1931, "That was really the end of the gay times of the New Negro era in Harlem." He soon revises his assessment: "the period . . . had begun to reach its end when the crash came in 1929 and the white people had much less money to spend on themselves, and practically none to spend on Negroes."[15] In a 1963 essay, Hughes provides yet another ending: "In the midst of the Depression I got a cable from Russia inviting me to work on a motion picture there. I went to Moscow. That was the end of the early days of Langston Hughes in Harlem."[16] Three years later, looking back from the Black Arts era of 1966, Hughes again emends Harlem's ending, surmising instead: "When Ralph Ellison came from Tuskegee to Harlem in 1936 and Richard Wright left Chicago the following year, I would say those migrations marked the tail end of the Negro Renaissance."[17]

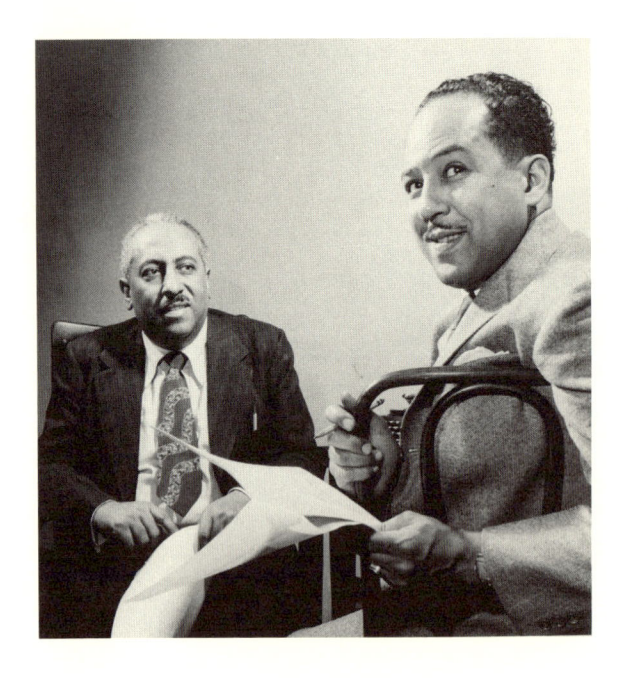

Arna Bontemps and Langston Hughes, circa 1948. Photo by Griff Davis.
Courtesy of Estate of Griffith Jerome Davis and the Yale Collection of American Literature, Beinecke Rare Book and Manuscript Library.

For Arna Bontemps writing a memoir essay for his 1972 edited volume, *The Harlem Renaissance Remembered*, the end was personal, 1932, when he left Harlem for Alabama a year after publishing *God Sends Sunday* and began "brooding over a subject matter so depressing that [he] could find no relief until it resolved itself as [his 1936 novel about a slave revolt] *Black Thunder*." For Alain Locke, whom Hughes called, "the granddaddy of the New Negro" though he was nowhere near that old, the end came in December 1934, when two of his protégés—Wallace Thurman and Rudolph Fisher—died in the same week.[18] And for Carl Van Vechten, who some would say was tossed out of the Renaissance at its apex—1926, when he published his controversial novel about Harlem, *Nigger Heaven*—the end came in 1938, when James Weldon Johnson, who shared Van Vechten's birthday, was killed in a car crash. "The golden days were gone," writes Bontemps nostalgically in 1972. "Or was it just the bloom of youth that had been lost?"[19]

It is noticeable that the women who were part of Harlem were less likely to write about its end—at least for many, many years. But the end, it is true, came nonetheless. Though perhaps, for them, the end seemed less poignant. And more absolute. Many were poor after they left Harlem. And many, it is said, stopped writing—or stopped publishing anyway. But that's a fiction too. Most kept at it for the rest of their lives.[20] Writers they were. Writers they remained. "Helen was very casual about her famous past. A kind of Boston shy arrogance," writes Helene (Helen) Johnson's daughter in a postscript to the posthumous collection of Johnson's poems, many of which were published, for the first time, a few years ago:

> I say arrogance because although she never told me who they were in history, by the time I was eight, she somehow expected me to know who Zora and Wally were. So I faked it. She would tell stories about Alain and Langston without ever giving their last names. Somehow I grew up not having any idea at all that these people were legends. To me they were characters in family stories.[21]

If contemporary critics now speak of *many* Harlem Renaissances—the New Negro one, the women's one, the queer one, the Red one, the blues one, the decadent one, the demotic one—we might think of Depression Harlem as a place that is similarly difficult to fix, but for reasons that have as much to do with the complexity of memory as with history, identity, economics, and myth.[22] Houston Baker has argued, "There was no 'Harlem Renaissance' (and certainly not a 'voguish' one comprised of disparate artists lumped under a single heading) until *after* the event."[23] While his point is open to some debate—one can point to the self-consciousness with which the Negro Renaissance was produced, for instance, or to the close interrelationships shared by the artists who so named it—Baker's emphasis on the retroactive production of Harlem is an important one and is as much as anything what distinguishes Harlem in Depression from its Renaissance, although chronologically the two moments (or, perhaps, movements) overlap.

As concepts, both Renaissance and Depression problematize the temporal relationships among present, past, and future. But while Harlem's retrospectively produced Renaissance relies on the promise of historical progress and atomizes distinctions between a glorious recent past (the New Negro 1920s), a mythical past (in Africa, Haiti, or the rural South), and an imperfect present (the 1930s, the Black Arts era, now), Depression disrupts any sense of opposition between past and present, since multiple refused, disavowed, and forgotten pasts bleed into and coexist with the present and indeed are the essential condition of its coming into being.[24] To believe in Renaissance, in the

"Signs in the windows of a Marcus Garvey club in the Harlem area," 1943.
Library of Congress, Prints and Photographs Division, FSA-OWI Collection. LC-USW3-024010-E.

promise of being reborn, is to indulge in the fantasy of freeing oneself from the burdens of memory while keeping history, or at least a concept of history, intact. But a depressive mindset acknowledges instead the melancholy of *not being able to forget*. Depressive Harlem is not just the Harlem that remembers; it is the Harlem that is haunted by and produced spectrally through an *inability to forget* what has been.[25] It is a self-consciously postlapsarian Harlem. Harlem reborn with a past.

The precision of Harlem's ending is unimportant, in other words; but the process of ending, the awareness of an ending, is what marks depressive Harlem. In *The Big Sea*, Hughes writes that with the exception of the debut and publication of a series of books by Zora Neale Hurston, who "blossomed forth in the midst of the Depression," during the 1930s "nothing much exciting happened, literarily speaking."[26] What did happen "literarily speaking" was remembrance. Not only in Hughes's 1940 memoir, but in Thurman's 1932 autobiographical novel about Harlem, the controversial *Infants of the Spring;* and in Richard Bruce Nugent's unpublished roman à clef, *Gentleman Jigger*, from the same period and his later essay "On Harlem," which he wrote for the WPA; in Claude McKay's 1937 memoir, *A Long Way from Home*; in Countee Cullen's 1932 autobiographical novel set in Harlem, *One Way to Heaven*; in Hurston's 1942 "autobiography" *Dust Tracks on a Road*; and in Roi Ottley's 1943 memoir, *New World A-Coming*; in the many oral histories of Harlem residents taken by members of the Federal Writers Project in the late 1930s; in the diaries and scrapbooks kept during the 1920s, 1930s, and 1940s by Gwendolyn Bennett, Alice Dunbar Nelson, Claude McKay, Arthur Schomburg, Van Vechten, and Hurston's friend and employer Fannie Hurst;[27] most spectacularly and comprehensively in the mammoth collection of scrapbooks put together by the Harlem rare book collector and salon host L. S. Alexander Gumby, who "collected newspaper items on everything. There was nothing too small, there was nothing too large but that he would follow it through in every detail, until he had every scrap of information published about it";[28] and, finally, in the institutionalization of memory with Schomburg's sale of his collection of materials on the history of blacks to the Carnegie Corporation in 1926 and his continued fostering of the collection at the New York Public Library's branch at 135th Street and Lenox Avenue, and with the establishment in 1940 of the James Weldon Johnson Memorial Collection at Yale University. Written, rewritten, and remembered in advance, Depression Harlem possessed a kind of *double vision*.[29] It looked outside and inside simultaneously, saving itself from hell while preserving itself for posthumous posterity.

second series: writing in blue pencil

Fragment of a letter from Langston Hughes in Monterey, California, to Carl Van Vechten, October 30, 1941:

> Dear Carl,
>
> You really should not tell me you are going to give all my letters to Yale because I will now become self-conscious and no doubt verge toward the grandiloquent. Besides I was just about to tell you about a wonderful fight that took place in Togo's Pool Room in Monterey the other day in which various were cut from here to yonder and the lady who used to be the second wife of Noel's valet who came to New York with him that time succeeded in slicing herself—but you know the Race would come out here and cut me if they knew I was relaying such news to posterity via the Yale Library.[30] So now how can I tell you?
>
> Meanwhile I have come across Miss Etta Moten's home address.[31]

Fragment of a letter from Langston Hughes at Yale University to Arna Bontemps, May 17, 1942:

> The Yale Library is the biggest campus library in the world—really enormous, almost the size of Radio City. Bessie Smith is now singing therein!
> Sincerely,
> Langston
>
> P.S. I would just as leave you did not give my letters away. How about yours? Do you want them to go to Yale? The ones of mine to Wallie look very juvenile now. I do not like the idea of writing to one's friends—for posterity and the world. Everybody seems so rich up here! (Harlem is worlds away! Maybe isn't at all.)[32]

Fragments of a letter from Carl Van Vechten to Langston Hughes, August 16, 1943:

> Dear Langston, What letters you write! Maybe I do too. Sometimes I wonder if OUR letters wont be the pride of the Collection . . . I haven't gotten around to sending yours to me yet, but will this winter!
>
> . . . You are right that Harlem is much more indignant about (and much more aware of) these [1943] riots than downtown and I dont know anyone more indignant than Pearl Showers and Mildred Thornton. So it isnt all Sugar Hill indignation. Roi Ottley came to be photographed Saturday and definitely we are getting the manuscript. When he saw your boxes, he almost swooned and exclaimed, "The Schomburg Collection doesnt keep things like this."
>
> Of course, nobody does and even Yale wouldnt, if I didn't do it myself.[33]

DOWN TO THE BRICKS

An inaugural scene: Harlem in cinders.[34] It is a moment best encapsulated by the publication and demise in 1926 of the avant-garde magazine *Fire!!: A Quarterly Devoted to Younger Negro Artists*. The magazine was jointly produced by Harlem's self-dubbed "Niggeratti"—Thurman, Hughes, Hurston, Gwendolyn Bennett, Aaron Douglas, Richard Bruce (Nugent), and John Davis—young artists who lived or congregated for a time in a New York rooming house at 267 West 136th Street. *Fire!!* was imagined from the start as a kind of rewriting and, as has often been noted, a revisionary and radical alternative to Locke's *New Negro* anthology, which came out the same year. Envisioned as a place to "burn up a lot of the old, conventional Negro-white ideas of the past," the little magazine was short-lived (it lasted one issue), ill-received, and put its editors in debt.[35] Because most of the unsold copies had been stored in the basement of an apartment that went up in flames shortly after they were put there, barely enough copies of the magazine survived to become the fodder of archives.[36]

Now, of course, *Fire!!* and its contributors have been recuperated by contemporary critics beyond the wildest dreams of the young artists who produced the magazine. (Reproductions of *Fire!!* are available for purchase on Amazon.com.) The magazine has become something of a touchstone in scholarship on Harlem's Renaissance, marking it either as the moment when the Renaissance went too far—or came out as queer.[37] And yet for some, such as the poet Melvin Tolson, who wrote a master's thesis for Columbia University in the 1930s, *Fire!!* and its equally short-lived successor, *Harlem*, represented no less than "the voice of the Harlem Renaissance."[38] More important perhaps, *Fire!!* served in later years—in later memories—as a crossroads for the artists who had produced it. At one time or another, beginning in the 1930s, most of the former Niggeratti recalled in memoirs and autobiographical sketches the circumstances and promise of the magazine's making and of their own complex relationships with Thurman, the "strangely brilliant black boy"[39] whom Dorothy West called "the most symbolic figure of the literary 'renaissance' in Harlem."[40] For it was Thurman who served as editor in chief of *Fire!!*, he who "prepared the magazine," "got a printer," "planned the layout," and footed most of the bill.[41] And it was he who died first.

If Harlem in Depression is a Harlem that had "grown up," as McKay put it, it is as well a Harlem that is constituted by and through the possessiveness, self-reflection, and temporal ambivalence of the present perfect.[42] It refers not to a Harlem that *was*, but rather to a Harlem that *has been* lived through, a Harlem that remains without remainder (wasn't everyone "passed" on?), is extinguished yet not gone. A cinder. "If a place [*lieu*] is itself surrounded by fire (falls finally to ash, into a cinder tomb), it no longer is. Cinder remains [*reste*], cinder there is [*il y a là cendre*]," writes Jacques Derrida, for whom

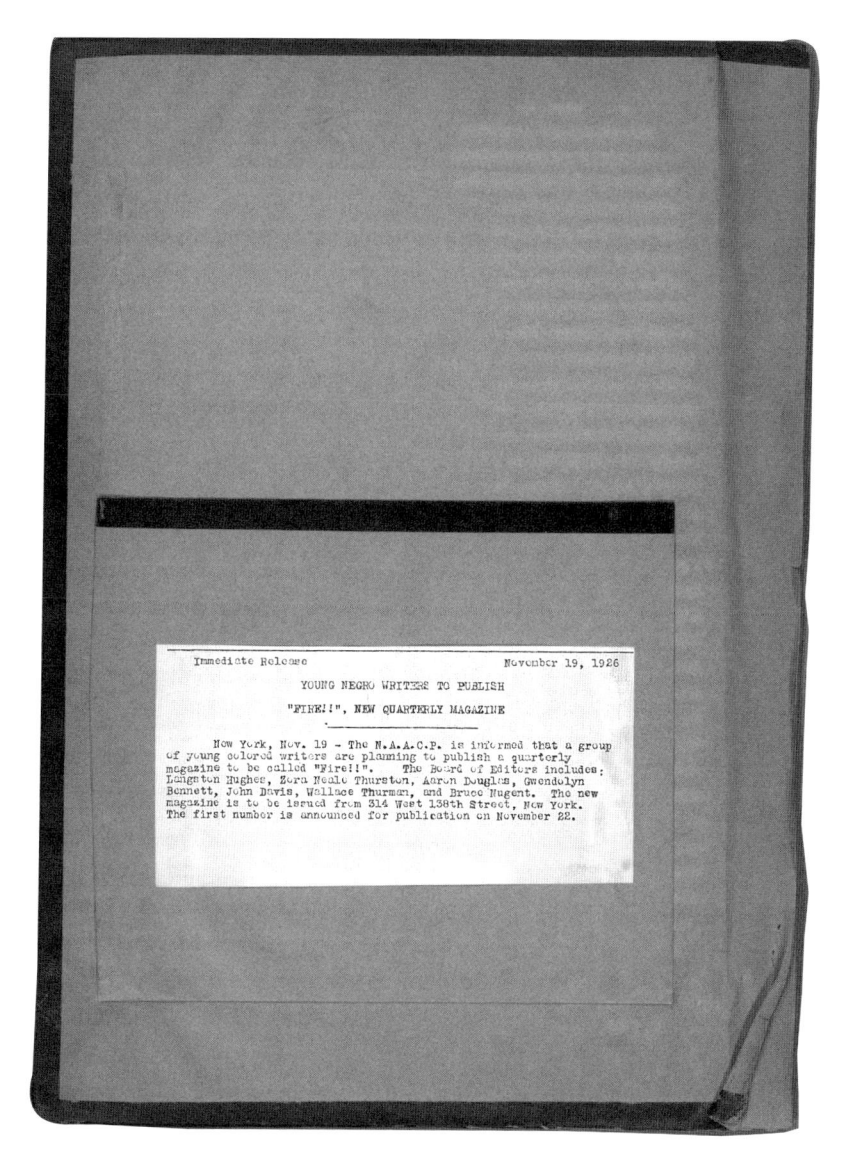

Press release for *Fire!!* 1926. Page from scrapbook no. 128, L. S. Alexander Gumby Scrapbooks.
Courtesy of Rare Book and Manuscript Library, Butler Library, Columbia University.

the cinder names the relation of the "difference between what remains [*reste*] and what is [*est*]."[43] Neither solely material nor metaphorical, actual or fantastic, the cinder—like the trace, like the corpse—signifies what has been. What is. And what is no longer. Ashes to ashes. Dust to dust.

The translation of *lieu* as "place" in Derrida's passage is therefore misleading. A better translation of the term is the less expansive word "site" or even "point."[44] By contrast, in *place* multiple and mobile strains of what is, what remains, what might be, what might have been comingle, rewrite, and overwrite each other. A place, in other words, is simultaneously site *(lieu)* and cinder *(reste/est)*. Harlem in Depression is a Harlem that must be read as a cinder and with an eye to its cinders, to its residues of newness (the New Negro) and self-declared youth (the "Younger Negro artists") alongside the spectral mishmash of the immediate past rising out of the ashes of archives. To encounter Depression Harlem, in other words, is to hear a Harlem confronted by a past that can no longer be defined by its ancestral ghosts—of the South, of enslavement and rebellion, of Africa—but instead is haunted by the shadowy presence of the viscerally and intimately known recent past and the past that will have been but as yet lingers on the horizon. Memory is part of it. As is forgetting. Depression Harlem is constituted in relation to a modernity that is not only aware of its newness, but of the *oldness of its newness*, of its remembrances of newness—and of the ways that newness has already been forgotten.[45]

Draft of "Harlem/Good Morning, Daddy" by Langston Hughes from *Montage of a Dream Deferred*.
© Harold Ober Associates. Yale Collection of American Literature, Beinecke Rare Book and Manuscript Library.

"In 1925 [Wallace Thurman] came hopefully from the West Coast. He was twenty-five and the Negro literary 'renaissance' was in full swing," writes West in a 1970 essay about her friend:

> He wanted to get on the crowded lift and not get off until it skyrocketed him, and such others as had his ballast of self-assurance and talent, to a fixed place in the stars. He died on Welfare Island ten years later, with none of his dreams of greatness fulfilled. Yet the name Wallace Thurman is more typical of that epoch than the one or two more enduring names that survived the period.[46]

Somewhat ironically she begins the next paragraph by renaming him: "He was Wallie to his friends."[47] There is, however, no more appropriate move. To read Harlem through *Fire!!* and its cinders is to read Harlem as a *blue-penciled* place, by way of an editor's aesthetic, through a model of spatiality, subjectivity, and authorship that is glossed by reinscription, remembrance, and the phantasmatic presence of Thurman's editorial hands. Thurman, West writes, "had no personal theory that could substitute for those which he rejected."[48] (And by all accounts, he rejected quite a few.) Instead, she sees personified in Thurman, Harlem in its youth—"immature" and "incomplete."[49] In fact, however, Thurman's practice of *refusal*—and, yes, the incompletion it implies—constitutes, if not a theory, a presence all its own.

Thurman was no stranger to blue pencils. He worked as an editor most of his adult life, first on the editorial staffs of *The Looking Glass*, *The Messenger*, and *The World Tomorrow*; then in 1928, at McFadden (publisher of twenty magazines, including the trashy *True Story*); and in 1932, at the Macaulay Company, serving for a time as editor in chief.[50] He was an uncompromising critic and rewriter, famously never satisfied with his own writing—and rarely with anyone else's. In a 1927 review called "Negro Literature" Thurman writes pointedly that his friend Hughes "needs to learn the use of the blue pencil and the waste-paper basket."[51]

Fire!!, in other words, contained its cinders from the start. An edited text is both a blue-penciled text and a black and blue text, bruised and double-written. It is haunted by its double nature, by the ghostly traces of blue pen-

1st 8/7/48 Keep together

Harlem

Good morning, Daddy!

I was born here, he said,

and I've watched Harlem grow,

colored folks,

until we spread

from river to river,

all across the middle of the island,

I've watched us spread

out of Penn Station

a new nation,

out of planes from Porto Rico,

and the holds

of boats from Cuba, chico,

Jamaica, Haiti, Panama,

out of busses from Georgia,

Florida, Louisiana, marked NEW YORK —

to Harlem, Brooklyn, Bronx, San Juan Hill,
but most of all to Harlem:

Montage of a dream deferred,

Tomorrow, ain't you heard?

a dream defered:

    Does it dry up like a raisin

    in the sun?

    Or fester like a sore,

and then run?

    Does it stink like rotten meat?

    Or crust, and sugar over —

    like a syrupy sweet?

    Or does it explode?

Maybe it just sags like a heavy load.

over) Has anybody heard // what happened to a dream defered?

cil scribbled over black standard type. It is not so surprising, then, that Thurman, in addition to editing, occasionally made his living as a ghostwriter for *True Story* and other pulp magazines. According to Hughes in *The Big Sea*, Thurman often renamed himself. Thurman wrote

> under all sorts of fantastic names, like Ethel Belle Mandrake or Patrick Casey. He did Irish and Jewish and Catholic "true confessions." He collaborated with William Jourdan Rapp on plays and novels. Later he ghosted books. In fact, this quite dark young Negro is said to have written Peggy Hopkins Joyce's *Men, Women, and Checks.*[52]

Editing, like ghostwriting, is a polyvocal act; it requires that one claim another's voice by superimposing on it one's own and then disavowing having spoken. At the same time, the specter of one's presence—as editor, as ghostwriter, and often there is little difference between the two—remains as a cinder, a blue-penciled trace. Ghostwriting, in fact, actually makes more visible the spectral quality of all modernist writing, which is mediated by the typewriter, the editor's hand, and the printing press. While modernist efforts to self-publish might be seen as an attempt to undermine this aspect of print culture, this resistance to the process merely underscores the ubiquity of it. The ghostliness of modern writing is a by-product of changes in technology and, more importantly, signals an epistemological and ontological transformation in the status of writing itself.[53] Indeed, Jean-Michel Rabaté posits a "spectral modernity" narrated by "ghostly writer[s]" who "[imagine themselves] posthumous so as to meditate between [the] past and future to judge the present."[54]

True, Thurman's practice of editing is not unique; the efforts of another heavy-handed modern editor, Maxwell Perkins, come to mind. However, because Thurman himself might be seen as a central figure and metaphor for modernist Harlem both in the fullness of presence—in all its erudition, energy, racial ambivalence, youth, bacchic decadence, male-centeredness, translocalism, bisexuality—and its spectral absence, his practice of refusal provides a way of reading the place. Thurman's editing and ghostwriting are not actively passive as much as passively active, intervening but effacing the act of intervening, being active while assuming the role of passivity. The present perfect—being absent and yet not gone.[55]

emendations

Fragment of an undated 1929 letter from Wallace Thurman to William Jourdan Rapp about Thurman's upcoming divorce from Louise Thompson. Rapp and Thurman collaborated on the 1929 Broadway play *Harlem*, an adaptation of Thurman's story "Cordelia the Crude," which he included in *Fire!!*:

Dear Bill:

I hardly know what to say about this Louise business. There is only one thing about which I am certain and that is: I will succumb to no more sentimental pleas that we "discuss matters between ourselves in an adult way." That's the reason I frankly stated my position to her and told her that I could not see the way clear at present to pay her expenses to Reno. . . . I will not pay her way to Reno and if she will not sign the agreement I will not make her another payment.

. . . If she brings up this homosexual business, she will get nowhere. She has already admitted to Swerling that after her operation all was well sexually between us and neither can she bring up that knowledge of that one incident in my life disgusted her so that she was unable to have further intercourse with me, for she did, on the very day I left New York, April the sixth.[56]

Fragment of a letter from Zora Neale Hurston to Dorothy West, postmarked November 5, 1928:

Dear Dorothy,
Wally should perk up. I know that it is annoying for his mother-in-law to keep on living and pestering him, but then there are gunmen down on the East Side who hire out for as low as $25.00. He should be a very happy man by Thanksgiving.[57]

Fragment of a letter from Carl Van Vechten to Langston Hughes, October 11, 1948:

A package from YOU goes to Yale today along with the Thurman letters. HE doesn't seem to have liked Louise much.
I am having my portrait painted (AGAIN) at midnight by a skater!
Hearts and Flowers[58]

ECHOES

For a long time the story of *Fire!!*'s beginning was better known than the little magazine itself. It began, so the story goes, not in Harlem, but in Washington, D.C., on a summer's night in 1925 when Richard Bruce Nugent met Langston Hughes at a party. As Nugent later wrote in his 1982 preface to the reprinted edition of *Fire!!*:

We left Georgia Douglas' together, since we each lived but a few blocks from her house. Besides, we were in the middle of a conversation. So he walked me to the corner of Thirteenth Street . . . and naturally, since we were again in mid-sentence, I walked him up to his house (near Seventeenth Street) . . . where again we had to walk back toward my house . . .

"New York's Harlem has its Housing Problems," 1946. Library of Congress, Prints and Photographs Division, *New York World-Telegram* and the *Sun* Newspaper Photograph Collection, LC-USZ62-115947.

and so the whole night went, because we never finished talking . . . to finish talking would never do. . . .

It was the beginning of many talking, walking evenings. I even wrote a poem.[59]

The passage, written nearly sixty years after *Fire!!* was published and not at all descriptive of the making of the magazine itself, is nonetheless reminiscent both formally and thematically of the long elliptical passages that make up Nugent's famous story "Smoke, Lilies and Jade." The story, which narrates the nighttime wanderings of a Harlem artist named Alex and his erotic encounter with another man, scandalized the little magazine's readers when it was published. It had been intended to do so. The story, included in nearly every anthology on the Harlem Renaissance, and nearly the only thing writ-

142 HARLEM

ten by Nugent that, until recently, anyone cited, is best known for being unabashedly queer.

Nugent's hallucinatory text is striated by ellipses, which become the subject of most critical readings of the story. For some readers, the long pathways of ellipses that "spiral from bottom to top of each page . . . evoke the ascending spiral of smoke of the title," according to Joseph Allen Boone; "and for others, [the ellipses evoke] Alex's desultory footsteps as he meanders throughout the city: the space of the text thus becomes a map of the city itself, imprinting a labyrinthine system of movement and flow that is constitutive of Alex's identity as a black man with gay desires."[60] For Boone, Nugent's story performs a "strategic queering of narrative that transforms modernist techniques for registering the flux of consciousness into a palimpsest of gay urban subjectivity in the making."[61] Yet the consciousness that Nugent's story negotiates cannot be seen as the "free associations" of an isolated voice. *Fire!!*, as edited by Thurman, belies the ideal of an individual authorial subject, voice, or personality. Rather, the ellipses in Nugent's story might be seen as a kind of trace for the excisions performed by Thurman's blue pencil—for the gaps of text cut out and the remaking of meaning that occurs in the process of manuscript editing. At the least, the gaps in Nugent's narrative suggest a kind of pause in conversation, a lull and waiting to respond, or an echo that reverberates between multiple voices, personalities, authors, and texts. Indeed, if Nugent's story can be seen as the energetic fulcrum of *Fire!!*, and to some extent it is, it is in part because it serves as a kind of switchboard or medium through which the multiple voices of *Fire!!* can converse.

Nugent's memoir of his nighttime walk with Hughes, which frames the reprinted edition of *Fire!!*, echoes Alex's night wanderings in "Smoke, Lilies and Jade." But the experience he describes of his walk with Hughes cannot be described as cruising. (Though, yes, admits Nugent many years later, they were never lovers, but there was always a *frisson* of excitement between them.) Nor is it Baudelaire's *flânerie*. (Though the young Hughes and, especially, Nugent would certainly enjoy the comparison.) Nor is it strolling. (That was an exact art, according to Loften Mitchell. "You had to walk with your right leg dipping a bit, resembling a limp. Your fedora was snapped smartly over your right eye.")[62] It might instead be seen as conversation. Call and response. Even writing and rewriting. Back and forth Hughes and Nugent went from apartment to apartment. They moved but went nowhere. They talked.

With an eye to Nugent's later framing of the reprinted magazine, it becomes easier to see how the individual texts that constitute *Fire!!* reverberate with one another. Nugent's story of sonic repetition and movement ("Alex walked and the clock of his heels sounded. . . . and had an echo . . . sound being tossed back and forth . . . back and forth . . .")[63] is echoed by Hughes's poem "Elevator Boy," found a few pages earlier ("Only the elevators/Goin' up and down,/Up an' down"),[64] as well as with Thurman's own story "Cordelia the Crude," about a promiscuous woman (a soon-to-be "street walker") who is about to accept her first paid client. Thurman's story, like Nugent's, ends with ellipses: "Still eager to speak, I followed and heard one of the girls ask: Who's the dicty kid? . . . /And Cordelia answered: The guy who gimme ma' firs' two bucks. . . ."[65] The path Cordelia follows is, like Alex's in Nugent's narrative, "to be continued," though to much more ill effect. The ellipses in Thurman's story suggest as well that Thurman's own "writing will be continued" and that Cordelia's story might be continued in the writings that follow. (Cordelia's story is literally "continued," of course, when Thurman rewrites it, in collaboration with Rapp, as the play *Harlem: A Melodrama of Negro Life in Harlem*, which opened on Broadway in February 1929.) The rhythms of walking are also repeated in Hurston's play *Color Struck*, which follows Thurman's story in the magazine, when Emma, the protagonist in Hurston's play, laments, "Us blacks was made for cobble stones," for street-walking, in other words, or for being walked on. In the play, Hurston also rewrites, and arguably reclaims, the degraded minstrel image of the "cakewalk."[66]

While the formal characteristics of specific texts—the trope of walking, the ellipses in Nugent's and Thurman's stories, the fragmentary quality of Hughes's poems, the dashes splattered throughout Hurston's writings—are not infrequently discussed by critics, they have almost always been read as indicative of the aesthetic, philosophical, and social struggles of individual authors or of individual authors' complicated relationships to recognizable categories of subjectivity. For example, Hurston's frequent use of dashes, ellipses, and narrative "circumlocution" in *Color Struck* have been interpreted as various "indices" of black women's discourse: as "literal and figurative cuts in the narrative" that display "the searing wounds of a violated and muted body" that cannot articulate "its history of injury";[67] as a "surplus of unattainable desires";[68] or as the "melancholy moment" that is constituted by a body "acting out a speechless articulation of desire and pain."[69] While such readings offer valid, even nuanced, insights into the writings of individual authors, they are incomplete by virtue of the fact that they focus on an individual writer's aesthetic negotiations and thus presuppose an a priori ideal of a solitary authorial subject.[70]

Fire!! has been largely read as a manifesto for artistic individualism honed from the young Harlem artists' desire to "express [their] individual dark-skinned selves without fear or shame,"[71] and without writing the thinly veiled propaganda for racial uplift and collectivism they saw being heralded as art by Harlem's more established leaders, Alain Locke, W. E. B. Du Bois, James Weldon Johnson, and Charles Johnson, at the helms of the Urban League and the NAACP.[72] When Raymond comments to Dr. Parkes (a loosely veiled Locke) in Thurman's *Infants of the Spring* that "one cannot make movements nor can one plot their course. . . . Individuality is what we should strive for. Let us each seek his own salvation," the argument is often taken as Thurman's own.[73] Though Thurman described himself as a "Nietzschean disciple" or even a "confirmed Neitzschean [sic]" (Thurman was a notoriously poor speller), according to some critics, he might more precisely be described as a follower of Nietzsche as glossed by H. L. Mencken.[74] This interpretation makes some sense. In his 1908 book on Nietzsche's philosophy, Mencken lays out a model of individualist morality that precludes that one person "in any way or form . . . judge or direct the actions of any other being."[75] Be critical, in other words—for Nietzsche, according to Mencken, "applied the acid of critical analysis to a hundred and one specific ideas"—but don't morally judge.

Thurman, in this view, becomes not as much a champion of individualism in a transcendental sense as suspicious of unself-conscious or programmatic moralism. Even Raymond in *Infants of the Spring*, a character often read autobiographically as Thurman himself, ascribes to a complicated individualism that is not incommensurate with mass movements, such as Communism. When Stephen asks Raymond, "How can you fight both for the masses and for the individual?" Raymond replies, "You have to improve the status of the masses in order to develop individuals. It is mass movements which bring forth individuals."[76]

However one describes individualism, the practice through which Thurman edited *Fire!!* must be seen as *dialogic*: "My idea of a foreward [sic]. What think you? Change or rewrite and special to me immediately," Thurman wrote to Hughes in October 1926, one of many such exchanges they had. But a better term for the aesthetic, subjective, and affective model that *Fire!!* performs is *dissociative*, as it resonates with turn-of-the-century French philosophies of memory, personality, hypnosis, and spiritualism. "I'm hell on bluepenciling the work of others, but much too soft with myself. Auto-intoxication I suppose," Thurman wrote to Hughes in 1929, asking him to read his manuscript and "actually correct anything which offends your eye or ear as far as words and sentences go."[77]

Using the term *dissociation* with regard to Thurman (or any of the Harlem artists) is not without its problems.[78] I should make clear that I am not using the term diagnostically, suggesting, for instance, that Thurman suffered from a dissociative personality disorder (multiple personality or a less extreme borderline personality) or even the bipolar disorder with which he has been posthumously diagnosed.[79] The diagnostic tradition of clinical psychoanalysis and psychology, which would see dissociation as a disorder of the ego, while not irrelevant here, is also not of primary importance. (Conceptually, depression and dissociative personality disorder share a genealogy. Late in his career, the French philosopher Pierre Janet, to whom many attribute the recognition of dissociative disorders, decided that most of the "dual personalities" he had hypnotized in the late nineteenth century had actually been suffering from manic depression.)[80] Instead, I use *dissociation* here to posit a historically and philosophically specific conception of modern subjectivity that disregards the limitations of embodiment and the desirability of an autonomous or integrated subject or voice. Thurman's blue-pencil practice is dissociative in that it presumes a form of subjectivity that is incommensurate with singularity—that sees the voice, ego, and skin not as boundaries, but as spectral and permeable spaces of exchange. Dissociation, in this sense, is marked by a continual and continually repeated feeling of estrangement and displacement, a perpetual re-forgetting of where you are—and who you are. This makes it a rather slippery, but also evocative, model for describing writing, subjectivity, or place.

Within this context, Nugent's story, though a monologue, should not be read as the insular words of a solitary voice.[81] Boone's suggestion that "some things are best left unsaid" is, after all, the necessary mantra of the practice of editing. While it is true that Nugent's narrative is "compulsively" littered with the names of Harlem's living artists—"Wallie . . . Zora . . . Clement . . . Gloria . . . Langston. . . . John. . . . Gwenny . . . oh many people"—as Boone observes,[82] read in relation to the other stories, poems, and essays that are included in *Fire!!* Alex's namedropping becomes less the effort of a fictional individual's attempt to claim his place among the ranks of other artists than a *telegraphic* (even *telepathic*) attempt to engage the rest of the Harlem Niggeratti, to send forth an echo that reverberates from story to poem to play across the surface of the magazine.

An echo implies a belated, partial, and repetitive return of sound, one that disrupts any conception of an original or solitary voice; it is precisely through repetition that both the original and the echo simultaneously come into being. Judith Greenberg argues that Ovid's story of Echo functions as a paradigm through which to read narratives of trauma: "Juno's punishment forces Echo to depend upon the speech of another; she needs to hear in order to speak."[83] We might also consider the dissociative quality of the echo as a way to understand the production of memory more generally.[84] Part of what these writers seek is a way to remember that, while not disavowing the inherited traumas of enslavement and racism, cannot be reduced to them.

In his essay about walking and memory, "A Berlin Chronicle," Walter Benjamin writes,

> The *déjà vu* effect has often been described. But I wonder whether the term is actually well chosen, and whether the metaphor appropriate to the process would not be far better taken from the realm of acoustics. One ought to speak of events that reach us like an *echo* awakened by a call, a sound that seems to have been heard somewhere in the darkness of past life. Accordingly, if we are not mistaken, the shock with which moments enter consciousness as if already lived usually strikes us in the form of a sound. It is a word, tapping, or a rustling that is endowed with

the magic power to transport us into the cool tomb of long ago, from the vault of which the present seems to return only as an echo.[85]

That there is a seductive as well as spectral quality to the echo cannot be denied. In "Smoke, Lilies and Jade," for instance, Nugent describes the echo as a kind of erotic foreplay, even a "libidinal current," in Boone's coinage of the phrase: "Alex walked and the click of his heels sounded . . . and had an echo . . . sound being tossed back and forth . . . back and forth. . . . . . someone was approaching . . . and their echoes mingled . . . gave the sound of castanets . . . Alex liked the sound of the approaching man's footsteps . . . he walked music also . . . he knew the beauty of the narrow blue . . . Alex knew from the way their echoes mingled . . . he wished he would speak . . ."[86] Acoustic erotics, yes. And for Nugent, the echo constitutes a percussive, masculine erotics. However, the words that Benjamin uses to describe the phenomenon of the echo in the preceeding passage—"tapping," "rustling," "magic," a "past life"—also reference the discourse of hypnotism and spiritualism that was associated with memory production in the late nineteenth and early twentieth centuries; issues that were not unknown to Nugent or to Harlem's other younger writers.

Thurman, in particular, read voraciously. "He would get from the library a great pile of volumes that would have taken me a year to read," remembers Hughes in *The Big Sea*. "But he would go through them in less than a week, and be able to discuss each one at great length with anybody."[87] Thurman

Langston Hughes and Wallace Thurman in California, circa 1934.
Courtesy of Yale Collection of American Literature, Beinecke Rare Book and Manuscript Library.

Langston Hughes and Dorothy West travelling to the Soviet Union in 1932.
Courtesy of Yale Collection of American Literature, Beinecke Rare Book and Manuscript Library.

Dorothy West and Helene Johnson, circa 1920s.
The Dorothy West Papers. Courtesy of the Schlesinger Library, Radcliffe Institute, Harvard University.

and, to a lesser extent, Nugent were impacted by Benjamin's muses, Proust and Baudelaire, as well as by other writers associated with nineteenth-century spiritualism and decadence, including Poe, Rimbaud, Verlaine, Wilde, Huysmans, Whitman, and Nietzsche. In *Infants of the Spring*, Thurman describes Paul Arbian (whose name plays on Richard Bruce Nugent's initials, R B N) as a hypnotist: "As usual when he spoke, everyone remained silent and listened intently as if hypnotized."[88] While hypnotism too does not lack seductive qualities, its connection with the nineteenth-century sciences of memory and personality is what is most important here. Indeed, a syncretism between folk traditions and the edgier Western philosophical models marks much of the work of the younger Harlem writers.

Rudolph Fisher's 1932 detective novel *The Conjure-Man Dies*, for example, takes as its project the dissolution of the boundaries between African "conjuring," psychology and psychoanalysis, criminology, and medical and scientific technologies, such as X ray and embalming. The dead man at the center of the story is a Harvard-educated native African king who makes his living as a Harlem "conjure-man," but who, it turns out, is also a Harlem undertaker in disguise. At one point, the hero, Dr. Archer, a young Harlem medical doctor like Fisher himself, explains to the working-class Bubber, "You see, while you have been ruminating in the depths of Frimbo's cellar, I have been ruminating in the depth's of my mind." To which Bubber replies, in a sly response to Freudian presumption, "I hope it 'taint as full of trash as that cellar was."[89] Solving the mystery of Fisher's novel involves a collapse between multiple modes of understanding and experience: An investigation of cellar trash provides the key to the novel's mystery. The cinders of what appears to be household rubbish turn out to be the burnt remains of the missing corpse.

on rewriting

I may as well admit it. This was the chapter I could not write. So I rewrote it. Again and again. I attributed my reticence to anxieties of influence. (So much has been said about Harlem before.) To trespassing. (New York is home. But Harlem is not.) To humiliation. (There was that ill-received talk.) To self-criticism. And perfectionism. And procrastination. To somehow, here, losing my voice—or being drowned by too many voices. So I listened. There was no way to hear everyone. So I listened to chatter, banter, the blue of the trace. Not to words exactly, but to echoes. To the shadowy mumblings of ghosts.

If we jettison prescriptions about the desirability of an autonomous or integrated subjectivity, voice, or cultural history, conflicts between Harlem's older generation of social scientists and philosophers, and its younger artists become much more visible.[90] The rupture lies not so much in marking the distinction between bourgeois propriety and avant-garde decadence—although that is part of it—but in an understanding of the complex nature and roles of personality, modernity, history, and memory. That this debate is staged in and through representations of Harlem makes a certain sense; as James De Jongh surmises in *Vicious Modernism: Black Harlem and the Literary Imagination*, Harlem is both topos and trope, it "has remained modernity's preeminent popular image of black racial being and interracial conflict."[91] That Harlem was represented by many white Americans—and, arguably, Van Vechten—as being inhabited by a population besot with the "bestial vivacity" of living in the moment that Nietzsche had heralded as an alternative to history is not beside the point here.[92] Nor is the fact that *Fire!!* closes with an editorial essay by Thurman that heralds Van Vechten's "sincerity" vis-à-vis his satirical and/or salacious depiction of "Negro life in Harlem."[93] The controversy within Harlem over Van Vechten's *Nigger Heaven* merely brought to the fore rifts that were philosophical and finely drawn. What is the past? Through what means can it be represented—if at all?

For Du Bois, Schomburg, Charles Johnson, and Carter G. Woodson, the so-called father of African American history, recuperating and renarrating a debased and often absent African American cultural past was of primary importance.[94] As Paul Allen Anderson observes, Schomburg, "gracefully captured the point in 'The Negro Digs Up His Past,' his essay for *The New Negro*. 'The American Negro,' Schomburg wrote, 'must remake his past in order to make his future. History must restore what slavery took away.'"[95] What they had in mind as the means through which to remake that past was, if not traditional, infused by the sort of teleological drive that might convey a Hegelian sense of progress.

Certainly, the *Fire!!* artists did not reject history wholeheartedly. While some of them may have aspired for a brief while to live artistically for and in the moment, good modernists that they were, they also wrote for posterity. And certainly, given the context in which he was writing, Du Bois's recognition of the value of a double or split consciousness was itself a controversial move, not wholly distinct from the philosophical dissociationism with which I link Thurman. In a critique of Warren Susman's influential argument about the impact of consumerism on the American personality, for example, Andrew R. Heinze locates late nineteenth-century changes in American popular understandings of personality in the impact of the new psychologies and understandings of the psyche. Debates about the shift in personality "centered on the dilemma of *dissociation* and *integration* in regard to the individual and the nation," he writes. "The shift was not from a moral world of character to a social world of personality; it was from a belief in the unitary and solid nature of personal and national identity to a sense of those identities as divisible and fragmented."[96] Heinze argues that conceptions of fragmented personalities, such as those laid out by Du Bois, were seen as threatening and nonintegrative, particularly for those who advocated for the assimilation of new immigrants.

In *Souls of Black Folk*, Du Bois is probably as much in conversation with William James as he is with Hegel and Booker T. Washington—and, in particular, he develops his concept of double-consciousness by drawing on James's integration of Janet's dissociative philosophy with Anglo-American associationist "double consciousness." In a section on hypnosis in *The Principles of Psychology*, for example, James, referring to Janet's observations of "certain hysterical somnabulists," extends the notion of double-consciousness to one that is reminiscent of Freud's conception of the consciousness/unconscious split, arguing that memories of the hypnotic state are "not simply organically registered, but that *the consciousness which thus retains it is split off, dissociated from the rest of the subject's mind.*"[97] Yet, even when read through the lens of James's writings, Du Bois's thinking cannot rightfully be called dissociative, in Thurman's sense. Arnold Rampersad rightfully notes that *Souls* represents a departure from "certain positivist goals of history and sociology"; but here, Du Bois complicates yet does not wholly reject a Hegelian ideal of synthesis or integration—as a collective as well as individual ideal.[98]

By contrast, Thurman's practice of blue-pencil authorship is radically nonintegrative, acknowledging, even embracing, breakdowns between self and Other, the living world and the world of spirits, *and* within a matrix of multiple selves, multiple others, and multiple conceptions of place.[99] "*I read your poetry and made a grand hit. From now on I substitute pour vous*," wrote Thurman to Hughes in 1926, a suggestion that we might take seriously. Thurman performs the substitution in his letter as a translation from English to French, but in doing so raises questions about who this "vous" is. Following the norms of French grammar, Thurman should address his close friend by the familiar "toi" rather than the formal "vous." Thurman's inappropriate use of "vous," inadvertent though it may be, might be seen as deferential; there is no doubt he envied Hughes's ability to write poetry, a task at which Thurman himself never excelled. (Although by all accounts Thurman was rarely deferential.) It also can be seen as a kind of wish fulfillment; Thurman did act as a "substitute" for Hughes on at least one more occasion—disastrously stepping in to rewrite *Mule Bone* with Hurston without first asking Hughes, who had been her coauthor.

Since "vous" is also the plural form of you, however, Thurman's slippery translation also suggests he substitutes for multiple subjects, bringing into relief Hughes's embrace of multiple lineages and subjectivities, a matter upon which Hughes insists over and over again in *The Big Sea*: "You see, unfortunately, I am not black," he writes. "There are lots of different kinds of blood in our family. But here in the United States, the word "Negro" is used to mean anyone who has *any* Negro blood at all in his veins . . . I am brown. My father was a darker brown. My mother an olive yellow."[100] Hughes uses similar phrasing later in the memoir when describing his "break-up" with "Godmother" (Charlotte Mason) in 1930: "She wanted me to be primitive and know and feel the intuitions of the primitive. But, unfortunately, I did not feel the rhythms of the primitive surging through me, and so I could not live and write as though I did. I was only an American Negro—who had loved the surface of Africa and the rhythms of Africa—but I was not Africa. I was Chicago and Kansas City and Broadway and Harlem. And I was not what she wanted me to be."[101] More obliquely, Thurman refers to the dissociative quality of modern writing in which the typewriter centrally figures. (Thurman himself typed most of his letters, even personal ones.) Critics such as Friedrich Kittler and Mark Seltzer have argued that the typewriter encouraged a disconnect between the formation of the subject and writing, mechanizing language and severing the link between "hand, eye, and text."[102] The "vous," in this sense, underscores the precarious link between man and machine.

Finally, and most important, however, Thurman's use of the second person plural, "vous," foregrounds the possibility that Thurman and Hughes might together produce a kind of fugal or dissociative authorship, in which Thurman functions as an alter ego who at times adopts and at other times superimposes his voice and personality on Hughes's.[103] Certainly, Thurman's understanding of the boundary between his writing and that of others seems flexible at best. Nugent's *Gentleman Jigger* was written at the same time in the early 1930s as Thurman's *Infants of the Spring* and describes many of the same incidents. "The fact that Thurman's novel was published, while Nugent's was not, does not mean that Nugent imitated Thurman," writes Thomas H. Wirth in his preface to the excerpts from the novel that he includes in his edition of Nugent's selected works. "Indeed, in interviews and in one chapter of *Gentleman Jigger* . . . Nugent alleged the opposite: that Thurman copied from him."[104]

Still, Nugent later insisted, it didn't matter much: "That was the sort of relationship we had, and others did it too without thinking too much of it." Nugent claims he had once taken a poem of Thurman's, and "Countee Cullen once published someone else's poem."[105] In another interview, Nugent describes how their friend Harold Jackman had been furious to discover Thurman's "plagiarism"—much more so than Nugent was himself. "Harold didn't know the relationship that existed between Wallie and me," he explains. "I had always written a lot of Wallie's stuff. Stuff that demanded color I had usually written. Wallie, as I say, was a wonderful editor and a wonderful fact

1

New Part —

Life at 267 was at least exciting. One was seldom bored. It was the conventional gathering place for all of the younger persons who felt it incumbent upon themselves, to keep the arts andscienxes alive. of course the seven who called thmselves 'The Niggeratti' gathered there. Howard, the artist who had absorbed so much occidentalized mysticizm as to be rendered fat over productive and plausible uncreative, would come and discuss his latest creative endeavor. Not because he thought that he could derive benifit from the pompous and unsound, tho apparently fundamental suggestions of ~~Wallie~~ Rusty, or the childish and naive oppinions of ~~Steward~~ Stuart. Or the knowing silences of Tony ~~Langston~~, or the irreverant and locquacious dialect wittiscisms of Nona ~~Zora~~, or the pedandic and latinized nonsenses of ~~Tim~~ Paul, or the inane and worthless opinions of ~~Gwendolyn~~ Theresa, ~~who~~ despite the fact that she was a teacher of the arts at one of the leading Negro colleges. On one score he agreed with ~~Steward~~ Stuart. That as far as art was concerned, meaning painting specifically, they were all imbeciles. He continued to visit 267. after all he was one of the seven

Steward, ~~joined~~ ~~belonged to~~ the gathering because he lived there. Because he thrived on excitement, and because, being the youngest of this most important group, had faith in them. Because he wanted to be an integral partof this new and excellent order. Because they formed a minority group and as such commanded attention, and Because he was still the exhibitionist. Because their opinios regarding him meant nothing also and place

~~Wallie because he~~ And Rusty had decided to become one of, if not the most, important Negro in America. Because he was an opportunist, ~~Because~~ he was facile and shrewed, and needed the ideas of these less aggressive imbeciles, to use as proof of his own creative ability. ~~Because~~ their opinions regarding him did ~~mean something~~ mean a lot. Besides, ~~Because~~ he had created the 'salon'

Anthony ~~Langston~~ because these were his freinds. Because their activities amused him. ~~Because~~ he could contribute his share as payment for the publicity he received in return. ~~Because~~ their opinions in regard to him meant nothing. But ~~because~~ they were his freinds and children amused him.

~~Zora because she could shine in un~~

writer but he wasn't very much on color. . . . You see Wallie and I had a relationship where we were really more or less the same person. So anything he couldn't do and I could, I did, and vice versa."[106]

Within this context, Thurman's performance of blue-pencil authorship might rightfully be said to be a kind of *blues* pencil authorship. Repetition as a form of rewriting has long been described as a hallmark of vernacular African American aesthetic forms, such as blues music. Albert Murray argues, for instance, that the virtuosity of blues musicians and blues music is performative; it derives not from the creation of an original form, but from imitation, variation, counterstatement, and elaboration of existing blues conventions.[107] Blues authorship therefore implies a kind of fluidity of ownership—and a suspicion of strict property relations. Unlike Hughes or others of his peers, Thurman did not adopt a formal style associated with the blues; but he did, like many of the younger generation of Harlem writers, combine a highly literate European, and particularly French, modernist aesthetic and philosophical sensibility with African American folklore and urban working-class idioms. The relationship between folk conjuring, blues aesthetics, and French mesmerism, hypnosis, and spiritualism are not so far afield. A hallmark of conjuring is that it functions in a way that might be described as dissociative in a literal sense, disrupting rigid demarcations among the minds and bodies of individual subjects and dissolving distinctions between earth, spirit, time, and space.

Thurman can advocate individuality, then, because to be an individual means something other than to be contained within a single body or ego. "If you ask Rapp and Thurman who wrote the dialogue, who developed the plot, or who decided on what atmosphere to accept or reject, they'll tell you they don't know," wrote Rapp and Thurman in an unpublished essay about their collaboration on the 1929 play *Harlem*:

> They claim individual collaboration for but one line each in the entire play. Everything else was created together. Thurman's line is that of the indignant father when he says, "You know what's wrong wid Harlem? Dey's too many niggers!" And Rapp's line is that of the janitress who when asked by the detective if she's the janitress, says, "Aw, I'm deh assistant superintendent!" And if you analyze these lines you'll discover that the first is white in its humor and thought content, and the second is typically Negroid. So figure it out, if you can![108]

Manuscript page from Bruce Nugent's unpublished novel "Gentleman Jigger."
© 2003 Thomas H. Wirth. Used with permission.

"Luxurious Condos"
in Harlem, New York
City, 2005
© Frank Jermann, Germany/
rAtgallery.com

THIRD SERIES: COLLECTING HARLEM

THE NEW YORK TIMES
November 19, 2000, Sunday
Harlem Journal: Gay White Pioneers, On New Ground
By Monte Williams

HARLEM, Nov 18—. . ."Harlem is on everybody's lips," said Willie Kathryn Suggs, a tough-as-wrought-iron real estate broker whose main turf is Harlem. "It's no longer a no man's land."

That fact has not been lost on whites, who seem to be moving into Harlem, the country's center of African-American culture, as fast as they can label their cardboard boxes.

One of the latest groups to make a beeline north is gay white men from the West Village, East Village and Chelsea, according to real estate brokers, residents and the men themselves. They are snatching up mint-condition, turn-of-the-century town houses in Hamilton Heights for $650,000 and up, and fixer-uppers and shells for $300,000 to $400,000. . . .

" . . . Gays have often been at the forefront of gentrification in New York City and elsewhere in the nation," said Charles Kaiser, author of "The Gay Metropolis, a History of Gay Life in New York" (Harcourt Brace, 1998).

"Gays are pioneers," he said. "They are outsiders already." Twenty years ago, he noted, gays from the West Village uplifted and refined Chelsea, then an industrial and commercial neighborhood that was not very desirable."[109]

"MY SWEET HUNK O' TRASH"

The fortieth volume of L. S. Alexander Gumby's 139-volume scrapbook "Collection of the American Negro" begins with an article on real estate, a 1922 *New York Times* depiction of the "black belt line." The many pages that follow document newspaper and other accounts of various inhabitants and happenings of Harlem—some well known, some forgotten—during the mid–twentieth century. Volume 41, also on Harlem, closes on a more downbeat note with stories about the 1943 riot, soldiers in World War II, and the Collyer Brothers, who died in a Harlem mansion stuffed with trash. More a series of collages than a catalogue, Gumby's books, assembled from "clippings, prints, documents, books and letters" that he collected between 1916 and 1951, aimed in Gumby's view to be "a complete history of the Negro in scrapbook form."[110]

While Gumby describes his assemblage as encyclopedic and claims a documentary authority garnered by visits to the "Congressional library in Washington and the public library in New York" and by studying the scrapbooks of well-known historical figures such as Theodore Roosevelt,[111] the scrapbooks nonetheless portray an encounter with the past that is imagistic and fragmentary rather than linear or totalizing. They capture a history that must be told in snapshots and scraps. In fact, Gumby's efforts to be exhaustive—to include everything he finds—allow for, even emphasize, the contingent nature of documentary and of historical narratives that preserve an absolute opposition between past, present, and future; that prioritize a solitary authorial or artistic voice; or that privilege any notion of history extricated from the exigencies of circulation, real estate, even the mail.

Susan Stewart argues that the scrapbook might more properly be considered a souvenir than a collection, transforming history into "private time," simultaneously authenticating the past and discrediting the present. The past is reconfigured and evoked through the efforts of a voluntary memory—as opposed to a Proustian *mémoire involuntaire*, those memories evoked, unwittingly, by the taste of a *madeleine*. "The nostalgia of the souvenir," Stewart explains, "plays in the distance between the present and an imagined, prelapsarian experience, experience as it might be 'directly lived.'"[112] The collection, by contrast, she argues, is metaphoric rather than metonymic; it "offers example rather than sample," replacing "origin with classification."[113] The collection, she writes,

> is a form of art as play, a form involving the reframing of objects within a world of attention and manipulation of context. Like other forms of art, its function is not the restoration of context of origin but rather the creation of a new context, a context standing in a metaphorical, rather than a contiguous, relation to the world of everyday life. Yet unlike many forms

ILLUSTRATED FEATURE SECTION—June 7, 1930

Unique Passion for Collecting Facts About Negroes

Alexander Gumby began compiling Scrapbooks of Negro History 22 years ago. Now he has one of the choicest collections in existence.

Alexander Gumby, whose passion for compiling scrapbooks has resulted in the accumulation of a rare collection of extraordinary and unusual facts about his race.

This is an interior view of Gumby's Negro Library. In the background can be seen the quaint and odd volumes which he possesses.

By John W. Douglas.

LET THOSE who consider the keeping of scrapbooks a children's pastime, pay attention to this story of Alexander Gumby. This man started compiling scrap-books twenty-two years ago. At first he just collected odds and ends that interested him—little items that he thought worth saving. Of course since he is a colored man his clippings are in a large part concerned with the doings of Negroes. It was not long before Gumby had become familiar with facts about the Negro race, facts that were little known to most of his friends. It was here that our friend stumbled on a sad truth.

He found that Negroes, even those relatively well informed, had a very meager knowledge of Negro history. When Gumby finally realized this, he decided to collect all of the race items that he could, regardless as to whether they referred to the past, present or future of the Negro race. That idea, was the basis of the Gumby collection, a history of the Negro depicted —

What a wonderful collection of items about Negroes this man has! Within the compass of sixty odd folios he has amassed material dealing with such topics as the Negro in Africa, slavery, Haiti, Liberia, current history, art, political crime, anthropology, drama, music, the N.A.A.C.P. and pugilism. There are also special books concerning Jack Johnson, Dr. DuBois, Frederick Douglass and Booker T. Washington.

It is a diversified and complete work. Of course it is impossible to adequately treat all of these topics within the limits of this short article. Our purpose will be to mention some of the interesting things that Gumby has collected just to show what his scrap books are like.

We have all given receipts for the sale of goods but how many have seen, receipts given for the sale of human beings. Gumby exhibited a paper yellowed with age when he acknowledged the payment of a sum of money for the sale of a Negro female slave. The woman was described with the same particularity as one would describe a typewriter. The white man who made the sale was so illiterate, that he had to make his mark instead of signing his name.

The subject of slavery in the United States forms an important part of the collection. Gumby showed copies of the American Anti-Slavery Almanac, published in 1836-37-36. In March, 1830 the Almanac states that a white man named George Storrs was arrested for delivering an anti-slavery address in a New Hampshire church. For the commission of this crime,

catechism which if in the form of questions and answers, which explains that this woman is killing her children rather than lose them grow up in the bonds of slavery.

Of course in dealing with this subject, one cannot omit the life of the Great Emancipator. Gumby has a small pamphlet, published in 1865, which prints in full the famous Cooper Union speech of Lincoln. Perhaps some readers remember the sad tragedy of Lincoln's death. They may recall that the newspapers printed special editions edged in black mourning. These editions are regarded as rarities today because so few are left.

French containing instructions from Toussaint L'Overture to his generals, an original letter written by Coleridge-Taylor, the famous Negro composer, and a manuscript by the eminent Reverend Alexander Crummell entitled, "Concerning Myself."

Whether all of our readers are interested in pugilism, I do not know, but Gumby's scrap book on Negro pugilists is worthy of note, aside from the sporting interest. When Jack Johnson (whom Gumby ardently admires) was signed to box Jeffries, the whole country was in a furor.

On turning the pages of this particular book we came across a clipping taken from a New York newspaper. The article was intended to show the difference between Johnson and Jeffries, from the view point of science. It was illustrated by showing the profiles of both men as compared with the profile of an ape. Jeffries had to be further developed from his ape type, while every street was put upon an alleged similarity between Johnson and the ape. The inference was, that Jeffries was the more intelligent and would easily defeat his opponent. Of course the result of that memorable contest at Reno is well known.

The continent of Africa has always aroused the interest of the outside world. Alexander Gumby has a huge geography devoted to a description of Africa. This book was published in 1670, which makes it two hundred and fifty-nine years old

Gumby has in his possession also many relics of former usage. In this picture appears an exotic looking vase and an exceedingly old-style piano.

Gumby has several old theatre bills which were used to advertise the appearance of "Mr. Ira Aldridge."

While we are on the subject of the theatre, it would be well to note the scrap book on "The Negro Drama." To all lovers of the theatre this book would prove a rare treat. It is filled with clippings concerning the accomplishments of Williams and Walker, Cole and Johnson, Florence Mills, Les Whipper, Ira Aldridge, Bert Williams, and a host of others. One may summon the whole panorama of Negro performers merely by going through this compilation.

Such is the very brief story of Gumby's "History of the Negro," in

Here appears a much-cherished announcement of an appearance of the great Negro actor, Ira Aldridge, in Othello. Ira Aldridge will be remembered as one of the most eminent dramatic interpreters of Shakespeare of his time.

no longer his hobby, but, as he terms it, scrap-books are his passion. He has gone to the Congressional Library in Washington, to the public library in New York, and he has studied the scrap-books of the late Theodore Roosevelt, so as to discover new ideas for the safe keeping of his clippings.

His enthusiasm has become so contagious that every Sunday his studio at 2144 Fifth Avenue, New York City, is filled with friends discussing Negro achievements. At the present time, they are preparing the "Gumby Studio Quarterly," which will be "A Journal of Criticism, Arts and Opinions Concerning the Negro."

This is another view of the interior of the famous Gumby Library.

scrap-book form. This description by no means gives the complete story, for to do so, would fill a small book. Consider, however, the pleasure and profit that Gumby has received from his books. They are

This picture indicates how systematically Gumby's remarkable collections of facts is filed.

Our friend was very fortunate to secure twelve issues of the *New York Herald*, published from the time Lincoln was shot, until the day he was buried at Springfield, Illinois.

Letters of great personages are always interesting to succeeding generations. The writers often reveal traits and angles of their character that are little known to the general public. While looking through the various folios, we saw several original letters written by Negroes whose names are famous. There was an epistle penned by the redoubtable Frederick Douglass, when he was in an angry mood, due to some deception practiced on him. He refers to his deceiver as a scoundrel. Gumby has an original message written in

It was dedicated to Charles II of England and contains an explorer's account of the Dark Continent. Naturally it is of no value today as a geography, but as a historical item, it is very rare.

The American Negro is rapidly being recognized as a powerful factor. Just recently certain London producers announced that Paul Robeson will play Othello in that famous play of Shakespeare's. Do not forget, however, that pioneer colored actor, Ira Aldridge, who played the part of Othello many years ago. He was a famous thespian at a time when only white actors were considered competent to play Negro parts. Consequently Aldridge's rendition of the part was superior to many of the burnt-cork whites who essayed the role.

Below, is the book-plate which identifies the Gumby congeries.

Storrs was sentenced to three months at hard labor.

In another part of the Almanac, there is a picture of a Negro mother killing her children. Underneath the picture is a little

---

RHEUMATIC PAIN BANISHED QUICKLY

The quickest way to banish rheumatic pain of the joints and muscles, gout or neuralgia is to get at the source of the trouble and remove the cause. Realizing that, a well-known physician formulated Prescription C-2223 and successfully treated thousands of cases. This effective prescription attacks the trouble at its source by helping to clear the system of accumulated waste matter and toxic acids. That is why you get such quick relief. Ask your druggist for the large size bottle of Prescription C-2223 today. If you fail to get relief after taking this prescription as directed, return this bottle to the druggist from whom you purchased it and your money will be refunded.

ASK FOR PRESCRIPTION C-2223

of art, the collection is not representational. The collection presents a hermetic world: to have a representative collection is to have both the minimum and the complete number of elements necessary for an autonomous world—a world which is both full and singular, which has banished repetition and achieved authority.[114]

What, then, can we make of the Gumby scrapbooks, which exhibit an attention to seriality, context, and the relationships between the objects collected —all hallmarks of the collection—but that aim as well to be encyclopedic and authoritative, not at the expense of, but through repetition, chance juxtaposition, coincidence, even redundancy? The scrapbooks are not nostalgic or welded to the past. The seventy or so categories around which they are organized include lynching, boxing, motion pictures, Countee Cullen, nightclubs, Jean Toomer, and Harlem. Neither are they so self-consciously artistic, playful, and present-directed as, say, Van Vechten's homoerotic scrapbook collages.

True to form, the scrapbooks document their own creation and situate Gumby and his work as central to African American and Harlem history. There are four volumes (numbers 35–38) on the Gumby Book Studio, 2144 Fifth Avenue, between 131st and 132nd streets, which functioned as a library, rare book store, literary salon, and, briefly, the publisher of an arts quarterly. The volumes on the studio itself are littered with correspondence, letters, envelopes, telegrams, invitations, photographs, and, at one point, the typescript of an article on Gumby's collections written by John W. Douglas, layered over photographs of the studio—and then the multiple printings of the article in various African American newspapers across the country. "Let those who consider the keeping of scrap-books a children's pastime pay attention to this story of Alexander Gumby," the article opens—and then reiterates again and again in the opening of the reprinted text on the scrapbook pages that follow.

The article depicts a self-conscious "race man" who has taken on the Herculean task of documenting the African American past. Though Gumby had begun simply by collecting "little items that he thought worth saving," he soon discovered that "Negroes, even those relatively well-informed, had a very meager knowledge of Negro history. . . ." Realizing this, "he decided to collect all of the items he could regardless as to whether they referred to the past, present or future of the Negro race." That idea was the basis of the Gumby collection a history of the Negro depicted in scrapbooks.[115] As Gumby tells it, in a brief essay published in 1951 at the request of the Columbia University library to which he donated his collection, the process began serendipitously—and much subject to chance. He began gathering clippings that interested him and eventually decided to organize them into scrapbooks; but "without experience in arranging such a vast amount of miscellaneous material," he writes, he "naturally made a botch of it"; so he took the

The Gumby Book Studio. Page from scrapbook no. 35, L. S. Alexander Gumby Scrapbooks.
Courtesy of Rare Book and Manuscript Library, Butler Library, Columbia University.

scrapbooks apart and remade them, this time classifying the material into groups.[116] It was later still that Gumby reorganized all the clippings once again and began his famous "Negroana" collection, first as a single scrapbook on "Negro items," eventually as a series. He rearranged clippings often, finally choosing loose-leaf binders to house the clippings because the pages could be easily reordered, materials could be added, and new themes could emerge.

Gumby had opened his bookstore in the mid-1920s, at the height of the New Negro Renaissance, with the help of his close friend and probable lover, the wealthy white stockbroker Charles W. Newman, with whom he shared a "staunch friendship... which as the years went by, grew ever stronger."[117] By the end of the decade, Gumby had assembled a collection of three hundred scrapbooks—some "devoted to Broadway," others to famous personages, such as Theodore Roosevelt, Abraham Lincoln, the Prince of Wales. By 1930, however, Newman had lost his money in the stock market crash. Gumby, sick with tuberculosis and "having spent all of his salaries in his studio and on artists (for his artists were his protégés, with all the expenses thereby entailed)," closed the bookstore down and took up residence in the City Hospital on Welfare Island.[118] Four years later, barely recovered, he went to retrieve his possessions from the basement of a stranger who had promised to protect them in exchange for "certain first editions," only to discover that most of his books and valuable Americana had been sold or given away and that a flood in the basement had turned many of his scrapbooks into mush. As the "Negro" collection "suffered the least damage," Gumby removed "all Negro items from scrapbooks that were not essentially Negroic and [added] them to the Negro collection."[119] It was those scrapbooks he continued to enlarge and revise.

Contingency, revision, and repetition actually come to constitute something like a formal logic of the scrapbooks. A case in point: Rather than responding to the Fiske University questionnaire about "Negro family life," Gumby pasted the whole of it in a scrapbook—along with the envelope it was sent in, and follow-up postcards reminding him that he had not yet responded to the inquiry. The questionnaire asks its recipients to "please give any memories of achievements of your ancestors which have been a source of family pride." By turning the material survey into a collectible, Gumby suggests that the questions being asked—the very fact of their being asked, the laying bare of what is askable—are more important than any data about Negro life and memory such a survey could produce. In preserving the questionnaire, and the means through which it circulates, rather than any so-called data it might glean, he performs an implicit critique of the progressive and objectivist historicist project of intellectuals such as Du Bois, Locke, Schomburg, and Woodson. (Du Bois, for instance, was no fan of scrapbooks. He once disparaged Charles Johnson's 1927 collection *Ebony and Topaz* by calling it a "sort of big scrapbook, quite without unity, even of race.")[120] Yet if Du Bois and Locke wanted to rewrite what they saw as the "history of the race," and younger writers like Thurman, Nugent, Hurston, and Hughes desire to build "temples for tomorrow," without having their accomplishments and even selves be subsumed into—or worse, be responsible for—a larger social discourse they see as self-evacuating, Gumby suggests that it is the disunity and nonlinearity of the scrapbook as a vernacular form that is most appropriate to the task of narrating the African American past.[121] A scrapbook history follows the make-do logic of a quilt stitched together from scraps or wall decorations made from the "glut of gaudy calendars, wall pockets and advertising lithographs" that Hurston observes "in the homes of the average Negro."[122] Such a history performs its relationship to the past through the mediation of the part-object, the remnant or scrap, the non-figurative figurative, which is subject to a "repetitive structure" that Patricia Yaeger sees as haunting southern fiction written by African Americans, but that must be seen as haunting black artists' attempts to represent Harlem as well.[123] The scrap is portable, ghostly, and eminently efficacious: It makes due with—and in doing so remakes—the materials at hand.[124]

Left unsaid, of course, in Gumby's inclusion of the blank questionnaire is the obvious fact that for him it cannot help but be unanswerable; his strongest attachments, like those shared by Harlem's other gay residents, were not represented by a questionnaire concerned with biological and marital ties. Finally, in preserving the envelope alongside its contents, which Gumby does here and elsewhere in the scrapbooks, he foregrounds his participation in the circulation of correspondence and production of commodities. The letters and clippings are haunted by the means through which they circulate and by the fact of circulation itself, the serial passage of texts from hand to hand, body to body.

The serial nature of Gumby's scrapbooks, both as artifacts and in the way the contents are ordered, implies a temporality that looks simultaneously to the future and the past. Viewed this way, the present seems to lack any presence at all, since the now of multiple presents is narrated in the scraps, preserved with an eye to their future importance and arranged vis-à-vis a context that can be produced only retrospectively, recognized after, as a result of the addition of a new artifact, it ceases to be. Yet if Gumby's scrapbooks fill in the gaps of the past through an expulsion of the present, they also herald the present by narrating intersecting series of moments that are thematically arranged, boxing, for instance, lynching, Harlem. And in this way the present is preserved and made thing-like.

Read as a whole, then—and this is no small task, and not even desirable—the scrapbooks become less like souvenirs than something of a precursor to postwar "assemblings"[125] and perhaps most explicitly to the artist Ray Johnson's "New York Correspondence School" works.[126] Throughout the 1960s,

Johnson sent out strips of new or recycled drawings or images to friends and acquaintances, asking the recipients to "add to the drawing" and mail it back; from those returned scraps he produced a collage, which bore the traces of multiple collaborators. "Let us not forget that 'Correspondances' is [also] the name of one of Baudelaire's poems," writes the conceptual artist Marc Bloch of Johnson's work. "In his *L'art Romantique*, Baudelaire says correspondences are 'the affinities which exist between spiritual states and states in nature; those people who are aware of these correspondences become artists and their art is of value only in so far as it is capable of expressing these mysterious relationships.'"[127] To situate Gumby —and Thurman—in this lineage is to suggest that they too adhere to an artform that privileges collaboration and communication (letters, that litter) over solitary artistic production. Their art of "correspondances" is a queer art, one that performs more than expresses those "mysterious relationships" that emerge among and between texts, ideas, and people.

In this context, however, these relationships are permeated by urban consumer culture and its institutions.[128] Certainly, for Gumby, who ran a "studio," bookstore, salon, and literary magazine, an ideal of a solitary, self-reliant artist isolated from the exigencies of commerce held little importance. Friends and acquaintances sent inscribed clippings to Gumby and, when he was sick, several kept up the production of scrapbooks in his stead. And Gumby was more than a bit indebted to the circulation of mail. A sometime butler and bellhop, Gumby took the postal examination in 1926; like Thurman and Bontemps before him, he became a post office clerk. With the income garnered from this position, an income generously supplemented by funds from Newman, Gumby rented the second floor storefront that was to become his salon and began to buy up "his eternal first editions, newspapers from which to clip articles, and, every now and then, a Chinese vase or cloisonné samovar."[129]

Though collaborative, neither Gumby's scrapbooks nor Thurman's blue-penciled writings can be considered collectivist works in the sense that we might read Nancy Cunard's encyclopedic and self-consciously Socialist *Ne-*

Correspondence addressed to Alexander Gumby on the Gumby Book Studio. Page from scrapbook no. 35, L. S. Alexander Gumby Scrapbooks.
Courtesy of Rare Book and Manuscript Library, Butler Library, Columbia University.

Untitled (f.x. profumo) by Ray Johnson. Letter postmarked 1948, large panel c. 1953–59, other elements c. 1970–80, mixed media collage, 20½ x 15½ x 1½ inches.
The Estate of Ray Johnson, Courtesy of Richard L. Feigen & Co., New York.

gro anthology from the same period. Gumby, even more than Thurman, was an elitist, a dandy. Gumby, writes Nugent, was "a sport. Fancy clothes, a perennial walking stick, pale yellow kid gloves, and a diamond stick-pin helped make him the Beau Brummel of his particular little group. He was a member of this group who was most cognizant of and familiar with the various and sundry arts, artists, and their lives."[130] Like Johnson after him and to a much greater degree than Thurman, Gumby emphasizes the conversational, even promiscuous, nature of his work. *Promiscuous* is the term that Wayne Koestenbaum uses in *Double Talk* to describe the homoerotic and evasive nature of modern male writers' collaboration. "Men who collaborate engage in a metaphorical sexual intercourse," writes Koestenbaum, "and the text they balance between them is alternately the child of their sexual union, and a shared woman."[131] Gumby's work, which entailed much more than producing scrapbooks, for, after all, he was a patron, a salon host, "the Great God Gumby" in Nugent's sardonic description, depended upon and commemo-

BLUE-PENCILED PLACE **161**

rated a series of successful seductions. Readers, spectators, artists, investors, hangers-on became participant-producers and collectors. Each in turn left a trace.

Gumby collected people as well as objects. It is precisely this quality that distinguishes his art of collecting, a self-acknowledged obsession, from the insanity of hoarding, collecting run amok. If hoarding is the specter that haunts any collector, for Gumby, perhaps, it came closer to home. Four stories figure prominently in press clippings in the pages of Gumby's two scrapbooks on Harlem (nos. 41 and 42). Depictions of the death and funeral of Florence Mills in 1927; articles that describe the 1935 and 1943 riots; and the bizarre 1947 saga of the eccentric, white Collyer brothers, Harlem's "ghosty men," who died buried under decades of junk.

the problem with collecting

A central problem: How does one set limits on collecting? Collecting, like writing, requires a sharp editorial hand. At each excision from the text, I feel simultaneously the pangs of loss and the euphoria that accompanies my extrication from the burden of words, from the burden of stuff.

Still, I am bombarded by letters and emails. From archivists, librarians, photographers, collectors, and the eccentric legal progeny of long-dead artists. "Due to equipment problems, we are unable to provide you with the prints and negatives . . . you ordered," one archivist writes. "Instead, we will provide you with digital images. . . . We have reassessed the charges as follows. . . . This amount is for imaging only. Permissions fees are issued separately." Writes another, "I've spoken with our permissions manager and he's preparing a contract for the use of this image, but needs to know where it will be published. Could you let me know the book's title, publisher, and print run if you have that information, and also where the image will appear?" Inevitably, there is a series of refusals: "This notice does NOT grant permission. Please be assured that we have carefully considered your request." No explanation is given and my later pleas on the telephone are to no avail; the conversation ends with a terse rejection: "Lady, this phone call is over." Collecting and writing are not enough. It takes a year—and a large grant—to get the right (or refusal) to print all this stuff.

SACRIFICING LUST

The two brothers, Homer and Langley Collyer, supposed descendents of Pilgrims, had lived in the twelve-room brownstone at 2078 Fifth Avenue near 128th Street since 1909, when Harlem was still a fashionable white enclave. Over the decades, the brothers stayed put, becoming increasingly isolated, infamous as the eccentric "ghosty men" or "hermits of Harlem." On March 21, 1947, Homer was found dead. He had gone blind in 1934 and was later crippled by rheumatism, rarely venturing out of the house in the last decade of his life. Langley, always the stranger of the two, had become his caretaker; Langley wandered the Harlem streets in tattered clothes, procuring food from garbage cans and buying oranges and meat for the special diet they had devised that was supposed to restore Homer's sight. But when the police uncovered Homer's body, Langley was nowhere to be found.

Days and weeks passed as two dozen policemen and New York City Housing Department workers excavated the mess and searched through the Collyer house for Langley—or his corpse.[132] Newspapers photographed, categorized, and quantified the odd objects found, as if they were on some kind of treasure hunt. "What is This?" the caption of an article pasted in Gumby's scrapbook reads. "A Cop is puzzled by his find. It is said to be an old potato peeler." The list of loot accrued: A baby carriage, radio loudspeaker, steering wheel, an automobile of ancient vintage, a twenty-year-old newspaper front page, "4 Violins, A Cornet, Trombone and Cello"; a two-headed baby in formaldehyde; thirteen mantel clocks; sheet music; an early X-ray machine; two human skulls. Finally, the findings were no longer described but quantified by weight: "Collyer House Yields 26 More Tons of Debris" reads one headline; "Junk Tonage Passes 100 at Collyer House" reads a second. Ultimately, the twelve-room house was emptied of 180 tons of stuff.[133] On April 8, Langley was finally found ten feet from where his brother had died. Turns out he had died first, trapped between a bedspring and a chest of drawers, felled by one of the many booby traps he had engineered throughout the house. "A suitcase, three metal bread boxes and bundles of newspapers rested upon the partly decomposed body, gnawed by rats," reported the *New York Times*.[134] From the many tons of junk taken from the house, 150 items were auctioned off, at a final price tag of $1,892.50. Six months later the Collyer house was condemned and torn down.[135] For years afterward all that was left was a litter-strewn lot. Today it is a park.

In documenting the story, Gumby did what he always had: Narrated events that caused Harlem to talk—and had kept it talking since the 1930s. But its prominence in the scrapbooks, as a kind of bookend to the promise of black Harlem posited in story after story in the first Harlem scrapbook, also seems to serve as a warning. The Collyers, two bachelor brothers descended from Pilgrims and dependent on each other in a way more incestuous than fraternal, performed more perfectly and completely than Gumby, or even Van Vechten, the encyclopedic promise of collecting everything. And in doing so they exposed the risk that all collectors run: When does collecting, even acquisition, become hoarding? Benjamin stated this problematic well: "There is in the life of a collector a dialectical tension between the poles of disorder and order. Naturally, his existence is tied to many other things as

The Collyer Hoard
Yields No Key to the Hermitage Mystery

WHAT'S THIS? Cop is puzzled by his find. It is said to be an old fashioned potato peeler. Searchers found no trace of Langley Collyer. Neighbors saw him last on Thursday.

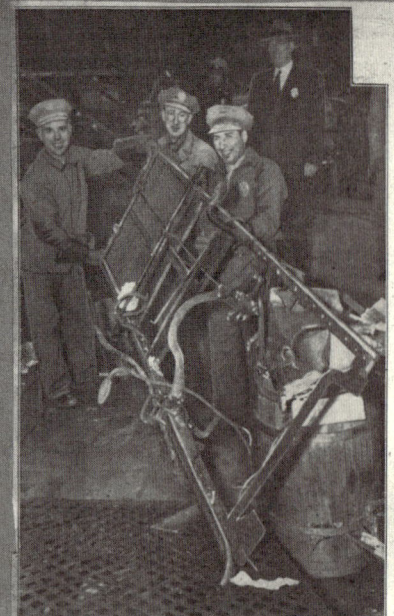

CHASSIS of an automobile of ancient vintage comes out of the basement. Searchers on Monday found a steering wheel. Cellar was searched for secret passages yesterday.

JUNKMAN'S DELIGHT. A cop catalogues some of the Collyer treasures piled on front porch. The junk includes parts of a baby carriage, an old suitcase, radio loud speaker and several old ba's.

BROWSING in book-lined library, a searcher looks over titles. "In Darkest Africa" and "Babylon and Nineveh" were two of them. Many of the books were on technical subjects.

FRONT PAGE news on June 13, 1927, was Lindbergh's New York welcome. Collyers probably never suspected they'd be front page news 20 years later.

well: to a very mysterious relationship to ownership . . . ; also, to a relationship to objects which does not emphasize their functional, utilitarian value —that is, their usefulness—but studies and loves them as the scene, the stage, of their fate. . . . Everything remembered and thought, everything conscious, becomes the pedestal, the frame, the base, the lock of his property."[136] Hoarding might be seen as acquisition without remembrance, fetishistic acquisition rather than acquisition with love. While collecting is directed toward pleasure in presence, a pleasure that is yet more full because the past is interpolated within it, hoarding eschews presence and the present; it seeks to preserve the past whole, unchanged indefinitely so as to stave off some as yet undefined future need; to stave off the future itself.

In the late 1930s, when the Collyer brothers gained notoriety in newspapers, they seemed to embody a threat more culturally resonant than what might be dismissed as individual eccentricity. Not accidentally, local rumor had it that the Collyers hoarded not just stuff, but cash. The *New York Times* reported in 1939 that the brothers were said to be wealthy and hid money in their house.[137] This was no incidental observation. The hoarding of cash was much on the minds of economists and politicians in the 1930s and early 1940s. Fearful of bank runs, Presidents Hoover, Roosevelt, and Truman all warned at points in their presidencies against hoarding. Hoover instituted National Thrift Week in January 1932 to encourage the "wise provision against future needs" but sent a message preempting criticism that he was encouraging hoarding.[138] The following month Hoover issued a "Statement on the Hoarding of Currency," which read:

The Collyer Hoard. Page from volume 41 of the L. S. Alexander Gumby Scrapbooks. Courtesy of Rare Book and Manuscript Library, Butler Library, Columbia University.

Collyer Brothers Park, Harlem, 2005. © 2006 by Joseph M. Scandura IV.

> There is now a patriotic opportunity for our citizens unitedly to join in this campaign against depression. Given such patriotic cooperation we can secure a definite upward movement and increase in employment. That service is to secure the return of hoarded money back into the channels of industry. During the past year and with an accelerated rate during the last few months a total of over 1,300 millions of money has been hoarded. That sum is still outstanding.[139]

For Hoover, hoarding gets configured not as saving but as debt. Two weeks later, Hoover reported an "entire turn in the tide," with $34 million returned to circulation.[140] But Hoover, still steeped in classical economics, had difficulty making the shift to John Maynard Keynes's view of saving, which the economist had begun to lay out in lectures in the United States in 1931. Keynes argued that saving was not the means through which one increases capital, as it had been in the economics of Adam Smith (and Hoover), but was driven by hoarding.[141] By 1933, Franklin D. Roosevelt, whose policies were much influenced by Keynesian economics, made the ills of hoarding (which he called an "exceedingly unfashionable pastime") the subject of his first Fireside Chat.[142] Later that year, Roosevelt issued several executive orders that prohibited the hoarding and exporting of gold; and following the outbreak of war in Europe in 1937, he declared a prohibition on the hoarding of sugar. Somewhat ineloquently, in a June 1945 news conference, before mentioning prisoners of war or relief efforts, Harry Truman declared, "It is a crime to—a terrible crime, in my opinion, to find these people who are hoarding money and living off the black markets, and things of that sort, when the sons of the rest of the population are out getting killed to save the country."[143] (Presumably he was against hoarding, not the finding of hoarders.) For the individual consumer, hoarding becomes both anti-American and antipatriotic.

According to Marx, "In order that gold may be held as money, and made to form a hoard, it must be prevented from circulating, or from dissolving into the means of purchasing enjoyment. The hoarder sacrifices the lusts of his flesh to the fetish of gold."[144] As Barbara Spackman observes, "Wealth is dependent upon exchange, so that what appears to be, in hoarding, an increase in wealth is in fact its decrease."[145] For Marx, capital relies on unceasing exchange, constant motion through circulation. Hoarding, by contrast, petrifies this motion. The hoarder comes to value money (or, by extension, a collectible, a letter, an artifact) not for its symbolic nature—as the means through which to mediate a process of exchange—but as a material object in itself. "For Marx, the miser's aim and the capitalist's are the same: both seek only to accumulate money," writes Matthew Rowlinson:

> For both, the antithesis of this aim would be to spend money on a commodity for use, whose value would drop finally out of circulation. Nonetheless, the formula by which Marx asserts this similarity of the capitalist and the miser also differentiates between them. Whereas the miser madly believes that money will magically accumulate (by breeding?) if it is hoarded, the capitalist rationally understands that money only accumulates if it is thrown away.[146]

Hoarding is constituted by a refusal to circulate and therefore might be seen as the antithesis of promiscuity, which is marked by excessive circulation. In psychoanalytic terms, the introjective quality of collecting constitutes it as an act of mourning, whereas hoarding is a melancholic act, associated with anal eroticism and the primitive.[147] Read in conjunction with Marx, however, hoarding might be seen to be associated not so much with anal eroticism as with the prohibition or sacrifice of anal desire: "The hoarder sacrifices the lusts of his flesh to the fetish of gold." For both Gumby and Van Vechten, foregrounding the conversational, interactive, even promiscuous aspects of their collections allows them to voraciously collect without evacuating the erotic from the mix. Indeed, the opening spread of the third of Van Vechten's erotic scrapbooks, its "Invitation Basket" flaunts the promiscuous ends to which he hopes his collection will be availed. Such is the promise

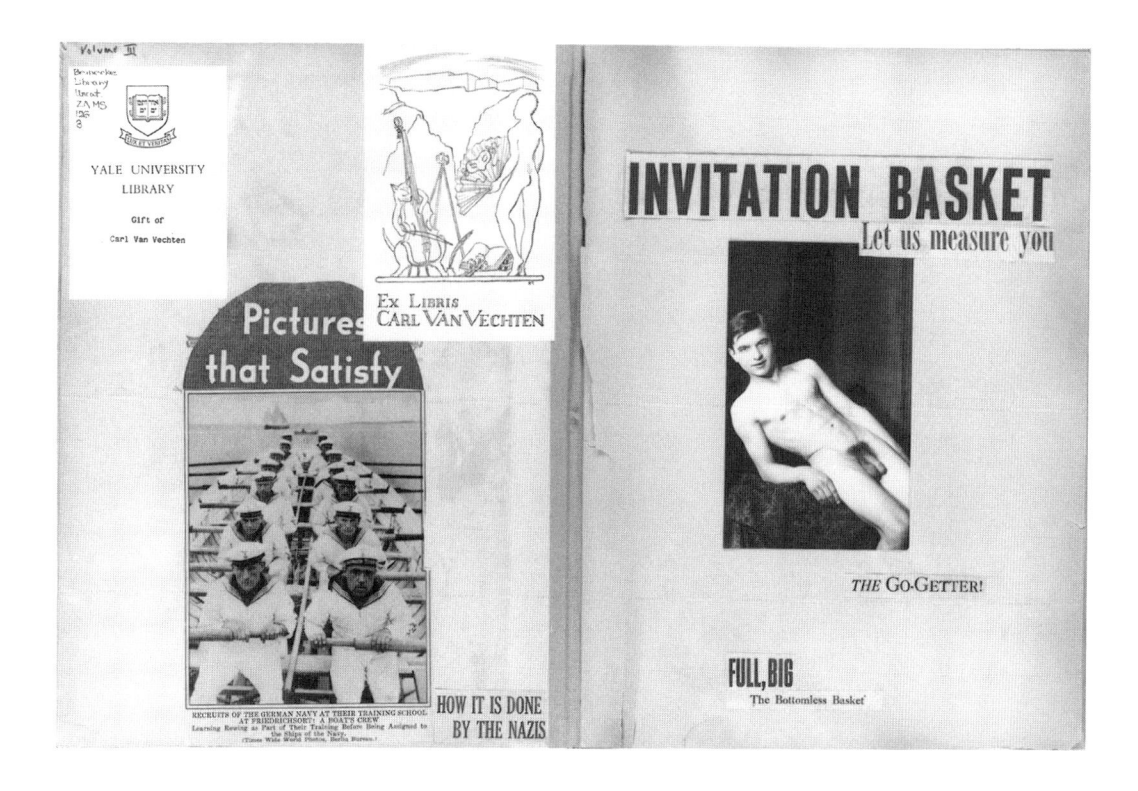

Pages 1–2 of Carl Van Vechten's Scrapbook III.

© Bruce Kellner. Courtesy of Yale Collection of American Literature, Beinecke Rare Book and Manuscript Library.

of definitive collections—they exist in order that their contents may induce the desire of multiple handlers. The more stringent an archive's prophylactic measures, the more desirable the collection might be said to be. Gumby's and Van Vechten's balancing acts between selective acquisition, promiscuous circulation, and primal acts of hoarding also suggest a kind of flirting with and undermining of modernist conceptions of the primitive. Where better to expose and resignify the so-called primitive urges of hoarding and promiscuity (both, I might add, stereotypically associated with blackness and femininity) than by situating them at the most elite and white of institutions, Columbia and Yale?

Gumby, the autodidact and dandy, reconfigures the amateur, vernacular, need we say primitivist production of history—a scrapbook—into the definitive history of African American life. And for Van Vechten, who was never forgiven by many of Harlem's elite for publishing *Nigger Heaven*, the creation of the James Weldon Johnson Memorial Collection of Negro Arts and Letters at Yale was payback of a different sort: He rejects the critique that he traded on racist conceptions of the primitive by claiming and remaking hoarding productive, reintroducing it as a central component of archiving and situating it in the province of the Protestant elite.

The *Times* article that describes the discovery of Langley ends ominously, as if the brothers' Pilgrim roots and bachelorhood provide an explanation: "The brothers, descendants of a family that came to America in 1640 on the

BLUE-PENCILED PLACE **167**

Speedwell, have at least forty cousins surviving them. They never married." Gumby donated his scrapbooks a few years after the Collyers died. "His newspaper clippings are still, despite the many hundreds which he lost during the five year internment in the tubercular hospital, more complete than even the Schomburg collection at the 135th Street Public Library," surmised Nugent. "He is an ardent anti-everything, and being biologically a complete revolutionary, he is fundamentally, essentially and totally correct in all of his judgments."[148]

scraps

Fragment of a March 1935 article in the *New York Times* pasted in scrapbook no. 41 of the L. S. Alexander Gumby Collection of the American Negro:

> The proprietor of a Chinese laundry at 367 Lenox Avenue shared the fears of other store owners on the street as hoodlums raged along the sidewalks shattering windows with bricks and stones.
>
> Then he noticed that Negro shopkeepers were painting on their display windows, in huge white letters, the word "Colored" to warn off the rioters. He adopted the idea and up went a sign: "Me colored too."
>
> The window was smashed.

THE DISORDER

It is, after all, disorder that makes possible the writing of history. And it is through disorder that new orders—even newness—become licensed to emerge. This is why disorder is both central to modernist projects and why it always seems to clog up the modernist machine. It is not without irony, then, that in the days after the 1935 riot in Harlem, the delicate term *disorder* became the description of choice. And disorder was seen as the cause. Over and over again in the last days of March, newpapers debated the cause of the riot, how to describe it, and whether or not race was a factor in the uprising. "The Harlem problem is a racial problem only to the extent that racial factors have intensified depression evils," observe the editors of the *New York Post* on March 30, 1935. "The disorders there cannot be properly termed race riots. They were rather a miniature uprising by the most depressed section of New York's unemployed."[149] One bit of advice the newspaper offers: "Clean up Harlem's rackets."

To be sure, disorder was not simply euphemism. A 1933 article in the Unemployment Council's newspaper, *Hunger Fighter*, laments, "Rain pours through the ceiling. Rats dart from great gaps in the walls, windows are smashed, sickness flourishes especially because the garbage is never collected from the dumbwaiters. These are some of the horrors of the Negro worker's life disclosed by the Upper Harlem Unemployed Council after canvassing only three houses at 16, 18, 20 West 116 Street."[150] In fact, the Mayor's Commission on the Conditions in Harlem estimated that at the time of the Harlem disorder "10,000 blacks lived in cellars and basements with no toilets or running water."[151] If economic depression was not new to Harlem, after the stock market crash it hit Harlem harder and longer than it did the rest of New York. Cheryl Lynn Greenberg observes that "while applications [for relief] by [New York] city residents rose 75 percent between 1929 and 1931, black applications tripled. Between 20,000 and 50,000 residents of Harlem were unemployed."[152] In 1936, George Schuyler comments, Harlem was a "checkerboard of crowded flats between an open sewer and a cliff."[153]

"Without exception the tenements of Harlem are filthy," writes Adam Clayton Powell, Jr., in the second of three articles he published in the *Post* at the end of March 1935 following what he called the "recent disturbances in Harlem":

> Landlords refuse to make janitors keep their houses clean, and how can they ask them to when he hires the man and his family for nothing per month except a basement to exist in and tells them to clean six floors, take care of the sidewalk and backyard, haul the garbage, stoke the furnace and make minor repairs?[154]

He begins the last article in the series with an even more evocative question:

> Have you ever eaten garbage? Dined, but not wined, on bones sucked dry by strangers' mouths, bread soaked in the juices of a garbage can, maybe a rotten tomato as a relish and a partly devoured orange to top off the meal, in which some of the pith still remains? If not, my friends, you are not a member of the new social "odor."
>
> Men and women comb the streets of pauper Harlem looking for cast off food. This I and others have seen.[155]

The slippery slope between ownership and disorder became central to the debates and central to prescriptives for repair. It is not insignificant, in other words, that the riot—or, rather, disorder—began with the accusation of a petty theft.

The story that incited the riot went this way: A young black boy had been beaten to death at Kresge's department store on 125th Street and 7th Avenue after being caught stealing a cheap penknife. Only part of the story was factual. But that was enough. For a sixteen-year-old Puerto Rican boy, Lino Rivera, had indeed been detained by Kresge's white store employees for shoplifting a pocketknife. In the struggle, he bit one of the employees on the thumb. The manager called an ambulance for the bleeding man. And the clerk who had been bitten, according to an account in the *New Republic*, screamed at the boy, "'I'm going to take you down to the basement and beat the hell out

Clippings on the 1935 Harlem riot in no. 41 of the L. S. Alexander Gumby Scrapbooks.
Courtesy of Rare Book and Manuscript Library, Butler Library, Columbia University.

of you!'"[156] The store employees did take Rivera down into the basement, but there, by most accounts, he wasn't beaten. He returned the knife, was released through the back door, and ran home.

Upstairs the story was different. Watching the struggle, a woman screamed that the boy was being hurt, and the crowd, hearing the threats, was outraged. White policemen, who had a long history of harassing black residents in Harlem, tried to break up the crowd, making matters only worse. The boy had not been seen again after being taken to the basement. Then, out of nowhere, an ambulance arrived at the store, which seemed to all but confirm the rumors. Forced by the police, the crowd dispersed, but only briefly. By 5:30 so many people had gathered in front of the store it was forced to close. Two hours later, the Young Communist League dispersed pamphlets claiming that a twelve year old who had been accused of stealing a piece of candy had been beaten to near death by the store's "special guard." The Young Liberators, a local political group, issued a leaflet that provocatively declared that a woman who had come to the badly beaten boy's defense had had her arm broken. Someone threw a rock through the store window, and the rioting and looting began.[157]

In the end, four people died, at least one shot by the police, and dozens were hospitalized. The largely white businesses in the area suffered damages in the hundreds of thousands of dollars. Afterward, it was agreed, the incident was simply the tinder that incited an explosion of anger long sublimated and long overdue. Mayor Fiorello LaGuardia's Commission of Inquiry, made up of "leading experts" from both the black and white communities, argued finally, "This sudden breach of public order was the result of a highly emotional situation among the colored people of Harlem, due in large part to the nervous strain of years of unemployment and insecurity."[158] Black resentment, according to the commission, lay in a history of police brutality, poverty, unfair rents, overcrowding, discrimination in work and school, "inadequate institutional care," and numerous other infractions. "It was not the unfortunate rumors," Alain Locke later wrote in *Survey Graphic*, "but the state of mind on which they fell."[159]

This state of mind was a retrospective one to be sure. But what was being remembered was more than lost promise or lost youth—but loss, as Freud might say, in a more ideal sense.[160] The city of refuge had become the city of refuse. Perhaps it always already was. In Hazel Campbell's story about the 1935 riot, written a few months after it occurred, a character remarks slyly, "Nigger heaven has turned into a living hell now." Then he is swallowed up by the crowd and crushed.[161]

The Harlem riot was not solely an action of spontaneous collective outrage, as McKay observes, it was directed toward a specific target, the stores on 125th Street. For him the reason was clear: The merchants on 125th Street had refused to hire black employees.[162] They had already been picketed by the Negro Industrial and Clerical Alliance; a Citizens League for Fair Play had been formed and endorsed by sixty-two organizations, including eighteen Harlem churches. The riot was in many senses, then, an economic revolt. A fight for the ability to work—and to shop. Indeed, underlying the riot in part (as it was part of the impetus behind the contemporary building of the Harlem U.S.A. mall) was the desire for a race-blind right to consume.[163] "The peculiar position of Negroes in America offers an opportunity," wrote Du Bois in 1935. "Negroes today cast probably 2,000,000 votes in a total of 40,000,000, and their vote will increase. . . . The consuming power of 2,800,000 Negro families has recently been estimated at $166,000,000 a month—a tremendous power when intelligently directed."[164]

Yet Du Bois, whose complete rejection of capitalism was still years away, did not fully understand the working people's plight. In the eyes of many of Harlem's poor, who could ill afford to buy food, much less the luxurious commodities they saw in shop windows, selling goods at an unaffordable price was not so different from the hoarding of gold. It was not consumers, or potential consumers, who had clogged up the system, but the shop owners who had stopped consumption in its tracks. As one resident explained in 1939 to Vivian Morris, who was taking a Life History for the WPA,

> An' I tell y'this. Some people gotta idea this was a race riot. I know it wuzn.' F'r instance during the evenin' a cullud liquor sore wuz busted into an' the guy who own the joint say he's cullud an' someone yells out. "He ain' no better, gittin' the gravy from us folk," so they goes on bustin' up the joint an' takin' out a bottle aliquor. What I'm tryin' t' say is that it wuzn' a question of culla. People wuz sore at the guys who lived ona gravy while they wuz starvin' t' death—[165]

Read through this lens, the riot might be seen as an attack on American capitalism and on the compulsory pursuit of private property. Looting necessarily attacks normative constructions of private ownership and also stages the breaking of these boundaries as revolt, not theft.

If one face of Harlem in Depression is that of the series, the mourner, the collector and the other that of the hoarder, disorder and mess, these facets of modern urban culture are inextricably linked. Disorder disrupts and in doing so makes it possible for new histories to be written and for ways of understanding the past to be revised. As both Hurston's Florida matrons and the Dadaists knew, hoards bring forth collections—refuse can be reused as ready-made—given the right context or frame.

It is as a result, in part, of the profligate collecting by Van Vechten and Gumby, for instance, that Harlem's history became ripe for rediscovery many years after the fact. In this, they were not alone. In the early 1980s, Bruce Nugent met Tom Wirth, who later became the executor of his estate. Perusing Wirth's collection of perfectly preserved "Afro-Americana," Nugent lent an eye to his own hoard of stuff: "I have the incurable habit of never throwing away things which more tidy people dispose of once they have finished using them," he explains in the introduction to the reissue of *Fire!!*. Discovered among his "paraphernalia" was

> a copy, battered and torn, of this ancient magazine [*Fire!!*] that, when I gave it to Tom to preserve in his inimitable way, triggered this present effort to share it with more people than the few who own the private collections or visit the closely guarded rarities in libraries. Langston, of course, and Langston's words—these come to mind. It was Langston who said that the Negro in America was like the phoenix and that some day he would rise from the fire to which America had consigned him.[166]

fourth series: surfacing

From Anita Scott Coleman's 1927 short story "Unfinished Masterpieces":

> Hand in hand, unmindful of her muddy ones, we skip around the old ramshackle house, back to the furthest corner of an unkempt yard, impervious to the tin cans, the ash-heap, the litter, the clutter that impedes our way, our eyes upon, our thoughts bent upon one small tin can. And row after row of mud. No, not mud—not merely mud, but things made out of mud. Row on row, drying in the sun.[167]

DOUBLE VISION

Four months before the riot, in the last week of December 1934, Wallace Thurman and Rudolph Fisher died. Because of the unfortunate proximity of their deaths, as well as their youth, verbal brilliance, and shared friends, they were to be forever connected in histories of Harlem—as symbols of its demise or of promise lost. Thurman died first at age thirty-two on December 22 "of tuberculosis in the charity ward, having just flown back to New York from Hollywood," where he had been writing several film treatments.[168] Fisher died unexpectedly four days later, at age thirty-seven, after his third operation for an "intestinal ailment."[169]

The first was a consumptive, then, who was predisposed to overconsume. Alcohol. Books. Sex. Conversation. "I've been reading far too much: Proust, Joyce, Dostoyevsky, Shakespeare's tragedies, Ibsen, Molière, Hardy, and Swift," wrote Thurman to Rapp in 1929. "Is it any wonder I'm depressed and enfeebled both mentally and physically?"[170] "I guess you know Wallace Thurman is in Welfare Hospital, with TB," wrote Hughes, then in Carmel, California, to Van Vechten in New York, on October 3, 1934. "If you have any new books or magazines that you don't want and have any way of sending them over to him, I know he'd like them. He says he doesn't get enough to read. (No wonder,—he can read eleven lines at a time. That's the way he kept his job at Macauley's as a reader.)."[171]

The second was a Brown- and Howard-educated doctor, a married family man who succumbed to cancer, contracted through overexposure to his own X-ray equipment, the very means by which he had diagnosed tuberculosis and sundry ailments in others. There were only 4 African Americans among the 1,250 specialists who were included on the *Journal of the American Medical Association*'s list of radiologists in 1934. Fisher was not on the list; the AMA had only recently begun to track and regulate medical specialization. He was, however, one of only a handful of African American radiologists in the early 1930s. By the year of his death, 1934, he had already closed down his private radiology practice, which had not been able to carry on through the

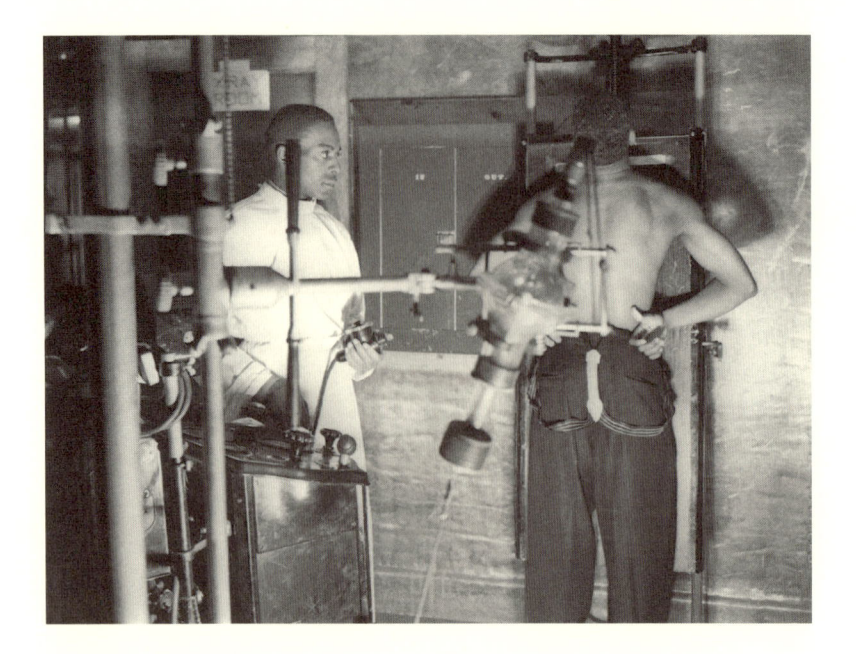

Technician taking an X ray in a Harlem clinic in the 1930s.
Library of Congress, Prints and Photographs Division, FSA/OWI Collection, LC-USW3-024010.

Depression economy, and was working for the New York City Health Department, not as a physician but as an X-ray technician.[172]

An editorial in the February 1935 issue of the National Urban League's journal, *Opportunity*, which memorializes the lives of the two men, describes Fisher's brilliance as an "engaging conversationalist, a competent pianist, a splendid singer, an able writer" but is reserved on the question of Fisher's placement in "the literature of his country"; it does not mention *Fire!!* or Thurman's *Infants of the Spring*. Instead, the article situates the two men within a historical trajectory of African American achievement as "young men who had begun the precipitous ascent to Parnassus . . . those of that eager hopeful company whose sudden emergence in the literary firmament gave birth to what has been designated the Renaissance of Negro Literature" and who "were undoubtedly the precursors of a number of yet unnamed [Negro writers] who even now eagerly gaze upon the distant summits of literary achievement."[173] Thurman's send-off in the *Amsterdam News* was less equivocal: "Perhaps it is too early to attempt an appraisal of his work in various fields of art," wrote Thurman's close friend Theophilus Lewis in his "Harlem Sketchbook" column. "I am ready to give out only one unqualified opinion. He wrote lousy poetry."[174] Immediately, Lewis revises his assessment: "On second thought, I hazard another opinion without reservation. As an editor, novelist and playwright, he was the most versatile of contemporary aframerican literary men."

In some ways, Thurman's and Fisher's nearly simultaneous deaths seemed a cruel repetition of the premature demise of Du Bois's firstborn son, who had died at eighteen months. (None of Du Bois's adopted sons—so many, a whole generation of writers—could fill the void of the child he called "the

Family portrait of W. E. B. Du Bois, Nina Gomer DuBois, and their son, Burghardt, who died at eighteen months from typhoid, circa 1897.
Special Collections and Archives, W. E. B. DuBois Library, University of Massachusetts, Amherst.

One." And Du Bois outlived almost all of them.) Could Du Bois have described "double-consciousness" without understanding the splitting of the self that constitutes remembrance? The death of a son fragments the body in time and space. Part of you is here. Now. Part of you remains. There. Then.

In other ways, the causes of Thurman's and Fisher's deaths can be seen as more broadly symptomatic of the economic collapse and social climate of Harlem in the mid-1930s. Both tuberculosis and cancer are, as Susan Sontag argues, engulfed by metaphors that interlace the economic with emotion and expressiveness.[175] Whereas tuberculosis has been considered a disease of "distintegration, febrilization, dematerialization," of weak will and self-destruction, excessive and hidden desire, and constitutional vulnerability, of too much feeling and too much consuming, she writes, cancer has been represented as a disease "of the failure of expressiveness," of the "repression of emotion," of the failure to consume enough.[176] While tuberculosis, with its excess, represents an inability to subscribe to the "necessity of regulated spending, saving, accounting, discipline," associated with earlier forms of capitalism, cancer becomes a disease associated with a kind of hoarding, a failure to master the late twentieth-century capitalist "irrational indulgence of desire."[177]

It seemed more than coincidence that two of Harlem's most promising writers died of diseases so steeped in the metaphoric dress of capital in the first years of the New Deal—at precisely the moment when economic discourse was beginning to shift in its understanding of the roles of spending and saving in the maintenance of capital. Indeed, the event was read by many who had been invested in the construction and promotion of the New Negro as a symptom of some kind of end or, retrospectively, as a precursor of the more ubiquitous ills made visible in the riot in March of the following year. Certainly, the divide between tuberculosis and cancer is not hard and fast. The writer of a 1929 article in the Ladies Home Journal, for instance, ascribes the supposed conquest of tuberculosis (at least among her middle-class readership) with improved mass production and, one would imagine, consumption as well: "What is the real cause of the conquest of tuberculosis?" she writes. "I believe we are justified in answering—the general distribution of cheap food supply. . . . Industrialism! Capitalism! That is what has conquered tuberculosis. Give capitalism credit for once. It gets enough blame."[178] Yet the discourse around cancer was not as richly wrought in the 1930s as it was in the 1970s when Sontag wrote about it. Cancer was still, in many ways, undiagnosed and unspeakable. (Fisher, remember, is said to have died of an "intestinal ailment.") In contrast, tuberculosis was undergoing a quite significant process of metaphorization at that time. The mayor's report on the 1935 riot concludes, in fact, that the uprising was partly due to high rates of disease. "In the Harlem area as in the country at large the Negro death rate is exorbitantly high in the very diseases in which lack of sanitation and medical care, and poverty are important factors," the writers of the report declare. Of these diseases, they rate tuberculosis as the worst. In 1934, when Gumby was recovering and Thurman dying from the disease, the report notes that the rate of tuberculosis for African Americans in New York was nearly four times that of whites, a disproportion that had grown progressively greater since 1910.[179] Harlem had its own so-called Lung Block, a phenomenon not usually associated with the Depression era, because so many cases had been found on that street.

Tuberculosis was contagious—it passed through bodies, oblivious to the boundaries that separated one from another. It thereby pushed to the limit the dissociative disregard for the bodily constraints of subject formation. To a larger extent than had been true in the nineteenth century, tuberculosis was both racialized and feminized and carried medical consequences and social stigma for those groups most affected: the working classes, immigrants, and African Americans. "A diagnosis of tuberculosis potentially made the patient vulnerable to intrusion, discrimination, or detention, depending upon his or her racial background and social status," writes Claudia Marie Calhoon.[180]

Into the 1930s, many physicians considered African Americans to be constitutionally more susceptible to the disease, as if the African American body were more permeable, less self-contained, and less able to ward off intrusions from without. In 1933, Du Bois felt compelled to write an article in The Crisis in order to correct this misconception, pointing out that "the susceptibility of Negroes to tuberculosis. . . . shows not any lack of 'racial' resistance, but the result of people who are poor and live in poor surroundings."[181] Two years later, in the wake of the 1935 riot, the surgeon and African American community leader Louis T. Wright published a similar article, also in The Crisis, arguing that the primary "factor controlling Negro Health," and tuberculosis in particular, was economic. "Colored people," he writes, "show high morbidity and mortality rates from [tuberculosis] alone due to bad housing, inability to purchase proper food in adequate amounts, having to do laborious work while ill, little or no funds for medical treatment."[182] While *Ladies Home Journal* may have felt justified in celebrating capitalism as the cure for tuberculosis, it was equally clear that capitalism was its cause.

The options for treatment for Africans Americans in New York were few. The East Harlem Health Center, which opened in 1920, was inadequate to meet demands; only a few people could afford to be treated in privately owned sanitariums that were open to African Americans, such as the black-owned Edgecombe and the short-lived Vincent Sanitarium.[183] Most of the services for those with tuberculosis were centered at Harlem Hospital, a veritable dump site that was overcrowded to the point that "patients were forced to give up their beds periodically; cots were placed in the hallways; couches were squeezed between beds; stretchers were used as bed; and some patients were forced to sleep on chairs"; and where

> the elevator which was installed for patients [had] been out of order for more than a year, patients are carried up and down the elevator which is used for garbage . . . the ventilating system in one of the kitchens had been out of order for over a year and . . . a refrigerator in one of the kitchens contained spoiled meat. The rubbish and roaches which were found in other units of the refrigerating system were characteristic of the general conditions of the kitchens which were cluttered with rubbish. In the yard of the hospital where garbage was stored, piles of rubbish furnished a happy hunting ground for scavengers in the neighborhood.[184]

To be sure, the disease was still metaphorically cloaked in its old artistic garb, though more often associated with poverty and filth. Writing to Hughes in July 1934, Thurman comments with characteristic sarcasm: "Yes, at last I'm a genius. I have T.B."[185] The statement seems to more comfortably situate his disease as an artistic legacy than as the plight of someone who suffers from either limited funds or insufficient will. In the 1930s, tuberculosis was, in fact, persistently associated with the psyche and temperament, though no longer in a way that Thurman might romanticize. In her book *Fevered Lives: Tuberculosis in American Culture since 1870*, Katherine Ott argues that the individualist psychologies of Alfred Adler, Hughlings Jackson, and Adolf Meyer, which were popular during the Depression, as well as the theories of some psychoanalysts, such as William A. White, suggested that personality type, behavior patterns, moods, or compromised libidinal energies might make one susceptible to tuberculosis. Some even suggested that tuberculosis might be a psychoanalytic condition.[186] While he lay in the men's pulmonary ward of Welfare Hospital, Thurman wrote a sketch about his fellow occupants, taking an almost journalistic position, finding the situation difficult to read: "It

I

Male X possessed one rather amazing peculiarity. Despite its sunlit spaciousness, it bore more than a slight resemblance to a tenement railroad flat.

Male X knew no privacy. It was at once a rectangular hospital ward, and an elongated corridor, through which there continually passed a variegated procession of septic people and antiseptic paraphenalia.

Physically there remained little else to criticize. True, 25 beds did tax the available space. But there was not too much congestion. And the sunlight and air drawn available from the six windows, was sufficient to please the most captious. Which was all to the good. For Male X was dedicated to the care & cure of pulmonary tuberculosis.

Among the 25 patients there were naturally a few characters. There was for instance the perky, little Scotchman, Macleish. He admitted being 67 years old. He insisted he was not inflicted with tuberculosis. He also insisted that Mr. Roosevelt's shenagling with the national currency was the direct cause of his indigence.

"Christ, man," he would say with an inimitable accent, "I've got $30,000 in stocks and bonds and can't even collect the principal."

The 25 beds were

It was seldom that any of the 25 beds were

can be seen that things were not dull in Male X. There was seldom a general outburst of hilarity and little horseplay. Neither was there much of the 'male talk' characteristic of a number of men isolated in one room. Nor was there an aura of deep depression. The atmosphere was one difficult to analyze. There was definitely an emasculation."[187]

Tuberculosis makes the body simultaneously readable and invisible. "TB makes the body transparent," writes Sontag. "The X-rays which are the standard diagnostic tool permit one, often for the first time, to see one's insides —to become transparent to oneself."[188] In other words, the disease makes the body a ghost and subject to ghosts. Certainly, X rays had long been thought ghostly. "Radiographic pictures . . . were often referred to as 'ghost pictures' or 'shadowgraphs,'" comments Sara Danius. X rays were "suffused with a rhetoric of death."[189] Early scientific articles connected them to the discourse associated with spiritualism and mesmerism.[190] Moreover, the viewing of one's own X-ray image asks for a kind of dissociation on the part of the spectator: "The X-ray asks us to view the 'self' as 'other,'" writes Allen W. Grove, "it forces us to identify the cold, alien, black-and white-image with our living bodies and in doing so reminds us of our own mortality."[191] All photography has this quality, however. What is unique about an X ray is that it forces you to simultaneously hold two living visions of yourself—one familiar, one unfamiliar—an inside that is defamiliarized because it bears no association with the internal workings of the mind, and an outside that one comes to recognize as surface, as skin. The X ray's primary function is to see through skin, to see the skeleton, which is normally visible only at death. It thereby becomes a tool that, potentially at least, might undermine what Frantz Fanon describes as the "racial epidermal schema"—or the displacement of the body by the skin—in constituting the black (male) subject through the gaze of the white spectator.[192]

Toward the end of the first decade of X-ray technology, in fact, some researchers suggested that combining X-ray treatment with radium would "bleach the skin of Negroes white," although efforts at the practice were short-lived and researchers made "no mention of the fate of these human subjects whose 'conditions' had been treated."[193] Still, because the X ray worked on the skin, both penetrating it and making it invisible, the technology was ripe for metaphorical exploitation by artists, most famously H. G. Wells in his 1897 novel *The Invisible Man* but also Thomas Mann, whose *The Magic Mountain* was one of Thurman's favorite books.[194]

In George Schuyler's 1931 satirical novel *Black No More*, the technology of "electrical nutrition and glandular control" that is employed to artificially and uniformly induce the pigment-stripping skin disorder vitiligo—and turn black skin white—does not specifically refer to X-ray technology.[195] The procedure is, however, reminiscent of X-ray treatment; beginning in the 1920s physicians would inject fluids like oil, iodine, and others into the spine or

Page of Wallace Thurman's draft of Male X." Courtesy of Yale Collection of American Literature, Beinecke Rare Book and Manuscript Library.

into the veins so as to be able to photograph organs as well as bone.[196] In Schuyler's novel, a black Harlem resident, Max Disher, decides to undergo the treatment by sitting in a "formidable apparatus of sparkling nickel" that "resembled a cross between a dentist's chair and an electric chair"; when he ends up after the treatment with "pork-colored skin" and blonde hair, he is "terribly weak, emptied and nauseated; his skin twitched and was dry and feverish; his insides felt very hot and sore."[197]

To some extent the X ray *did* make black skin white—or at the very least irrelevant. In peeling away the skin, X rays seemed to obliterate racial distinctions. And yet the X ray, especially early X rays, always retained a trace, a spectral presence, of the flesh they penetrated. *What could the X ray see?* "Many Victorians seemed to believe that X rays could . . . strip the fleshly mask from a person and expose his or her naked character," writes Grove. From early on, in fact, X rays were associated with erotic knowledge, even voyeurism.[198] In the 1920s, Bettyann Holtzmann Kevles notes, "neuroradiologists, who were beginning to see the interior of the living brain, competed with Freud and his psychoanalytical colleagues to make their own maps of the seats of 'sexual repression' and 'sexual desire.'"[199] The radiologist, Fisher suggests in *The Conjure-Man Dies*, is akin to an analyst, mind reader, and detective. He too can decipher hidden desires and read the psyche.[200] There is a telling moment in Hughes's *The Big Sea* when his doctor suggests he go to Fisher for "x-ray photographs" to diagnose his nausea, but Hughes, ever protective of self-exposure, decides to go elsewhere. He explains, "I knew that my writer-friend, Bud [Fisher], would be full of clever witticisms of the sort that I could never find repartee for when I was in a normal state of mind, let alone now—with my mind in the far-off spaces and my stomach doing flops. So I went to another Harlem specialist I did not know."[201]

If the X ray undermined an easy association between the body's appearance and its internal structures, psyche, desires, spirit, even essence, then it also simultaneously helped to reinforce a carceral social order and calcify increasingly mobile conceptions of the subject. At the same time, the spectral nature of the X ray lies in the fact that it makes the body's insides visible, while not wholly erasing the body's outside. The surface remains as a presence, a trace. It is this dual nature that makes the X ray simultaneously an *event* (being while seeing) and a *thing*; it is both proposition and expression. Present and absent. Here and gone. We might, in fact, see the collapsing of Thurman's and Fisher's coincidental deaths in Harlem discourse in the months before the riot not so much as a historical coincidence between different metaphorically loaded diseases as an encapsulation of the struggle for understanding that the X ray elicits: How does one hold onto presence, to immediacy, when shrouded by a ghost—and finding it one's own? A cartoon by Chase published in the *Amsterdam News* the week after Thurman's and Fisher's deaths is titled "Death Writes a Book" and shows the shrouded figure inscribing the names of the writers on the pages of an open book. The dead are written. The dead write their own names in the book.

"So Thurman lived and died, leaving no memorable record of his writing, but remaining the most symbolic figure of the literary 'renaissance' in Harlem," writes West of Thurman's death, the culmination of six months of dying, largely alone, in the incurables' ward on Welfare Island. "His death caused the first break in the ranks of the 'New Negro.' Assembled at the funeral in solemn silence, older, hardly wiser, they were reminded for the first time of their lack of immortality."[202]

And still he never left. Thurman wrote to Hughes a month before he died, "Thurman is distinctly a has been—so many people have already buried him. Woe betide 'em when I am resurrected."[203] Hughes includes a section called "Death in Harlem" in his 1942 collection of poems *Shakespeare in Harlem*, a book he dedicates "to Louise," his friend Louise Thompson, Thurman's former wife. Among these is a poem called "Death Chant" about the burial of a character named Cordelia, the name of the title character in Thurman's story in *Fire!!*[204] Another poem is titled "Cabaret Girl Dies on Welfare Island," in which the dead speaker laments,

> Rather die the way I lived—
> Drunk and rowdy and gay!
> God! Why did you ever curse me
> Makin' me die this way?[205]

"Death Writes a Book," *Amsterdam News* cartoon by Chase pasted in no. 128 of the L. S. Alexander Gumby Scrapbooks.
Courtesy of Rare Book and Manuscript Library, Butler Library, Columbia University.

Hughes had revised the poem from an earlier version, published first in a 1931 collection, *Dear Lovely Death*, and published once again revised in *Opportunity* in 1933, when Thurman, Harlem, and his youth still seemed quite alive. The poem had been titled "The Consumptive."[206]

"a moment of dignity"

From the typescript of a February 4, 1960, article for the *Fort Pierce News Tribune*:

> SEEK $ FOR ZORA'S FUNERAL
> Howard Shapp
>
> Funeral services for Zora Neale Hurston, 52, leading Negro writer and anthropologist, will be held Sunday afternoon at 3 o'clock from Peek Funeral Home chapel. She will be buried in Genesee Memorial Park.[207]

Last known photo of Zora Neale Hurston (seated at center). It was rescued from the fire after her death. From the Zora Neale Hurston Manuscript Collection. Courtesy of the Department of Special and Area Studies Collections, George A. Smathers Libraries, University of Florida.

The Florida-born author died last Thursday in Memorial Hospital, penniless and almost forgotten after a literary career that included the writing of best-selling books, articles and biographies for the Saturday Evening Post and scripts for Warner Bros. studio in Hollywood.

Herbody [sic] will lie in state at Peek Funeral Home from noon Saturday until funeral service time. Officiating will be the Rev. W. A. Jennings, pastor of St. Paul's A.M.E. Church, the Rev. H. W. White, pastor of Friendship Baptist Church and the Rev. W. J. Cliffion, pastor of Mount Olive Baptist Church. . . .

. . . A fund-raising drive is under way in the Lincoln Park area to raise money to pay for Miss Hurston's funeral. Persons wishing to help may contact Mrs. Paige at the Lincoln Park Academy, HO 4-1424.

Miss Hurston was born at Eatonville, near Orlando . . .[208]

"LITTERED SILENCES"

In the end, there are scraps. Those things not written. Objects that haunt. And objects missing. Missing people as well. "I am trying to find Helene Johnson who put a box of papers in storage for me. She has something Eliza-

182 HARLEM

beth [Hull] wants to see," writes Hurston to Van Vechten in 1937. "I find that she has lost her job, broken up her home and some say that she is in Boston. Anyway some one says that they will locate her by Monday if she is in town and if in Boston she will get me her address."[209] "Very little is known about Johnson, although she participated extensively in New York and Boston literary circles," comments Maureen Honey in 1989 in the short biography that accompanies her collection *Shadowed Dreams: Women's Poetry of the Harlem Renaissance*. "As of the 1960s, she was living in Brooklyn with her husband and children."[210]

Johnson wasn't lost, of course. Or married very long.[211] There were three who lived to old, old age: Bruce Nugent. Dorothy West. And Helene (though she had returned to her birth name, Helen, by then). Nugent recorded his musings on tape for historians and turned over a lifetime of drawings, writings, and loot to be preserved with an eye to the future. In 1995, at age eighty-eight, West finally found fame when she published *The Wedding*, a novel she dedicated to her editor, *the* Jackie O. But Johnson kept to herself. She published her last poem in 1935 and died a footnote to Harlem history, leaving behind her fifty years of unpublished writing, "stacks and stacks of handwritten works all over the room, under the bed, in closets, in drawers, behind bureaus," and a daughter, Abigail, who "gathered up" the scraps and put them into boxes.[212]

Johnson had always been a scrap collector. ("I can hardly wait to see you," she writes to West in December 1932 when West was in the Soviet Union with Hughes and Thompson. "I've read lots and I've got lots of excerpts to copy and send you. You won't read them but I'll love sending them.")[213] But her late-life poetry is taut, scraped clean to the bone. If in their last days Nugent was given to bravado and West to overglossing the past, Johnson seems clear-eyed in understanding the dilemma of living haunted by myth. Of living and remembering not nostalgically and not with glitz. Of being old when somehow you were supposed to stay captured in a photograph of youth. Of being not of a place, Harlem—which after all, had had many lifetimes after you—not a biographical anomaly, but a poet, who lives even in death. Of living finally with and amidst remains. "Give me a moment of dignity," she begins a six-line poem that closes, "before I nestle pleasantly/into the rubbish." She did not nestle quietly. In "Time After Time," she rewrites T. S. Eliot's "The Love Song of J. Alfred Prufrock" with the fervor of Bessie Smith:[214]

> It need not be that way, old woman.
>
> Skip the lonely flicks. Mix. Tremble the air! Resemble!
> Declare! Inhale! Exhale! Blare! Blare loudly! Louder than
>   the crowd!!!
>
> Ignore the meek. They have no fervor.
> They die from murmured violence, littered silences.

They die at the end of queues, mewing, waiting, waiting in
>   good faith,
>   unembittered.

"Helen used to accuse me of 'ghetto thinking,' and because we were black and we lived in a housing project in Brooklyn, I always assumed that it meant thinking from the bottom up instead of from the top down," remembers her daughter Abigail in an afterword to Johnson's first collection of poems, published posthumously, in 2000. "It was not until I was about ten years old that I discovered what she meant. She meant that my thinking was controlled by boundaries, that I was encircled by limitations in the same manner that a geographical ghetto is within boundaries. What she wanted me to realize is that with the imagination there are no limitations to thought."[215]

This is ghostwriting. Bodies and places unbounded by thought. Life is complicated, writes Avery Gordon, it asks people to move "between furniture without memories and Racism and Capitalism."[216] Haunting, Gordon calls it. Haunting is what happens when "that which appears not to be there becomes a seething presence."[217] Seething no. Laughing perhaps. When Hurston died she ordered her papers burned. And they were. Then someone walking by extinguished the fire and salvaged the scraps from the flames.[218]

Helene Johnson reading to her daughter, 1940s.
The Dorothy West Papers. Courtesy of the Schlesinger Library, Radcliffe Institute, Harvard University.

the crypt

All the while, I think of the bones. You remember them. They were found near New York City Hall back in 1991. Digging a foundation for a new federal office tower, construction workers came upon skeletons, hundreds of them, twenty feet below the surface of the street. Turns out it was a colonial graveyard for enslaved Africans: "The Negros Burial Ground," just outside the city's limits. Forensic anthropologists swarmed the place and unearthed four hundred bodies, half of them the remains of children. They shipped them off to Howard University for analysis. Bit by bit the remains revealed stories of how the people lived and died. There were updates periodically in the news. The last of the remains were buried, with much fanfare, more than a decade after they'd been found.

At the time the remains were discovered, however, it was much more dramatic. All of a sudden, New Yorkers realized they were walking on bones. Decayed corpses, perhaps thousands of them, of enslaved blacks and indentured or destitute whites were entombed beneath buildings and park grounds across the city. Not just downtown. "Walking through the lobby [of the General Services Administration Tower, now a national landmark], it is impossible not to think of the dead beneath one's feet and—by extension—of the nameless and unremembered dead all over Manhattan," wrote Brent Staples in a May 22, 1995, editorial in the *New York Times*.[219] "It is as if these African dead have claimed an otherwise anonymous Government building as their own." Bones upon bones all over New York.

Malcolm X Boulevard, New York City, February 2005
© Frank Jermann, Germany/rAtgallery.com.

BLUE-PENCILED PLACE **185**

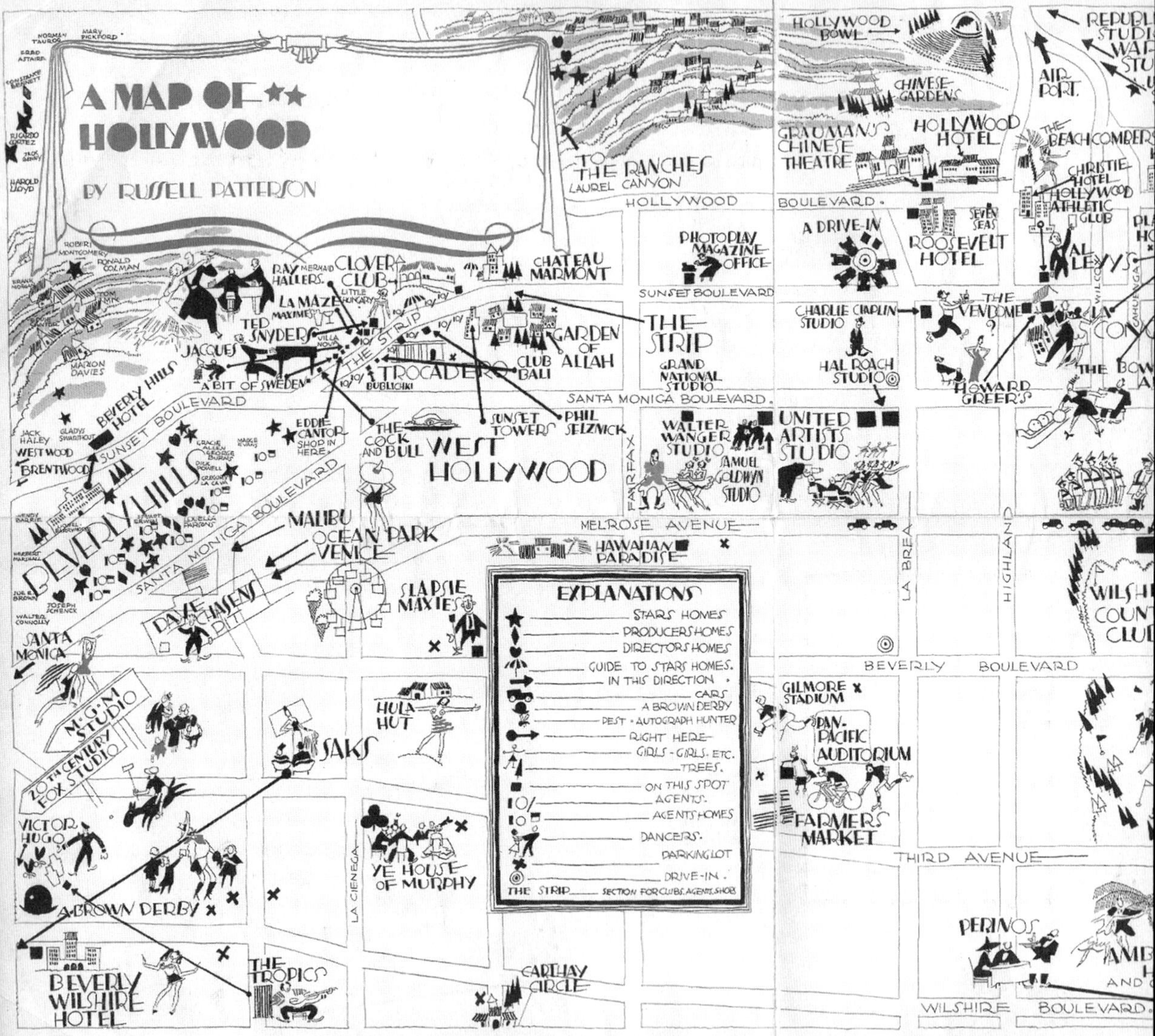

A MAP OF HOLLYWOOD
BY RUSSELL PATTERSON
HOLLYWOOD BOWL
CHINESE GARDENS
AIR PORT.
REPUBLI STUDI
TO THE RANCHES
LAUREL CANYON
GRAUMAN'S CHINESE THEATRE
HOLLYWOOD HOTEL
THE BEACHCOMBERS
CHRISTIE HOTEL
HOLLYWOOD ATHLETIC CLUB
HOLLYWOOD BOULEVARD.
A DRIVE-IN
SEVEN SEAS
ROOSEVELT HOTEL
AL LEVY'S
PHOTOPLAY MAGAZINE OFFICE
CHATEAU MARMONT
RAY HALLERS.
MERMAID
CLOVER CLUB
LITTLE HUNGARY
LA MAZE
MAXIMES
TED SNYDERS
VILLA NOVA
JACQUES
THE STRIP
TROCADERO
BUBLICHKI
CLUB BALI
GARDEN OF ALLAH
A BIT OF SWEDEN
SUNSET BOULEVARD
THE STRIP
GRAND NATIONAL STUDIO
CHARLIE CHAPLIN STUDIO
HAL ROACH STUDIO
THE VENDOME
HOWARD GREER'S
THE BOW
SANTA MONICA BOULEVARD.
BEVERLY HILLS HOTEL
EDDIE CANTOR SHOP IN HERE
THE COCK AND BULL
SUNSET TOWERS
PHIL SELZNICK
WEST HOLLYWOOD
WALTER WANGER STUDIO
SAMUEL GOLDWYN STUDIO
UNITED ARTISTS STUDIO
FAIRFAX
NORMAN TAUROG
MARY PICKFORD
FRED ASTAIRE
CONSTANCE BENNETT
RICARDO CORTEZ
JACK BENNY
HAROLD LLOYD
ROBERT MONTGOMERY
RONALD COLMAN
TOM MIX
MARION DAVIES
JACK HALEY
GLADYS SWARTHOUT
WESTWOOD
BRENTWOOD
BEVERLY HILLS
GRACIE ALLEN GEORGE BURNS
DICK POWELL
MARGIE
WENDY BARRIE
JOE E. BROWN
JOSEPH SCHENCK
WALTER CONNOLLY
LOUELLA PARSONS
SANTA MONICA BOULEVARD
MALIBU
OCEAN PARK
VENICE
MELROSE AVENUE
HAWAIIAN PARADISE
LA BREA
HIGHLAND
WILSHI COUNT CLUB
DAVE CHASEN'S PIT
SLAPSIE MAXIE'S
EXPLANATIONS
STARS HOMES
PRODUCERS HOMES
DIRECTORS HOMES
GUIDE TO STARS HOMES.
IN THIS DIRECTION
CARS
A BROWN DERBY
PEST - AUTOGRAPH HUNTER
RIGHT HERE
GIRLS - GIRLS - ETC.
TREES.
ON THIS SPOT
AGENTS.
AGENTS HOMES
DANCERS.
PARKING LOT
DRIVE-IN.
THE STRIP — SECTION FOR CLUBS, AGENTS, SHOPS
SANTA MONICA
M-G-M STUDIO
20TH CENTURY FOX STUDIO
HULA HUT
SAKS
BEVERLY BOULEVARD
GILMORE STADIUM
PAN-PACIFIC AUDITORIUM
FARMERS MARKET
THIRD AVENUE
VICTOR HUGO
A BROWN DERBY
YE HOUSE OF MURPHY
LA CIENEGA
PERINOS
BEVERLY WILSHIRE HOTEL
THE TROPICS
CARTHAY CIRCLE
WILSHIRE BOULEVARD.

4

Hollywood(land)

WAX, FIRE, INSOMNIA

ISN'T HOLLYWOOD A DUMP, IN THE HUMAN SENSE OF THE WORD. A HIDEOUS TOWN, POINTED UP BY THE INSULTING GARDENS OF ITS RICH, FULL OF HUMAN SPIRITS AT A NEW LOW OF DEBASEMENT.
—**F. SCOTT FITZGERALD** TO ALICE ROBERTSON, JULY 29, 1940

A STUDIO BACK LOT FULL OF BROKEN DOWN STREET SETS, AND DESERTED EMPTY STAGES, IS INDEED A SAD SPECTACLE TO CONTEMPLATE. FORTUNATELY, HOWEVER, FOR THE MOTION PICTURE INDUSTRY, ALL THOSE CONNECTED WITH IT, SUCH SCENES OF UTTER DESOLATION ARE COMPARATIVELY RARE.
—**LEO KUTER**, *HOLLYWOOD REPORTER*, CIRCA 1940S

PLACE

Hollywood is "nowhere."[1] It is not so much a "place without a place,"[2] but more like the "idea of a place."[3] For there is no *there* to Hollywood—at least not materially—even if it is somewhat imperfectly designated on all Los Angeles maps, even if it was heralded with fifty-foot-tall letters embossed on Mount Lee: HOLLYWOOD(LAND). "While 'Hollywood' is commonly used to designate the motion picture industry as a whole," notes the author of the entry on Hollywood in the WPA *Guide to California*, "most of the major producing units are not in the Hollywood District, but are scattered in the outlying areas."[4] Hollywood-as-place refers as much to an industry and means of production as to any location in space. A 1930s Los Angeles tourist map, for example, highlights movie stars' private homes as well as parks, museums, and the Griffith observatory. To "go Hollywood" (or as a character in Paramount's 1936 film *Hollywood Boulevard* puts it, "Too much too soon too bad") was an expression used frequently in studio-era films. But it meant that one contracted a state of mind rather than demonstrated an affinity to a material site.[5]

Depression-era Hollywood is not only where absurd human "masquerades" live alongside "middle westerners" who have "come to California to die," as Todd Hackett observes in *Day of the Locust*; it is a place where no one can die because no one has ever been.[6] Burial seems superfluous. Then again it is the only truly important event. (Bad publicity functions as a kind of symbolic death. But it's still better than having been forgotten.) Paramount Studios fittingly backs up against the Hollywood cemetery where Rudolph Valentino, John Gilbert, and, the authors of the WPA *Guide to California* note, William Desmond Taylor are buried (the last of these most permanently).[7] "Doesn't anybody live here now?" Kathleen asks Monroe Stahr in *The Love of the Last Tycoon* as they stroll through Hollywood in the late 1930s. "'The studios moved out into the country,' he said, 'What used to be the country. I had some good times here though.'"[8]

Ask someone in Hollywood how long something —or someone—existed and there are always disputes. Some people say, for instance, that the mammoth Babylon sets from D. W. Griffith's 1916 epic *Intolerance* stood at the corner of Hollywood and Sunset boulevards for the better part of a year; others assert that they were left there for four years; still others insist that the sets stood intact for fifteen.[9] (These disputes arise even in the face of documentation. But,

← "A Map of Hollywood."
Cartoon, 1930s.
Author's collection.

Hollywoodland poster, 1924.
Courtesy of Bison Archives.

then, Hollywood has never gone in much for documentation, despite the current movie industry's lip service to preservation.) The Margaret Herrick Library of the Academy of Motion Pictures, for instance, is a lovely place, a few blocks from the Beverly Center mall and funded by the likes of Martin Scorcese, Harrison Ford, and Tom Cruise. Yet it is oddly bureaucratic for an archive—somehow too clean—more like, yes, the idea of a library than a library, though its collections are quite impressive. There is little of the chumminess that usually develops between scholar and librarian over weeks of intensive work. And at the UCLA film archives, near Gold's gym, just off Hollywood Boulevard, you sit mostly alone in a hot, darkened closet of a room, winding short reels of crackling films around the spools of ancient projectors. Unlike the wood-paneled rooms of the overly air-conditioned Charles E. Young Research Library on the UCLA campus in Westwood, these archives are a tomb of sorts—and a death trap. Curators regularly throw out reels of disintegrating films to keep them from liquefying and incinerating the rest.

This is not to say that Hollywood is without its landmarks. Films about Hollywood in the 1920s and 1930s identify the place primarily with location shots: The street signs that mark the intersection of Hollywood and Vine, a movie premiere at Grauman's Chinese Theater, the façade of the Brown Derby restaurant on Vine Street, (and in later years, of Schwab's drugstore on Hollywood Boulevard), perhaps the Hollywood Bowl, and, inevitably, studio gates—those at Paramount, for instance, or some place like that.[10] In contemporary films, "location shots" of Hollywood are usually restricted to signage: a long shot of the lights of Los Angeles looking down from the Hollywood hills or a reverse shot of the rebuilt (and abbreviated) Hollywood sign, now made permanent in steel.[11] To look at Hollywood as a place with a past, as a place *in* the past, is to issue forth ghosts, not ghosts of people, certainly, not of things, but of the city itself. It means to excavate the condition of what Michel de Certeau, Luce Girard, and Pierre Mayol call the "true city " in its most elemental form. Hollywood embodies the "ruins of a city that had never been, the traces of a memory that [has] no specific place."[12] Hollywood is the true city because Hollywood is the city without site.

Indeed, the studios were themselves self-contained cities of a sort. A 1941 article, "A City within a City," in MGM's magazine *The Lion's Roar*, boasts,

> Metro-Goldwyn-Mayer's make-up department can handle an average of 1,200 makeups an hour; its telephone exchange has 898 stations, and handles as many long distance calls as could the exchange in a city of 50,000; it has its own telegraph office and direct teletype to the offices in New York, a complete emergency hospital operated by a licensed physician, dental offices; a music department staffed by experts and noted composers, that maintains a music library of 2,000,000 items; a research department, in which experts answer an average of 500 unusual questions that

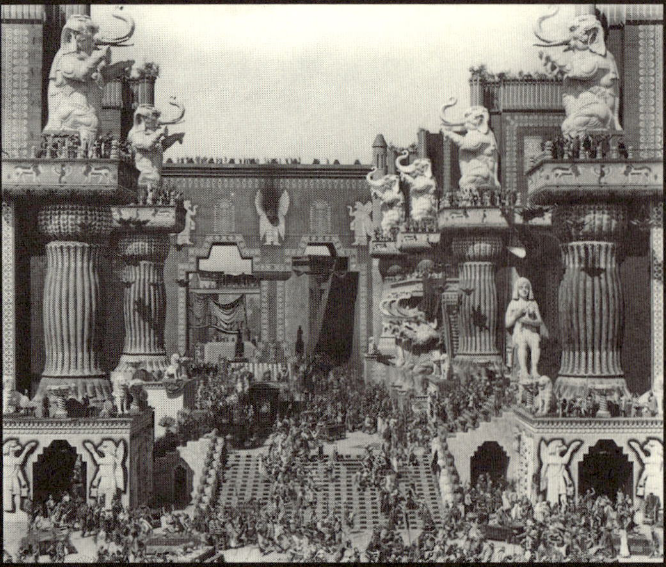

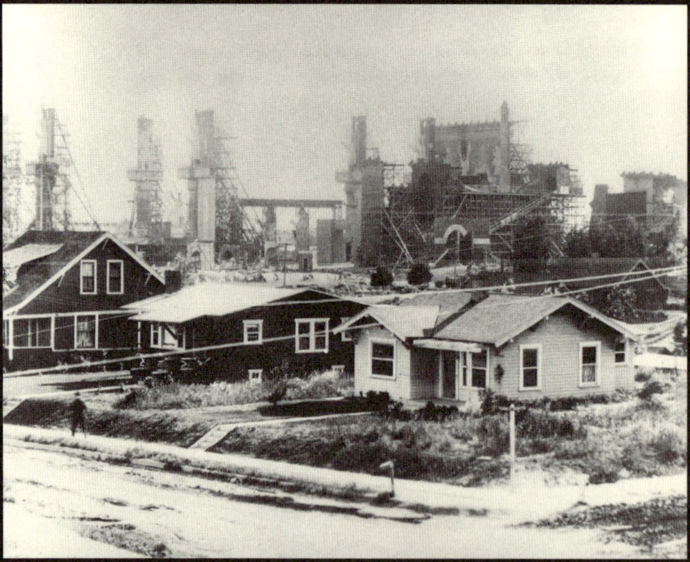

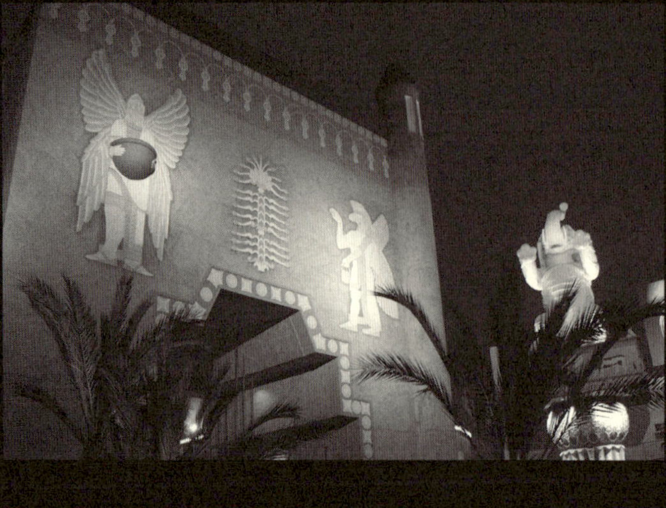

come up in film making daily; its own symphony orchestra, a complete transportation department, art department staffed by artists and architects who design the settings for its pictures, a "sound library" of the recorded effects that run into thousands of items, a reading department that reads about 12,000 novels, plays, and short stories yearly, providing a synopsis of each, a casting department that has about 20,000 portraits of players in its reference files, highly developed recreational facilities, a group insurance unit, a safety council; and a commissary that takes rank as one of the best restaurants in America.[13]

Hollywood's relation to place and place making is, in other words, a complicated one—in part because the industry that produced it and was produced by it relies on the construction and remaking of spatial and temporal illusion. Even the five-hundred-acre Hollywoodland development that gave the "film colony" its name and panache in 1923 was constructed as a massive illusion. Housing styles were a rehashing of European originals: Tudor Revival, Spanish Revival, French Normandy Revival, and so on. "Give the kiddies a chance," crowed magazine ads, " . . . crowded boulevards, dangerous corners, unknown companies are an ever-present danger to children of big cities. Come to Hollywoodland." And if it wasn't the financial success the developers had dreamed of, it nonetheless was touted as "one of the showcases of the world."[14]

If Hollywood was (and is) notable for its inability to be easily locatable, it was also identifiable by its pastiche of borrowed styles. In *The Day of the Locust*, Claude, a successful screenwriter who dons a ridiculous confection of Confederate garb, lives in a "big house that was an exact reproduction of the old Dupuy mansion near Biloxi, Mississippi"; the narrator, Todd, notes that on the "corner of La Huerta Road was a miniature Rhine castle with tarpaper turrets pierced for archers. Next to it was a highly colored shack with domes and minarets out of the *Arabian Nights*"; and Homer Simpson rents a "queer" "Irish"-style cottage: "the house was cheap because it was hard to rent. Most of the people who took cottages in the neighborhood wanted them to be 'Spanish.'"[15] In Robert Florey's 1928 experimental short film *Life and Death of 9413: A Hollywood Extra*, the film cuts suddenly to what looks like a newsreel shot of Montmartre. A homage to the bohemian life of Florey's native France, perhaps? No, it is soon clear the footage is of a *set* of Montmartre on a studio back lot.

Much was made of Hollywood filmmakers' concern for realism in creating set designs. ("Nothing could be more minutely authentic than the African jungle backgrounds, construction of the native villages, implements, decorations and proper presentation of native customs and pronunciation of the Swahili," comments the writer of "Tarzan Fact and Fiction," in MGM's *The Lion's Roar*. " . . . In contrast to the native village sets, Tarzan's treetop house is sheer invention. It was felt that a modern touch could justifiably be intro-

Still of the temple at Babylon from D. W. Griffith's *Intolerance*, 1916. Courtesy of the Academy of Motion Picture Arts and Sciences.

Babylon set amid Los Angeles bungalows, 1916. Courtesy of Bison Archives.

Kodak Theatre, Los Angeles, 2005. © Stephen Bay, bayimages.com.

MOVIES

HOLLYWOOD REPRODUCES THE RIVIERA

One hundred and twenty tons of sand were dumped into this corner of stage No. 1 of the Hal Roach studio, Culver City, Calif., for the big Riviera beach scene in *Topper Takes A Trip*. Director Norman McLeod (in white slacks, arms folded, in front of foremost group at left) is about to shoot a scene in which Constance Bennett, as a ghost, pulls the bathing trunks off an Italian count who is courting Topper's wife. Stand-ins for Billie Burke and Alexander D'Arcy are under the second umbrella from the left. At bottom, left to right, are a prop man (*with suspenders, seated*), an electrician, a group of assistant directors, an actor (*in trunks*), another electrician. A still photograph is being taken at left center. Beside the camera, in a straw hat, stands Roy Seawright, wizard of camera tricks, whose "materializations" and "dematerializations" of two impertinent ghosts made *Topper* (LIFE, July 26, 1937) one of 1937's funniest comedies. Now, in its sequel, he uses more tricks, achieves even more hilarious screen magic. Even this production shot was turned over to him when Director McLeod finished it. To see what he did with it, turn the page.

duced into the deep jungle, because of Tarzan's mate, Maureen O'Sullivan, a product of civilization.")[16] Still, as Beverly Heisner points out, "Realism meant, in one form or another, a world that the audience recognized."[17] Heisner quotes an anecdote by the art director William Cameron Menzies about designing the set for a Mary Pickford picture: "We had to have a Spanish city near Toledo and I put the Campanile of Toledo in it to make it authentic. As you know, Madison Square Garden in New York copied this campanile, and so many people recognized it and asked what Madison Square garden was doing in the picture, that I had to change it."[18] For designers like Menzies, who had dabbled in avant-garde and expressionist film in addition to making mainstream cinema (he worked with Florey on the short film, *The Love of Zero*), the difference between avant-garde set design and commercial design was one of degree more than of content. "In many cases," he is quoted as saying, "authenticity is sacrificed, and architectural principles violated, all for the sake of the emotional response that is being sought."[19] Studio-era Hollywood, it might be said, was the rightful ancestor of Disneyland (which was, not incidentally, designed by studio set designers, as was much of the 1933 World's Fair and 1950s Las Vegas). It was imagined and built through a play of facades as a kind of ever-expanding set and collective dream that permeated the whole of the United States.

"Hollywood Reproduces the Riviera," in *Life* magazine, January 2, 1939.

In the mid-1930s, the director George Cukor reportedly urged "filmland's writers [to] park their cosmopolitan frames [once a year] in Eb's general store, and hear the proprietor swap yearns with Eph, as he nods wisely from his seat atop the cracker barrel."[20] But when Brian Marlow, a screenwriter and playwright, took Cukor at his word and spent a month in Hog Junction, Arkansas, he discovered that "there isn't just one Hollywood anymore, but 10,000 Hollywoods. The only difference is that this one has cameras and more horses and you hear something else besides what the stars do and wear."[21] That Hollywood was everywhere, and yet could still be referred to as "this one," *here*, suggests a transformation in the way that place is understood. It has become commonplace to say that cinema shifts perceptions of time and space, but how that impacts the way that place is known and experienced is distinct. Film presents the illusion of movement but is entirely composed of still images—twenty-four frames per second of film.[22] Place, on the other hand, presents the illusion of stillness but is always in flux. Place, one might say, is both constituted and undermined by its flicker-effect. There is some irony, then, that Hollywood, a place that has become synonymous with filmmaking, comes to allegorize the paradoxical nature of place perception. Hollywood is here, *ici*, fixed in place. Hollywood is everywhere, flickering. Narrated in both universal and particular terms, as both site-specific and ubiquitous, Hollywood place making performs a tap dance back and forth between the virtual immediacy of presence and the lethargy of matter-clotted historicity.

Then again, perhaps it is the other way around.

FAÇADE

> X-From_: rothx002@tc.umn.edu Mon Apr 21 13:56:10 2003
> Date: Mon, 21 Apr 2003 13:56:09 -0500 (CDT)
> From: Marty Roth <rothx002@tc.umn.edu>
> To: jani@umn.edu
> X-Umn-Remote-Mta: [N] garnet.tc.umn.edu #+LO+NM
>
> Jani,
>   Although I have no idea what you're doing in the chapter, I do have a never-to-be-finished article on how D. W. Griffith's INTOLERANCE sets wrote the city, Los Angeles. If you'd like to look (or loot) just ask.
>   I was thinking about surface and depth in Hollywood on the way home and the image that kept occurring to me is that of Bill Holden floating on the surface of the star's swimming pool at the opening of SUNSET BOULEVARD, but after a few minutes Wilder reverses and has his camera, now located a few feet down in the water, shoot up at that surface.
>   I hope to see you from time to time. Marty

INSIDE/OUTSIDE

In Hollywood's early days, filmmakers often shot interior scenes outdoors in order to benefit from natural light and to minimize the contrast between outdoor location shots and artificial interiors.[23] After lighting technology improved, and especially after the advent of sound recording, outdoor scenes were filmed inside on sound stages. An August 31, 1939, headline in MGM *Studio News* announces, "Desert is Moved to Studio for Big Reno Dude Ranch" and goes on to describe the spectacular design of the set of *The Women* (MGM 1939): "Based upon actual photographs of fashionable divorcee hosteries, the ranch required three weeks to construct and covers approximately 2700 square feet on one of the studio's largest sound stages," the article reports. "Fifty truckloads of desert sand were brought to the studio and spread across the locale chosen for the scene. Twenty-five live pine trees, and as many varieties of shrubs, natural to that part of the country, were also transported to the studio."[24]

While such transpositions of inside and outside, depth and façade can most easily be read as by-products of technological necessity, they are also hallmarks of a larger spatial disconnect endemic to modernity. Walter Benjamin argues that the act of making the inside outside and vice versa is nothing less than a symptom of bourgeois arrogance. In the "dream house" of modernity, "the domestic interior moves outside," Benjamin writes:

> It is as though the bourgeois were so sure of his prosperity that he is careless of façade, and can exclaim: My house, no matter where you choose

to cut into it, is façade. Such façades, especially, on the Berlin houses dating back to the middle of the previous century: an alcove does not jut out, but—as niche—tucks in. The street becomes room and the room becomes street. The passerby who stops to look at the house stands, as it were, in the alcove.[25]

In contradistinction to the bourgeois house in Berlin, Benjamin describes the nineteenth-century Parisian arcade as an inside with "no outside." It is this element that makes the arcade, for Benjamin, also like a dream. The hallucinatory qualities of the arcade are less important than the fact that these qualities reveal themselves through spatial disorientation. As Benjamin well knew, like dreaming, the experience of watching film has been described as subjecting one to a kind of spatial and temporal confusion—in which outside becomes inside, top becomes bottom, beginning becomes end. Such disorientation is a primary component of the spectatorship of narrative and realist cinema, which dominated (and dominates) Hollywood filmmaking. "Hollywood invented an art which disregards the principle of self-contained composition," writes Béla Balázs in *Theory of the Film*, "[it] not only does away with the distance between the spectator and the work of art but deliberately creates the illusion in the spectator that he is in the middle of the action reproduced in the fictional space of the film."[26] This is a point Benjamin alludes to in "The Work of Art in the Age of Mechanical Reproduction" when he argues that film spectatorship fundamentally changes the perceptive relationship between audience and the object upon which it gazes.[27]

Not surprisingly, then, the ways Benjamin describes the "dream city" of Paris as a city of scraps, "an aggregate of all the building plans, street layouts, park projects, and street-name systems that were never developed," are reminiscent of how Cecelia Brady describes the studio back lot in F. Scott Fitzgerald's *The Love of the Last Tycoon*.[28] "Under the moon," the locations, the African jungles and the French châteaux, look "like the torn picture books of childhood, like fragments of stories dancing in an open fire."[29] In comparing the sets to narrative fragments and, in particular, to fragments of childhood stories, stories that an audience already knows well, Cecelia suggests that the film set is not metaphor (a substitute), but synecdoche (a *stand-in*).[30] The part, as glimpse, fragment, sketch, façade, stands in for the whole, concept, narrative, memory, locale.[31]

It is notable, then (not to say a bit sad), that the fragmentary set flirts with the threat of self-immolation. Cecelia describes an image as it is about to go up into flames. We might, therefore, consider it a moment of cinematic self-reflexivity par excellence that when Norman Maine (Fredric March) walks *out* of the curtain-framed double doors of his living room to go for a swim in the ocean in his fateful last scene in MGM's 1937 film *A Star Is Born*, he does so as if entering *into* a movie screen.[32] (To underscore the diegetic connec-

Jean Harlow at Grauman's Chinese Theater, September 1933.
Courtesy of Bruce Torrence Hollywood Historical Photograph Collection.

tion between cinema and suicide, the next shot is of Maine's footprints in the sand—yes, he's "all washed up," Hollywood is not afraid of the literal in its simplest form. The moment is purposefully reminiscent of an early scene when Esther Blodgett/Vicki Lester [Janet Gaynor] steps into his footsteps at Grauman's Chinese Theater.) By the time he drowns himself, Norman Maine has performed a triple play, serving simultaneously as a figure for actor (albeit a failed one), spectator (Vicki Lester, the newborn star has taken center stage), and spectacle (a drunken sideshow). The spatial-temporal reversal that he performs and that constitutes his becoming-cinema, moreover, suggests that the spectator's performance, like that of the actor's, is always also a drive to death.[33] More pointedly, it alludes to the medium's own drive to chemical self-destruction—and the necessity of that destruction to the production of cinema as institution.

Film, we might say, is a constitutively melancholic medium. Nitrogen-laced celluloid plastic, which was used to make most film before the 1950s, is a semisolid, impermanent material that is in the process of self-destructing from the moment it is made. It transforms first into a gelatinous goo, close in composition to nitroglycerin, and then to an explosive powder.[34] The dangers of storing and projecting nitrate film were known almost from the start. Fires were not infrequent. In 1929, a chemist at the Bureau of Mines warned that "stored nitrate cellulose film presented a triple menace of fire, explosion, and wholesale gas poisoning."[35] Eight years later a nitrate fire at a storehouse in Little Ferry, New Jersey, destroyed most of the silent films produced by the Fox Film Corporation and killed a thirteen-year-old boy who lived nearby.[36]

For some, there is poignancy in film's evanescence. A headline for an October 2002 article in the *New York Times Magazine* reads coyly: "Martin Scorcese and others may plead for the preservation of decomposing film stock, but a radical new film shows that there's unexpected beauty in those self-immolating archives."[37] The film, *Decasia: The State of Decay*, is the best-known work by the filmmaker Bill Morrison, who created the precisely edited montage from scraps of decomposing nitrate film stock culled from archives around the country. "Who knew that decay itself—artfully marshaled, braided, scored, and sustained—could provoke such transports of sublime reverie amid such pangs of wistful sorrow?" reflects the *Times*'s author Lawrence Weschler, describing the blurred, indistinct, and haunting images of film that has been captured in the process of turning to dust. More explicitly than *Decasia*, however, two short films, *Light Is Calling* and *The Mesmerist*, which Morrison produced in 2003, pay homage to cinematic necrophilia. To watch the melting images of the sepia-tinted *Light Is Calling* is to stare into flames. The film incinerates—violently, sweetly—before your eyes. You become witness to, complicit in, seduced by the spectacle of cinematic death.

And thus its birth. It is "the destruction of moving images that makes film history possible," writes Paolo Cherchi Usai in *The Death of Cinema: History, Cultural Memory and the Digital Dark Age*:

> That is to say, the Present is indivisible and overwhelming, while the Past presents us with a limited set of choices on which to exercise such knowledge as we are able to glean from the range of perspectives that remain

Image from Bill Morrison's film *The Mesmerist* (2003, 1926).
Courtesy of Hypnotic Pictures.

WAX, FIRE, INSOMNIA **197**

[XLIV].³⁸ If all moving images were available, the massive fact of their presence would impede any effort to establish criteria of relevance—more so, indeed, than if they had all been obliterated, for then, at least, selective comprehension would be replaced by pure conjecture.³⁹

If one of the problems of doing research on and in Hollywood lies in a simultaneous abundance and absence of materials to study, we might say that this paradox is part and parcel of writing history—or thinking place. It is both a limiting and enabling condition of possibility. Transhistorically, Mary Ann Doane argues, film has been constructed by a fundamental but (not incompatible) tension between its conceptualization as performance/display/the instant and as record/archive/"stored time."⁴⁰ Death and the drive toward death lurk in cinema, are inherent to it; indeed, cinema might be said to serve as its sign or at the least as a sign of inaccessibility with which death coincides.

copy

From June 8, 1940, notes on "Set Designing" by the Publicity Department at 20th Century Fox:⁴¹

> Art, as a rule, is created for preservation by prosperity. But there are artists at 20th Century-Fox who were expressly commissioned to create art for the purpose of destruction.
>
> As far as the story of "The Great Profile" is concerned, the xxxx oil paintings in question were supposed to be the work of the character played by John Barrymore. In a stage play within the picture, he plays the role of an artist, intent on creating masterpieces.
>
> The canvases for this purpose turned out by the art department were very fine examples indeed, worthy of hanging in any parlor. But the script required their utter destruction. In one scene Barrymore is supposed to become disgusted and slash one to ribbons. In another, Mary Beth Hughes is the disgusted person, and she causes the canvas to hang around his neck by the force of impact.
>
> Two canvases, of course, would not be sufficient. The art department had to prepare spares in case of emergencies.
>
> The job was handed to Artist Leo Quijano, who made the original sketches from which the art staff made the finished paintings. One was a very colorful job of a South American negress with a basket of fruit on her head. This was the one to be slashed, and as the scene was an intricate one, no less than fifteen of this one were painted. . . .

None of this is to suggest that we can read place like a film. Instead, it is to underscore that the fact that we *do* read place is worth further reflection. Along these lines, Doane argues that with the rise of the industrial system, "time becomes a value," sharing the logic of capital as something to be "read, calculated," even worn as a prosthetic.[42] Because cinema performs the tension between the static instant (the present) and continuous movement (presence)—it is both, according to Doane—it has an "apparent capacity to *represent* the contingent" and therefore is a "crucial participant" in rethinking the nature of temporality in modernity.[43] But so too is cinema critical to understanding modern place and place making. It is not too far-fetched to suggest that Hollywood produced itself and was produced in the image of its chosen medium of representation, film. Or perhaps it is enough to say that in Hollywood the film medium found its most complementary material home.[44] (There is always, as I have suggested in earlier parts of the book, an intrinsic though imperfect mimetic relationship between place-shaped imaginaries and the aesthetics of place representation.)

In Hollywood, the interplay between materiality and place-produced metaphor is sometimes unexpectedly coherent. Consider, for instance, that the winner of the 1934 Academy Award for Best Short Film (novelty) was a one-reel documentary named *The City of Wax*. Part of a successful series of nature films produced by Horace and Stacy Woodward (Educational-Fox), the film charted the life of a honeybee. It was remarkable for its use of microscopic camera filming technology and the evocation of what Balázs has called the "hidden life of little things" heretofore invisible.[45] "The close-up," writes Balázs "has not only widened our vision of life, it has also deepened it. In the days of the silent film it not only revealed new things, but showed us the meaning of the old." Unlike the theater, in which "the living, speaking human being has a far greater significance than dumb objects," he points out, in film, "both man and object [are] equally pictures, photographs, their homogeneous material [is] projected onto the same screen, in the same way as in a painting, where they are equally patches of colour and equally parts in the same composition. In significance, intensity, and value men and things were thus brought on to the same plane."[46] Early cinema, in this view, produces a different relationship between subject and object and a transformation of the way that the thing may be known.

All film, it might be said, is close-up, since cinema brings into view locations, people, and objects that are out of view—even to those who are filming them. Moreover, the drama of cinema also implies a drama of scale: It makes large that which is tiny and miniaturizes that which is so immense it cannot be fully seen unaided by the eye, at least not without a change of physical location. Yet the way scale was manipulated for the screen image, and its concomitant impact on the way that objects and place were produced, changed substantially with the advent of recorded sound in cinema and with the consolidation of production authority in the major studios and the rising importance of art directors within that system.[47] The simple theatrical backdrops designed by painters and prop men for film in the first decades of the twentieth century gave way to the elaborate, immense film sets of the late silent era. These sets, though more ornate than their predecessors, largely found their genesis in stage design. Griffith's famous *Intolerance* sets, for instance, were designed by a theater scenic designer, Walter L. Hall.[48] Even the most sophisticated sets of the late silent era tended to be coherent and close to full scale; they were designed as elaborate façades that could be shot from different angles.

The fragmentary, stylized, and miniaturized sets of the studio era, by contrast, needed to accommodate the more complex spatial constraints of sound recording, in particular, the use of stationary microphones that were ill equipped to filter out ambient noise. These settings were increasingly designed by men (few women had authority in art departments) who had been trained as architects, not as painters. The shift in training and orientation of setting designers was arguably a side effect of work shortages. The motion picture industry was one of the few places outside of the WPA in which architects and builders could find work during the Depression. (Carl Jules Weyl, who designed the Hollywood Brown Derby restaurant, for example, became an art director for Warner Brothers during the Depression after his architecture practiced failed. He won an Academy Award for *The Adventures of Robin Hood* in 1938 and was the art director for *Casablanca*.)[49] The increasing prevalence of architects in art departments also pointed to a heightened importance of the visual setting to the film scenario. "Studio heads were faced with the undisputable fact that a large number of people came into theatres to see settings, as well as actors. The Art Director and Set Decorator ceased to be looked upon as an experiment," writes George James Hopkins, who had been a set decorator for both silent and sound films, in a 1952 issue of *Production Design*.[50]

Much as it is indisputable that Hollywood set styles impacted American architecture and interior design more generally,[51] it is perhaps more important to note the subtler epistemological shift that was necessitated by the visible/invisible sleights of hand that mediated the making of place in Hollywood cinema. For many reasons, of which the constraints of budget and technology were only two, early sound films were almost exclusively made on studio lots, on fragmentary sets that were open-roofed to facilitate overhead lighting and sound equipment. Building multiple versions of the "same" place in multiple scales—or in different states of disarray or décor—became standard practice for big-budget A pictures. By the mid-1930s, few films could do without the special effects of miniatures, deep-focus photography, matte shots, and cycloramas.[52]

The project for the new "architectural" art directors, then, was to construct a group of permeable and fragmentary material sites that could be sutured cinematically into a coherent and closed visual statement. For instance, the illusion of grandeur of the manor Manderley, where Laurence Olivier and Joan Fontaine play out Daphne du Maurier's domestic drama in the 1940 film *Rebecca*, was produced by building and shooting multiple versions of the manor at different scales. "We figured that the only way to do it really effectively was to build the largest-scale miniature that had ever been built; then another miniature half that scale; and then sections of it full scale," recalled Ray Klune, who worked in the Selznick production department. Selznick "gave the go-ahead and we built the biggest miniature first. . . . It was so big and it took up so much of the old unsoundproofed stages that we couldn't really get far enough away from it to get a full feeling of the scale of it, so that's why we needed a smaller one . . . to show the scale of the whole estate."[53]

It was only through the mediation of the camera, in other words, that these new sets came into being; the filming and editing processes could bring together that which was materially distinct and create an illusion of distance between sites that were materially quite close. It is less important, therefore, to note that motion picture producers could produce or perform acts of enlargement, miniaturization, or simulation with increasing sophistication, than it is to recognize that cinematic narrative became increasingly dependent upon the spectators' *mis*reading of scale and place. The 1933 film *King Kong*, for example, has often been cited both for its innovative use of spe-

Lyle Wheeler, his assistant, and the miniature of Atlanta for *Gone With the Wind*.
Courtesy of the Harry Ransom Humanities Research Center, University of Texas at Austin.

cial effects and for its inconsistent rendering of scale. The gigantic ape had to seem big enough to be frightening, but he could never seem so large as to be unable to interact with the actors. His scale changed several times in relation to the setting, most strikingly so that he appeared about eighteen feet tall in the jungle scenes, but twenty-four feet tall in the scenes in Manhattan, where the immense tip of the Empire State Building, which had been built close to actual size, seemed to dwarf the ape models that had been filmed at the original proportion.[54] While the success of the film visibly depends upon its spectators' willingness to ignore these inconsistencies, which are most visible in the dramatic last scene, this dependency is nothing new. Indeed, *King Kong*'s mismanagement of scale merely makes obvious a prerequisite of cinema spectatorship more generally. To watch cinema, at least realist cinema, spectators must be willing to misread place and spatial scale and to simultaneously misrecognize (or misremember) that they are doing so.

In a time when the abstraction of set design was little understood by spectators, Hollywood cinema produced a concept of place that was extricated from the material in a way that previously had been considered to be fundamental to spatial abstraction, rupturing any notion of an a priori opposition between space and place, or of an inherent affinity between place and matter or space and the abstract.[55] Hollywood-the-place followed a similar logic, seeming both deceptively readable, "a perfectly zoned city so you know exactly what kind of people economically live in each section from executives and directors, through technicians in their bungalows right down to extras,"[56] and hopelessly abstract, a decentered, nowhere and everywhere—what Ralph Carson, the narrator of Horace McCoy's 1938 novel *I Should Have Stayed Home*, fears will be "a cheap town filled with cheap stores and cheap people, like the town I had left, identically like any one of ten thousand other small towns in the country."[57]

interior decoration

Letter to MGM, August 1938:

Aug. 8 1938
Metro Goldwyn Mayer
Film Exchange,
Walton Street,
Atlanta, Ga.

Gentlemen:

I was so charmed by your setting for "Merrily We Live" that I have been to see it several times and have bombarded our local theatres for pictures of the beautiful house. They have referred me to you, as to where I may secure pictures of the sets.

I am planning a house and am so anxious to have the beautiful door way in my house.

After my several attendances to the show I still can't remember enough of the details to put them on paper. Please Sirs, can you help me. I must have that door in my house.

Thanking you in advance for your courtesy.

I am,

Very Sincerely

Mrs. Fred L_____.

S_____, Tenn.[58]

Letter from MGM Distributed by Loew's Incorporated to Hal Roach Studios:

Sept 2, 1938
Hal Roach Studios
Culver City, California

Dear Sirs:—

We are attaching a letter received in the Exchange quite some time ago which is self-explanatory. We had only one still on hand which we forwarded to Mrs. L_____ but it did not give her the front view which she desires.

If you have any photos or any other material that you would care to send us, we would be very glad to forward it on to Mrs. L_____.

Yours very truly,

LOEW'S INCORPORATED[59]

WAX

Given the changing relationship between matter and place in Hollywood, the reference to wax—and particularly to a *city* of wax—in the earlier-mentioned short film *The City of Wax* is instructive. If Hollywood cinema raises questions about how we define materiality, it is an inquiry for which wax is perhaps the most famous metaphor. In his *Meditations on First Philosophy*, René Descartes uses wax as an analogy to ask, "What is the essential property of an object?" (After all, wax can change shape or even chemical form and still be recognized as wax.) Extricating material properties and sense perception from essence, Descartes subordinated the material world to cognition and transformed the way in which matter could be thought. Wax can be seen as a kind of originary metaphor for nonanalytic forms of cognition, those that are not so much outside of thinking as outside of the forefront of consciousness and yet still connected to the "I": the wax seal serves as sign of the *signature* and the absence of the subject;[60] the wax tablet and wax grooved phonograph record functioned as metaphors for memory and the unconscious and, later, for language and the trace.[61]

Film, like wax, is pliable, clear, and capable of being imprinted. It is also, like many things modern, both more efficient and more dangerous than its Enlightenment counterpart. The relationship between cinema and wax is, in other words, not an incidental one. Vanessa R. Schwartz has argued, for instance, that the process of walking through serial displays at nineteenth-century wax museums like the Musée Grévin in Paris introduced audiences to the forms of spectatorship later required by realist narrative cinema.[62] Giuliana Bruno makes a similar point about the centrality of popular wax exhibits at fairs to the development of early cinema spectatorship.[63] Notably, talking cinema would not have been possible without refinements in wax sound recording technology.

In a reading of Warner Brothers' 1933 horror film *The Mystery of the Wax Museum*, Michelle E. Bloom discusses the tension between the film's narrative depiction of melting wax figures and the technique of cinematic dissolve. The "dissolution of wax [is not] portrayed through dissolves," she observes; instead, "the prevalence of cuts provides a counterpoint to the dissolution of wax."[64] To overlay the vision of wax melting with a dissolve would be redundant, she points out, noting that in French, the dissolve is called *fondu enchaîné* or a "melted connection" from the infinitive *fondre*, which means "to melt." Thus, she surmises, "the dissolution and resolidification of wax [in the film] functions as a paradigm for the diegetic tension of the Hollywood film and its formulaic resolution."[65] In other words, things fall apart and then, this being Hollywood, they get put back together again—if only incompletely. However, dissolve in Hollywood cinema serves as more than a paradigm for narrative resolution; it is a self-reflexive tool that draws attention to the limitations of the cinematic medium itself. The dissolve is generally used to mark a similarity between two places, events, or characters or a flashback or memory. It foregrounds, even as it disrupts, the time-space narrative of the film. Yet almost from the moment of its invention, the dissolve, in contrast to the cut, seemed a technique that was imperfect to its task. In his 1926 book *The Mind and the Film: A Treatise on the Psychological Factors in the Film*, Gerard Fort Buckle argues (presciently perhaps) that dissolve is disposable. It represents a failure of the scenario; he writes, "by starting from the correct angle of conception, the dissolve and flash-back could almost be eliminated."[66] Because the dissolve signifies, to some degree, aesthetic failure, it often functions as a metaphor for transformations in film aesthetic technologies.

The failure of dissolve, in other words, might also be said to be its success. While the cut propels traditional filmic narrative forward in time, compelling the spectator to suture its fragments into a coherent whole,[67] the dissolve instead offers the possibility of temporal reversibility or simultaneity and thereby undermines the progressive thrust of most Hollywood cinema.[68]

Film still from *The Mystery of the Wax Museum*, 1933, Warner Brothers Pictures, Inc. Courtesy of the Stills, Posters and Paper Collections, Motion Picture Department, George Eastman House, Rochester, New York.

Dissolve, in other words, overthrows time for place. While the dissolve seems to disrupt the diegetic present by making narrative reference to another *time*—the past, future, or irrational temporality of the dream vision—it does so by making visual reference to another *place*. And unlike the cut, which demonstrates the boundedness of the cinematic frame and the precision of the filmmakers' technique, dissolve tends to emphasize the imprecision and ephemerality of cinema and motion picture production. Dissolve is messy; it calls attention to its own imperfection. While the cut might be said to mimic the sequential narrative of waxwork display, the imprecision of dissolve can be found only in cinema. Dissolve announces, even licenses, the most cinematic aspect of a film as technology. (It is perhaps a bit too bold in this regard, and for this reason veers close to camp.) Therefore, dissolve might also be seen to function as a metaphor for film both as medium and technology, alluding in particular to the volatile and transitory nature of film. (Is it a coincidence that the demise of the dissolve technique, which became relegated to lowbrow flicks and television, coincided with the movie industry's switch to the less volatile acetate film in the 1950s?)

Dissolve is why MGM's 1939 classic *The Wizard of Oz*, a film that allegorizes many things, might be said to be a preeminent allegory of studio-era Hollywood. Dorothy's immersion into the dream world of Oz is precipitated by a merging of dissolve with montage—a close-up and prism shot of Dorothy "superimposed over shots of the whirling cyclone and the house whirling through space." The purpose, the screenplay announces, is to "suggest the sensations of a person going under gas or ether."[69] Salman Rushdie remarks in his reading of the film, "This device—the knocking out of Dorothy—is the most radical and in some ways the worst of all the changes wrought in Frank Baum."[70] (In Baum's story, it is never clear whether or not Oz is a real place.) Yet it is precisely this moment, Rushdie notes, that produces Dorothy as a spectator and that simultaneously anchors the film's allegorical connection to MGM's "dream factory" and to the history of motion picture production more generally.[71] "What she sees through the window is a sort of movie," Rushdie writes, "the window acting as a cinema-screen, a frame within a frame—which prepares her for the new sort of movie she is about to step into."[72] But before Dorothy "steps into" this new film, she must watch a miniaturized history of filmmaking technique projected before her with newsreel-like precision—introducing her to montage (the lady knitting in her rocking chair, then a cow, then two men floating by in a rowboat); parallel editing (a long shot of the exterior of the "house spinning up in the swirling funnel of the cyclone" is followed by a long shot of Dorothy inside "screaming as the bed spins and rolls around the floor," which is followed by a long process shot of the house falling); special effects (Miss Gulch on her bike transforms into a witch on a broomstick, Dorothy's house whirls in the tornado and lands); and synchronized sound (the witch "gives a wild, weird peal of laughter").[73] Finally and more dramatically, the film announces the arrival of TECHNICOLOR. Color does not dissolve in gently—it announces itself in *"a blaze"* when Dorothy opens her front door to enter the scene/screen.[74]

Dorothy goes inside, however, by walking outside. Rushdie points out that Dorothy's "homelessness, her *unhousing*, is underlined by the fact that, after all the door-play of the transitional sequence, and having now stepped out of doors, she will not be permitted to enter any interior at all until she arrives at the Emerald City."[75] And if, as it seems perfectly reasonable to suggest, the assembly line production that goes on inside the Emerald City, where beauticians can "even dye [Dorothy's] eyes to match [her] gown," serves as a kind of false front for the behind-the-screen machinations of the Hollywood studio, then when Dorothy goes "outside" to go "inside," she is not entering a movie screen but leaving one.

While the explicit problem for Dorothy in *The Wizard of Oz* is dislocation, nonetheless Dorothy's desire to go home is, as Rushdie remarks, "the least convincing feature of the film." (After all, Kansas *is* a dump; and Dorothy, with Judy Garland's big girl voice and garish red slippers, seems ill-suited to inhabit it, despite her saying she pines for it.) The resolution of the film lies not in thwarting the stumbling blocks (the twister, the Wizard, the Witch) in the way of bringing Dorothy home, but by raising questions about the fallacy of apparent "spatial reconciliation" in Hollywood cinema.[76] The spiraling close-up of Dorothy in dissolve clicking the heels of her ruby red slippers to return to Kansas reproduces the more theatrical dissolution of the Wicked Witch: "I'm melting! Melting! Oh, what a world! What a world! Who would have thought a good little girl like you could destroy my beautiful wickedness! Ohhhh! Look out! Look out! I'm going! Ohhhhh—Ohhhhhhhhhh!" the Wicked Witch shrieks as she descends into an elevator under the sound stage, leaving her costume and hat smoldering on the floor. It reproduces as well as the "hazardous and technically unexplainable journey into the outer stratosphere" made by the Wizard, who floats away in the balloon "and passes out of sight."[77] For Dorothy, in other words, going back to Kansas, that nonideal idealized home, means moving one step closer to the inaccessible, one step closer to death. Dorothy's final words before the "fade out" are themselves a kind of dissolve; she acquiesces to her family's disbelief: "Oh, but anyway, Toto, we're home—home! . . . And. . . . oh, Auntie Em, there's no place like home!" It is no accident that Dorothy sounds a bit like the Witch (not to mention Molly Bloom) in her dying throes. Kansas does not take Dorothy outside the scene-dream—there is no outside. (Remember Hog Junction?) Nor can it be said that the film makes the outside inside, in which Kansas becomes a production of Oz, nor Oz a production of Kansas. Oz, like Kansas, like Hollywood, becomes a nonoriginary origin, a home that is not "at home," but which is instead a perpetual substitute and deferral. Dorothy's "dissolve" in this final scene comes to allude less to transformations of cinema technology, in other words, than to their concomitant death throes.[78]

By the time *Sunset Boulevard* was made by Paramount in 1949, the dissolve had become codified as an allusion to cinematic failure and to the confusion between inside and outside that is cinema's false front. *Sunset Boulevard* begins at the end, with the vision of a speaking corpse, which, floating in a pool, is both outside and inside; it ends with an eerie and silent close-up of a face, Norma Desmond's, filmed primarily from inside, going outside into a dissolve. The writer Gillis (William Holden) has dubbed the pathetic has-beens from the silent era who play bridge at Norma Desmond's "her Wax Works,"[79] but it is clear from the first shot that Gillis is also one of the waxworks, as is Norma herself (Gloria Swanson). If Hollywood cinema in the 1930s might be seen as a melancholic cinema, haunted by self-produced effigies from the days before voice, Hollywood-the-place was imagined as populated by the living dead: Nathanael West's transplanted (homeless?) "middle western" locusts, alongside the petrified (if pliable) casualties of the contingencies of sound technology.

"We who have witnessed the birth of an art," wrote the infamous film historians Maurice Bardèche and Robert Brasillach of the arrival of the voice in cinema, "may have also witnessed its death."[80] The dissolve, which unsettles the opposition between inside and outside, subject and object, presence and having been, comes to stand in for the specter of death—and denial of death—that is associated with the arrival of sound and might be said to perform technically the spectrality of Hollywood itself. "Ever since the telephone and gramophone made it possible to isolate voices from bodies, the voice naturally has reminded us of the voice of the dead," writes Michel Chion, " . . . and those who witnessed the birth of those technologies were aware of their funerary quality." Charles Brackett, describing the writing of *Sunset Boulevard*, comments that "[Billy] Wilder, [D. M.] Marshman [a *Life* reporter] and I were acutely conscious of the fact that we lived in a town which had been swept by a social change as profound as that brought about in the Old South by the Civil War. Overnight, the coming of sound brushed gods and goddesses into obscurity."[81]

No wonder Hollywood went all abuzz with the making of *Gone With the Wind*. It was in Atlanta, not Oz, that Hollywood found its best allegory.

SERIES

INTEROFFICE MEMO[82]
To: Mr. Menzies
From: Mr. Selznick
Subject: Backings GONE WITH THE WIND
Date: Nov 20 1938

. . . We must bear in mind that we cannot have a single phoney-looking foot of film in GONE WITH THE WIND. On the other hand, if we take this to mean we should spend the maximum amount of money to make everything perfect, regardless of whether it is going to be appreciably visible, we will all be out of business. . . .

SELZNICK INTERNATIONAL PICTURES, INC.
To: Messrs. Wheeler, Menzies, Lambert, Coles and Mrs. Leone
Date: December 6, 1938
From: Mr. Klune
Subject: GONE WITH THE WIND
Retention of material.

Further in connection with Mr. Selznick's note concerning the retention of miniatures, sketches, special props, etc. used in GONE WITH THE WIND, for the time being it is important that all of these be kept in as good condition as possible, and that nothing be disposed of without my authorization, including rejects.

Later on we will select one point at which to accumulate and assemble all of the material that may possibly be needed for the display at the World's Fair, which we have been asked for.
Rak

INTEROFFICE COMMUNICATION
To: Messrs. Menzies, Wheeler and Platt
Date: 1/30/39

My discussion with you today about the general size and character of the sets, and about going somewhat further toward theatricalism, applies to Rhett's home also.
DOS

INTEROFFICE COMMUNICATION
To: Messrs. Cukor, Menzies, Lambert, Plunkett
cc. Mr. Klune
SUBJECT: Authenticity
DATE: 2/8/39

There is no question in my mind but that to date we have seriously hurt the beauty of our production by letting authenticity dominate theatrical effects. There is such a thing as carrying authenticity to ridiculous extremes and I feel that in our sets and in our costumes in the future, where authenticity means a loss of beauty, we should take liberties, and considerable ones, with the authenticity. The first people to complain about the lack of beauty will be the Southerners that we are trying to satisfy with authenticity.
dos

INTEROFFICE COMMUNICATION
To: Mr. Cosgrove, cc. Mr. Menzies, Mr. Fleming
SUBJECT: GONE WITH THE WIND
Date: 3/13/39

In connection with the shot which you are going to do of the wounded men in the square, with the line of wounded extending beyond actual bodies and dummies that we will be using, and with the tracks going off into the distance, I wish you would see the reference on page 292 of the book to the "rails shining in the sun." I wish you would go after this effect.

I am also hopeful that Mr. Menzies will be able to contribute some ideas

to Mr. Fleming for ways and means to get this effect of merciless sun and intolerable heat throughout this sequence. We will also bear it in mind in checking through the script on this sequence.
DOS

INTEROFFICE MEMO
To: Mr. Menzies
From: David O. Selznick
Date: 3/21/39

Just as we are planning on carrying out your excellent idea of the green light in the operation room, I wonder if we couldn't do something similar with purple light in the scenes in which Rhett is grief-stricken over Bonnie. I write you about this now, because you might like to bear it in mind in planning the windows, lampshades and other color values of the sets in Rhett's home. I think we could get something really eerie and an atmosphere of gloom if we went in for a purple effect in these scenes.

INTEROFFICE COMMUNICATION
To: Mr. Selznick
Subject: Dance Scene in Bazaar Set
From: Wm. C. Menzies
Date: March 24, 1939

Due to the limitations of the size of the Bazaar set I don't think we were able to get an exciting, swirling finish to the dance, but I have an idea that if it is worth it I would like to build the upper part of the set and the ceiling in miniature and make a whirling plate of this, possibly with a shadow of the dancers thrown against the miniature by using cut-out dolls, or Jack might even be able to burn some people's faces in back of them if we are whirling fast enough. The only thing against it might be that we probably would be a little low on Leigh but I think with the movement and the shortness of the scene she wouldn't suffer too much.

INTEROFFICE COMMUNICATION
SELZNICK INTERNATINAL PICTURES, INC.
To: Mr. Menzies–cc: Messrs. Klune, Wheeler and Kern
Date: 3/31/39

Just as the extra Cosgrove of Ellen's arrival at Tara ought to add value, I think there is a chance for another shot that will add value and one which, as a matter of fact, I am afraid we will need—which is a Cosgrove shot of Twelve Oaks in the late afternoon to precede the scene of the girls asleep

upstairs. This could be entirely or almost entirely painting, with the long afternoon shadows falling over the grounds. I wish you would give this some thought and possibly get up a sketch.
DOS

INTEROFFICE COMMUNICATION
To: Mr. Menzies and Mr. Wheeler
Date: April 3, 1939
From; R.A. Klune
Subject: Sets

Mrs. Selznick has suggested that in the event we should need any additional bedrooms in TARA other than Scarlett's, we use the two bedrooms built for TWELVE OAKS for this purpose.
Rak

INTER-OFFICE COMMUNICATION
To: Mr. Klune—Mr. Menzies[83]
Date; 4/24/39

Curiously, there is a carriage shot with Errol Flyn from the viewpoint of a window in "DODGE CITY" which is almost exactly like that which we planned of Rhett in Scarlett's bedroom. This ought to be seen so that we don't exactly duplicate the shot.
DOS

INTEROFFICE COMMUNICATION
To: Mr. Wheeler
Subject G.W.T.W.
Date: 5/1/39

Do the interiors of Rhett's home check in size and in type of architecture with the exteriors on the Fox lot?
DOS
SELZNICK INTERNATIONAL PICTURES

INTER-OFFICE COMMUNICATION
To Mr. Selznick
From: Lyle Wheeler
Date: May 2, 1939
Subject: Ext. Butler House
The exteriors of Rhett Butler's house, of which I showed you sketches the other day, are to be Matte shots which Jack will make to tie in to an exist-

ing garden set at Fox. In designing the exteriors, I have kept in mind the size and type of the interiors.

    Lwr

INTEROFFICE COMMUNICATION
To: Mr. Kern—cc: Mr. Klune, Mr. Forbes
Date: 6/24/39
From David O. Selznick

We decided last night that we could probably get just the long shot we wanted of the river boat to precede the River Boat Sequence in the Honeymoon by using the night shot in "Tom Sawyer"—the one with all the stars—and Jack felt he could put the river boat into this in place of the raft . Please follow up on this as I would like to have it for preview because otherwise the River Boat Sequence won't make any sense. We also should have some sort of track of negroes singing to go under this long shot and also under the scene itself. I should think you could dig up a stock track of some kind for preview purposes.

    DOS

FIRE

In 1903, Thomas Edison's and Edwin S. Porter's seven-minute biography, *Life of an American Fireman*, introduced narration to cinema. As Cecil B. DeMille tells it, the introduction was simple: "Although this whole stirring biography took only seven minutes in the telling it was the longest American film ever made, and it pointed the way," DeMille writes. "The public decided that it wanted films to tell stories with plots, and fiction came to the screen."[84] Yet just as the image of the locomotive would forever recur in films as an ambivalent homage to *The Great Train Robbery* (and the concomitant dangers of technology and progress it signified),[85] the choice to construct a film in which fire played a fundamental narrative role was not without consequences. "We have only to speak of an object, to think that we are being objective," writes Gaston Bachelard in the opening paragraph of *The Psychoanalysis of Fire*. "But, because we chose it in the first place, the object reveals more about us than we do about it."[86]

Fire, like film, is constituted by a problematic materiality. Both are dangerous and somewhat elusive. Both require a kind of restraint and faith on the part of the spectator. They are simultaneously spectacle and its allegory. One must see and believe, but one can touch only at one's peril. "Fire is for the man who is contemplating it an example of sudden change or development and an example of a circumstantial development. . . . it links the small to the great, the hearth to the volcano, the life of a log to the life of a world,"

Bachelard continues. "The fascinated individual hears *the call of the funeral pyre*. For him destruction is more than a change, it is a renewal."[87] While fire connects the modern world to the ancient and even primeval ones, it is also, for Bachelard, the apotheosis of modern temporality—symbolic of the beauty and blow of sudden expected, yet unpredictable transformation.

Bachelard published *The Psychoanalysis of Fire* in 1938, the year before Nathanael West published *Day of the Locust*. The two texts were produced in exceedingly different circumstances (one in the intellectual milieu of Dijon and Paris on the brink of World War II, the other in the commercial and artistic atmosphere of studio-era Hollywood, albeit a Hollywood populated by German-Jewish socialists who had barely escaped Hitler's regime). It is unlikely, though not impossible, that West could have been influenced by Bachelard. West knew French, having lived in Paris for two years, and was familiar with the French avant-garde and intellectual scene. But this is not really the point. More significant is how each text in its own way meditates on the erotics of apocalypse.

Bachelard's project in his book about fire was to posit a phenomenological and psychological critique of empirical science—to consider, in other words, how unconscious values affect and are shaped by scientific knowledge.[88] He chooses to talk about fire at the moment when its function as center and hearth of the house is becoming anachronistic, when the fireplace begins to be seen more as a decorating option than a necessity. Fire, as Bachelard points out, is "more a *social* reality than a *natural* reality."[89] It is both the sign of first civilization and a sign of civilization destroying itself: modernity at its most virulent. Moreover, it is, according to Bachelard, a primal object of prohibition. Since "fire is initially the object of a *general prohibition*"—*don't touch!!*—"the social interdiction is our first general knowledge of fire." ("The problem of obtaining a personal knowledge of fire is the problem of *clever disobedience*.")[90] Bachelard calls the relationship humans have to fire one of *rêverie* (daydream or fantasy), which he distinguishes from the *rêve*, or dream state. *Rêverie* suggests a trancelike, almost unwitting spectatorship, but also a distracted consciousness (musing) and a divine or sacred awe. It requires, then, a form of spectatorship much like that which Siegfried Kracauer describes of cinema: not only dreamlike but daydreamlike.[91] And yet with a bit less spontaneity and a good deal more wonder. In other words, fire is both a threat to film (it is small wonder that the wax figures in *The Mystery of the Wax Museum* dissolve into flames) and its necessary precursor, not because it made technology possible but because it taught people how to watch.

By the time Bachelard and West wrote their books, fire had already become part of the mythos of Hollywood. Long before Los Angeles burned live on CNN in 1992 in the wake of the Rodney King ruling and thousands of acres of the California coastline erupted into flames in October 2003, many, many

Fire at Warner Brothers, 1952. Courtesy of Bison Archives.

fires had already burned.[92] As Mike Davis points out, Westlake, near downtown Los Angeles, has the highest urban fire incidence in the United States, and Malibu has the highest rate of wildfires in North America.[93] Studios were not immune. Century film company caught fire in 1926. Warner Brothers had a fire on its back lot in 1952. Universal Studios burned down in 1967, razing what was then Hollywood's oldest set: The cathedral built for Lon Chaney's 1923 film *Hunchback of Notre Dame*, which had been used in many films.[94] Paramount had a fire in 1983 that burned the five-acre New York Streets standing set. And the old sets of 20th Century Fox were also razed by fire.

Davis attributes West's vision of a burning Los Angeles to the torrential 1930 Decker Canyon fire, which the county supervisor feared might incinerate the city.[95] More likely, West was impacted by multiple sources. In 1939 Hollywood, there was much ado about fire, what with mishaps on the *Wizard of Oz* set and the filming of the famous fire scene for *Gone With the Wind*.[96] And certainly, West's apocalypse was glossed by the tumult in a Europe and Asia about to self-immolate. None of these events on their own provide a satisfactory explanation for the potency of the metaphor.

The relationship of fire to cinema is overdetermined by virtue of the fact that fire is for film a constitutive threat—and necessary precursor. There is no doubt that a mix of fear and reverie marked early cinema spectatorship. If *Life of an American Fireman* introduced narration to cinema, it did so in a nonlinear fashion. As researchers discovered in the 1970s, in the original version of the film, the fireman's rescue of a mother and her child is shown sequentially, from two points of view that are supposed to occur simultane-

214 HOLLYWOOD(LAND)

ously: first, an interior shot shows the fireman rescuing the mother and baby from a smoke-filled room; next, an exterior shot shows the fireman breaking down the door to enter the burning building while other firemen work to squelch the fire outside. Noël Burch attributes this narrative disruption to the "alterity of the relationship these early films entertained with the spectators who watched them."[97] For Burch, this discomfort is marked by a spatial unease, an anxiety about the mobility of the camera. And, Mary Ann Doane remarks, responding to Burch, "concerns about the stability of point of view [and spatial fixity] seem to outweigh the disadvantages of temporal" incongruity.[98] Mark Garrett Cooper argues further that "the instant critical attention shifts from the placement of the camera [and point of view] to the spaces represented by the mise-en-scène, it becomes clear that the shots figure a complementary relationship between inside and outside in order to stage a competition between the two. The shots each depict two distinct spaces and at the same time insist on a permeable barrier between them."[99] But the film also posits different forms of spectatorship, as constituted not by the perspective one sees (inside/outside) or the temporal disconnect/connection between the two scenes (some of it occurs simultaneously, some not), but by the extent to which each scene is made visible.

The film institutes a spatial and temporal division between smoke (which clouds the room inside) and fire (which rages outside) and, implicitly, between interiority and exteriority, private and public, femininity and masculinity, melodrama and the epic, the passive and the active, the atemporal or even extemporal and the temporally bound. It is through the juxtaposition of smoke and fire that the placelessness and problematic materiality of film are played out. If the watching of fire is associated with cinematic spectatorship, smoke might be said to presage questions about cinematic materiality: What is smoke? Is it a thing or not a thing? Can it be located? Contained? Smoke can only be "captured" on film, an equally nebulous medium, and therefore it is filmed quite a lot. Smoke presupposes fire, serving either as its precursor, its remainder, or, in the case of the witch's demise in *The Wizard of Oz*, its substitute. *Stand-in*, if you will. Smoke in cinema serves as a residue of the first narration and thereby might be said to serve as a sign of cinematic history, or at the least of a narratable past. But smoke, and more so the act of smoking, also suggests a kind of exteriority, the making of place outside the subject, and alludes to the accompanying confusion of insides and outsides on which Cooper remarks.

Smoking "is the most exterior thing to our understanding," writes Georges Bataille. "Insofar as we are absorbed in smoking we escape ourselves, we slip into a semi-absence, and if it is true that a concern for elegance is always connected to waste, smoking is elegance, is silence itself."[100] If fire elicits a kind of reverie for Bachelard, the "semi-absence" Bataille sees in smoke and smoking —"we escape ourselves"—suggests a concomitant act of being/not being that

The Brown Derby at Hollywood and Vine, circa 1930s.
Author's collection.

Hollywood Brown Derby, 2005.
Photograph © Terrah Johnson Photography.

is also constitutive of film spectatorship. Watching a film can be an out-of-body experience, a momentary escape from the burdens of being a subject. But such an escape is also its risk.

On the page previous to the one mentioned above, Bataille writes (it is crossed out on the manuscript, but not in the published text): "[All communication among men is rich with garbage. It is natural to want to avoid filth, garbage, ordinary trash. But a little simplicity reveals that a foul smell also marks the presence of life.]"[101] He is talking about "authenticity" in the "spiritual contact between humans," about what functions as a substitute in the crass and secular order of modern culture for the ancient sacred sacrifice of animals. If fire alludes to the inaccessible and to indirect knowledge, to that which can be named but is forever out of touch, smoke is even one step more removed, evoking the simulation of sacrifice, codified as waste. "This is why I think it is not too much to ask anyone who persists in wanting to live completely not to put on too many airs and, as there is always filth where there is life, to get used to filth," Bataille writes before the crossed-out passage; then he adds a disavowal: "I am not saying this to rid myself of a problem."[102] Implicit in studio-era Hollywood's production of place is the residue of disavowal, a disassociation from the very materiality it seeks to simulate.

Remember the Brown Derby? There were four Brown Derby restaurants, actually, the first one on Wilshire Boulevard, designed in the shape of a bowler hat. But the Hollywood Brown Derby, which opened at 1628 Vine Street in 1929, was the famous one in movie lore. It stuck around for quite some time, closing in 1985, long after its heyday. The building caught fire soon after it closed. As I write this, its run-down remains house a nail salon.

Plans are in the works to tear it down and break ground on a 305-room hotel, luxury condominium, and shopping mall. Still, you can eat at its stand-in, a replica at the Disney-MGM Studios' theme park in Orlando.

studio

The tour of Universal Studios' back lot is a tour of natural disasters. Fires, floods, earthquakes, you get to experience them all—albeit in miniature. Unlike the back lot tour at Warner Brother's, the Universal tour doesn't pretend to reveal much about film production. Sure, your guide drives you past the house from Alfred Hitchcock's *Psycho—it looks so small*—you can see how the scale was manipulated to evoke distance. At the bottom of the hill, somehow ironically, is the bloated set of Whoville from Jim Carey's overwrought *Grinch* film. Your guide points out the swamp from *Gilligan's Island*, making it clear that the castaways were even dumber than they looked not to escape from that small pond. And yes, your guide explains how DeMille manufactured the parting of the Red Sea—not once, but twice, the first time (in 1923) by running the film in reverse, and in the 1956 Charlton Heston version, mechanically. But while you drive through a sound stage, you never really feel you're seeing what is going on behind the screen. You don't get the feeling that many films are made on the lot anymore, and if they are it is clear the tour bus avoids them. (A commercial *is* being made the day you take the tour, but it is for a new Universal Studios theme park in Japan.) For the function of this tour is not to make tourists feel like actors or producers, but to allow them to experience a kind of apotheosis of spectatorship. The tour extends the limits of the film diegesis, moving participants not behind but into the screen. There is no outside here—it is all so loud. You too become a hologram, like the 3-D projections of the Terminator at the show in the amusement park just off the back lot. You too fall into the screen while the soundtrack runs at full volume in your head.

STAND-IN

The burning of Atlanta in *Gone With the Wind* was the first episode of the film that was shot. It was reasoned that the most cost-effective way to clear old sets from the forty-acre back lot of Selznick studios so that new ones could be built was to torch them.[103] (The fire also made for a "sensational stunt," which David O. Selznick compared to the "Chariot Race in *Ben Hur*.")[104] The burning "boxcars" of Atlanta were therefore produced by redecorating, and then incinerating, the remains of the 1933 *King Kong* Skull Island set, which had itself been created by redecorating the massive Temple of Jerusalem set that had been left over from DeMille's 1926 biblical epic *The King of Kings*.[105]

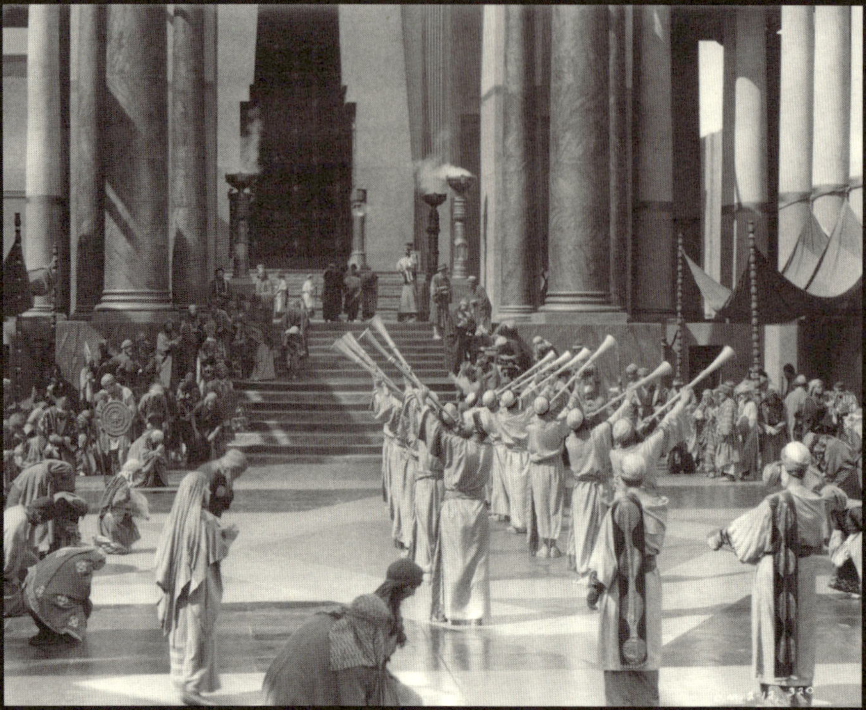

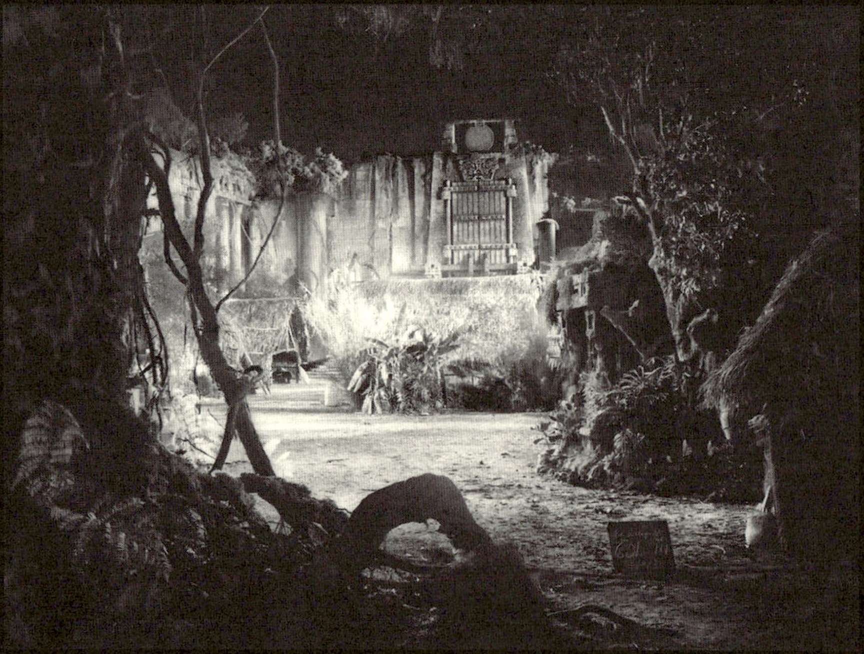

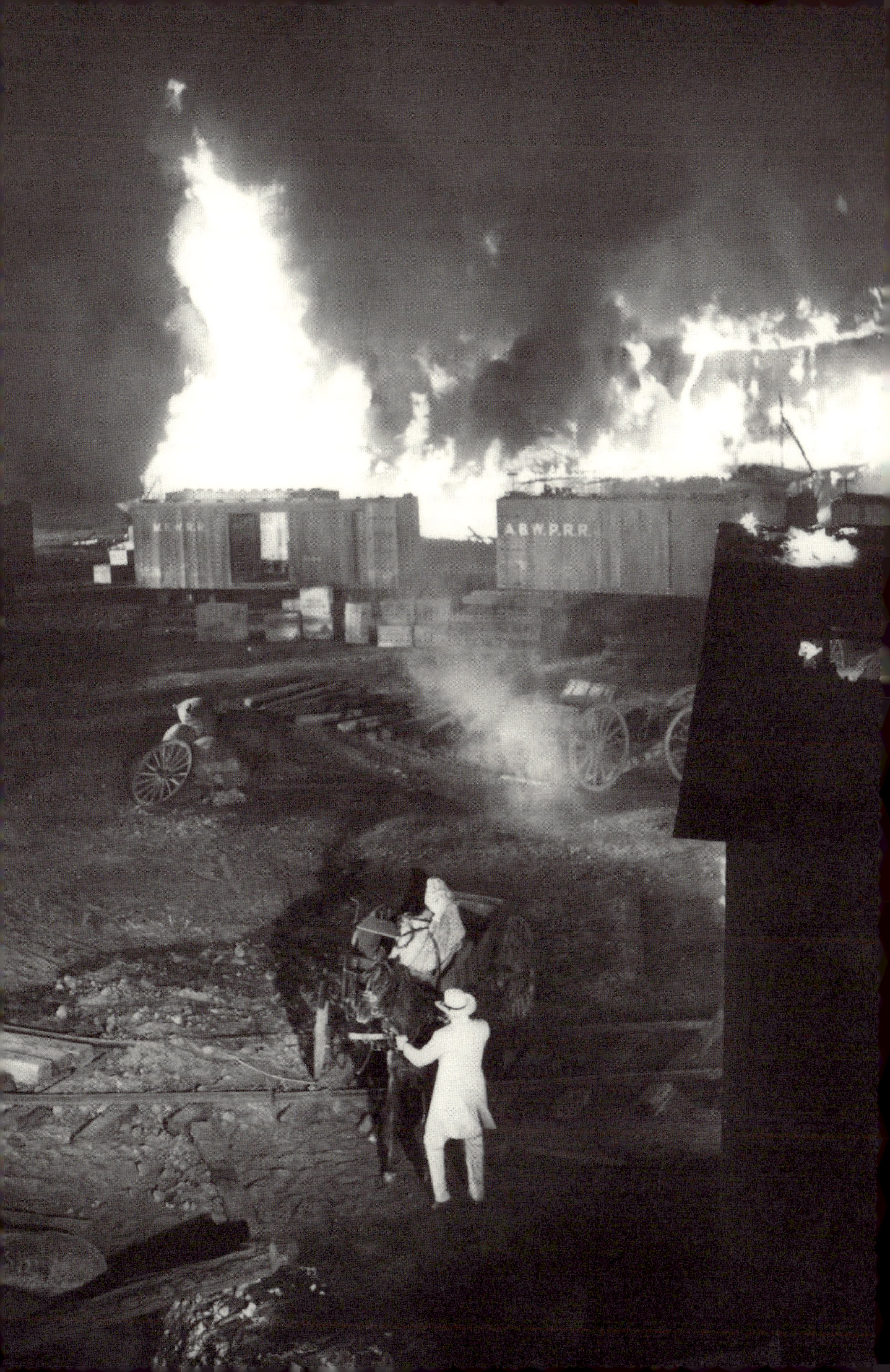
A.B.W.P.R.R.

(previous spread)

Temple in the *King of Kings*, 1926.
Courtesy of the Academy of Motion Picture Arts and Sciences.

Jungle in *King Kong*, 1933.
Courtesy of sculptureone.com.

The burning of Atlanta in *Gone With the Wind*, 1939.
GWTW Images/MGM Collection, Academy of Motion Pictures Arts and Sciences.

Rhett and Scarlett were played by stand-ins, since the role of Scarlett had not yet been cast.

The making of the scene, while singularly spectacular, follows a more generalized logic of substitution, citation, and seriality that is constitutive of Hollywood film production as well as to place making more generally. The recycling of back lot sets by dressing and redressing them had been standard practice in Hollywood since 1915. "Nowadays there are very few standing sets except for television," commented Robert Boyle, who worked in the Art Department at Paramount under Hans Dreier in the 1930s, in an oral history recorded in the 1980s. "The standing sets, however, in those days [studio era] were left and then you would revamp them and revamp them. Now they're inclined to just go in and bulldoze the whole thing out and the next company comes in with a different situation, because so many of the studios are rentals, now. You get space, so they sell space. And that's more valuable than keeping an old set around."[106] Even for expensive pictures, sets and parts of sets such as staircases were ripped apart, redecorated, and reused, reshot from different angles in order to create the illusion of newness.[107] (Bette Davis, so the story goes, descended the same staircase in three Warner Brothers' pictures; when she was directed to again walk down them in a fourth film, she balked.)[108] B movies and serial films, in particular, were made recognizable by a continuity of actors and set environments. They were also distinguishable by a singularity that could be read only against the frame of repetition. They could be viewed as new, in other words, only if you already knew what was old about them.

"French Street." MGM standing set, 1939.
Courtesy of Bison Archives.

220 HOLLYWOOD(LAND)

The logic of the standing set—and even the set or set element that has been remade, reshot, or reused—is of a "not quite" presence similar to what Ann Chisholm describes as constitutive of Hollywood body doubles and stand-ins. The stand-in, like the latter-day body double, is a "dangerous supplement," she argues, referring to Derrida's notion of supplement as "the outside of the inside" that is already "within the inside."[109] The problematic transposition of inside and outside arises again, this time as a kind of necessary masking. "There are two absences necessary to the economy of body doubling," writes Chisholm, "the absence of the star's body and the absence of the body double's body" since the body double not only masquerades as the star, but the "star masquerades as the body double."[110]

When he comes across a photograph of four stand-ins dressed up in the familiar costumes for the stars of *The Wizard of Oz*, Rushdie observes,

> Stand-ins know their fate: they know we don't want to admit their existence: Even when our rational minds tell us that in this or that difficult shot—when the Witch flies, when the Cowardly Lion dives through a glass window—we aren't watching the stars, yet the part of us that has suspended disbelief insists on seeing the stars and not their doubles. Thus the stand-ins are rendered invisible even when they are in full view. They remain off-camera even when they are on-screen.[111]

Hollywood's use of set renewal and the stand-in are economic: preservation of the star's energy, perceived image, or bodily integrity or of the labor and costs of spatial illusion. (In big-budget pictures like *Rebecca*, the setting serves as a star in its own right or, at the least, as a supporting actor that sets off the star but hopefully does not steal the show.) But Hollywood cinema relies more generally on a stand-in economy, one that is induced by and induces the simultaneous pleasure and denial of the "*not quite the same* in which we recognize the *same*," the way Lesley Stern describes smoking tobacco—or the funeral of a first husband when he is no longer your husband.[112]

The logic of the stand-in is possible only within a late modernist economy already so accustomed to the vicissitudes of mass production that spectators can perform nuanced distinctions between objects and events that are the same and yet not the same. This is, like Reno-vation, *repetition with a difference*. Or repetition *as* difference. The 1930s, remember, brought marketing to its mature state so that the serial reproducibility of Fordism was replaced by the every-changing sameness of progressive obsolescence. The mature star economy, and the studio system more generally, presuppose an audience that is sophisticated enough to make infinite distinctions between infinitely substitutable images and narratives, while simultaneously recognizing the nuances of and their complicity in, a mass cultural economy that such perceptions require. It becomes no longer enough to distinguish between, say, a Norma Shearer picture and a Bette Davis film, but between MGM's and

Stand-ins for Cary Grant and Katharine Hepburn. Set still from *Bringing Up Baby* (1938).
Courtesy of the Academy of Motion Picture Arts and Sciences.

Warner Brothers' cinematographic and spatial styles.[113] Infinite substitutability, in other words, becomes the central drama of Hollywood narrative, and perhaps of Depression itself.

Substitutability is the primary joke of the 1928 King Vidor film *Show People*, in which Marion Davies plays a Hollywood hopeful and talented slapstick comedienne (Peggy Pepper) who turns into an insufferable (and awful) dramatic starlet (Patricia Peppoir). The film, like most films of the Hollywood-on-Hollywood genre, is liberally doused with cameo appearances by actors and directors playing themselves but is intriguing because the comedy also anticipates and spoofs its audience's knowledge of scandal sheet rumors about Davies herself.[114] Davies was William Randolph Hearst's hardly hidden lover; her failed acting career has often been attributed to Hearst, who, it has been claimed, ruined Davies's career by funding her exclusively in the dramatic roles he preferred instead of encouraging her to play the comic roles at which she excelled. One of the highlights of the film is a trick shot in which, shortly after her arrival in Hollywood, the ingénue Peggy Pepper recognizes and then disdains the tennis-skirt-clad Marion Davies—the actress playing herself. More subtly, the film pokes fun at Davies's role as a central figure in the unsolved shooting of the producer Thomas Ince aboard Hearst's yacht in 1924. (Rumor had it that Hearst shot Ince by mistake while aiming at Charlie Chaplin, with whom he believed Davies was having an affair.) The joke in the film, then, is one of nonrecognition: Peggy Pepper, standing next to Chaplin at a movie premier, doesn't recognize the actor (her lover?) without his makeup, hair dye, and costume.[115] Then again, who would?

A scene about a story meeting in Fitzgerald's *The Love of the Last Tycoon* serves as an even more pointed metaphor for this narrative economy: "'Let each character see himself in the other's place,' [Boxley] said. 'The policeman is about to arrest the thief when he sees that the thief actually has *his* face. I mean show it that way. You could almost call the thing "Put Yourself in My Place."'"[116] Identification, the novel suggests, relies on a kind of infinite substitutability; place making is revealed as *re-placement*. And love becomes a recognition not of singularity, but of similarity. When Stahr sees his lover-to-be for the second time, he thinks, "There she was—face and form and smile against the light inside. It was Minna's face—the skin with its peculiar radiance as if phosphorus had touched it, the mouth with its warm line that never counted costs—and over all the haunting jollity that had fascinated a generation."[117] The passage is itself a repetition of an earlier one in the novel: "Smiling faintly at him not four feet away was the face of his dead wife, identical even to the expression."[118] Of course, it is *not* Minna Davis, the dead film star who had been Stahr's wife and creation, but Kathleen Moore, a "stray," who had "followed a truck in through the gate" and gotten caught in a studio flood. Stahr first sees her floating in the flood, clinging to the top of a prop, "a huge head of Siva."[119]

What prevents Kathleen from being Minna's double is her voice. She is, in other words, "the same with a difference." When Stahr greets Kathleen, he hears "another voice speak that was not Minna's voice."[120] While the voice seems to be the measure of authenticity, it must be recognized that in cinema there is no such thing as an authentic voice. Even a voice that is directly recorded is a reproduction, and, as Chion notes, "The idea of dubbing [replacing an on-screen character's voice with the voice of another] was born with the sound film itself."[121] He cites as an example Hitchcock's decision to adapt his 1929 film *Blackmail* for sound by having an English actress, Joan Barry, stand outside the frame with a microphone and speak the dialogue, which he listened to through headphones, while the German-speaking main actress, Anny Ondra, "pantomimed the words" for the camera.[122]

When Rushdie writes, "We are the stand-ins now," then, he suggests more than the identification a film spectator has with a film actor; he refers to the ambivalent relationship American (and global) culture has to Hollywood as a cultural as well as cinematic phenomenon, to the ways in which Hollywood produced and produces the modern, and now global, subject.[123] "In looking over a group of about 35 extras called for atmosphere work in 'The Truth About Hollywood,' which he is directing for RKO," comments a 1932 article in *Film Daily*, "George Cukor says he found eight former directors, a dozen former leading women, four former stars and one former boxing champion."[124] Fitzgerald's Stahr is himself a stand-in, after all. His character had been modeled after MGM's famous producer Irving Thalberg. (Thalberg, like Stahr, had married a film actress, Norma Shearer; although Thalberg, unlike Stahr, had died before his wife.) Moreover, the modern subject might be said to be formed through an ambivalent desire for and resistance to the stand-in. Or, in Adam Phillips words, "The same things and 'the same things done up in a different fashion,' become [both] the modernist problem and the modernist solution." (Freud, he notes, had already made this point.)[125] This tension between singularity and the stand-in is played out in the Hollywood narrative again and again, reaching an apotheosis in the 1933 World's Fair exhibition of "shooting a scene," in which spectators stand in for extras, simulating their not quite presence behind the screen.

And still, of course, there were those who were even more forgotten. Or, if not forgotten, made to stand in in a more ontological sense. "We don't call them anything especially," Stahr says to Kathleen of the unnamed pail-carrying black man who comments to Stahr that he doesn't let his children see movies, "because there's no profit." Stahr comments, after he thinks a bit, "'They have pictures of their own.'"[126] From then on, however, he submits ideas for films to a fictive vision of "The Negro," who stands in for his most discriminating critic.

"Met James Cruze, who is quite anxious to see a script of *Harlem*," writes Wallace Thurman to William Jourdan Rapp in June 1929.

> Has long wanted to do a first class colored movie and showed me countless stories he has considered. He wants to star Evelyn Preer, which is alright by me so long as he buys the movie rights. I'll wire you immediately any developments. Bowman is also here andhe [sic] likes her, so I made a grand little sales talk on how he could make use of both of them in Harlem. Believe it or not I still have conferences on the average of once a week with various Pathe officials. I have come to the conclusion that they must like to talk to me, or that they are trying to gain some knowledge. I thus talk quite guardedly, for fear should I be led into a discussion of Negro life, a dictaphone might be around which could realy [sic] my talk to a voracious scenario hound. This may sound fanciful, but you dont [sic] know Hollywood.[127]

sleep

Obituary in the *New York Times*, October 2, 2002:

> Allen Parkinson, a star-struck entrepreneur who developed an over-the-counter sleep aid and built a wax museum dedicated to Hollywood legends, died on Aug. 19 at his home in Warwick, R.I. He was 83.
>
> Mr. Parkinson was the creator of Sleep-Eze and the original owner of Movieland Wax Museum in Buena Park, Calif.
>
> With all the hoopla of a Hollywood premiere, Mr. Parkinson opened

the wax museum in May 1962, complete with searchlights, bleachers holding thousands of fans and the arrival of stars in black limousines. . . . During its peak years in the 1960's Movieland drew as many as 1.2 million visitors annually.

Mr. Parkinson was working as a salesman for a wine company in 1948 when he noticed an advertisement in a Canadian newspaper for a sleep aid called Persomnia.

Plagued by insomnia himself, Mr. Parkinson thought that the idea of a sleep aid was good, but that the name was terrible, and he came up with Sleep-Eze.

Fellow insomniacs turned the nonbarbiturate product into a best seller . . . [128]

INSOMNIA

Between 1929 and 1932, the Payne Fund, a philanthropic organization in Cleveland, in cahoots with the conservative Motion Picture Research Council, financed nearly twenty studies on the health and behavioral effects of movie watching on children.[129] Eight volumes on the studies were published by Macmillan between 1933 and 1935, covering such topics as *Motion Pictures and Standards of Morality*, *Movies and Conduct*, and *Boys, Movies, and City Streets*. The findings were summarized in a polemical book in 1933, *Our Movie Made Children*, which became a best-seller.[130] The Payne studies, controversial at the time and considered by some to have "as much scientific value as a recipe for noodle soup," were nonetheless hugely influential and widely accepted and are even now considered a landmark in social science research as the first scientific investigations of the impact of mass media on people.[131]

The most important aspect of the studies, at least in terms of cinema history, however, is the fact that they were inspired by and provided legitimacy for the early 1930s movements that sought to increase government regulation of film content. The moralistic Production Code had been established in Hollywood in 1930 as a means to "preserve movie purity," but it had been largely ineffective until the Catholic Legion of Decency, galvanized in part by the results of the Payne studies, launched a campaign to boycott "immoral" movies. In July 1934, Will Hayes, president of the industry trade association, the Motion Picture Producers and Distributors of America, created a new censorship office, the Production Code Administration (PCA), with Joe Breen at the helm. The PCA's task was to scrutinize every script and film image for supposed improprieties and, if the material was approved, to issue its seal of approval, which was required for a film to be shown in theaters.

Against this backdrop, the sleep study, conducted by three psychologists at Ohio State University who investigated the impact of movie watching on

Still from *The Wizard of Oz* (1939).
MGM Collection, Academy of Motion Pictures Arts and Sciences.

the sleep habits of 170 children living at a state children's home, seems a good deal less provocative than those linking film spectatorship to increased rates of drinking, violence, petty crime, race prejudice, and promiscuity. The study was most notable for being a disaster of scientific design. The scientists divided the children into two groups: they took the first group to see movies every evening; the other group saw no films, although occasionally they went on other excursions. The scientists then recorded both groups' movements during the night by wiring their bedsprings. Although the data from the experiments "showed few patterns," according to the authors of *Children and the Movies: Media Influence and the Payne Fund Controversy*, the Ohio State scientists nonetheless "categorized nonmovie [watching] children who slept soundly through the night as well rested, but ... intimated that movie stimulation could induce a drug-like stupor in film-viewing children. They construed tossing in bed at night as healthy for nonmovie children and for moviegoers as the physical manifestation of disturbing, movie-inspired dreams."[132]

What is most remarkable about the study, then, is not its findings, but the assumptions that led the researchers to associate sleep problems with film spectatorship. To be sure, the connection they were making between film watching and sleeping was not theirs alone. From the early days of cinema, the association between film viewing and sleeping, especially dreaming, has been a central, if at times contested, concern of almost all sociological and aesthetic analyses of film spectatorship. Jane Addams, the director of Chicago's Hull House, for instance, aptly titled her chapter about children's movie watching in her 1909 book *The Spirit of Youth and City Streets* "House of Dreams."[133] Hollywood was itself often dubbed a "Dream Factory"[134] which manufactured Horatio Alger stories of success or, by contrast, was portrayed as a dystopian "dream dump," allegorized by West by the ever-expanding heap of partly demolished sets on studio back lots.[135]

Even early studies of cinema take for granted that an association between dreaming and film watching can be made. "Film is the dream . . . which makes one dream," writes Siegfried Kracauer, citing the psychoanalytic critic Serge Lebovici.[136] It was, in fact, the supposed dreamlike quality of film viewing that distinguished it from the experience of going to the theater. "A cinema audience is not a corporate body, like a theatre audience, but a flowing and inconstant mass," writes Iris Barry in her 1926 book *Let's Go to the Movies*. Barry continues,

> To go to the theatre is to buy an experience, and between experience and dream there is a vast difference. That is why when we leave the theatre, we are galvanized into a strange and temporary vigour, why so many people run home and act and strut in their own rooms before the wardrobe mirror. But we come out of the pictures soothed and drugged like sleepers wakened, having half-forgotten our own existence, hardly knowing our own names. The theatre is a tonic, the cinema a sedative.[137]

Drug-induced intoxication is in fact a common trope used to mediate the transformation of cinematic characters into metaphorical film spectators who mimic the supposed identification between film audiences and the cinematic diegesis. Dorothy's becoming-spectator in *The Wizard of Oz* is predicated, as I noted earlier, on an association between cinema spectatorship and the druglike induction into a dream-state by visually suggesting through dissolve, "the sensations of a person going under gas or ether" as a preparatory event. The sedative-induced transportation of the New Deal hobo-turned-extra Al Babson from the film set of Ali Baba to ancient Babylon in the 1937 Eddie Cantor film *Ali Baba Goes to Town* performs a similar collapse.

Widespread acceptance of the narcotic effects of film spectatorship legitimated the anxieties of those who advocated increased scrutiny of film content (there is indeed something suspect about semidrugged strangers sitting together in the dark), even as this collapse was alluded to and often undermined in Hollywood cinema. It was, moreover, the supposed drugged, dreamlike state induced by film watching that was heralded by avant-garde filmmakers such as Luis Buñuel and Sergei Eisenstein, who were interested in tapping into the resources of the unconscious, in the experimentations of the psyche that concerned the Surrealists and Expressionists. And it was the transformation in perception engendered by film watching, "reception in a state of distraction," in Benjamin's words, that scientists, politicians, artists, and critics found interesting—or threatening—depending upon their understandings of the psyche and relationships to bourgeois and mass cultures.[138] Benjamin, for instance, while intrigued by the potential transformation in perception engendered by cinema, argues that it transforms the masses into "absent-minded" and passive critics who have honed modes of perception that might make them more acquiescent to the twin tyrannies of capitalism and fascism.

Despite these collapses, even classic film theorists are careful to point out that dreaming and film watching are not wholly comparative states. "The dreamer does not know that he is dreaming; the film spectator knows that he is at the cinema: this is the first principle difference between the situations of film and dream," writes Christian Metz. "We sometimes speak of the illusion of reality in one or the other, but true illusion belongs to the dream and to it alone."[139] Metz, like Kracauer, acknowledges nonetheless that the experience of watching a film can seem to blur the boundaries between the waking and dreaming states: "The spectator lets himself be carried away—perhaps deceived, for the space of a second—and by the anagogic powers belonging to a diegetic film, and he begins to act; but it is precisely this action that awakens him, pulls him back from his brief lapse into a kind of sleep, where the action had its root, and ends up by restoring the distance between the film and him."[140] For Metz, then, film spectatorship is constituted by a kind of repetitive and enforced awakening, the disruptive and serial dosing and alertness that is a hallmark of daydreaming rather than of dream sleep. Because film watching is associated with motor inhibition, Metz surmises, it might best be likened to "a kind of sleep in *miniature*, a waking sleep."[141]

It helps to remember, of course, that dreaming and waking are not oppositional states. "It is one of the tacit suppositions of psychoanalysis," muses Benjamin in *The Arcades Project*, "that the clear-cut antithesis of sleeping and waking has no value for determining the empirical form of consciousness of the human being, but instead yields before an unending variety of concrete states of consciousness conditioned by every conceivable level of wakefulness within all possible centers."[142] In fact, even the Payne sleep study researchers are ambivalent about cinema's supposed sedative effects. They argue that cinema watching induces dreaming—and dreaming means restless sleep. But so too, they point out, do cinema watchers risk *not* falling asleep. Watching motion pictures, the Payne researchers surmise, is in fact more likely to cause nighttime restlessness in children than would drinking several cups of coffee before bed: "Parents who would strongly protest against their children ingesting from 4 to 6 grains of caffeine between the hours 6:00 and 9:00 P.M., nevertheless permit attendance at motion pictures whose effects on sleep mobility may be as great or greater than that of coffee and possibly more lasting in influence."[143] In a 1920 self-help book designed to "help the sleepless sleep" and "to instruct them on a few principles of right living," William S. Walsh, M.D., advises readers to "patronize the better [motion picture] theaters" and warns that "prolonged attendance or frequent attendance at motion picture entertainments may cause eye strain, [a primary cause of insomnia] particularly in those whose eyes are sensitive."[144]

That insomnia is a cohabitant of the "dream world of mass consumption" is not surprising. Filippo Marinetti heralds insomnia in the "Manifesto of Futurism" as one of the glories of the machine age: "We intend to exalt aggressive action, a feverish insomnia, the racer's stride, the mortal leap, the punch and the slap."[145] From the commercial filmmakers' standpoint, the heralding of insomnia makes a certain sense. If "film is a dream . . . that makes one dream," it cannot be a dream that puts one to sleep.[146] At least not completely. The sleeping screening room spectator who finds his way into so many films about filmmaking represents as much an anxiety about the risks of producing an art form that people watch while lounging half-asleep in the dark, as any kind of diegetic critique.[147]

"Hollywood, California. Girl on the Street," 1942. Photograph by Lee Russell. Library of Congress, Prints and Photographs Division, FSA-OWI Collection. LC-USW3-022834-E.

There are several ways one can read the presence of insomnia in discourse about Hollywood cinema and in Hollywood cinema itself. On one hand, it seems to allude to an anxiety about production and about the subject's relationship to production. On the other, insomnia might be said to allow for a different model of cinematic spectatorship vis-à-vis the subject. In a fragment on insomnia in his essay "Pure Happiness," Bataille laments, "I need to produce and I can only rest while granting myself the feeling of increased production."[148] Unlike Marinetti, who associates insomnia with action and increased production, Bataille suggests that insomnia is associated instead with anxieties about one's production and about the bind between modernity's impetus for ever-increasing production as a means for "living" and the problematic that one cannot think/represent living without action. "To live without acting is unthinkable," he writes. "In the same way, I can only represent myself as *sleeping*, I can *only* represent myself as *dead*."[149]

If Hollywood narratives are populated by cinematic *daydreamers*, such as Faye Greener in *Day of the Locust*, for whom "all these little stories, these little daydreams of hers, were what gave such extraordinary color and mystery to her movements,"[150] or by the sleepy clients of the Brown Derby restaurant, which is described by Fitzgerald in *The Love of the Last Tycoon*, as "a languid restaurant patronized for its food by clients who always look as if they'd like to lie down,"[151] Hollywood cinema is depicted as being produced by famous insomniacs. *The Last Tycoon*'s Monroe Stahr (who, like Irving Thalberg, after whom he was scripted) was "born sleepless without a talent for rest or the desire for it."[152] When his doctor asks him shortly before he dies if he is "get-

WAX, FIRE, INSOMNIA **229**

ting any sleep," he replies, "No—about five hours. If I go to bed early I just lie there."[153] And prominent among all of John Dos Passos's sleepless moderns in the *USA* trilogy, is Margo, the film-starlet-to-be in *The Big Money*, who requires an aspirin at bedtime because she is "too excited to sleep" the night before beginning the film that will be her big break."[154] Yet when she falls into an "aspirin"-induced sleep, she dreams cinematically of "finishing the *Everybody's Doing It* number and the pink cave of faces was roaring with applause."[155]

Insomnia seems to imply the temporal irreversibility and ever-increasing production constitutive of progressive modernity for which, Doane argues, cinema is a most potent metaphor. Yet the relationship between dreamlike sleepiness and sleeplessness in Hollywood narratives is rarely clear-cut. For example, when Homer Simpson, in *The Day of the Locust*, first settles in his new home in Los Angeles he is overcome by sleepiness despite the fact that "he was afraid to stretch out and go to sleep" because "he was afraid he would never get up."[156] The longer he stays in Hollywood the more his terror of staying awake overpowers his fear of falling asleep:

> His thoughts frightened him and he bolted into the house, hoping to leave them behind like a hat. He ran into his bedroom and threw himself down on the bed. He was simple enough to believe that people don't think while asleep.
>
> In his troubled state, even this delusion was denied him and he was unable to fall asleep. He closed his eyes and tried to make himself drowsy. The approach to sleep which had once been automatic had somehow become a long, shinning tunnel. Sleep was at the far end of it, a bit of a soft shadow in the hard glare. He couldn't run, only crawl toward the black patch. Just as he was about to give up, habit came to his rescue. It collapsed the shinning tunnel and hurled him into the shadow.[157]

The difficulty with insomnia is that it is representable only as that which eludes that which is not. "It is sometimes so difficult to sleep!" writes Bataille. "I tell myself: I am finally falling. The feeling of falling asleep escapes me. If it escapes me, I am, in effect, falling asleep. But if it subsists . . . ? I cannot fall asleep and I must tell myself: the feeling that I had deceived me. . . . I cannot arrive at the experience of 'what does not happen,' except through 'what happens.'"[158]

Insomnia is, in effect, the dream from which one cannot awaken. For one is not really asleep. To be kept a-wake is to be kept in a perpetual state of mourning—always present at the wake, yet never dying, never dead.[159] For Emmanuel Levinas, writing in a Nazi work camp in Germany in the early 1940s, the "*horror*" of insomnia is that it happens to no one. It is, in short, a "state without a subject" and a "state that is impossible to recount."[160] "In insomnia one can and one cannot say that there is an 'I' which cannot manage to fall asleep," Levinas writes. "The impossibility of escaping wakefulness is something 'objective'; independent of my initiative. This impersonality absorbs my consciousness; consciousness is depersonalized. I do not stay awake; 'it' stays awake.... In the maddening 'experience' of the 'there is' [*il y a*], one has the impression of a total impossibility of escaping it, of 'stopping the music.'"[161] In the French, Sara Guyer notes, Levinas uses the verb, *veiller*, in its double sense, as both wakefulness and watching or witnessing, to describe this phenomenon.[162] One watches, witnesses—despite oneself—and in doing so risks becoming "some-thing."[163]

The dread of silence (death/sleep/the unknowable) is supplanted by the *horror* of sound (wakefulness). Insomnia might be said to lead to a kind of synesthesia, in which enforced *watching* is propelled by a bombardment of inescapable *sound*. Watching, one cannot "stop the music" and thereby becomes an *it*. Indeed, the advent of talking cinema, which solidified Hollywood's cinematic reign, according to Chion, brought with it a kind of cinematic death. "It's not so much the *absence of voices* that the talking film came to disrupt," he writes, "as the spectator's freedom to imagine them in her own way.... We're no longer allowed to dream the voices—in fact, to *dream period*."[164]

For Levinas, in other words, insomnia constitutes a kind of heightened awareness not so much of death or even the death drive, but of that dreadful waiting and longing for a sleep/death that never seems to arrive, indeed can never arrive, and over which one has no control. This state is the *other* of consciousness, of which sleep and awakening are constitutive parts; it is, as I noted, what Levinas calls the "there is" (*il y a*), which he uses to designate that which resists the personal, or "being in general."[165] Consciousness, by contrast, the sense of the self as a subject, as an "I," of being at home [*chez soi*] is *here*; it is found not in abstract space, but in the phenomenon of localization and of sleep. To sleep, for Levinas, is not only to find a place, but to lie down and thereby "limit existence *to a place*, a position."[166] Sleep and dreaming are not separate from, but forms of existence, not the "reverse of consciousness ... it is a mode of being in the world."[167]

Dreaming then takes place in the realm of the subjective and particular, a point to which Freud alludes when he suggests that while general rules may hold for dream symbols, these symbols are culturally prescribed; and dreams have meaning only within the context of an individual's life. We might argue, then, that "to lose oneself" in a film is not a condition of dreaming, when one is most fully inside oneself, but rather it is to be wakeful. To watch, without "watching over." It means to lose one's place, one's base or "condition of being," in Levinas's terms, and thereby to lose oneself as a subject. What is peculiar, however, and what Levinas does not take into account when he "praises" insomnia, is the kind of double play Hollywood films often perform.

Pointing out that "the work of Georg Simmel, Walter Benjamin, Siegfried Kracauer, and Theodor Adorno ... presumed that a distracted perception was central to any account of subjectivity within modernity," Jonathan Crary argues perceptively that "modern distraction was *not* a disruption of stable or 'natural' kinds of sustained, value-laden perception that had existed for centuries but was an *effect*, and in many cases a constituent element, of the many attempts to produce attentiveness in human subjects."[168] Crucial to this point is not that spectators (or critics) confuse the enforced watchfulness of cinematic insomnia with distraction or dreaming, but that a viewer's extrication from subjectivity spiraling off into the "abyss" of nonplace, the "there is" (*il y a*), occurs at precisely the moment she imagines herself most a subject, most individual, most *here*, in place, *chez soi*. It is, in fact, the interplay between these two states that makes one's induction into the impersonality of a collective film audience feel like an individual subjective experience. What Levinas constitutes as an experience outside of being is reconfigured by Hollywood cinema to be constitutive of being.

Mark Garrett Cooper and Michael Tratner have recently argued that while most film theory presupposes an individual spectator at risk for overidentification with the film spectacle, post-1910 Hollywood cinema appealed to a "'universal' heterogeneous mass audience" and defined cinema as a "'universal language' that, [apparently] paradoxically, was also supremely American."[169] A reading of cinematic insomnia, however, suggests that the supposed opposition between the individual spectator-as-subject and the nonsubjectivity of the cinematic crowd merely refers to two sides of the same coin, much like awakening and sleep, since both the individual subject and the public are constituted through being. Instead, we might see Hollywood cinema as masking the nonbeing, the "there is" of the insomniac, framing it instead as the supreme moment of being "at home."

"*It wasn't a dream, it was a place*," Dorothy protests at the end of *The Wizard of Oz*. "A really truly live place! Doesn't anyone believe me?" Rushdie writes, "Many, many people did believe her." Dorothy's plaint is the plaint of the spectator. There is no place like home in *The Wizard of Oz*, because home, in Levinas's terms, *is* sleep. And Dorothy does anything but sleep in Oz. (Yes, the Wicked Witch gives her some respite in a field of red poppies, but the Good Witch Glinda takes care of that.) Like a good spectator, Dorothy is not so much awakened *as kept awake*—to return home, where, she is told, she has never left. But the unemployed and depressed extras in Horace McCoy's 1935 novel, *They Shoot Horses Don't They?*, who "couldn't get inside" the studio gates to find work and "can't get registered by Central [Castings Bureau]," cannot help but fail at Hollywood's game.[170] They stay awake for 879 hours in a rigged dance marathon in the hopes that someone from the "Hollywood crowd" will spot them. "'When this marathon is over,' I told myself [the nameless narrator muses], 'I'm going to spend the rest of my life in the sun. I can't wait to go to the Sahara Desert to make a picture.'"[171] By staying awake he hopes to shift his subject position from consumer to producer, from spectator to spectacle. Yet what he is unwilling to give up, what he clings to until the moment he kills his dance partner, Gloria Beatty, is his status as a subject, his being at home, *here*, in Hollywood. "I know where I stand . . ." comments Gloria as she looks "down the ocean toward Malibu," where, the narrator has told her, "all the movie stars live."[172] The narrator responds, "I didn't say anything looking at the ocean and thinking about Hollywood, wondering if I'd ever been there or was I going to wake up in a minute back in Arkansas and have to hurry down and get my newspapers before it got daylight."[173]

Then he shoots her.

live burial

Beneath the sand of the Nipomo Dunes, in Guadalupe, California, a town 170 miles north of Los Angeles, fragments of the largest movie set ever built lay buried. You wouldn't know it. It looks like any number of Pacific coast beaches—albeit a bit more dramatic, what with its wide expanse of white sand dunes (which are, not incidentally, protected by The Nature Conservancy). In Hollywood's heyday, directors came here to shoot the Sahara desert scenes for films like Rudolph Valentino's *The Sheik* (1921) and Marlene Dietrich's *Morocco* (1930), carefully severing the waves of the Pacific coastline from the frame.

It was here that Cecil B. DeMille brought a crew of sixteen hundred laborers to build his spectacular 110-foot-high, ten-acre City of the Pharaoh Ramses for his 1923 film *The Ten Commandments*. It was here on the dunes that the twenty-five hundred actors and forty-five hundred animals who took part in the production set up camp "on location" at a price tag of forty thousand dollars a day. And it was here after filming was finished a month later that DeMille ordered the set bulldozed and buried beneath the sand. The site was discovered in 1990 by a documentary filmmaker, Peter Brosnan, who had spent most of a decade trying to find it and is now still trying to cobble together money to do a formal excavation.[174] Some of the set's remains have already been salvaged, packaged, and preserved in the Hollywood Studio Museum in DeMille's tiny "barn" across the street from the Hollywood Bowl. But for untrained scavengers who dig in the dunes, privileges are few (not to say illegal). When exposed to the air, the damp plaster fragments of DeMille's buried set crumble to dust in your hands.

Nipomo Dunes, 1990s. Photograph and © by Lynn Radeka, radekaphotography.com.

41 MARINE TERMINAL
BLUE & GOLD FLEET
THE ONLY WAY TO "THE ROCK"
ALCATRAZ
SAUSALITO
VALLEJO
ANGEL ISLAND
TIBURON
OAKLAND
ALAMEDA
PREPAID TICKETS
PREPAID TICKETS
PREPAID TICKETS
BAY CRUISES & FERRIES
ALCATRAZ
EARLY BOAT
SPECIAL
BEFORE NOON
AND SAVE MONEY

Afterword

THE PRISON AND THE PENTAGON

> DISSIMULATION, SECRETIVENESS APPEAR
> AS A NECESSITY TO THE MELANCHOLIC.
> —**SUSAN SONTAG,** *UNDER THE SIGN OF SATURN*

> THE CARCERAL NETWORK DOES NOT
> CAST THE UNASSIMILABLE INTO A CON-
> FUSED HELL; THERE IS NO OUTSIDE....
> IT IS UNWILLING TO WASTE EVEN WHAT
> IT HAS DECIDED TO DISQUALIFY.

THE ROCK

When Franklin Delano Roosevelt introduced his New Deal in 1933, he embraced a model of prison reform that sought to rehabilitate prisoners through work training, counseling, and education. Under Roosevelt's tutelage and the strong arm of J. Edgar Hoover, the Bureau of Prisons, created by Congress in 1930, adopted a classification program in which a review board interviewed each new prisoner, studied his record in an effort to design a suitable program of rehabilitation, and then placed the prisoner in an institution that housed convicts of similar type.

In order for this model of segregation and rehabilitation to succeed, however, the bureau needed to construct an alternate prisoner, one who was irredeemable and could not easily reenter society. To meet this demand, the federal penitentiary Alcatraz was born, built upon the foundations of a nineteenth-century military blockade and prison. Like Key West, Alcatraz was nicknamed "The Rock," though this tiny island was located on the western edge of the United States, three miles offshore in the bay outside of San Francisco. The most famous of all American prisons, in its twenty-nine-year existence as a federal penitentiary, Alcatraz never housed more than 250 prisoners at any one time.

← San Francisco Ferry Terminal, circa 2000. © Mike Long.

Alcatraz, outside view, circa 1930s. Bureau of Prisons Photograph. Courtesy of National Archives and Record Administration.

The new super prison was designed to be self-contained and needed little from the world outside: The warden and guards and their families lived on the island.[1] Prisoners worked in various on-site industries, made their own bread and garments, and dry cleaned the guards' uniforms. Mail privileges were limited, reading material was censored, visits from family members were infrequent and highly regulated; prisoners had one brief period a day during which they could converse. Work in the prison industries was counted as a privilege. Few outsiders could get in to see the day-to-day inner workings of the institution; and those prisoners who were released were forbidden from speaking of their experiences there. No one, it was said, could escape.

A 1937 editorial in the *Philadelphia Inquirer* suggested that Alcatraz was like "some dark chapter out of medieval lore [where] the most hardened and desperate criminals in the country [are confined] under the most rigid system of discipline ever

Clothing factory on Alcatraz, circa 1930s. Bureau of Prisons Photograph. Courtesy of National Archives and Records Administration.

enforced in America."[2] Others claimed that the horror of Alcatraz lay precisely in its modernity. It was called a scientific prison, Taylorized to an extreme.[3] Every hour of every day was programmed—and repetitious. "Men slowly go insane under the exquisite torture of routine," a former inmate claimed in a 1938 article in the *Saturday Evening Post*.[4]

Both medieval and modern, Alcatraz, like its famous inhabitants, seemed to exceed classification. It defined only itself. "Alcatraz is not a penitentiary," the former associate warden Edward J. Miller remarked, "Alcatraz is Alcatraz."[5] Part penal colony, part factory, Alcatraz simultaneously embodied both the disciplinary mechanisms of the Foucaultian carceral city and was itself the logical fulfillment of Le Corbusier's utopian "Contemporary City," in which mass-produced apartment "cells" were made for mass-produced living.[6] But the utility of Alcatraz lay not in its effectiveness as a prison for so-called incorrigibles, a population that contained more than its fair share of men convicted of sodomy, but in its potency as a New Deal symbol of centralized federal authority.[7]

The Rock was, of course, the dumping ground for the most renowned and romantic of gangsters, desperados, and traitors, among them Al Capone, Baby Face Nelson, and Machine Gun Kelly. It was built not to contain the most violent and destructive of prisoners, in fact, so much as to hide the most famous of federal prisoners from the mythologizing gaze of the public. Notorious public enemies were secretly/not-so-secretly brought in the night on a heavily guarded train dubbed the Alcatraz Express. If Alcatraz prisoners could not be rehabilitated, they could be rejected. For only through their refusal could the fiction of disciplinary rehabilitation be preserved. So risky was the move to exceed the definitional boundaries of classification, however, that Director Sanford Bates objected in a January 1933 letter to Attorney General Homer Cummings, "to putting too much emphasis upon the irreclaimability [and one might say singularity] of the men who are sent to the institution."[8] While the new classification of the Alcatraz prisoner as "irredeemable" seemed to frame him as outside the boundaries of classification, it instead served to renarrate the meaning of classification and thereby exposed a fissure in the system of normalization through classificatory individualization. The classification of Alcatraz prisoners might be best described not as irredeemable, but as unforgettable. They could be normalized and redeemed only by being extricated from celebrity status by being made obscure.

The economy of power that circulated in Alcatraz was figured by secrecy and secreting, yet it was also dependent upon the gaps in those codes. Ruptures in the system of silence—the smuggled stories of released prisoners, the anonymous talk of the disciplinarians—built the very walls that reinforced it and were necessary for Alcatraz to succeed as a symbol. Shocking official narratives about the place were leaked carefully and continually: "Press releases and speeches issued from the Justice Department emphasized the extraordinary security measures that would be necessary to hold the country's worst desperadoes."[9] Bureau of Prisons publications boasted: "The establishment of this institution . . . has had a good effect upon the discipline in our other penitentiaries also."[10]

The construction of secrecy that produced Alcatraz therefore served to reinforce the disciplinary mechanisms not only of the prison, but of the so-called free population. It served to make those outside "beg for admission," to know the secret, to peer inside, to desire, in a sense, to incarcerate themselves.[11] (Even today, long after it has been closed as a prison, people stand in line to catch a glimpse. Alcatraz is the most popular tourist site in San Francisco, hosting one million visitors a year.) Alcatraz, as prison and tourist site, anticipates what Jean Baudrillard argues is the seductive power of the secret, which has nothing to do with the retrieval of some "hidden information." Instead, the secret derives its power from an "allusive and ritual power of exchange" between complicit partners who know each other's secrets and know that their secrets are known but cannot acknowledge it.[12] If, as Foucault argues, the "carceral archipelago" transports the normalizing processes of penitentiary technique to the entire social body, then the collapse of classification into celebrity at Alcatraz serves as a sign of a transformation of the mechanisms of normalization that were socially available.[13] The disciplinary economy of American Depression relies on self secreting, on the production of a population that believes in its own freedom and that nonetheless begs for self-imprisonment; it paradoxically believes that that is where freedom lies.

BIGNESS

Nine years after Alcatraz opened and on the brink of World War II, the federal government financed a rushed construction of a super office building situated outside of Washington, D.C., that was to consolidate seventeen separate defense department buildings and become the brain center of the American military. Built on "nothing more than a wasteland, swamps and dumps,"[14] the Pentagon, like Alcatraz, was a place that exceeded classification. Although critics argued that the five-sided shape merely made the place look more like what it was, "the largest target in the world for enemy bombs," Roosevelt himself backed the controversial design as a model of modernity: "Nothing like it had ever been done before."[15] In fact, the style of the structure—Stripped Classicism—embraced an aesthetic model of building that blended the new with the "essential lines of the old," which Roosevelt had employed as metaphor to introduce his Second New Deal.[16] At Roosevelt's request, the building was constructed of concrete, not marble. If it was considered by many to be extraordinary only in its ugliness, it was also praised for its focus on utility and its functional design. Much was made of the fact that one could walk to any office on any floor without traveling more than eighteen hundred feet.

The Pentagon was a monument. Certainly. But more than that—it was big. From the start, it was narrated in terms of superlatives: It was a "five-sided, four-story, mile-around structure that . . . housed 40,000 workers. It ha[d] its own park; its own bank; its own office to issue railroad tickets; its own taxicab and bus terminal; a cafeteria that seat[ed] 6000; a telephone exchange with more than 86,000 miles of inside trunk wires and 300 operators,

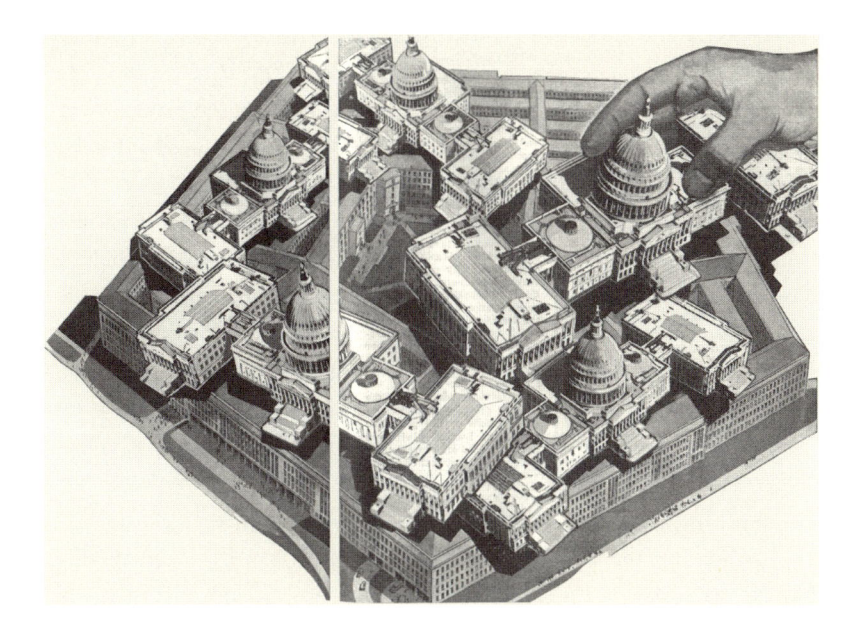

Sketch of five U.S. Capitol Buildings contained inside the new War Department Building.
Popular Mechanics, 1943.

THE PRISON AND THE PENTAGON

enough to serve Wichita or Trenton."[17] It covered "more space than all the buildings in Radio City put together, [was] three times as large as the Empire State Building."[18] It was "one and a half-times as spacious as the Sears Tower in Chicago. It had [16 ½ miles of corridors], enough pavement for a 49 miles long roadway, and parking space for 8,000 cars."[19] *Reader's Digest* dubbed it "a city within a Pentagon."[20] The *Saturday Evening Post* called it simply, "Hell-and-Gone."[21]

Built at a cost of $85 million—well exceeding the price expected—the Pentagon was the butt of innumerable jokes, most of which concerned its size. To a *Life* magazine reporter, the place looked like a "Cecil B. DeMille backdrop."[22] When the Pentagon opened for business the Navy Department (not generally known for its sense of humor) issued a tongue-in-cheek memo: "Personnel are cautioned not to become panic-stricken by the great expanse of corridor. Rumors concerning lost safaris in the Pentagon are hereby discounted."[23]

Compared simultaneously to a "desert" and "a fortress without windows," the Pentagon pushed the limits of spatial comfortability. Psychologists told *Newsweek* reporters when it opened, "The place is so vast and yet self-contained that it obviously will bother . . . both those who fear being alone and those who fear being smothered."[24] The Pentagon wasn't simply, like Alcatraz, a "Big House" that conveyed the power of the federal government on a national scale, but rather was, quite literally, the "biggest house," a structure which conveyed the power of the war-ridden nation on a global scale.

Its bigness meant that it could not help but be an allegory for the city, for the nation. Its bigness served not only to allegorize the disciplinary authority of the federal over local governments, as Alcatraz did, but also to materially perform the disciplinary authority of the American military over both the executive and legislative branches of government and, more so, over the world. Spatially, the Pentagon dwarfed both the White House and Capitol buildings. In doing so, it recentered the seat of Washington power. Symptomatically, a March 1943 edition of *Popular Mechanics* displayed a sketch of five Capitol buildings contained inside the structure.[25]

"It seems incredible that the size of a building alone embodies an ideological program independent of the will of the architects," writes Rem Koolhaas in his manifesto "Bigness."[26] Yet Koolhaas argues persuasively that the ideological program embedded in bigness is that of disinformation. "Where architecture reveals, Bigness perplexes; Bigness transforms the city from a summation of certainties into an accumulation of mysteries," he writes. "What you see is no longer what you get."[27] Thus, according to Koolhaas, "bigness no longer needs the city: it competes with the city; it represents the city; it preempts the city; or better still, it is the city."[28]

Significantly, the sprawl of the deceptively huge, low Pentagon building, like the now familiar megamalls that are its legacy, no longer reveals what happens inside. As important, however, and unlike the skyscrapers Koolhaas studies, the Pentagon reveals its outside only when mediated by the lens of a camera. Unlike skyscrapers built in the previous two decades, the bigness of the Pentagon was apparent only from above. "You have to fly over the structure to realize that it actually consists of a veritable concentric nest of five five-sided rings of narrow connecting buildings," commented a journalist in *Newsweek*, though flying over the structure was (and is) not allowed.

"DEFACEMENT"

Henry Pringle's 1943 *Saturday Evening Post* exposé on the Pentagon" bears the tantalizing blurb, "A former inmate guides you through the fabulous maze where pretty secretaries protect military secrets and even generals get lost."[29] Inhabitants of the Pentagon, the article suggests, become spatial prisoners in a world-turned-upside-down, a world in which women guard secrets and even the rulers are trapped. But outsiders, like Pringle, have the worst time of all. "An escort must accompany [a visitor] to the first office they want to reach," he writes. "After that, if they have other calls to pay, they are left on their own, as long as they do not wander into some restricted area, whereupon, presumably, they are shot."[30]

Though the comment Pringle makes is sardonic, the narrative of restriction that underlies it is not. The presumption of restriction is precisely what makes the Pentagon succeed. The collapse in meaning between classification and secrecy that had been made in the early 1930s with the construction of Alcatraz, which made outsiders want to break in, came to fruition with the building of the Pentagon, in which even insiders had always already broken in and even so were nonetheless lost. The Pentagon protected secrets and was itself a secret, unmanageable, unforgettable, unclassifiable because it was classified. Following the building of the Pentagon and the concomitant consolidation of U.S. military authority and its secrets under one roof, it became no longer necessary to say that a protected document was classified as top secret, for to be classified meant it was secret, and to be secret meant not that it was unknowable, but that it was knowable only to a select few.[31] The shift in signification of the term *classified* as it emerged during the construction of Alcatraz and transformed during World War II became in the Cold War period an everyday part of American vernacular speech. That this secrecy often protected nothing—as the release of the classified Warren Report papers revealed—is, of course, not the point and exactly the point.

The cultural and historical shift that occurred between the building of Alcatraz as a model prison du jour and the building of the Pentagon as the national Big House is less a rupture than a logical fulfillment of post-Enlightenment rationality. If, today, one visits Alcatraz-the-museum in order to experience what Andrew Ross calls the "Alcatraz Effect" of postmodernity, in which we escape by imagining we cannot escape, knowing all the while that we already have, we visit the Pentagon to imagine that there is something to escape from, that there is something there behind all the blandness. Today, in visiting the Pentagon, tourists must follow a long list of prescriptions—you can't stray away from the pack, can't photograph offices with open doors, can't use the restroom. When you are directed to look at banal paintings on gray-tinged walls, however, you are suggestively seduced into believing you are being given misinformation, that you are being directed away from seeing what is really there, that there is a secret you know exists, but to which you have no access. Nowadays, with few exceptions, you have to be part of a school group and make a reservation to get in.

When you go in 1998, your guide tells you a story. For years during the Cold War, he says in a chummy way, as if he has just thought of this, the Soviets targeted a nuclear missile onto the hot dog stand at the center of the courtyard at the center of the Pentagon. It wasn't until the American government showed the Soviets enough photographs and proved that the structure was nothing more than a hot dog stand that they ceased to make it a target. The guide, an Aryan-looking fellow who is part of President Bill Clinton's honor guard, ostensibly tells you this anecdote to expose the misplaced aggression of the Soviets during the Cold War. And the story, you imagine, is also told in order to induce you to suspect that the hot dog stand really did contain a nuclear arsenal; and that, somehow, "we Americans" (and one must show ID to go on this tour) duped the Soviets into believing otherwise. What you cannot—are, in fact, disallowed to—suspect is that the hot dog

Lunchtime in the Pentagon Building courtyard, April 17, 1943.
Courtesy of National Archives and Records Administration.

242 AFTERWORD

Old airplane hangars on the site of the Pentagon, 1941. United States Army Photographic Agency. Courtesy of National Archives and Records.

stand at the center of the Pentagon really is and always was just a hot dog stand. And that the tour of the Pentagon is nothing more than a tour of a mile of hallways with institutionally painted rectangular walls, bad portraiture, and shiny linoleum floors.

What was built at the center of the Pentagon and what is allegorized by its bigness, then, is not a culture of secrecy, but one that produces and relies on "not telling" and not knowing, a culture produced through what Eve Sedgewick refers to as "strategic ignorance" and what Michael Taussig has called "public secrecy," the knowing of what not to know.[32] We are interpellated into a culture in which we are prepared always to be disinformed—and are always prepared to disinform. The spatial narrative of the Pentagon delineates a form of meaning production that not only makes it not surprising but also makes it absolutely essential that the president who disclosed the secret of not telling by instituting a don't ask, don't tell policy for gay soldiers was impeached for not telling the truth.

HOMELAND SECURITY

And then there is September 11. One hour after the Twin Towers are hit, the Pentagon is penetrated by a low-flying airplane. Mourning and recognition of the massive slaughter of those in the World Trade Center go on for months.

Those killed in the Pentagon are barely a footnote. The military closes ranks. Governmental secrecy is not only legitimated, it's legislated. In Europe conspiracy theories abound. A Website displays photos culled from satellites cameras and remarks enticingly, "The Associated Press first reported that a booby-trapped truck had caused the explosion. The Pentagon quickly denied this. The official US government version of events still holds. Here's a little game for you: Take a look at these photographs and try to find evidence to corroborate the official version."[33] "Can you explain how a Boeing 757-200, weighing nearly 100 tons and traveling at a minimum speed of 250 miles an hour only damaged the outside of the Pentagon." "Can you find debris of a Boeing 757-200 in this photograph?" "Can you explain why the County Fire Chief could not tell reporters where the aircraft was?" "If you begin to question whether a Boeing really did crash on the Pentagon then, no doubt, you'll be wondering what happened to the aircraft that disappeared," it concludes. "You will probably ask yourself why the US government even told you this story in the first place and you'll start asking yourself lots of other questions besides."

The governmental conspiracies Americans are invested in uncovering seem to be of a different sort: Did the government have information—and ignore it? Could the attacks have been prevented? If the American version tries to uncover what Gilles Deleuze and Félix Guattari call a secret of content, which underlies a modernist certainty that something is there to be found, the European version tries to uncover a postmodernist and paranoiac secret of form: "a non-localizable something has happened."[34] If both versions inadvertently reinforce the power of the state apparatus, suggesting that there is, if imperceptibly, an underlying system at work, the state is invested in yet another model.

In January 2002, Vice Admiral John M. Poindexter, former national security advisor under Reagan and convicted for his role in the Iran-Contra affair, was brought in to oversee a new office, housed in the Pentagon. That office developed a new surveillance technology system, Total Information Awareness, whose function was to search for "hidden patterns of activity" culled from commercial and governmental computer databases. In introducing the system, the spokeswoman for the agency, Jan Walker, claimed that the project would "revolutionize the ability of the United States to detect, classify, and identify foreign terrorist activities." But the headline of the *New York Times* article in which Walker was quoted reads alarmingly, "Pentagon Plans a Computer System That Would Peek at Personal Data of Americans."[35] That summer, after the new surveillance technology was introduced, the George W. Bush administration, which cut social programs with giddy enthusiasm, proposed a new one: the Terrorism Information and Prevention System (Operation TIPS). Neighbors were encouraged to spy on neighbors. Neo-McCarthyism lurked. It didn't pass, and things settled down only to resurface again three years later.[36] By late 2005, it turned out that the executive branch had been eavesdropping on Americans' phone calls all along.[37]

Then things became clear: The Pentagon is impenetrable not because there is no outside but because any notion of inside and outside is itself anachronistic. "To secret" is to constantly *dis*-place. There is no room for standstill—or for the insight associated with it. There is only the refusal at all costs to dwell.

Notes

INTRODUCTION

"The significance of insignificance" is from Barthes, "The Reality Effect," *The Rustle of Language*, 42.

1. Johnson, "Dumping Ends at Fresh Kills, Symbol of Throw-Away Era," 1:1. Editorial, "Rethinking Garbage," 14:1.
2. See Barry and Waldman, "A Nation Challenged."
3. See Verlyn Klinkenborg, "The Other Graveyard," 53:3.
4. See Barry and Waldman, "A Nation Challenged."
5. Ibid.
6. Ibid.; Dewan, "From 9/11 Rubble, Unclaimed Mementos"; Kelley, "A Nation Challenged: The Relics."
7. Lee, "Plucking 9/11 Objects."
8. In this I follow Benjamin in his critique of Hegel's and Marx's adoption of a teleological account of history and of the inevitability of historical development. See esp. Hegel, *Lectures on the Philosophy of World History*, 124–50, and Marx and Engels, *The German Ideology*.
9. Barry and Waldman, "A Nation Challenged."
10. Lee, "Neighborhood Report: Staten Island Up Close."
11. For more on the relationship between America and modernity, see the introduction to Jani Scandura and Michael Thurston, eds., *Modernism, Inc.: Body, Memory, Capital*.
12. I refer here to Walter Benjamin's multiple uses of "standstill" and "idling" (in *The Arcades Project* as well as *The Origin of German Tragic Drama*). These, he implies, are not without movement but follow a form of movement and transformation that does not progress forward, that belies the modernist imperative of irreversible time. I refer also to Bessie Smith's song "I'm Down in the Dumps," written by L. Wilson and W. Wilson and accompanied by Buck Washington and his band. Recorded on November 24, 1933, New York.
13. Jackson, *Melancholia and Depression*, 5–7. Unless otherwise noted, etymologies derive from the *Oxford English Dictionary*.
14. McElvaine, *The Great Depression: America, 1929–1941*, 175.
15. Ibid., 177.
16. The American suicide rate increased in 1932 to 17.4 individuals per 100,000, up from 14 per 100,000 in 1929. Ibid., 369. From United States Chamber of Commerce, Bureau of the Census, *Historical Statistics of the United States, Colonial Times to 1970*, 58.
17. Ann Douglas characterizes modern American culture as inflicted with symptoms of manic-depressive disorder. However, Douglas, focusing on the 1920s relative boom economy and high modernism, is concerned predominantly with the manic phase of American cultural *cyclothymia* (the contemporary medical term for the mood disorder). She cites an impressive list of modernist artists thought to be afflicted with bipolar or manic-depressive symptoms, if not the disorder itself, including F. Scott Fitzgerald, Ernest Hemingway, Al Jolson, Elinor Wylie, Sinclair Lewis, Hart Crane, Robert Sherwood, Dashiell Hammett, Eugene O'Neil, John Barrymore, Jed Harris, Maxwell Bodenheim, Walter Winchell, Van Wyck Brooks, Lewis Mumford, S. J. Perlman, Edmund Wilson, Wallace Thurman, Dorothy Parker, Robert Benchley, Louise Brooks, Sara Teasdale, and Louise Bogan. Her suggestion that all but Jolson, Sherwood, Brooks, and Mumford were alcoholics or addicts also implies an intimate connection between manic depression and overconsumption. To figure modern American culture as manic-

depressive or even depressive, however, is not so much to impose an absolute psychological diagnosis on a diverse group of individuals as to suggest that Americans mapped these symptoms onto their own culture and sought compensatory cures. Douglas, *Terrible Honesty: Mongrel Manhattan in the 1920s*. Douglas includes an outstanding review of literature that includes these parallels. See especially 167–76, 472–75 and 524–25. For more on this aspect of modernism, see also the introduction to Scandura and Thurston, eds. *Modernism, Inc.: Body, Memory, Capital*.

18. These are the moments that make visible the operation of what Lauren Berlant calls "The National Symbolic," to refer to those discursive practices that transform those born within "a geographical/political boundary . . . into subjects of a collectively held history." See Berlant, *The Anatomy of National Fantasy*, 20.

19. This is why, in part, the discursive impact of the term *depression* is so profound for Americans. It is not only because of New Deal financial reforms that there have been no official economic depressions in the United States since the 1928–41 depression, though several preceded it. Part of what the United States cannot work through is its own building on the back of an economy of enslavement. See, for instance, Michael Rogin's chapter, "Two Declarations of Independence: The Contaminated Origins of American National Culture," in *Blackface, White Noise*, 19–44. Rogin looks at the "*mésalliance*" in American political theory of a "Declaration of Independence, demanding freedom from enslavement to England for a new nation built on slavery." Ann Cheng draws on Rogin to argue that "dominant white identity in America operates melancholically—as an elaborate identificatory system based on psychical and social consumption-and-denial." See Cheng, *The Melancholy of Race*, 10.

20. Until recently, most studies on place have come out of geography departments. Throughout the 1970s and much of the 1980s, a phenomenological approach to place, which was brought to prominence by Yi-Fu Tuan and Edward Relph, dominated discourse in humanistic geography. (See especially Tuan, *Space and Place: The Perspective of Experience*; and Relph, *Place and Placelessness*.) While these geographers were responsible for invigorating a field that had been dominated by positivism and for opening up questions about the symbolic and metonymic qualities of place that had been ignored, feminist and poststructuralist critics have critiqued their phenomenological readings of place. Feminist geographers, in particular, have critiqued the opposition in much geographical discourse between the notion of a masculinized, universal, abstract, and scientific space and a femininized, subjective, existential, and localized notion of place. (See, in particular, Massey, *Space, Place, and Gender*; and Rose, *Feminism and Geography: The Limits of Geographical Knowledge*.) The 1990s brought a revived interest in place studies by both cultural and, to a lesser degree, Marxist geographers. Far from being fixed, cohesive, or bounded—materially, ideologically, or otherwise—these critics argue that "the identity of place is always and controversially being produced." In *Place and the Politics of Identity*, an anthology that greatly influenced literary scholarship, Michael Keith and Steve Pile posited "a different sense of place . . . no longer passive, no longer fixed, no longer undialectical . . . but, still, in a very real sense about location and locatedness." (See Keith and Pile, *Place and the Politics of Identity*, 1993; and Pile and Keith, *Geographies of Resistance*, 1997. See also Cresswell, *In Place/Out of Place*; and Adams, Hoelscher, and Till, eds., *Textures of Place*.) Social and cultural geographers have tended to be more interested in questions about space and spatiality in recent years and have largely framed questions about place through studies on "spatial scale" and "locality" or have read place as a vehicle through which to perceive social relations. (With regard to movements in Marxist geography, I refer here to work following David Harvey's influential book *The Condition of Postmodernity* as well as to a variety of works by Neil Smith, Derek Gregory, Doreen Massey, Edward Soja, Henri Lefebvre, and the sociologist Anthony Giddens and others. For more on these debates, see, Johnston, Gregory, Pratt, and Watts, eds., *The Dictionary of Human Geography*, 456–60.) Edward S. Casey lays out a useful philosophical history of place in *The*

Fate of Place: A Philosophical History. J. Nicholas Entrikin also takes a philosophical approach and introduces French geographers' use of milieu as place/context in *The Betweenness of Place: Toward a Geography of Modernity*. What has been understudied, until recently, is the complex social, epistemological, and aesthetic impact of this very opposition with regard to theorizations of modernity. Works by scholars in a variety of fields, including Delores Hayden, Christine Boyer, James Duncan ad Nancy Duncan, Tim Edensor, Steve Pile, Karen Till, and others have pushed the envelope of place studies, incorporating nuanced theoretical discussions of memory, ruin, affect, embodiment, and technology, particularly with regard to cities and modernity. See Boyer, *The City of Collective Memory*; J. Duncan and N. Duncan, *Landscapes of Privilege*; Edensor, *Industrial Ruins*; Hayden, *The Power of Place*; Pile, *Real Cities*; and Till, *The New Berlin: Memory, Politics, Place*.

21. While some geographers, for example, Denis Cosgrove and James Duncan, have argued that landscape is a "way of seeing" or even a kind of text, others critique these views by claiming, for instance, "space is metaphor *and something else*." Yet what most historical and geographical narratives use to anchor their claims are not so much an uncomplicated view of reality as an effort to preserve *materiality* as distinct from—and as a more significant place holder for the real—than the discursive. See especially Cosgrove, *Social Formation and Symbolic Landscape*; and Duncan, *The City as Text*. See also Mitchell, *Cultural Geography: A Critical Introduction*, and "The Lure of the Local: Landscape Studies at the End of a Troubled Century," 269–81. For a summary of this debate in geography, see Till, "Political Landscapes," in Duncan, Johnson, and Schein, eds., *A Companion to Cultural Geography*, 347–64.

22. See, in particular, Deleuze, *Bergsonism*.

23. Bergson's concept of *durée* changes in his writings; crucial to all his conceptions is the way *durée* functions simultaneously as a noun and the past participle of a verb. Here, I refer primarily to his use of it in *Matter and Memory*, since I am most interested in how Benjamin extends from this work. Bergson, *Matter and Memory*, 134. Originally published in French as *Matière et Mémoire* by Presses Universitaires de France in 1896.

24. See Benjamin, *The Arcades Project*, 388–89, 462–64. Wyndham Lewis blames Henri Bergson, who "put the hyphen between Space and Time" (408), rather than preserving space and time as discrete entities and for the diminishment of space. For Bergson, Lewis argues, conceived of time as "mental as opposed to physical," leaving, one might suggest, the physical to space. "Space," Lewis writes, "[is] becoming the 'Nothing' of the modern European" (418). Benjamin's unhyphenated, interpenetrating conception of *Zeitraum* preserves the wholeness of time and space but not as discrete entities (space *and* time), or as an oppositional hyphenation (space-time), but within an invisible relation still to be thought. See Lewis, "Space and Time," 408–18.

25. Benjamin, "On the Theory of Knowledge, Theory of Progress," *The Arcades Project*, 475. While Benjamin too grounds his notion of place in dialectical opposition—"standstill" emerges when the tension between dialectical opposites is greatest—it is with an awareness of the nondialectical binary that history posits between the past and the present. See also 247, fn. 12.

26. Karen Till explores the tension between the material presence of place and its phantasmatic quality. She argues, "places of memory both remember pasts and encrypt unnamed, yet powerfully felt, absences—absences that might be considered modernity's ghosts of the nation." Such places, she continues later, "give shape to that which is . . . absent through material and imagined settings that appear to be relatively permanent and stable in time." See Till, *The New Berlin*, 9–10.

27. Buhite and Levy, eds., *FDR's Fireside Chats*. See also the America Presidency Project document archive (APP), (http://www.presidency.ucsb.edu).

28. The terms Roosevelt uses to describe the qualifications of his chosen "architects and builders" are important ones. The builders of the office—and hence of the New America—are men of "common sense," a reference that may be indebted to Thomas Paine, who mused as well on "the present state of American affairs," but that might more productively be read through Antonio Gramsci. To refer to "common sense" as self-evident or as a "confirmation of truth" is, in Gramsci's terms, absurd; for common sense is itself unstable and ambiguous, an ever-evolving set of popularly held unquestioned beliefs which tend toward conservatism. Gramsci distinguishes between "common sense" and "good sense," which is not rigid and immobile, but which refers to the "incoherent set of generally held assumptions and beliefs common in a given society." See Gramsci, "Problems of Marxism," *Selections from the Prison Notebooks*, 323–43, 419–30.

29. Anthony Giddens argues, "The counterfactual, future-oriented character of modernity is largely structured by trust vested in abstract systems—which by its very nature is filtered by the trustworthiness of established expertise." The crucial point for Giddens is that under the circumstances of modernity, "expert knowledge" "*creates* [rather than explains] the universe of events." Roosevelt certainly is not alone in appealing to a panel of experts, his aptly named "brain trust," who do the facework for a more abstract phenomenon of policy; what makes Roosevelt interesting, however, is his rhetorical prowess. See Giddens, *The Consequences of Modernity*, 79–111.

30. My position on Roosevelt and his administration is, not surprisingly, an ambivalent one. There is no doubt that Roosevelt's New Deal rejected the elitism of Hoover's Uncommon Man in favor of the more populist Forgotten Man and that it instituted work programs and organizations that acknowledged governmental responsibility in feeding and employing its people, a people who had suffered from the fallout of industrial self-management. Admittedly, the New Deal sponsored art programs to a degree that the federal government had not previously—or has since. Moreover, the Socialist left and labor unions gained an unprecedented political agency, if not under Roosevelt's tutelage, at least not in strict opposition to it. The New Deal attempted, though inadequately and with short-term impact, to begin to address the rights of black and women workers, as well as to pay at least some homage to traditional belief structures of Native Americans.

It funded, albeit briefly, bilingual theaters (I refer specifically to the Spanish language WPA theater that opened briefly in Tampa, Florida). However, it is also under the New Deal administration that Jim Crow laws continued to thrive (even in administering WPA benefits), that 120,000 Japanese-Americans were imprisoned in War Relocation Authority camps after Roosevelt signed Executive Order 9066, that 82,000 Mexican immigrants and Mexican Americans were repatriated between 1929 and 1935 and some 500,000 forced or persuaded to emigrate to Mexico in state and federal attempts to ban them from the labor force, and that J. Edgar Hoover, who had taken over as director in 1924, was able to vastly expand the authority and influence of the FBI administration, instituting an era of heightened surveillance that included FBI taping and Internal Revenue Bureau investigations of political opponents (and others). See Badger, *The New Deal: The Depression Years, 1933–1940*, 178–81; Balderrama and Rodriguez, *Decade of Betrayal: Mexican Repatriation in the 1930s*; and Weber, *Dark Sweat, White Gold*.

31. Consider the critique of Foucault by the *Hérodote* editors, Mark Wigley's analysis of Derrida's reliance on spatial metaphor in deconstructive discourse in *Derrida's Haunt*, Descartes' reliance on a narrative of scholarly isolation in *Discourse on Method*, and even Plato's famous cave dwellers. Remember also that Bill Clinton rebuilt the White House offices during his first term—his staff leaking provocative statements about how outdated they had become, statements that also served as not-so-veiled critiques of the previous twelve years of Republican stewardship in the executive offices. Among the many social geographers who have discussed this issue is David Harvey in *The Condition of Postmodernity*, and elsewhere.

32. See Foucault, "Questions of Geography," 70, 77.

33. In his book *Rubbish Theory*, Michael Thompson argues that in any battle over rubbish, cultural value is always at stake. "The residual, marginal category of rubbish," he suggests, "is the point of connection between two conflicting codes," transience or durability. On one hand, modernity's quest for newness might be

said to be marked most visibly by a buildup of the transient—a category that encompasses the rotating doorways of fashion and mass-produced products; wandering expatriates; and the influx of immigrants and emigrants; trains, planes, and automobiles (and in the United States, the motor lodge); free love, cross-dressing, and its cousins; the urban housing and U.S. stock markets; war; musical performance; the avant-garde; and film. On the other hand, modernity's twin pull toward durability reveals itself in its Cartesian impulses, its nostalgia and utopianism; its heralding of folk traditions, museums, heritage and preservation projects; its love of High Art; in the fetishization of the nuclear family and American democracy; in immigration restrictions and Jim Crow laws; in German fascism; in census taking, citizenship and IQ testing; and in race and gender classification. For my purposes *refuse* is a more useful term than *rubbish*.

34. See Benjamin's work but also Roosevelt, above.

35. Schmidt, "Refuse Archeology: Virchow—Schliemann—Freud," 212, emphasis added.

36. Schmidt draws on Mary Douglas's definition of *filth* as "matter out of place" and reframes it to describe the "idea of refuse as it emerged in Western industrial societies in the nineteenth century." See Douglas, *Purity and Danger*. See also Lacan's reading of Poe's short story, "Seminar on *The Purloined Letter*," in Muller and Richardson, *The Purloined Poe: Lacan, Derrida, and Psychoanalytic Reading*. Lacan's seminar is considered to be such an important text to poststructuralist and psychoanalytic thought that this anthology, published in the late 1980s, includes over a dozen essays from the debate. Schmidt makes ingenious use of the essay as a way to think about refuse, but he drops the analysis before fully considering the implications of the suggestion he makes.

37. Lacan, "Seminar on *The Purloined Letter*," 38.

38. Schmidt, "Refuse Archeology," 211.

39. Lacan, "Seminar on *The Purloined Letter*," 38.

40. Schmidt, for instance, traces the etymology of the German term for refuse, *Abfall*, to argue that "the idea of refuse" is most likely a nineteenth-century invention. Schmidt, "Refuse Archeology," 219. Scanlon similarly argues (35–36) that *garbage* "provides a shadow history of modern life."

41. See Benjamin, "Theses on the Philosophy of History," 257.

42. Franklin D. Roosevelt. "The Forgotten Man." Radio address, April 7, 1932 (APP), fn. 27. It could be argued, by contrast, that Hoover's political failure in the early part of the Depression was exacerbated by his inability to recognize the resonance of refuse within the depressed national imaginary—a failure ironized in the naming of city transient camps as Hoovervilles. However, Roosevelt's use of the metaphor of the "forgotten man" required some canny forgetting of its own; William Graham Sumner's 1883 "forgotten man" referred to a man of Emersonian self-reliance, a "worthy, industrious, independent, and self-supporting" middle-class individual who "minds his own business, and makes no complaint" and not to the unemployed, destitute man in need of state social assistance to whom Roosevelt seemed to refer. Though it was not Roosevelt who inserted the term in the speech, the two conceptions of the forgotten man are not so far removed, as has been suggested. Roosevelt continually relied on a narrative of self-reliance in promoting his social programs. FERA work relief programs, for instance, offered "help to those who help themselves." Roosevelt also explicitly recontextualizes the "pursuit of happiness" in American discourse to mean more than a pursuit of capital.

43. During the Depression, the National Park Service employed out-of-work architects through the Historic American Buildings Survey, which "documented the architectural structure and detail of historic buildings" (Barthel, *Historic Preservation*, 21). The Historic Sites and Buildings Act of 1935 was the first American law to regulate the preservation of built spaces. See Murtagh, *Keeping Time*, 174–75.

44. Barthel, *Historic Preservation*, 32.

45. See Hildegarde Hawthorne's laudatory, descriptive history of the renovation: *Williamsburg*, 105–52. This passage is cited in Hawthorne from a speech by Rockefeller regarding the project, 24.

46. Ibid., 128–29.

47. Barthel, *Historic Preservation*, 38.

48. Hawthorne, *Williamsburg*, 128–29.

49. Diane Barthel argues that Colonial Williamsburg is a "Staged Symbolic Community," a symbol that "stands curiously out of time" to perform "community" in a society "where organic communities are a thing of the past, if, indeed, they ever existed" (*Historic Preservation*, 36–37).

50. Shanks, Platt, and Rathje, "Modernity and the Archaeological," 70.

51. I borrow the term "the forgettery" from Studs Terkel, who used it for the Depression in *Hard Times: An Oral History of the Great Depression* (New York: New Press, 2000).

52. Grail Marcus. *Lipstick Traces*, 5.

53. Dietmar Schmidt argues that "refuse is systematically generated in the execution of cultural procedures without forming a part of that particular culture. Refuse thus brings the reverse side of culture into view. In being useless, refuse manifests itself on the edge of a cultural order and forms its silhouette." See Schmidt, "Refuse Archeology," 210–32.

54. Vismann. "The Love of Ruins," 201.

55. Ibid., 201–03.

56. Schmidt notes that when the nineteenth-century archeologist Rudolph Virchow used the term *refuse (Abfall)* in his writings about refuse archeology, it had a new connotation. Previously, the word had meant "the process of falling down or the state of having falling down" or "an infidelity or breach of trust" during the first third of the nineteenth century. See Schmidt, "Refuse Archeology," 219.

57. Shanks, Platt, and Rathje, "Modernity and the Archaeological," 65.

58. Schmidt also asks this question—but suggests, misleadingly I think, that "refuse archeology" is one response.

59. Benjamin, *The Arcades Project*, 460.

60. Benjamin, "In Almost Every Example We Have of Materialist Literary History," 547. Fragment unpublished in Benjamin's lifetime. Originally published in the collected works: *Gesammelte Schriften*, vol. 6, ed. Rolf Tiedemann and Hermann Schweppenhäuser (Frankfurt: Suhrkamp Verlag, 1972–89), 172.

61. Jacques Lacan in his "Seminar on *The Purloined Letter*," references Joyce's jeu de mot. See Muller and Richardson, *The Purloined Poe*, 40.

62. In her reading of Poe's story, Lacan's seminar on it, and Derrida's response to Lacan, Barbara Johnson argues that the literal emerges in these texts as the most "problematically figurative mode of all." That is, the letter, as a literal object, "acts as a signifier not because its contents are lacking, but because its function is not dependent upon the knowledge or non-knowledge of its contents . . . the letter cannot be divided because it functions only as a division. It is not something with 'an identity to itself inaccessible to dismemberment.'" The difficulty of making sense of the letter lies not in the fact that it is "problematically figurative," though this may be true, but in the fact that it is not *merely* problematically figurative. Johnson is correct to suggest that the letter does not have an identity that is not able to be "dismembered," but incorrect in remaining within the literal–figurative dyad. The difficulty with which Lacan, Derrida, Johnson, and elsewhere, Paul de Man struggle with literal, only begins to suggest some of its complexity. See Johnson, "The Frame of Reference: Poe, Lacan, Derrida," in *The Purloined Poe*, 213–51, and "Disfiguring Poetic Language," in *A World of Difference*, 100–115.

63. For an interesting use of this, see Altieri, "Taking Lyrics Literally: Teaching Poetry in a Prose Culture," 259–81.

64. Brown, *A Sense of Things*, 1–19.

65. Ibid., 7.

66. Ibid., 8–9.

67. Ibid., 11.

68. I refer to Jennifer Ashton's essay "Modernism's 'New' Literalism," in *Modernism/Modernity*, 381–90, which reviews, among other things, Marjorie Perloff's book *21st-Century Modernism: The 'New' Poetics*. Perloff coins the phrase "the new literalism" in her 1981 book *The Poetics of Indeterminacy*. Perloff identifies L=A=N=G=U=A=G=E poetry as "literalist poetry," and Michael Fried first describes as "literalist art" the visual art movement later known as minimalism in his 1967 essay "Art and Objecthood." See also Fried, "An Introduction to My Art Criticism" and "Shape and Form," in *Art and Objecthood*, 1–99, 148–73.

69. Ashton, "Modernism's 'New' Literalism," 387–88.

70. Ibid., 384–85.
71. Ibid., 389.
72. I thank Michael Hancher for making this connection.
73. Elizabeth Bishop, "The Sea and Its Shore." *Collected Writings* (New York: Farrar, Straus and Giroux, 1984), 172.
74. Ibid., 163–74.
75. Ibid., 179–80.
76. Ibid., 170.
77. Gilles Deleuze and Félix Guattari play on this connotation in the introductory pages of *A Thousand Plateaus*.
78. For more on the relationship between Freud and Janet, see Sprengnether, "Reading Freud's Life," 9–54. See also Hacking, *Rewriting the Soul*, and Haule, "Pierre Janet and Dissociation: The First Transference Theory and Its Origins in Hypnosis," 86–94.
79. For a summary of the transformation of Hume's work to the dissociationists and Jung, see Haule, "From Somnambulism to the Archetypes: The French Roots of Jung's Split with Freud," 635–59. Economic Associationism was a separate strain of post-Hegalian thought to which I refer in the section on Harlem.
80. Ibid., 639.
81. Ibid.
82. The lynchpin of Janet's analytic process was hypnosis, a technique he never rejected, which he used to induce in patients a state of *somnambulism*, the definition of which he extended beyond sleep walking to include any activity that usually belongs to waking consciousness but that is "pursued while in a dissociated condition," that is, "while the individual's consciousness is inhabiting a dreamscape." It was through exploring the "dissociative" logic that emerged in a patient's hypnotized state that Janet believed he could effect a cure. Reading backward, through Janet, for instance, we might add the hypnotist to Benjamin's collection of allegories; it is not a stretch to conceive of capitalist modernity as a kind of quack hypnotist who induces witless moderns into the waking dream of *somnambulism*. The critic, on the other hand, becomes something like the analyst, who brings into relief the hidden connections and associations within the mental archive of a somnambulant European bourgeoisie. See Haule, "Pierre Janet and Disassociation," and Janet, "L'influence somnambulique et la besoin de direction," 423–80, originally published in 1898. Benjamin spends quite some time critiquing Jung in *The Arcades Project*. See, for instance, convolutes K in the English edition, "[Dream City and Dream House, Dreams of the Future, Anthropological Nihilism, Jung]" in Benjamin, *The Arcades Project*, 388–404.
83. Bergson, *Matter and Memory*, 164–65.
84. Ibid., 134.
85. Ibid., 164, emphasis added.
86. Ibid., 165.
87. Deleuze, *Bergsonism*, 17.
88. Ibid.
89. Benjamin, *The Arcades Project*, [N 1, 3] 456.
90. Reno has shifted over time from being the second and third section of the book. At the moment, it follows the introduction.
91. Quoted from "Debris," in Fearing, *Complete Poems*. Originally published in *Dead Reckoning* (New York: Random House, 1938).

1 RENO

1. See Parmer, *After Divorce?*, 31.
2. Nevada's residency requirement for citizenship, voting, and divorce was the shortest in the nation. Designed in the nineteenth century to benefit a mobile mining population, the lenient legislation took on new meaning in the first decades of the twentieth century when an increasing number of easterners—mostly from New York, where the divorce laws were especially stringent—began to make the quest West for a Reno "quickie" divorce. As the Nevada economy became more and more dependent on divorce revenue, divorce protesters became incensed at this ill-reputed moneymaking operation. Arguments for catering to a divorcing clientele were largely financial; those against were largely moral. In February 1913, divorce protesters stormed the state capital and demanded the passage of a bill that required a one-year residency of all divorce petitioners. Two years later, pragmatism won and that bill was overturned. Under pressure from the Reno Businessmen's Association, the governor signed a bill that reinstated the

six-month residency requirement. The residency requirement was reduced twice, from six months to three months in 1927 and from three months to six weeks in 1931. For more information on Nevada divorce laws, see Riley, *Divorce: An American Tradition*, 135–38. See also Blake, *The Road to Reno*, 135, 157–59.

3. The train quest and arrival at the Reno train station is a standard trope in the divorce novel and film genres.

4. Eliot appropriates vernacular tropes but employs them in order to make a universalizing and transhistorical statement about modernity and its spaces. Indeed, "The Wasteland" seeks to erase the cultural, spatial, and historical particularity of individual place-texts. When "The Wasteland" is read for its vernacular peculiarities, the poem reveals Eliot's collapse of vernacular spaces, such as the English pub, into both Western classical history and Eastern philosophy. The poem sublimates Eliot's American national identity and those histories outside of imperial Britain that not only contribute to, but have been the victim of Anglo-American industrial modernity's waste. More potently, the poem's appropriation of "all history" as English modernist history and its suggestion that English modernist history is "all history" become a form of imperialism that mimics Britain's cultural imperialism, an imperialism that, albeit self-destructively, is nonetheless nostalgically in decline.

5. For more information on the Pickford divorce and on divorce sensationalism, see Stevens, "Social Utility of Sensational News: Murder and Divorce in the 1920s," 53–58. See also Morris, *Not So Long Ago*, 138. Morris argues that the frequent stories about divorce suits by young women against "rich and famous men" suggested that the public was "watching celebrities in order to clarify its own attitude toward divorce," see p. 57. Morris contrasts the blasé attitude with which the public accepted Charlie Chaplin's 1925 divorce with the uproar surrounding Mary Pickford's 1920 divorce. Neither Stevens nor Morris remarks on the influence of gender on the public's perception of divorce. Yet gendered constructions of divorce and the divorcée are embedded in any social critique. It is impossible to consider the Reno divorce without taking gender into account. For a more detailed account of the Pickford-Moore divorce, see Lillard, *Desert Challenge*, 346–47.

6. That year a total of 183,695 divorces were granted in the United States (17 percent of the married population).

7. Ryan, "The City That Sex Built," 12–17, 79–82.

8. Mining and ranching had always overshadowed divorce as the main staples of the Nevada economy; but the Depression hit the mining industry especially hard. The divorce industry had little overhead and a high profit margin, making it attractive to financiers during the 1930s. Gambling did not make as large a contribution to the Nevada economy until Las Vegas took precedence over the state in the 1950s. In the years just after World War II, gambling was estimated to bring in just $330,000 to the city annually. In the 1930s, the gambling industry relied upon and was inextricably linked to the divorce economy. For more information on the history of gambling in Nevada, see Lewis, *Sagebrush Casinos*, 115.

9. Lillard, *Desert Challenge*, 341.

10. "Passion in the Desert," 101. Private rooms could be had for as little as fifteen dollars a month. But apartment houses that catered to divorcées usually ranged in 1930 from fifty dollars a month for a tiny efficiency to two hundred dollars and up for a suite at the Riverside Hotel. (See "Letters from a Richmond Wife in Reno," 44–45.) In later years, chic stays at Dude Ranches could cost between thirty and seventy-five dollars a week for meals, lodging, and the use of a saddle horse. From the "Nevada Dude Ranch Association" brochure.

11. Over the years, the divorcing glitterati included Tallulah Bankhead, Constance Bennet, Liz Whitney, John Gunther, Doris Duke, Cornelius Vanderbilt, Jr., Ethel DuPont, Jack Dempsey, Franklin D. Roosevelt, Jr.'s wife, and many others.

12. Divorce narratives were plentiful in the United States during the late nineteenth century and early twentieth, and divorces took place in a variety of locales (particularly Paris) during the nineteenth century. For a summary of some of these works, see: James Harwood Barnett, *Divorce and the American Divorce Novel, 1858–1937: A Study in Literary Reflections of Social Influences*.

See also, Donald Nelson Koster, *The Theme of Divorce in American Drama, 1871–1939*. Ph.D. dissertation, University of Pennsylvania, 1942. Reno novels and stories perform cultural work that expands beyond the strictures of the divorce novel genre. The earliest book published about the Reno divorce colony was probably Leslie Curtis's eclectic compilation, *Reno Reveries* (1910); the last of the relevant novels is Jane Rule's lesbian romance, *Desert of the Heart* (1964). Reno texts include: Lilyan Stratton, *Reno: A Book of Short Stories and Information* (1921); Cornelius Vanderbilt Jr, *Reno* (1929); John Hamlin, *Whirlpool of Reno* (1931); Rupert Hughes, *No One Man* (1931); Grace Hegger Lewis, *Half a Loaf* (1931); Kathleen Norris, *Second Hand Wife* (1931); Earl Derr Bigger's Charlie Chan thriller, *Keeper of the Keys* (1932); Dorothy Walworth Carman, *Reno Fever* (1932); Charles Parmer, *After Divorce* (1932); Marian Sims, *Call It Freedom* (1937); Leslie Ford, *Reno Rendezvous* (1939); Faith Baldwin, *Temporary Address: Reno* (1940); Elswyth Thane, *Remember Today: Leaves from a Guardian Angel's Notebook* (1941); Mary Warren, *Reunion in Reno* (1941); Walter Van Tilburg Clark, *City of Trembling Leaves* (1945); Latifa Johnson, *Sheila Goes to Reno* (1952); Dean Evans, *No Slightest Whisper* (1955); and Jill Stern, *Not in Our Stars* (1957). These are largely forgotten texts, too popular at publication to be accorded the cultural privilege of preservation. Once disposable, they now are rarely accessible, available occasionally at used bookstores specializing in "pulp," in online bookshops and eBay, or through the arduous (and often unsuccessful) help of Interlibrary Loan. For a more detailed description of the plots of some of these novels, see Ann Ronald. "Reno: Myth, Mystique, or Madness?" Reno divorcées figure in the plot of many other novels, plays, and films, including John O'Hara's *Elizabeth Appleton* (1963) and Don Siegel's 1956 film, *Invasion of the Body Snatchers*, but Reno is not central to these texts.

13. Cavell. *Pursuits of Happiness*.
14. Most of these were B pictures, starring lesser-known actors and filmed on cheap sets. Often they were titled, simply and aptly, *Reno*. Warner Brothers produced at least three B films devoted to Reno between 1927 and 1946: *A Reno Divorce* (1927); *Merry Wives of Reno* (1934), which is a more middle-class version of the socialite narrative of the world of *The Women*; and *Reno-vated* (1946). "Reno" films also include, among others, *Reno* (Son Art World Pictures Inc. 1930), an adaptation of his novel of the same name by Cornelius Vanderbilt Jr., which is notable for location shots of the city; *Peach o' Reno* (RKO 1931); *Reno* (RKO 1939); *Charlie Chan in Reno* (1939); *The Women* (1939), MGM's adaptation of Clare Boothe's 1937 play of the same name; *The Opposite Sex* (1956), an MGM musical remake of *The Women*; *Maisie Goes to Reno* (MGM 1944); *Vacation in Reno* (RKO 1946); a film version of the 1931 Kathleen Norris novel, *Second Hand Wife*; John Huston's dystopic Western, *The Misfits* (1961); and *Desert Hearts* (1985), Donna Dietch's adaptation of Jane Rule's novel *Desert of the Heart*. Reno is mentioned in many 1930s screwball comedies, including *Libeled Lady*, *Mr. and Mrs. Smith*, and others.
15. Buck-Morss, *The Dialectics of Seeing*, 92.
16. Under the conditions of "competitive capitalism," speed was only one of the "advertisements" of progress, according to Buck-Morss who argues that abundance or excess, monumental size, and expansion (industrial and imperial) were also crucial metaphors. Ibid., 91.
17. Kristeva, *Powers of Horror*, 65.
18. *The Century Dictionary and Cyclopedia*, vol. 9 (New York: Century, 1911). The *Century Dictionary* refers largely to American usage.
19. The term is Max Horkheimer's and Theodor W. Adorno's. They argue that this rubbish is force-fed to the masses by the culture industry. Horkheimer and Adorno, *Dialectic of Enlightenment*, 134.
20. Miller, *Reno*, 25.
21. See Buck-Morss, *Dialectics of Seeing*, 104–05.
22. Hegger Lewis, *Half a Loaf*, 337.
23. See Hamlin, *Whirlpool of Reno*, 132.
24. Ley, "Modernism, post-modernism, and the struggle for place," 52.
25. Also called the "Bridge of Meditation." Newly "processed" divorcées supposedly tossed their wedding rings from the bridge into the Truckee River.
26. Also called the "Castle of Lady Luck" and "The House of Divide."

27. Lillard, *Desert Challenge*, 341.

28. I draw on Mark Wigley's use of the term *unbuilding* as it is deployed in deconstructive architectural theory. Wigley argues, "Just as Heidegger displaces philosophy's sense of itself as a construction standing on a stable ground in favor of philosophy as a constructing-through-unbuilding, he also displaces the sense of the structures that philosophy describes. Although following the tradition's understanding of being as a certain kind of 'standing,' it is no longer standing on a stable ground, but a standing based on a loss of ground, a construction built on an 'abyss.'" See Wigley, *Derrida's Haunt*, 41.

29. See Smith, "New City, New Frontier: The Lower East Side as Wild, Wild West." 61–93, as well as other writings.

30. John Urry makes four claims about contemporary constructions of place: (1) places are increasingly being restructured as centers for consumption; (2) places are themselves consumed, particularly visually; (3) places can be "literally" consumed, i.e, "what people take to be significant about a place (industry, history, buildings . . .) is over time depleted, devoured or exhausted by use"; (4) localities can consume one's identity." See Urry, *Consuming Places*, 1–2. Reno is a particularly interesting place in which to explore the neo-Marxist paradigms of much of contemporary cultural geography which relies on the premise that space, as Henri Lefebvre most influentially put it, is socially produced. Yet the notion of spatial production enacted in modern Reno is an inherently deconstructive one: The Reno divorce factory produced production. Thus, Reno becomes an interesting place in which to test out assumptions about the relationship between place, production, and consumption in modern and postmodern culture. Indeed, the central cities of Nevada—Virginia City, Reno, and Las Vegas—seem to sequentially perform the social and economic trajectories of early modernity (corporatization, pre-Fordist industry), late modernity (Fordism, progressive obsolescence), and postmodernity (late capitalism, globalization).

31. Robert David Sack argues that a "place of consumption" creates "the impression that it has little or no connection to the production cycle and its places." See Sack, *Place, Modernity and the Consumer's World*, 103–4.

32. Reprinted by permission of Special Collections Department, University of Nevada, Reno. Enclosed in Judge Bartlett's papers.

33. In Johnsen, *Selected Articles on Marriage and Divorce*, 19–20, 28–39. The subhead title, "mass culture as woman," is from Huyssen, *After the Great Divide*, 52. In the late nineteenth and early twentieth centuries, Huyssen writes, "the fear of the masses in this age of declining liberalism is also a fear of women, a fear of nature out of control, a fear of the unconscious, of sexuality, of the loss of identity and stable ego boundaries in the mass." The conflation of woman and mass gets played out in Reno, which is anthropomorphized as feminine, hypersexual, and unstable.

34. Cahen, *Statistical Analysis of American Divorce*, 129.

35. Antonio Gramsci points this out, as I address in this essay, but also see Barrett, "Americanization from the Bottom Up," 162–86. For more on the narrative implications of the Taylorization of domesticity, see Banta, *Taylored Lives*.

36. Wollen, "Cinema/Americanism/the Robot," 45. See also, Antonio Gramsci, "Americanism and Fordism," in *Selections from the Prison Notebooks*.

37. Kessler-Harris, *Out to Work*, 259.

38. Ibid., 259–261.

39. Ibid., 256. She cites Cousins, "Will Women Lose Their Jobs?," 14.

40. For a summary of these measures, see Kessler-Harris, *Out to Work*, 256–61.

41. The anachronistic term *mill* is a holdover from the earliest Reno cartoons at the turn of the century. It also suggests that divorce itself is anti-progressive, a reversion of the twentieth-century Fordist factory to a nineteenth-century mill.

42. Although MGM's *The Women* (1939) references Reno's ideological connection to the Fordist factory, it is Sydney's, the Taylorized New York beauty salon-spa, that frames the film, which is produced as a Fordist factory and becomes the center for the mass circulation of gossip. Mary Haines hears of her husband's indiscretion because the gossipy manicurist provides the same narrative to all her clients, just as she paints all their nails "jungle red."

43. Hegger Lewis, *Half a Loaf*, 375.
44. Ibid., 377–78.
45. Hegger Lewis, *Half a Loaf*, 387.
46. Parmer, *After Divorce?*, 93.
47. Smith, *Making the Modern*, 57.
48. Hegger Lewis, *Half a Loaf*, 378.
49. Clel Evan Georgetta, 1969. Courtesy of the Nevada Historical Society.
50. Lillard, *Desert Challenge*, 341.
51. In "The Truth About Reno" (n.p., n.d.), 24. Divorce-era tourism pamphlet courtesy of the Nevada Historical Society.
52. Carman, *Reno Fever*, 66.
53. Ibid., 128.
54. Reproduced by permission of Special Collections Department, University of Nevada, Reno, Judge Bartlett Papers.
55. Gramsci, "Americanism and Fordism," 302, 297.
56. Ibid., 297–98. Gramsci wrote this essay while in prison. It is one of his few works that deals with the immediacy of contemporary events and suggests a reliance on mass-cultural representations of divorcées, such as those found in popular magazines.
57. Ibid., 306.
58. Ibid., 304, 296.
59. The War Department shut the houses down in 1942. The photo reproduced on page 47 was taken shortly after the Stockade closed.
60. By the early 1920s, legal prostitution was almost entirely disbanded in the United States as a result of Progressive era morality quests. Reno attempted to follow suit. In early 1922, bolstered by the League of Women Voters and religious and education groups, Mayor Harry Stewart declared the red light district, then housed at Front and Second streets and in nearby Chinatown, closed down. The following year, however, with a new mayor in office, the city council passed a compromise amendment. Brothels could legally operate in the city at a distance of 250 yards from any major road. A 1923 Nevada law additionally stipulated that brothels be located at least 500 yards away from any church or school. The Reno red light district was located near Commercial Row in what was called the Riverside "restricted district" on North Second Street. The Stockade building, by then the River Apartments, was demolished in 1977.
61. The cribs contained a private door and two functional rooms: a front sitting room in which to make deals and a rear bedroom.
62. See Lillard, *Desert Challenge*, 330–31.
63. Ibid., 327–32. See also "Reno: Bother over Brothels."
64. Baldwin, *Temporary Address: Reno*, 200. Baldwin was one of the most popular romance writers of the time.
65. Lillard, *Desert Challenge*, 29. For more on the relationship between film sets and place making, see the section on Hollywood in this book.
66. Ibid., 330.
67. Ibid.
68. Ryan, "The City that Sex Built," 16.
69. Baldwin, *Temporary Address: Reno*, 200.
70. Zanjani, *The Unspiked Rail*, 343.
71. Carman, *Reno Fever*, 219.
72. Hegger Lewis, *Half a Loaf*, 378.
73. Parmer, *After Divorce?*, 38–39.
74. Courtesy of the Nevada Historical Society.
75. See Smith, *Making the Modern*, 28.
76. Gambling becomes an important subtext in this exchange. One writer comments, "'A man gambles when he marries—and he gambles at whatever business he is engaged in,' Wingfield told me." See "George Wingfield and Nevada's Peculiar Institutions," 195.
77. Lillard, *Desert Challenge*, 330.
78. Buck-Morss, *Dialectics of Seeing*, 184–85. She cites Benjamin on Baudelaire, part 5 of *The Arcades Project*. See ibid., 430nn147–50.
79. Hamlin, *Whirlpool of Reno*, 129.
80. See Lillard, *Desert Challenge*, 372. For more on Taylorism and the evolution of scientific management of fatigue, see Anson Rabinbach, *The Human Motor*.
81. Irigaray, "Women on the Market" and "Commodities Among Themselves," in *This Sex Which is Not One*, 170–97. Rubin, "The Traffic in Women."
82. Lillard, *Desert Challenge*, 330.
83. Stuart Ewen describes this phenomenon in

All Consuming Images, 244. See especially Ewen's chapter "Form Follows Waste," 233–58.

84. Carman, *Reno Fever*, 130.

85. Ibid., 98.

86. Harding, *Roads to Reno*.

87. Wajcman, *Feminism Confronts Technology*, 114.

88. Le Corbusier, *Towards a New Architecture*, 7.

89. Sims, *Call It Freedom*, 14.

90. In the postwar era, constructions change but the message stays the same. Playing off of the post–World War II boom in academia, *The Opposite Sex*, MGM's 1956 musical remake of *The Women*, transforms Reno into a "college" full of cozy sorority sisters who hook up back in New York after receiving their "diplomas" (divorce decrees) for friendly "class reunions." But in an era in which one quarter of white, urban college women married while still in school, the divorcées offer an ironic counterpart to the imagined 1950s coed. The Reno diploma didn't offer what was considered an ideal "woman's degree"— marriage to an educated man—but "unmarriage" and the depressing prospect of employment.

"What's happening, it's frightening," cries an unnamed divorcée from the hallway of the guesthouse at Lucy's divorce ranch. Bathrobe-clad ranch guests rip open their bedroom doors and stare down the hall, like sorority sisters in a college, at the brawl between Sylvia and Gloria that threatens to wreck the ranch kitchen. The potential destruction of this kitchen space is so disturbing it is likened to "another Atom-bomb test," then prevalent in southern Nevada. For more on sex and "the Bomb," see Elaine Tyler May's seminal work on American women during the Cold War era: *Homeward Bound*, esp. 79–83.

91. Hamlin, *Whirlpool of Reno*, 193.

92. Ibid., 18.

93. Ibid., 61.

94. For "the desert of the real," see Baudrillard, "Simulacra and Simulations," in *Selected Writings*, 166.

95. Virginia City was considered a "ghost town" and visited by tourists in the 1930s.

96. Case, *The Singing Years*, 52. A Reno minister's wife's memoirs. (Incidentally, Vantage Press had published *Sheila Goes to Reno* the previous year.)

97. See Taylor, "Introduction," in Taylor, ed., *The Turner Thesis*, vii.

98. Turner makes his point by quoting a passage from Peck's *New Guide to the West* (Boston, 1837); see Turner, "The Significance of the Frontier in American History" 15–16.

99. Ibid., 27.

100. Ibid.

101. See Limerick, *The Legacy of Conquest*.

102. Harding, *Roads to Reno*.

103. See Lewis, *Sagebrush Casinos*, 117.

104. Riley, *Divorce: An American Tradition*, 135.

105. Nelson Manfred Blake provides a good history of this legislative debate in *The Road to Reno*, 173–88.

106. Migratory divorce was really never much of a statistical issue. Only between 3 and 20 percent of divorces in the pre–World War II era "were obtained in states other than the state of marriage and only a few of these involved spouses who had purposely migrated to obtain a divorce." See Riley, "Sara Bard Field, Charles Erskine Scott Wood, and the Phenomenon of Migratory Divorce," 251–59.

107. Hughes, *No One Man*, 235.

108. See Zanjani, *The Unspiked Rail*, 23.

109. This special issue of a Duke University law journal covers some of the debates: *Law and Contemporary Problems*.

110. From *Century Dictionary and Cyclopedia*.

111. From Hegger Lewis, *Half a Loaf*, 371; and "Letter from a Richmond Wife in Reno."

112. See McCarthy, *The Company She Keeps*, 3. The "potential divorcée" is having an extramarital affair and speculates on the impending demise of her marriage and the potential glamour of becoming a young divorcée after going "West" to Reno. For more on McCarthy within the context of the 1930s, see Rabinowitz, *Labor and Desire*, esp. 10–15.

113. Carman, *Reno Fever*, 80. See also Hamlin, *Whirlpool of Reno*, 176.

114. See Lewis, *Sagebrush Casinos*, 117.

115. Hegger Lewis, *Half a Loaf*, 83.

116. Ibid., 370.

117. Carman, *Reno Fever*, 46–47.

118. *Reno Divorce Racket*, 15.
119. A 1931 *Vanity Fair* article makes explicit the connection between the Mann Act and Reno divorce. In a fictional scenario, a man's attorney informs the man's wife's attorney that the man has both divorced his wife and remarried. "Well, I'll have him prosecuted for violating the White Slave Act, traveling with the lady from state to state," the woman's attorney threatened. "You can't do that," was the reply, "because he didn't travel back with his new wife." See Hays, "When Is a Divorce Not a Divorce?," 34–35, 74. For more information on the Mann Act, see Langum, *Crossing Over the Line*.
120. See Foucault, *Discipline and Punish*, 242.
121. "Medico-Dental Building" brochure, 1927. Courtesy of the Nevada Historical Society.
122. Parmer, *After Divorce?*, 33.
123. Ibid.
124. See Schmitt, *Back to Nature*, 12–14.
125. Theodore Roosevelt, "The Strenuous Life," 80.
126. See Schmitt, *Back to Nature*. See also Nash. *The Nervous Generation: American Thought, 1917–1930*.
127. Carman, *Reno Fever*, 91.
128. Ibid., 5.
129. *Letter from a Richmond Wife*, 51.
130. "Reno: Answers to Physicians and Health Seekers" (Washoe County Medical Society, 1915). Courtesy of the Nevada Historical Society.
131. Hughes, *No One Man*, 208.
132. Miller, *Reno*, 50.
133. Ibid., 107.
134. *Letter from a Richmond Wife*.
135. Hegger Lewis, *Half a Loaf*, 380.
136. Lillard, *Desert Challenge*, 342.
137. I refer to those laid out by Claude Lévi-Strauss in *Elementary Structures of Kinship*, and critiqued by Gayle Rubin in "The Traffic in Women."
138. Carman, *Reno Fever*, 149.
139. Ibid., 149.
140. Ibid., 113. Not coincidentally, Ray's dog is named Sappho.
141. I refer to the unscripted alternative sexual economy that is possible whenever "the goods get together," to borrow from Luce Irigaray. See Irigaray, *Speculum of the Other Woman*. See also Butler, *Gender Trouble*, 41.
142. Carman, *Reno Fever*, 186.
143. Ibid., 201.
144. It is not until Jane Rule's 1964 novel *Desert of the Heart* that lesbian desire is brought to fruition. In the classic lesbian film based on the novel, *Desert Hearts* (1986), Vivian Bell, a Barnard College professor, doesn't find solace in the inevitable Buck, a handsome cowboy who gives another divorcée a little "understanding," or in Walter, ranch owner Frances Parker's smitten son—or even in the husband she left. Instead, she falls in love with Kay, an openly lesbian casino worker, who helps Vivian trade in her gray New York dress suit for a more masculine Western shirt and jeans and later drives her (a bit obviously) "over the state line." It is significant that although the women violate Nevada residency statutes, they don't violate the Mann Act, which doesn't acknowledge the possibility of erotic desire between women.
145. Carman, *Reno Fever*, 150.
146. Ibid., 241.
147. Pechinksi, "The Landscape of Memory," 129.
148. The connection between consumption and femininity has a long and well-charted history in modernity. See Todd, "Art, the 'New Woman,' and Consumer Culture," 127–54.
149. See especially Felski, *The Gender of Modernity*, 61–90.
150. Michel Aglietta defines Fordism as "the principle of an articulation between process of production and mode of consumption." Renovation is perhaps the more explicitly gendered explication of that articulation, and a mode through which women are interpellated as subjects through the abstraction of the ideal female consumer. See Aglietta, *A Theory of Capitalist Regulation*, 116–17, 161. Cited in Kalaidjian, *American Culture Between the Wars*, 12, 269nn34–35.
151. Surveillance takes two forms: in matters of taste, as middle-class women start buying ready-to-wear clothes they need to mark class affinity with increasingly subtle codes—fit of dress, fabric content, etc.—and in the later image of the frugal

housewife, who is actually a hypercomsumer, consumed with consumption played out through "bargain hunting."

152. In *The Women* that threat is embodied by the indomitable perfume clerk Crystal Allen (Joan Crawford).

153. Parmer, *After Divorce?*, 30.

154. Doreen Massey, Luce Irigaray, Edward Casey, Elizabeth Grosz, Gillian Rose, and others point out that place is a gendered and bodily event. As Casey writes, responding to Irigaray, woman becomes "place *as such*, at once physical and metaphysical—without the opportunity to be a sexually specific body/locus that is neither mere 'thing' nor exalted essence" (327). See Casey, *The Fate of Place*; Irigaray, "Place, Interval: A Reading of Aristotle, *Physics IV*"; Grosz, *Space, Time, and Perversion*; Massey, *Space, Place, and Gender*; Rose, *Feminism and Geography*.

155. See Butler, "Imitation and Gender Insubordination," 13–31. See also Butler, *Gender Trouble*; and Butler, *Bodies that Matter*.

156. Carman, *Reno Fever*, 37.

157. Today, the space is the site of the new Washoe County courthouse.

2 KEY WEST

1. The title of this section is from Herbst, *The Starched Blue Sky of Spain*, 135.

2. Letter from Robert Frost to G. R. Elliott, December 17, 1934, in Thompson, *Selected Letters of Robert Frost*, 413.

3. Arthur Duke, "Key West, Revamped by Stone, Goes in for Varied Customs Including Shorts and Siesta," *Orlando Reporter Star*, May 13, 1935. From WPA scrapbooks, Key West, Monroe County Public Library (MCPL).

4. On July 10, 1934, the *Tallahassee Daily Democrat* declared, "Unique Experiment in Progress at Key West." A March 30, 1935, headline in the *Philadelphia Enquirer* left no doubt as to who was in charge of the place: "Key West Practically Run by FERA; Seen as 'Laboratory,'" in WPA scrapbooks, MCPL.

5. "Uncle Sam Revives," in *Philadelphia Record*, May 16, 1935; "Key West, Broke and Asleep," in *Atlanta Constitution*, June 20, 1935; "Bankrupt Key West," in *Washington Post*, April 22, 1935. From WPA scrapbooks, MCPL.

6. *Buffalo Courier-Express*, July 7, 1935. From WPA scrapbooks, MCPL.

7. "Key West Gambling Goes Under Ban," in *Tampa Daily Times*, July 19, 1934. From WPA scrapbooks, MCPL.

8. Courtesy of MCPL.

9. Stone, "Remaking a City," *Tampa Morning Tribune*, January 17, 1935. From WPA scrapbooks, MCPL.

10. See "Vacations Put Jobless Key West In Prosperity Class in Year," in *Christian Science Monitor*, July 5, 1935. From WPA scrapbooks, MCPL.

11. Tschumi, *Architecture and Disjunction*, 72–73.

12. Putnam, "South from Miami," 34.

13. Letter to Frederic G. Melcher, December 30, 1934. From Thompson, *Selected Letters of Robert Frost*, 415. Also reprinted in Murphy, *The Key West Reader*, 11.

14. See Susan Sontag's analysis of tuberculosis (or consumption) in *Illness as Metaphor*.

15. Hemingway, *To Have and Have Not*, 96.

16. Barnard, *The Great Depression and the Culture of Abundance*, 1995.

17. Cabell Phillips argues, "To fully comprehend [the mass unemployment of the Depression], you have to both see the figures and feel the emptiness." See Phillips, *From the Crash to the Blitz, 1929–1939*, xii. Cited in McElvaine, *The Great Depression*, 171.

18. Herbert Hoover, "Annual Message to the Congress," AAP. Cited in Crouse, *The Homeless Transient in the Great Depression*, 51.

19. Allen, *Since Yesterday*, 123.

20. Badger, *The New Deal*, 21.

21. Browne, *Key West*, 162. (Facsimile reproduction of 1912 edition.) See also Miller, *Topographies*, 1995. Miller argues that "like many place names, 'Key West' contains within itself in miniature the history of its human occupation, building and naming, in this case from the Native American inhabitants to the Spanish conquerors to the English-speaking Americans who changed 'cayo' to 'key'" (261).

22. Browne, *Key West*, 8–9.

23. Benítez-Rojo, *The Repeating Island*, 214–17. He specifically refers to the myth that when one dies he takes two others with him, since the pirate captain Henry Morgan killed three of his men "in order to bury them, as gatekeepers beyond the grave, beside the treasure he took in the sacking of Panama." Hemingway employs this trope when his Depression-era Harry Morgan kills three Cuban revolutionaries and is himself killed in an effort to bring stolen funds to Cuba. By drawing on the Morgan myth, Hemingway figures Morgan as both proletariat revolutionary and pirate, who sacrifices his own people for gain in the afterlife.

24. Burg, *Sodomy and the Pirate Tradition*.

25. Rediker, *Between the Devil and the Deep Blue Sea*, 297–98. Cesare Casarino reads the nineteenth century "sea narrative" through Deleuze, Marx, and Foucault as constitutive of a crisis of modernity and "as an attempt to produce the space of the ship as the thought of an unthinkable unthought, as the inside of an unrepresentable outside, as the fold-effect through which the immanent cause of the outside comes into being as a form in the world and comes to disrupt the history of forms—in short, as an attempt to produce the space of the ship as heterotopia." Casarino, *Modernity at Sea*, 12–13. Key West artists might be said to engage in a similar negotiation, but less with an eye to the ship than to the island. Nor is the impetus strictly narrative, in fact, as in most cases writings resist narrativization.

26. Davis, "New World Symphony," 64.

27. Sontag, *Under the Sign of Saturn*, 124.

28. Pérez, *Cuba*, 276.

29. For a more complete history of this tumultuous period, see ibid., 251–75.

30. See ibid., 270.

31. See ibid., 230–12.

32. This fact is mentioned in Longenbach, *Wallace Stevens*, 156–57.

33. See Kaplan, "Romancing the Empire: The Embodiment of Masculinity in the Popular Historical Novel of the 1890s," 659–90.

34. Berman, *All That Is Solid Melts Into Air*, 15–21.

35. Benjamin, "Theses on the Philosophy of History," in *Illuminations*, 257–58.

36. A definition in the *Shorter Oxford Dictionary*, 3d ed. (London: Oxford University Press, 1955): "Conch \konk\: (also Conk) a nickname for the lower class of inhabitants of the Bahamas and the Florida Keys, etc. for their use of conchs for food." The reason for the name actually is unclear. Some say Key West locals are called conchs because they survived by consuming the meat of that prickly crustacean; others attest that early inhabitants posted conch shells as a sign outside their doors that announced deaths and births.

37. From Bishop, "Seascape," *The Complete Poems*, 40.

38. "Jerónimo's House," ibid., 34.

39. Bishop, from "The Florida East Coast Railroad; Dawn," Vassar Library Special Collections (VLSC), box 67.12. The line is itself in flux as if the material fluidity of the place she describes has infused the poetic process itself: "The light was lavendar. The unpainted houses/were almost the color of the air" and beneath that a change, "unpainted house, air-color, almost." Recently published as "Something I've Meant to Write About for 30 Years," in Bishop, *Edgar Allan Poe and the Juke-Box*, 137–39.

40. From "Full Moon, Key West," VLSC, Key West Notebook (KWN), I (enclosures), box 75.1. See also ibid., 59–60.

41. From Bishop, "Pleasure Seas," *The Complete Poems*, 195.

42. From "Florida," ibid., 32.

43. McCabe, *Elizabeth Bishop*, 40.

44. Darden, "The Architecture of Exhaustion," 19.

45. Plans included placing a ton of coral gathered from Florida reefs into fish tanks planted with natural vegetation and housing a variety of the one thousand or more tropical fishes indigenous to the area.

46. Information reported in the following newspaper articles in the MCPL collection: Dewitt, "New Building First of Kind in All World," *Miami Daily News*, September 2, 1934; "Aquarium Director Sees Dream Unfold," *Philadelphia Inquirer*, September 1934. From WPA scrapbooks, MCPL.

47. From Ratner and Altman, *John Dewey and Arthur F. Bentley*, 74.

48. Paul Giles astutely argues that the pun provides a key to Crane's aesthetic. Giles, *Hart*

Crane, esp. 6–18. Giles argues that the pun is a "bridge between alternative meanings" and is the structural principle behind Crane's long poem "The Bridge."

49. For a summary of the rationale for the exclusion of the "Key West" poem (along with five others) from the "Island Sheaf" collection, though they were found in the same manila folder, see Marc Simon's editorial notes to Crane, *The Complete Poems of Hart Crane*, 237–39, and Crane, "Key West," ibid., 126.

50. Djuna Barnes's insistence that she "was not a lesbian," although she loved women, and Laura Riding's plaint that she "was not a poet," although she wrote poems, are gestures seeking a similarly fluid identic space.

51. For Hemingway, in an excised portion of *To Have and Have Not*, Crane's suicidal leap becomes simultaneously a symptom of the ailments of the "Lost generation," and a personal indictment. "Built the way he was, under what system would he have thrived?"

52. The most pertinent example of this kind of elision is in Wallace Stevens's famous reference to Ramón Fernandez in "The Idea of Order at Key West." Critics have long argued over whom Stevens referred to, most suggesting it was the Mexican-French philosopher by that name, whose book *Messages* had a large readership among Anglophone intellectuals during the 1920s and 1930s. (See Miller, *Topographies*, 262). There is some evidence that there was a newspaperman in Key West named Ramón Fernandez who wrote a weekly column at the time Stevens visited. But the gesture to particularize the identity of Fernandez misses the point. Stevens claimed that his Ramón had no corresponding source in the real world. Dehistoricizing the individual, Stevens tries to have it both ways: Ramón Fernandez becomes a dehistoricized hybrid who represents both French philosophy, Cartesian tradition, and Western aesthetics *and* the vernacular, popular, quotidian, Latin, Caribbean traditions. To ask Ramón Fernandez, "tell me, if you know" is to simultaneously evoke the Anglo-European and Latin-Caribbean traditions that continually drift into each other in Key West.

In making this gesture a universalized evocation to poetic inspiration, however, is to deracinate the politics and power embedded in scraps upon which he relies. Stevens, "The Idea of Order at Key West," in *The Collected Poems*, 128–30.

53. By contrast, his masculine "North" is unfixed, unnarratable, a mobile "wintry slime" where "men are moving as the water moves." See Stevens, "Farewell to Florida," ibid., 32.

54. There has been much recent work on Stevens's politics of gender and sexuality—and on the politics of reading Stevens in a straight or "purple" light. See especially Lentricchia, *Ariel and the Police*, and Edelman's response to Lentricchia in *Homographesis*, 24–41.

55. From Stevens, "Theory," in *The Collected Poems*, 86.

56. This is the last line of Stevens, "The Idea of Order at Key West," ibid., 130.

57. This subsection's title is from Gertrude Stein, "He and They, Hemingway," in Dydo, *A Stein Reader*, 449.

58. Hemingway commented on his inclusion in the FERA map in "The Sights of Whitehead Street: A Key West Letter." Reprinted in White, *By-Line*, 192–204.

59. The late Harvard professor Robert Fitzgerald recorded this comment in an interview on November 6, 1984 in Hamden, Connecticut. Reproduced in Fountain and Brazeau, *Remembering Elizabeth Bishop*, 365–66n12. The story is "After the Storm," a tale that Hemingway claimed his captain Bra had told him while on a sailing trip to Dry Tortugas with Waldo Peirce and John Dos Passos.

60. Letter from Bishop to Frani Blough, 4 January 1937. VLSC, box 16.4.

61. Key West has long attracted gay writers and artists, including Hart Crane, Elizabeth Bishop, Tennessee Williams, and others.

62. From KWN I, VLSC, box 75.3b, 189.

63. From *The Nation* 145 (October 23, 1937), 339–40. Reprinted in Meyers, *Hemingway*, 236.

64. From *Southern Review* 3 (Spring 1938): 769–82. Reprinted in Meyers, *Hemingway*, 243–56.

65. From Kazin, "New York Herald Tribune

Books," 3. Reprinted in Meyers, *Hemingway*, 229–32.

66. I draw here on Catherine Gallagher's analysis of the evanescence of texts, which, even more than commodities, constantly waver between materiality and ideation. See Gallagher, *Nobody's Story*, xxiii.

67. Douglas Darden explores what he calls the architecture of exhaustion, a deconstructive architecture that reflects modernist physical principles of quantum mechanics. He writes, "Neither form nor form-giver act any longer as substance, but must 'drift' as a possibility, an emanation, and as something which always has the potential to become something else" (18). The approach, which he finds in the theoretical and architectural works of Bernard Tschumi and Peter Eisenman, destabilizes the lens through which one can view material culture and the built world in general. Darden, "The Architecture of Exhaustion," 13–22.

68. I use *mestizo* in José Martí's sense of the term in "Our America" and elsewhere as a condition of "mixedness," that refuses the boundaries of race. It is particular to this moment in Key West and in modernism and is thus rightfully subject to the very critiques that have been leveled at Martí. I borrow the term *twilight* from Simon Gikandi, *Writing in Limbo*.

69. "Full Moon, Key West" has been recently published in Bishop, *Edgar Allan Poe and the Juke-Box*, 59–60.

70. Gikandi refers to Creolization here, which is a different, though not unrelated discourse to that of *mestizaje*. However, his point about modernization, aesthetics, and conditions of mixedness is useful here. He makes a related point in a reading of the Cuban novelist Alejo Carpentier later in his text. Ibid., 18.

71. Ibid.

72. Benítez-Rojo, *The Repeating Island*, 26–7.

73. Somewhat ironically, perhaps the best remembered local Key West artist from the 1930s is Gregorio Valdes, a former cigar worker, sign maker, and amateur painter in whom Bishop and her partner Louise Crane took an interest. Crane, whose mother was chair of the Museum of Modern Art (MoMA) in the 1930s, eventually helped include Valdes's work in a MOMA exhibition on "primitive art." Bishop eulogized Valdes in her story, "Gregorio Valdes." See Bishop, *The Collected Prose*. Betsy Erkkila argues that "through the work of Valdes Bishop defines a literal, mimetic, working-class art that is both embedded in the material conditions of Key West life and that nevertheless slips almost imperceptibly through the local knowledge and desire of the factory worker/sign painter/painter into a kind of magical realism, a perspective that is 'mysterious,' uncanny, and alluring. In doing so Bishop perhaps comes closer to negotiating the putative conflict between proletarianism and aesthetics than other more earnest commentators on the respective claims of politics and art." See Erkkila, "Elizabeth Bishop, Modernism, and the Left," 292–93. However, As Susan Rosenbaum notes, Bishop's conception of Valdes as a "true primitive," i.e., one who "lacks awareness of matters of taste and value" is both racialized and class-based. See Rosenbaum, "Elizabeth Bishop and the Miniature Museum," esp. 84, 94.

74. To my knowledge there is only one book that even begins to attempt to uncover African American history in Key West. See Wells, *Forgotten Legacy*.

75. Stevens recognizes this aesthetic drive in "The Idea of Order at Key West," in which his poetic muse "sang beyond the genius of the sea." But, as we have seen, Stevens himself resists it.

76. The struggle embodied in this effort is symptomatic of what Kristeva calls, "the ultimate condition of being with others." For Kristeva, this condition is embodied in the figure of the "foreigner," that serves as the "scar" between the "citizen and the man." In this sense, then the effort at salvaging performed by Key West writers and artists becomes an effort to remember the "foreigner" as scar, but also, preserve a subjective condition of being "at home." See Kristeva, *Strangers to Ourselves*, 192, 197–98. See also, Ziarek, "The Uncanny Style of Kristeva's Critique of Nationalism."

77. See Lombardi, *The Body and the Song*, 21. References to salvaging and shipwreck arise frequently in criticism on Bishop. Susan McCabe

describes Bishop's work as "homemade art" that "scavenges from among what has been left behind," even fragments of her own work. See McCabe, *Elizabeth Bishop*, 87. And Marilyn May Lombardi remarks that in later years, as a result of Robert Lowell's frequent breakdowns, her lover Lota's suicide, and her own alcohol-induced depressions, "Bishop had come to think of herself as a Dorothea Dix for the literary world, an architect of asylums and a rescuer of shipwrecked souls." See Lombardi, *The Body and the Song*, 219. She notes biographical similarities between Bishop, whose great-grandfather had been lost at sea in a storm off Sable Island, near Nova Scotia, and Dix, who worked on behalf of asylum patients and shipwrecked sailors in the same place and at about the same time Bishop's ancestor perished. Lombardi argues that "Dorothea Dix's evangelical mission of salvage was translated by Bishop into a secular poetic of reclamation and recovery." Lombardi, *The Body and the Song*, 227. Both of these observations, while astute, are limited by the narrow focus of the studies, both of which deal with only one poet. McCabe likens Bishop's "homemade art" to that of Jerónimo and Gregorio Valdes, about whom Bishop writes, but McCabe ignores the possible connections between Bishop's aesthetic and the Latin Caribbean art forms she describes. And Lombardi performs a biographical criticism that considers Bishop's poetics of "reclamation and recovery" in her later works, ignoring that the earlier poems of *North and South* juxtapose representations of two wrecking colonies, Nova Scotia and Key West.

78. From Bishop, *The Collected Prose*, 62.

79. Bishop proposes a similar model of reading in her story "The Sea and Its Shore," in which the main character is a scavenger who places preeminent value on scraps of reading matter as things. His privileging of the "misuse" value of things is reminiscent of what Bill Brown sees in a short story by Virginia Woolf about a shard of glass, except Bishop makes more explicit the suggestion that to "thingify" objects is a productive model of reading. See Brown, "The Secret Life of Things (Virginia Woolf and the Matter of Modernism)."

80. Raul's Club Miramar on East Roosevelt Boulevard near the East Martello Tower was advertised in the WPA tourist brochure as a place where "trained fish will eat from your hand." The owner of the club, Raul Vasquez, was active in the Cuban underground, which overthrew Machado and helped install the (then) leftist future president Fulgencio Batista.

81. Interview recorded in Key West. August 1995.

82. See especially James Clifford's well-known essay on salvage ethnography, "On Ethnographic Allegory," in Clifford and Marcus, *Writing Culture*, 98–121. Theodor Adorno remarks on Kant's attempt to "salvage" metaphysics. As Rolf Tiedemann notes in his edition of Adorno's text *Kant's Critique of Pure Reason*, though Kant uses salvaging only in a casual manner, "the concept of *salvaging, rescuing [Rettung]* is crucial to Adorno's interpretation of Kant. . . . For Adorno the nominalism that both accompanies and conditions the history of the increasing domination of nature terminates in the abolition of metaphysical entities and reaches a culminating point at which the entire process goes into reverse: the *Kantian* urge to *rescue* the intelligible sphere." See Adorno, *Kant's Critique of Pure Reason*, 2, 239n.

83. Hemingway, *To Have and Have Not*, 39.

84. Stevens, *The Collected Poems*, 47–48.

85. Guillén, *Obra Poética 1920–1958*, 170. "West Indies, Inc." was published originally in a collection of the same name in 1934.

86. Translation by Benítez-Rojo, *The Repeating Island*, 128.

87. Ibid.

88. For a critique of the gendering of the "cross-cultural synthesis" called *mestizaje* in Cuban poetry and nationalism, see Kutzinksi, *Sugar's Secrets*, esp. chaps. 5, 6.

89. Bishop, *The Complete Poems*, 32–33.

90. Ibid., 46. Margaret Dickie notes Bishop's problematic "poetic possession of the dispossessed" and particularly her "recurrent need to identify with people of colour [and] . . . to project onto them an exuberant variety of her own artistic endeavours." See Dickie, "Race and Class in Elizabeth Bishop's Poetry," 46.

91. Goldensohn, *Elizabeth Bishop*, 87.

92. For an extended view of the architectural interpretation of this term, see Vidler, *The Architectural Uncanny*, esp. 3–14.

93. I refer to the standard definition of *etcetera* as "a number of unspecified additional persons and things" and "unspecified additional items: ODDS AND ENDS."

94. The title of this section is from Bishop's poem "Late Air," a passage of which reads, "Five remote red lights/keep their nests there; Phoenixes/burning quietly, where the dew cannot climb." See Bishop, *Complete Poems*, 45. Originally published in *North and South*.

95. From Fountain and Brazeau, *Remembering Elizabeth Bishop*, 78.

96. Interview, Key West, August 1995.

97. See "Immortal Kisses Were His Goal."

98. Smith, "The Man Who Loved a Corpse," 90–92.

99. "Aged Key Wester Used 'Body' To Gratify Sex Passion!" Courtesy of MCPL.

100. The article (*Fantastic Adventures* 9:5 (September 5, 1947)) was republished by Rod Bethel in Key West in 1988 as *A Halloween Love Story*. Citation from page 76.

101. Harrison, *Undying Love*, 137. This excerpt was reprinted from Von Cosel's narration of the events, "The Secret of Elena's Tomb," 8–77. It included a title page blurb, "Can the dead be brought back to life? This is the true story of a scientist who believed it could be done—and did it!"

102. Bethel, *A Halloween Love Story*, 54.

103. De Certeau, *The Practice of Everyday Life*, xiv.

104. That it also required the feminization of the nation was not so problematic for the national imaginary—since the feminization of the nation is a common, if problematic, trope.

105. In 1921, Manola Cabeza was lynched by the Key West Ku Klux Klan for living with a mixed-race woman. No one was ever punished for the murder. This section's title is from Steven's "O Florida, Venereal Soil," *The Collected Poems*, 47. Typescript printed with permission of Stetson Kennedy and courtesy of MCPL.

106. Kristeva, *Powers of Horror*, 8. Ewa Ziarek astutely observes that "abjection can be described as a perpetual displacement, disrupting even a temporary crystallization of identity." She cites Kristeva's essay, "Women's Time," 210.

107. Hemingway, "Who Murdered the Vets? A First-Hand Report on the Florida Hurricane," in Murphy, *A Key West Reader*, 117.

108. Hemingway, *To Have and Have Not*, 205–06.

109. Hemingway revealed in a letter to Max Perkins following the hurricane that the man who served as a model for the rummy Eddy was drowned in the tempest. The secreting of Eddy's death in the novel, like that of the homeless and desperate veterans in Freddy's bar serves to underscore its inevitability, indeed, its necessity.

110. See "Warn of Possible 'Race Riots' in Key West Strike," *Polk County Record* (December 6, 1935). WPA Scrapbooks, MCPL.

111. From Bishop's unfinished poem "Key West," VLSC, box 66.2. See also Bishop, *Edgar Allan Poe and the Juke-Box*, 51.

112. FERA's institution of carnival was a response to Caribbean and Latin American carnival traditions. For more on the Caribbean carnival, see Roach, *Cities of the Dead*. See also Bakhtin, *Rabelais and His World*.

113. From Giroux, *One Art*, 68.

114. Letter to Frani Blough, May 2, 1938. Giroux, *One Art*, 72.

115. Letter to Marianne Moore, November 20, 1939. Ibid., 85.

116. Letter to Marianne Moore, May 5, 1938. Ibid., 73.

117. From Luis Palés Matos, "Plena de menéalo" (Shaking it) from the 1928 collection "Danza negra" (Black Dance). Cited in and translated by Kutzinski, *Sugar's Secrets*, 145–46.

118. Weber, *The Letters of Hart Crane*, 316.

119. Crane, *The Complete Poems of Hart Crane*, 124. In contrast, Archibald MacLeish's much later poem "Hurricane" (1967) adopts a Caribbean Creole grammar to imply the futility of racial revolution: "Door go jump like somebody coming:/let him come. Tin roof drumming:/drum away—she's drummed before." From MacLeish, *Collected Poems*, 461–62.

120. VLSC, box 68, box 75.4.

121. See Cavendish, "Key West Fears Its Most Serious Economic Blow if F.E.C. Extension Is Abandoned." The article reveals the fears of many Key West leaders about the prospect of replacing the railroad with a highway.

122. Wigley, "Prosthetic Theory: The Disciplining of Architecture," 8–9.
123. From Williams, "Homage to Key West," 161. In plucking out his artificial eye, Regis also refuses the artifice of figurative language, the frustrating inability of words to speak for matter.
124. Ibid., 164.
125. See Bataille, *Visions of Excess*, 61–72.
126. The ear also allegorizes a violent privileging of the image over language, suggesting a desire to refuse the symbolic sphere of culture and remain in the fragmentary world of images. The self-portraits van Gogh obsessively painted in the aftermath of his self-mutilation can be seen as an almost celebratory refusal to hear. He substituted the image not for what is unspeakable, but for what is unhearable, shifting agency from the actor to the receiver.
127. See Caruth, *Unclaimed Experience*, 16–19. Freud's theory of trauma developed through an analysis of a train wreck.
128. Bataille, *Visions of Excess*, 17–19.
129. Kroker and Cook, *The Postmodern Scene*, 79.
130. Mitchell, "Holy Landscape: Israel, Palestine, and the American Wilderness," 207.
131. Ballou, "Key West." Benedict Anderson argues that "having to 'have already forgotten' tragedies of which one needs unceasingly to be 'reminded' turns out to be a characteristic device in the later construction of national genealogies." The smoothing over of the rupture between Key West and the mainland performs the forgetting that is constitutive of nation building in Anderson's terms. See Anderson, *Imagined Communities*, 201.
132. Hemingway, *To Have and Have Not*, 252.
133. Ibid., 253.
134. Typescript included in the Hemingway Archives, John. F. Kennedy Library, Boston.
135. Culler, *On Deconstruction*, 135. A deconstructive materialism compels one to explore the slippage between material and linguistic grafts—the graft *between* grafts.
136. I draw here on John Cage's concept of noise as undifferentiated sound as well as that of the Futurist composer Luigi Russolo, of whose work Hemingway was surely aware.

137. I draw on Caruth's terminology. See *Unclaimed Experience*, 8.
138. Hemingway, *To Have and Have Not*, 92.
139. Ibid., 79.
140. From KWN 2, box 75.4a, 57, VLSC.
141. Page, "Recording a Life: Elizabeth Bishop's Letters to Ilse and Kit Barker," 201.
142. Ibid., 197.
143. Miller, *Topographies*, 268.
144. Hemingway, *To Have and Have Not*, 252.
145. Ibid., 261–62. Hemingway thereby concedes his own inability to speak for these forgotten corpses and particularly for those female corpses who must go "dead inside." The novel thus anticipates its own encryptment, its exclusion from the modernist canon, and its ultimate reception as one of Hemingway's worst works. But can it be a surprise that, even when created by so-called High Modernist artists, works that employ an aesthetic of salvaging are rendered marginal, transitional, unfinished, unpublished mistakes? Can we wonder at the reception of Stevens's most famous, most lauded, most emblematic poem, "The Idea of Order at Key West," when we consider that it formally refuses these alterior forms?
146. Hemingway, *To Have and Not Have*, 225.
147. Key West seceded for one day to protest the roadblocks set up where the Overseas Highway intersects the mainland of Florida. The roadblocks were used to inspect cars coming off the Keys for drugs and illegal aliens but caused such congestion in traffic that they were hurting Key West tourism. Key West's gesture was largely symbolic, but it succeeded in stopping the inspections.

3 HARLEM

1. In 1941, Edith Halpert began to represent Lawrence and exhibited his "Great Migration" series. Lawrence was the first African American artist to be represented by a white downtown gallery. For the title of this section, see Hughes, "My Early Days in Harlem," 62–64.
2. Lawrence's biographical series paintings portrayed historical narratives that, if not strictly linear, progress to some kind of denouement. While clearly acting as counternarratives to

official U.S. histories, Lawrence's series paintings are nonetheless indebted to (even as they battle) a Hegelian notion of historical progress. See Nesbett and Dubois, *Jacob Lawrence, Paintings, Drawings, and Murals (1935–1999)*, 70, 206.

3. The editors of the *Catalogue Raisonné* cite a passage from a letter Lawrence wrote to Lynn Igoe (January 29, 1979) and note that Lawrence reconfirmed this interpretation in an interview with the series authors on June 7, 1999. See Peter T. Nesbett and Michelle Dubois, *Jacob Lawrence: Paintings, Drawings, and Murals (1935–1999): A Catalogue Raisonné* in *The Complete Jacob Lawrence*, vol. 2, 70.

4. Lawrence, like Romare Bearden, was influenced by the color space theory of the painter Stuart Davis, which held that "through color the artist could create a planar relationship that established the way the spectators would read colors spatially on a two-dimensional plane." Murray, *The Blue Devils of Nada*, 181.

5. His paintings were often described in terms of film as well, as "shooting scripts" or like storyboards for motion pictures that integrate "verbal and visual media." Transcript of interview, Downtown Gallery Records, 1824–1974, Archives of American Art, Smithsonian Institution, reel 5549, frame 365.

6. *Series* comes from the Latin *seris*, which means a row or chain, and the French *serre*, to join, connect.

7. Lawrence did distinguish his Migration Series from his earlier works. The Migration Series was not historical, he claimed, as much as an interior portrait of contemporary life. Nonetheless, he considered them to be a series. He comments in an interview, "It was such a part of me I didn't think of something outside. . . . It was a portrait of myself, a portrait of my family, a portrait of my peers. . . . It was like a still life with bread, a still life with flowers. It was like a landscape you see." See Nesbett and Dubois, eds., *Jacob Lawrence*, vol. 2, 70.

8. Spivak, "Harlem," 136.

9. In September 1943, *Vogue* reproduced five of the paintings. Elizabeth McCausland, "Jacob Lawrence," typescript, n.d., Downtown Gallery Records, 1824–1974, Archives of American Art, Smithsonian Institution, p. 10, reel 5549, frame 363.

10. See, in particular, his paintings *Tombstones* (1942) and *The Undertakers Do a Good Business* (1943), but funeral iconography shows up elsewhere. In the painting *Pool Parlor* (1942), for instance, a pool cue crosses the arm of a man reaching for the ball on the pool table to form a cross quite similar to the cross found among the tombstones in his *Tombstone* painting; a similar cross shows up in the arm that crosses the stripes on the bag in *Woman with Grocery Bags* (1942), in the chairs and windows of *They Live in Fire Traps* (1943), in the bed of *The Apartment* (1943), and in boxes outside the shop in *Harlem Scene (Butcher Shop)* (1943); and in the crosses atop churches that figure prominently in *Harlem* (1942), *Harlem Street Scene* (1942), and *This is Harlem* (1943). There is also a cross on the minister—though it is miniaturized, albeit central—in *There Are Many Churches in Harlem The People Are Very Religious* (1943), but crisscrosses are completely absent from *The Undertakers Do a Good Business* (1943).

11. See, for instance, Lefebvre on the *mundus* in *The Production of Space*, 241–46. Lefebvre also argues that "spatiality is characterized by a death instinct inherent to life." Ibid., 135.

12. The title of this subsection is from Claude McKay's poem "Flame-Heart," published in 1922 in McKay's volume of poetry *Harlem Shadows* and in James Weldon Johnson, ed., *The Book of American Negro Poetry*.

13. Florence Mills's performance in the 1922 Miller and Lyle black-cast musical *Shuffle Along* helped kick off the New Negro Renaissance. This oral history was taken on July 14, 1939. The original manuscript is part of the Folklife Collection of the Library of Congress, Manuscript Division, WPA Writer's Project Collection, 1936–40. Part of the interview is reprinted in Bascom, *A Renaissance in Harlem*, 179.

14. Wallace Thurman and William Jordan Rapp in Singh and Scott, *Collected Writings of Wallace Thurman*, 22.

15. Hughes, *The Big Sea*, 247.

16. Langston Hughes, "My Early Days in Harlem," 62–64.

17. Hughes, "The Twenties: Harlem and Its Negritude," 11–20. Reprinted in Wintz, *The Harlem Renaissance 1920–1940*, 403–12.
18. Hughes in Wintz, ibid., 403.
19. Arna Bontemps, "The Awakening: A Memoir," in *The Harlem Renaissance Remembered*, 26.
20. Recent scholarship has refuted this myth. See, for example, Carla Kaplan, ed. *Zora Neale Hurston: A Life in Letters* (2002); Verner D. Mitchell, ed., *This Waiting for Love: Helene Johnson, Poet of the Harlem Renaissance* (2000); and Verner D. Mitchell and Cynthia Davis, eds., *Dorothy West: Where the Wild Grape Grows: Selected Writings, 1930–1950* (2005). To my knowledge, there has not yet been a reassessment of the last of the "Niggeratti" women, Gwendolyn Bennett.
21. Abigail McGrath in Mitchell, *This Waiting for Love*, 128–29.
22. See, for example, recently, Cherene Sherrard-Johnson, *Portraits of the New Negro Woman: Visual and Literary Culture in the Harlem Renaissance* (2007); William Maxwell, *New Negro: Old Left* (1999); Catherine Capshaw Smith, *Children's Literature of the Harlem Renaissance* (2006); Mark Naison, *Communists in Harlem During the Depression* (2004); Theodore Kornweibel, *Seeing Red: Federal Campaigns Against Black Militancy, 1919–1925* (1999); Venetria K. Patton and Maureen Honey, eds., *Double-Take: A Revisionist Harlem Renaissance Anthology* (2001); George Chauncey, *Gay New York: Gender, Urban Culture, and the Making of the Gay Male World, 1890–1940* (1995); A. B. Christa Schwarz, *Gay Voices of the Harlem Renaissance* (2003); Gary Edward Holcomb, *Claude McKay, Code Name Sasha* (2007); and Cheryl A. Wall, *Women of the Harlem Renaissance* (1995).
23. Houston Baker, *Modernism and the Harlem Renaissance*, xvii.
24. Certainly, this is the case in psychoanalytic conceptions of melancholia/depression, which posit depression as an inability to reconcile the past with the present, while becoming subject to the past as a result.
25. In this formulation, I am influenced by Karen E. Till's concept of places of memory as haunted places: "Places of memory are created by individuals and social groups to give a shape to felt absences, fears, and desires that haunt contemporary society." See Till, *The New Berlin*, 9–10. See also Maurice Halbwachs, *On Collective Memory*, and Pierre Nora, *Realms of Memory: The Construction of the French Past*, vol. 1.
26. Hughes, "The Twenties: Harlem and Its Negritude," 406.
27. Even Nancy Cunard's encyclopedic 1934 anthology *Negro* might be read as a scrapbook of sorts.
28. See Nugent, "On Alexander Gumby," 223–26. Gumby's scrapbooks are now held in the Special Collections at Columbia University.
29. Ann Pellegrini uses the term "double vision" to describe what she sees as Frantz Fanon's attempt in *Black Skin, White Masks* to propose "a general theory of collective consciousness that remains attentive to historical and cultural particularities," that is, a theory that is methodologically attentive to local and specific conditions but that nonetheless describes the existential, philosophical, and psychological crisis of being black and a man. See Pellegrini, *Performance Anxieties*, 89–107. The term "double vision," with its affinity to the mysticism of hypnosis and "second sight" has a linguistic resonance with dissociation in particular.
30. He refers to Noel Sullivan, a California art patron who offered Hughes writing sanctuary on Hollow Hill Farms, his estate in Monterey.
31. Bernard, *Remember Me to Harlem*, 193.
32. Nichols, *Arna Bontemps–Langston Hughes Letters*, 98–99.
33. Bernard, *Remember Me to Harlem*, 222–23. He is referring to the 1943 riots in Harlem and Detroit.
34. "Down to the bricks" is a "Harlemism," defined by Thurman as "to the limit." Thurman and Rapp wrote "Harlemese" in 1929 and distributed it with the playbill at performances of their play *Harlem*. See Singh and Scott, *Collected Writings of Wallace Thurman*, 64–66.
35. Hughes, *The Big Sea*, 235.
36. Ibid., 237.
37. See, for example, Cobb, "Insolent Racing, Rough Narrative: The Harlem Renaissance's Impolite Queers," and Knadler, "Sweetback

Style: Wallace Thurman and a Queer Harlem Renaissance."

38. Tolson, *The Harlem Group of Negro Writers*, 47.

39. Hughes, *The Big Sea*, 234.

40. West, "Elephant's Dance: A Memoir of Wallace Thurman," 227.

41. Hughes, *The Big Sea*, 236.

42. McKay titles his chapter on the Harlem of today (1930s Harlem), "The Negro Quarter Grows Up" in McKay, *Harlem*, 21–31.

43. Derrida, *Cinders*, 39.

44. Geographers have long noted the problematic translation of *lieu* in French poststructuralism when it is translated into English as "place." The French Annales school argues that *milieu* is a better translation of the English *place*.

45. In this context, Nietzsche's observation in *On the Advantage and Disadvantage of History for Life*, is pertinent: "So: it is possible to live with almost no memories, even to live happily as the animal shows; but without forgetting it is quite impossible to *live* at all. Or, to say it more simply yet: *there is a degree of insomnia, of rumination, of historical sense which injures every living thing and finally destroys it, be it a man, a people or a culture.*" The collapse between history and insomnia becomes more pertinent in my following chapter on Hollywood. See Nietzsche, 10.

46. West, "Elephant's Dance," 215.

47. Ibid.

48. Ibid., 227, 215. See also Marks and Edkins, *The Power of Pride*, 235–47.

49. See West, "Elephant's Dance," 225.

50. See Amritjit Singh's introduction, "Wallace Thurman and the Harlem Renaissance," in Singh and Scott, *Collected Writings of Wallace Thurman*, 3–5.

51. Wallace Thurman, "Nephews of Uncle Remus," *The Independent*, September 24, 1927. Reprinted in Singh and Scott, *Collected Writings of Wallace Thurman*, 203.

52. Hughes, *The Big Sea*, 234. Joyce was a socialite and celebrity.

53. I am indebted to Pat Crain for our long discussions on ghostwriting and phantom literacies.

54. Jean-Michel Rabaté, *The Ghosts of Modernity*, 3.

55. Thurman's mode of refusal is distinct from that described by Maurice Blanchot. Blanchot associates refusal with the passivity and infinite patience of Melville's Bartleby the scrivener, whose repeated refusal "I would prefer not to," Blanchot argues, situates Bartleby outside of being. Blanchot, *The Writing of the Disaster*, 16.

56. Letter from the James Weldon Johnson Collection, Beinecke Rare Book and Manuscript Library, Yale University. Reprinted in Singh and Scott, *Collected Writings of Wallace Thurman*, 142–43.

57. Collected in Kaplan, *Zora Neale Hurston*, 129.

58. Collected in Bernard, *Remember Me to Harlem*, 254.

59. Nugent, "Lighting FIRE!!" introduction to Thomas Wirth's 1982 reprinting of *Fire!!*

60. See Boone, *Libidinal Currents*, 224–25, emphasis added.

61. Ibid., 232.

62. Mitchell, "Harlem Reconsidered," *Freedomways*, 473–75. Cited in Greenberg, *Or Does it Explode?*, 16, who has a long footnote on other instances of strolling.

63. Bruce, "Smoke, Lilies and Jade," in Wirth, ed., *Fire!!*, 36.

64. Hughes, "Elevator Boy," ibid., 15–17.

65. Thurman, "Cordelia the Crude," ibid., 5–6.

66. Recounting the story of Hurston's own cry, "Color Struck," at an awards party, Michael North argues that "color struck" is a "term for [Emma's] obsession—but also for the retreat it causes: in military terms, she strikes the colors and leaves the field." Thus, what had been "denoted as retreat and shame becomes [for Hurston] a cry of triumph" and a reclamation of the southern folk. North, *Dialect of Modernism*, 176.

67. Hartman, *Scenes of Subjection*, 108. See also Krasner, *A Beautiful Pageant*, 125.

68. Tate, *Psychoanalysis and Black Novels*, 13. See also Krasner, *A Beautiful Pageant*, 125.

69. Krasner, *A Beautiful Pageant*, 125–26. Krasner does a good job summarizing Tate and Hartman's arguments, and I draw on his readings.

70. Stephen Knadler argues that Thurman "developed a new philosophy for the New Negro that linked sexual deviance with the blurring of the 'perpetual bugaboo' of identity-based thinking:

the sweetback style." While Knadler identifies this philosophy with the introduction of a "politically volatile" and unpredictable "queer black body," the "sweetback," who is a kind of "black dandy," ambiguously gendered and sexualized, exhibitionistic and bohemian. I read Thurman as making an even more radical move than the "sweetback," who strives for something like the sex and gender ambiguity that Hart Crane and other white queer modernists were after. He seeks to blur not only sexual boundaries or the boundaries of identity and social formation—but the boundaries of the material body itself, so that what constitutes the "I" of the subject is no longer constrained within the boundaries of a single body covered by a single, impermeable skin. See Knadler, "Sweetback Style," 899–908.

71. Hughes, "The Negro Artist and the Racial Mountain." Reprinted in various collections, including Patton and Honey, *Double-Take*, 40–44.

72. Locke's and Du Bois's criticisms of *Fire!!* and *Harlem*, the journal that Thurman edited a few years later, have been often noted. Du Bois was concerned in particular by Nugent's unabashed depiction of homosexuality; and Locke, a self-identified gay man, critiqued what he saw as these artists' embrace of the social vacuum of decadence. He wrote in an article that Thurman had asked him to submit to *Harlem*, "Not all of our younger writers are deep enough in the sub-soil of their native materials. Too many are pot-plants seeking a forced growth according to the exotic tastes of a pampered and decadent public. It is the art of the people that needs to be cultivated, not the art of coteries." Locke, "Art or Propaganda?," 12.

73. Thurman, *Infants of the Spring*, 240.

74. Eleonore van Notten argues that there is no evidence Thurman actually studied Nietzsche, though he had read Mencken's book on Nietzsche's philosophy while a student in 1922. She writes, "[Thurman's] knowledge came almost exclusively through Mencken's individual interpretations and adaptations of Nietzsche's philosophy for an American readership." Mencken's book was the first published on Nietzsche in English. See Van Notten, *Wallace Thurman's Harlem Renaissance*, 109.

75. Henry Louis Mencken, *The Philosophy of Friedrich Nietzsche*, 23.

76. Thurman, *Infants of the Spring*, 218.

77. Letter to Langston Hughes from Wallace Thurman, Monday, n.d. [ca. July 1929], in Singh and Scott, *Collected Writings of Wallace Thurman*, 120–21.

78. The model I am describing for Thurman is not wholly akin to either Janet's model or to Henri Bergson's, although Bergon's suggestion that the body is an instrument of action, not substance, is an important one. But Bergson's model is racialist. In *Matter and Memory*, for instance, Bergson, who drew on Janet's dissociationism to develop a model of memory, makes his case about the "apparent diminution of memory, as intellect develops," by offering the following anecdote: "A missionary, after preaching a long sermon to some African savages, heard one of them repeat it textually, with the same gestures, from beginning to end." Bergson, *Matter and Memory*, 154.

79. See, for instance, Douglas, *Terrible Honesty*.

80. Hacking, *Rewriting the Soul*, 133. He refers to Janet's 1919 three-volume edition of *Psychological Healing*, vol. 3, 125.

81. Boone, *Libidinal Currents*, 219–20. The ellipses show up in works by other Harlem writers who are clearly attempting to negotiate desire—most prominently in Mae Cowdery's 1928 story "Lai-Li" and in several of the homoerotic love poems she includes in her 1936 collection of poems *We Lift Our Voices*.

82. Bruce, "Smoke, Lilies and Jade," in Wirth, *Fire!!*, 36.

83. Greenberg, "The Echo of Trauma and the Trauma of Echo," 319–47.

84. It can be argued that there is no such thing as an unechoic memory, since trauma is produced as a repetition through memory. See Caruth, *Unclaimed Experience*, esp. 1–57.

85. Benjamin, "A Berlin Chronicle," in *Reflections*, 59.

86. Bruce, "Smoke, Lilies and Jade," in Wirth, *Fire!!*, 36.

87. Hughes, *The Big Sea*, 234.

88. Thurman, *Infants of the Spring*, 44.

89. Fisher, *The Conjure-Man Dies*, 254. The novel was originally published in 1932.

90. It is a mistake to overstate the similarities between Du Bois and Locke. Leonard Harris argues that Locke and Du Bois had distinctly different views of the role of the aesthetic. By the 1920s, Harris argues, the sociologist Du Bois saw art primarily as a means of propaganda, whereas the pragmatist Locke "believed that art could form a propaganda role, but that there were other criteria, associated with notions of beauty as a pragmatic good, due consideration as criteria of evaluation." Harris is correct in arguing for a more nuanced reading of the distinctions between Locke and Du Bois, especially with regard to the role of the aesthetic. However, I think he overstates his case about Du Bois—although this is certainly the view that many of the younger artists had of his position. See Harris, "The Harlem Renaissance and Philosophy," 381–85.

91. James De Jongh, *Vicious Modernism*, 2, 210. In an international survey of literary depictions of Harlem, De Jongh divides the construction of the "Harlem motif" into three phases: the "Black Awakening of the 1920s," narrated by seers, in which Harlem emerges as myth; in the second "period of adjustment," the "emerging ghetto" of the 1930s and 1940s, Harlem undergoes "mythification in historical and sociological time, in defiance of the existential actualities of an obscured and oppressive past and an uncertain present"; and the third "turbulent phase" initiated by the Harlem riot of 1964 is constituted by a "celebratory reworking of the ontology of black Harlem," 209–17.

92. Nietzsche, "On the Uses and Disadvantages of History for Life," 8–10.

93. For more on the role of sincerity in the production of modern authorship, see Rosenbaum, *Professing Sincerity*.

94. Woodson was the so-called father of African American history. He founded *The Journal of Negro History* and initiated Black History Week in the 1930s.

95. Anderson, *Deep River*, 2–3. Arthur A. Schomburg, "The Negro Digs Up His Past," in Locke, ed., *The New Negro*, 231.

96. Heinze, "*Schizophrenia Americana*: Aliens, Alienists and the 'Personality Shift' of Twentieth-Century Culture," 227–56. Heinze's essay strives to dismantle Warren Susman's influential argument that the turn-of-the-century shift among Americans from belonging to a "culture of character" to a "culture of personality" is largely attributable to economic factors, particularly the rise of consumerism, claiming instead that character and personality were by no means considered opposites in American psychologies between the 1890s and 1930s.

97. William James, *The Principles of Psychology*, vol. 2, 614.

98. Rampersad, "Slavery and the Literary Imagination: Du Bois' *The Souls of Black Folk*," 104–24. The debate about DuBois's relationship to Hegelian teleology and scientific positivism is extensive and changing. See for example, Winfried Siemerling, "W.E.B. Du Bois, Hegel, and the Staging of Alterity," and the fall 2000 special issue of *boundary 2* 27.3.

99. Hughes, *The Big Sea*, 238.

100. Ibid., 11.

101. Ibid., 325.

102. See Friedrich A. Kittler, *Discourse Networks*; Mark Seltzer, *Bodies and Machines*; and Morag Shiach, "Modernity, Labor and the Typewriter."

103. I use the term *fugue* in a precise sense here, as it resonates both with music and psychoanalytic models of dissociation or multiple personality.

104. Wirth, *Gay Rebel of the Harlem Renaissance*, 163

105. From Richard Bruce Nugent, taped interview, David Levering Lewis, September 1974, May 1977, Library of Congress, Washington, D.C. Cited in van Notten, *Wallace Thurman's Harlem Renaissance*, 289–90.

106. Cited from one of the fifteen taped, ninety-minute interviews with Nugent, dated from 1983, held in the private collection of Thomas Wirth, Nugent's executor, in New Jersey. Here, as above, I am indebted to van Notten's prodigious research of unpublished sources for *Wallace Thurman's Harlem Renaissance*.

107. And yet it is the repetitive nature of the blues that has gotten the critical bum rap. The so-called originality of particular songs, an originality based on the virtuosity of improvisation, and therefore individuality, becomes the way in which blues critics largely elevate some blues forms over others. In a move that Adorno would have found agreeable—though Adorno wasn't much for popular music, and certainly no advocate of jazz—the country blues and the masculine nonlyrical urban blues (largely based in Chicago) are often privileged over the feminine urban blues (largely based in Harlem), which are dismissed at best as watered-down versions and at worst as sellouts. Robert Palmer argues, for instance, that the more instrumental "delta blues" are "the purest and most deeply rooted of all blues strains." And as Angela Davis surmises, "studies of blues have tended to be gendered male." Women's classic blues songs were more strictly narrative, voice centered rather than instrument centered and therefore presumably more easily digested by white audiences. The female blues singers did sing in those vexed and segregated nightclubs instead of at rent parties and dives. And blues songs sung by women were more often pressed into race records and were sold to white audiences. See Palmer, *Deep Blues*, 18. See also Davis, *Blues Legacies and Black Feminism*, xiv; Murrary, *Stomping the Blues*, 82.

108. Thurman and Rapp, "The Writing of Harlem: The Story of a Strange Collaboration." The essay is included in James Weldon Johnson Collection, Beinecke Rare Book and Manuscript Library, Yale University. It was unpublished until Thurman's collected works were edited by Singh and Scott in 2003, 376–77.

109. Monte Williams, "Harlem Journal."

110. Browser, "A Negro Documentarian."

111. Douglas, "Unique Passion for Collecting Facts About Negroes." Courtesy of the Rare Book and Manuscript Library, Columbia University (BCLU).

112. Stewart, *On Longing*, 139.

113. Ibid., 153.

114. Ibid., 151–52.

115. Douglas, "Unique Passion for Collecting Facts About Negroes." 116. Gumby, "The Gumby Scrapbook Collection of Negroana," *Columbia Library World* 5, no. 1 (January 1951): 4, BLCU.

116. Gumby, "The Gumby Scrapbook Collection of Negroana," *Columbia Library World* 5, no. 1 (January 1951): 4, BLCU.

117. Ibid.

118. Nugent, "On Alexander Gumby," in Wirt, ed., *Gay Rebel of the Harlem Renaissance*, 225.

119. Gumby, "The Gumby Scrapbook Collection of Negroana," 4.

120. W. E. B. Du Bois, "The Browsing Reader," 165. Cited in Goeser, "The Case of Ebony and Topaz," 87.

121. Langston Hughes, "The Negro Artist and the Racial Mountain."

122. Zora Neale Hurston, "Characteristics of Negro Expression," in Cunard, ed., *Negro*, 9–46. Originally published by Nancy Cunard in London at Wishart, 1934.

123. Patricia Yaeger argues that the scrap or remnant that "haunts" southern black women's fiction "becomes an add-on that is at once necessary and missing, an increment that gestures toward a person, community, or world-that-would-be: a space that cries out for increase, appendage, addendum. This conjured or asked-for supplement stands in for the integer, the individual who should already be there, who should be constitutive, whose absence defines a system that unravels whole human beings. What travels in this space, what haunts its fictions, is often fragmented or partitioned: instead of the thing or person in itself (the woman who is losing her life hour by hour, the child torn from mother or habitus), we meet an object-memory that flashes up with the force of what's loved, a loss that signals the return of the dispossessed" (95–96). See Yaeger, "Ghosts and Shattered Bodies," 87–108.

124. See also Brathwaite, *The History of the Voice*, 19. Braithwaite argues for what Yaeger calls the "portability of black culture." I was directed to this citation by Yaeger's essay, cited above.

125. See Saper, "Intimate Bureaucracies and Infrastructuralism."

126. The "New York Correspondence School" is usually dated between 1962 and 1973, but Johnson argued he began this practice much earlier.

127. From paragraph 25 in Marc Bloch's "Rayocide: 67 paragraphs on the death of Ray Johnson," 1995, at http://www.panmodern.com/rayjohnson/rayocide.html.

128. Gumby, like Johnson, draws on a different Baudelaire from T. S. Eliot, whose "objective correlative" reifies as lyrical property the correspondences between nature and the human psyche. Not incidentally, some have read the objective correlative as a symptom of closetedness. My thanks to Maria Damon for mentioning to me Harold Norse's lecture on T. S. Eliot's objective correlative as symptom of closeted gay desire, Naropa Institute, August 1980. See also Wayne Kostenbaum's *Double Talk*. Kostenbaum argues that Pound's collaboration with Eliot on "The Wasteland" is "emphatically homoerotic." See chapter 4, "*The Waste Land*: T. S. Eliot's and Ezra Pound's Collaboration on Hysteria," 112–39.

129. Nugent, "On Alexander Gumby," in *Gay Rebel of the Harlem Renaissance*, 225.

130. Ibid., 223.

131. Koestenbaum, *Double Talk*, 3. Feminist critics such as Bette London and Holly A. Laird have taken Koestenbaum to task, arguing that this model of collaboration does not adequately describe women's literary collaborations and coauthorships. While Zora Neale Hurston, in particular, is a complex figure in the discourse of Harlem and collaboration, Koestenbaum's insights are quite on point for the coterie of young gay male writers and artists working in Harlem in the late 1920s and 1930s. On women's collaboration, see London, *Writing Double*, and Laird, *Women Coauthors*.

132. Lidz, *Ghosty Men*, 123.

133. Ibid., 9.

134. Faber, "Body of Collyer Is Found Near Where Brother Died."

135. Lidz, *Ghosty Men*, 153. The City of New York acquired the vacant lot in 1998 and turned it into Collyer Brothers Park.

136. Benjamin, "Unpacking My Library," *Illuminations*, 61. See also Stewart, *On Longing*, 153–54, 162–63. Stewart cites William James's reading of hoarding in *Principles of Psychology*, vol. 2.

137. See "Gas Company Seizes Meters of Hermits."

138. Hoover, "Message on National Thrift Week," released January 17, 1932, dated January 16, 1932. Message to Mr. J. Robert Stout, National Thrift Committee, 347 Madison Avenue, New York City. From the American Presidency Project document archive (APP).

139. Hoover, "Statement on the Hoarding of Currency," February 3, 1932. The White House held a conference on the "hoarding of currency" three days later, APP.

140. Hoover, "Statement on Hoarding of Currency," February 16, 1932, APP.

141. In a 1931 lecture at the New School in New York, John Maynard Keynes warned of the risk of declining consumer confidence after he observed widespread hoarding among consumers in New York and began to develop the influential economic theory that would shape the Roosevelt administration. In contrast to classical economics, which saw interest rates as determined by hoarding and dishoarding (saving and investment), Keynes argued they were more influenced by the supply and demand for money—that is, people's ability to buy things. In contradiction to contemporary views of Keynesian economics as being counter to government intervention to offset unemployment, Keynes called for public spending in certain dire circumstances. See Keynes, "Mr. Robertson on Saving and Hoarding," and "An Open Letter to President Roosevelt." See also Richard J. Kent, "Keynes's Lectures at the New School for Social Research."

142. See also Franklin D. Roosevelt. "First Fireside Chat (Banking)," March 12, 1933, in Buhite and Levy, eds., *FDR's Fireside Chats*, and APP.

143. Statements from "The President's News Conference of Harry S Truman." June 1, 1945, APP.

144. Marx, *Capital: A Critique of Political Economy*, vol. 1, 230–31.

145. Spackman, "Marfarka and Son: Marinetti's Homophobic Economics," 99.

146. Rowlinson, "Reading Capital with Little Nell," 347–80.

147. See, in particular, Freud, "Mourning and Melancholia," and Melanie Klein, "A Contribution to the Psychogenesis of Manic-Depressive States."

148. Nugent, "On Alexander Gumby," in Wirth, ed., *Gay Rebel of the Harlem Renaissance*, 226.

149. From *New York Post*, March 30, 1935. Found in the L. S. Alexander Gumby Collection of the American Negro, vol. 41, BLCU.

150. See Greenberg, *Or Does it Explode?*, 47. From James Hubert (Urban League), Testimony before the Mayor's Commission on the Conditions in Harlem, April 20, 1935, La Guardia Papers, new box 3770. Cited in the Unemployment Council's newspaper, *The Hunger Fighter*, 1933.
151. Mayor's Commission on the Conditions in Harlem, "The Negro in Harlem" 44–45, La Guardia Papers, box 2250. Cited in Greenberg, *Or Does It Explode?*, 184.
152. Ibid., 47. See also Osofsky, *Harlem*, 136–37.
153. George Schuyler, "Harlem Tempo." Mss. November 10, 1936, Schuyler Papers, Schomburg Center Special Collections.
154. Powell, "Harlem Declares Its Rent Too High," *New York Post*, March 1935. Found in the Alexander Gumby Collection, vol. 41, BLCU. Powell wrote the articles in the *Post* following the riot; these represented his entrée into politics.
155. Powell, "Harlem Demands Jobs for Starving," *New York Post*, March 29, 1935. Found ibid., BLCU.
156. Basso, "The Riot in Harlem." Quoted in Anderson, *This Was Harlem*, 245–46.
157. For a summary of the 1936 riot, see the published version of the La Guardia Commission Report, Fogelon and Rubenstein, eds., *The Complete Report of Mayor La Guardia's Commission on the Harlem Riot of March, 19, 1935*, 7–18. There is a reprint of the "Young Liberators" leaflet, p. 10. See also Greenberg, *Or Does It Explode?*, 3–6.
158. Cited in Anderson, *This Was Harlem*, 246.
159. Locke, "Harlem: Dark Weather-vane." Originally published in *Survey Graphic*, 457–62, 493–95.
160. See Freud, "Mourning and Melancholia."
161. Campbell, *Part of the Pack*, 341–52.
162. See McKay, "Harlem Runs Wild," *Nation* 140 (April 3, 1935): 382–83. Reprinted in Huggins, *Voices from the Harlem Renaissance*, 381–84.
163. Du Bois, "A Negro Nation with the Nation," *Current History* 42 (June 1935). Reprinted in Huggins, *Voices from the Harlem Renaissance*, 384–90.
164. Ibid. Du Bois's ideas about the role of capitalism in racial inequality were in transition in 1935, the year he published *Black Reconstruction in America* and after he separated from the NAACP. He did not join the Communist Party until 1961.
165. This interview on the "Harlem Riot" was conducted by the WPA by Vivian Morris on July 7, 1939. The interview subject was not named. Transcript in the WPA Life Histories Collection, Library of Congress. Courtesy of the Library of Congress.
166. Nugent. "Lighting Fire!!" Preamble insert to Wirth's 1982 reedition of *Fire!!*
167. Coleman, "Unfinished Masterpieces," 159–63. Originally published in *Crisis*, March 1927.
168. Hughes, *The Big Sea*, 241.
169. Perry, "The Brief Life and Art of Rudolph Fisher," 1–20.
170. Singh and Scott, *Collected Writings of Wallace Thurman*, 148–49.
171. Collected in Bernard, *Remember Me to Harlem*, 124–25.
172. See Oestreich, "Radiographic History Exhibit, 1934," 1013–20.
173. "Rudolph Fisher and Wallace Thurman," *Opportunity: Journal of Negro Life* 13.2 (February 1935): 38–39.
174. Theophilus Lewis in *Amsterdam News*, January 5, 1935. Cited in Singh and Scott, eds., *Collected Writings of Wallace Thurman*, 289.
175. See Sontag, *Illness as Metaphor*.
176. In the nineteenth century, tuberculosis was the romantic province of artists and the upper classes, a "vehicle for excess feeling." It was only in the last quarter of the century, when tuberculosis became recognized as an infectious disease—and a contagious one—that it took on a more "sinister" cast. Sontag, *Illness as Metaphor*, 13.
177. Ibid., 63.
178. Clendening, "Breakfastless Children and Tuberculosis Youth," 121. Cited in Ott, *Fevered Lives*, 141.
179. *The Complete Report of Mayor La Guardia's Commission on the Harlem Riot of 1935*, 92.
180. Calhoon, "Tuberculosis, Race, and the Delivery of Health Care in Harlem, 1922–1939," 104.
181. Du Bois, "The Health of Black Folk," 31. Cited

in Calhoon, "Tuberculosis, Race, and the Delivery of Health Care in Harlem, 1922–1939," 108.

182. Wright, "Factors Controlling Negro Health," 283. Cited also in Calhoon, "Tuberculosis, Race, and the Delivery of Health Care in Harlem, 1922–1939," 112.

183. Calhoon, "Tuberculosis, Race, and the Delivery of Health Care in Harlem, 1922–1939," 107.

184. *Complete Report of Mayor La Guardia's Commission on the Harlem Riot of 1935*, 98.

185. Wallace Thurman to Langston Hughes, July 10, 1934, in Singh and Scott, eds., *Collected Writings of Wallace Thurman*, 129–30.

186. Ott, *Fevered Lives*, 143–45.

187. "Description of a Male Tuberculosis Ward" from handwritten notes in the Thurman folder at the Beinecke Library, Yale University, written between July and December 1934, in Singh and Scott, eds., *Collected Writings of Wallace Thurman*, 93.

188. Sontag, *Illness as Metaphor*, 12.

189. Danius, *The Senses of Modernism*, 78.

190. Grove, "Röntgen's Ghosts: Photography, X-Rays, and the Victorian Imagination," 141–73.

191. Ibid., 162.

192. See Fanon, *Black Skin, White Masks*, 112. See also John Mowitt, *Percussion*, 156–62.

193. Kevles, *Naked to the Bone*, 49. She quotes several articles, including "X Ray to Turn Black Men White," *New York American*, December 28, 1903; *Boston Globe*, January 24, 1904; and David J. DiSantis, "Wrong Turn on Radiology's Road to Progress," 1121–38.

194. For more on the X ray's impact on modern art, see Kevles, *Naked to the Bone*, 116–41.

195. Schuyler, *Black No More*, 27. Originally published in 1931 by the Macaulay Company, where Wallace Thurman later served as editor in chief.

196. Kevles, *Naked to the Bone*, 100–110.

197. Schuyler, *Black No More*, 34–35.

198. Kevles argues that early on X rays were associated with a kind of eroticism, both because they could visually penetrate women's bodies—and lay bare the mysteries therein—but also because, for women, "this new ability to see through their bodies was a path to freedom." *Naked to the Bone*, 118–22.

199. Ibid., 122.

200. See also Fisher, "John Archer's Nose," in *Joy and Pain*, 149.

201. Hughes, *The Big Sea*, 328.

202. Dorothy West, "Elephant's Dance," in *The Richer, the Poorer*, 227.

203. Wallace Thurman to Langston Hughes, November 1934, in Singh and Scott, eds., *Collected Writings of Wallace Thurman*, 132.

204. Hughes, "Death Chant," in *The Collected Poems*, 71.

205. Hughes, "Cabaret Girl Dies on Welfare Island," in *The Collected Poems*, 66.

206. Hughes, "The Consumptive," in *The Collected Poems*, 157, see n. 640. "A moment of dignity," the title of the following subsection, is from the title of Helene Johnson's posthumously published poem, in Verner D. Mitchell, ed., *This Waiting for Love. Helene Johnson: Poet of the Harlem Renaissance*, 74.

207. Hurston had just turned sixty-nine when she died but had been shaving years off her age for most of her life.

208. Courtesy of the Zora Neale Hurston Collection, George A. Smathers Libraries, University of Florida, Department of Special Collections.

209. Hurston is referring to Elizabeth Hull, who is Van Vechten's niece. The letter, dated October 23, 1937, is in Kaplan, ed., *Zora Neale Hurston: A Life in Letters*, 407–8.

210. Honey, *Shadowed Dreams*, 230. In fall 2006, Rutgers University Press published a revised and expanded second edition of *Shadowed Dreams*, which includes a more detailed biography of Johnson.

211. According to Verner Mitchell, Johnson left her husband in 1941.

212. Johnson died in 1995. West, a few months her junior, died three years later.

213. Letter to Dorothy West, December 8, 1932, in Mitchell, ed., *This Waiting for Love*, 115–19.

214. In a review of the posthumous collection of Johnson's poems, *This Waiting for Love*, Leslie Wheeler comments that in this poem Johnson "unmistakably conjures the ghost of J. Alfred Prufrock." See Wheeler, 340–42. Johnson does so in engaging with the possibilities of passive

old age, but the ferocity with which she turns the poem around in the tenth stanza, "It need not be that way, old woman," also recalls Bessie Smith's reversal of the trope of the slave suicide by drowning in the last verse of "I'm Down in the Dumps" (lyrics by Leola P. Wilson, music by Wesley Wilson. Recording of 1933, Oken, from *Complete Recordings*, vol. 5: *The Final Chapter* [Columbia/Legacy 57546]):

> I'm twenty-five years old, that ain't no old maid
> I got plenty of vim and vitality, I'm sure that I can make the grade
> I'm always like a tiger, I'm ready to jump
> I need a whole lot's of lovin' 'cause I'm down in the dumps.

215. Abigail McGrath in Mitchell, ed., *This Waiting for Love*, 127.
216. Gordon, *Ghostly Matters*, 4.
217. Ibid., 55. See also Yaeger, "Ghosts and Shattered Bodies."
218. These are held at the George A. Smatters Libraries, University of Florida Department of Special Collections, Gainesville.
219. Staples, "Manhattan's African Dead: Colonial New York, From the Grave," A14.

4 HOLLYWOOD(LAND)

1. I borrow the phrasing from Ralph Ellison, who titles his 1948 essay on the Lafargue Psychiatric Clinic "Harlem is Nowhere." Clearly, however, the "nowhere" that is Hollywood is somewhat different from the "nowhere" that is the Harlem to which Ellison refers. See Ellison, *Shadow and Act*, 295–96.
2. Michel Foucault calls these spaces "adjacent to, but experientially detached from and 'absolutely different from' everyday life," heterotopias. He includes the cinema, museums, fairs, the beach, and other locations in his depiction. Hollywood both is and is not a heterotopia in Foucault's terms. See Foucault, "Of Other Spaces," 22–27, and *The Order of Things*, xviii. See also Cesare Casarino's astute reading of the concept of heterotopia, modernity, and the sea narrative in *Modernity at Sea: Melville, Marx, Conrad in Crisis*. Casarino writes, "Heterotopias are forms of representation that disturb and undermine representation: within such aphasic spaces, the fabular language of representation fails, flounders, encounters the unspeakable, faces the unrepresentable" (14). While Hollywood might be said to be unmoored and flirting with unrepresentationality (how can one represent what does not exist?), its mechanism is somewhat different. I draw also on Mary Ann Doane's comments on Foucault's use of heterotopia with regard to the cinema in *The Emergence of Cinematic Time*, 138–39.
3. A paraphrase of how Elizabeth Bishop describes a house in her story "The Sea and Its Shore," *Collected Prose*, 171–72.
4. WPA *Guide to California*, 195.
5. To "go Hollywood" is to become conceited, self-important, and superficial as a result of public attention. See, in particular, *Broken Hearts of Hollywood* (Warner Brothers 1926); *Show People* (MGM 1928), *Showgirl in Hollywood* (First National 1930); *The Royal Family of Broadway* (Paramount 1931); *What Price Hollywood?* (RKO Pathé 1932); *Going Hollywood* (MGM 1933); *365 Nights in Hollywood* (Fox 1934); *Hollywood Boulevard* (Paramount 1936); *Hollywood Hotel* (Warner Brothers 1938)
6. West, *Miss Lonelyhearts and Day of the Locust*, 60. Hereafter referred to as *Day of the Locust*.
7. William Desmond Taylor (né William Cunningham Deane-Tanner) was a Paramount film director who was mysteriously murdered in February 1922. The murder, which became famous, has never been solved but was one of a series of events (including the trial of the comedian Roscoe "Fatty" Arbuckle and the death of the actor Wallace Reid) that eventually led to the creation that year of the Motion Pictures Producers and Distributors Association under the direction of William H. Hayes.
8. Fitzgerald, *The Love of the Last Tycoon*, 76.
9. Martin Roth, in an unpublished paper on the *Intolerance* sets, writes that the number of years attributed to the set changes between one and four or more years in different reports. He cites Robert Sklar, who writes that, "For a year after *Intolerance* was finished the Babylonian set remained, dominating the Hollywood skyline. Then, in the

fall of 1917, it came down, and sections of it found their way into the back lots of other studios" (Sklar, *Movie-Made America*, 64). Roth also writes in a footnote of other accounts: "One of Griffith's assistant directors on the film, Joseph Henabery, makes it four or five" (119), and Griffith's cameraman, Billy Bitzer, claimed the set remained standing until the 1930s (135). The actress Miriam Cooper testifies that the sets were "solidly constructed and lasted for years. When I was back in Hollywood in 1940 the sets were still standing" (98). Since, as Roth points out, the sets were "dismantled and parts of them survived in other locations, it is hard to know exactly what is being referred to in the various claims of endurance," the instability of these claims is precisely the point. The places of Hollywood and Hollywood as place resist any model of narrative closure or linearity. In Roth, "Griffith's Walls," 30n2.

10. Opening with the "footprint ceremony" outside of Grauman's Chinese Theatre is probably the most common location shot. It is found in films about the rise of a star, from minor films such as *Hollywood Speaks* (Columbia 1932) to famous films such as *What Price Hollywood?* (RKO 1932), *Hollywood Boulevard* (Paramount 1936), and *A Star Is Born* (Selznick 1937). But many films, such as *Breakfast in Hollywood* (United Artists 1945), use an image of the street signs at the intersection of Hollywood and Vine.

11. Despite what Robert Venturi, Denise Scott Brown, and Steven Izenour suggest in *Learning from Las Vegas*, Las Vegas learned first from Hollywood. As did Disneyland, built by set designers in the 1950s—and produced for television. See Venturi et al., *Learning from Las Vegas*.

12. See Michel de Certeau, Luce Girard, and Pierre Mayol, "Ghosts in the City," in *The Practice of Everyday Life*, vol. 2: *Living and Cooking*, 143.

13. "A City Within A City," in *The Lion's Roar*, 2–3. Courtesy of the Margaret Herrick Library at the Academy of Motion Pictures (MHL).

14. Williams and Williams, *Hollywoodland*, 3, 13, 16.

15. West, *Day of the Locust*, 68, 61, 80.

16. "Tarzan Fact and Fiction," in *The Lion's Roar*. Courtesy of MHL.

17. Heisner, *Hollywood Art*, 4–5.

18. Heisner cites William Cameron Menzies, "Pictorial Beauty in the Photoplay," in Kozarski, *Hollywood Directors, 1914–1940*, 245. See Heisner, *Hollywood Art*, 46.

19. Cited in Heisner, *Hollywood Art*, 5.

20. Quoted from Scrapbook 1, Film in the George Cukor collection, MHL.

21. Quoted from "EXPEL FILM SCENARISTS ANNUALLY, SAYS GEORGE CUKOR, "Cracker-Barrel Spirit Lacking, Claims Director" (n.s., n.d.), and "Scribblers Claim 'Sticks' Worse for Gossip, Night Life." "By the Snooper," in Scrapbook 1, Film in the George Cukor collection, MHL. Probably dated 1932–33.

22. The metric films of the Austrian independent filmmaker Peter Kubelka make this illusion visible. In constructing his highly structured "metric films," Kubelka rejects Eisenstein's focus on the shot as the essential element of cinematic articulation, arguing instead that the frame is cinema's most elemental unit.

23. Heisner, *Hollywood Art*, 9, 15.

24. From "Flashes from World Premiere of 'The Women' at Grauman's Chinese Theatre, August 31, 1939" in "MGM Studio News," in Scrapbook 3 from the George Cukor collection, MHL.

25. Benjamin, "L Dream House, Museum, Spa," in *The Arcades Project*, 406.

26. Balázs, *The Theory of Film*, 50.

27. Benjamin, "The Work of Art in the Age of Mechanical Reproduction," in *Illuminations*. This also suggests that we might think differently about reading surface—and about surface readings or what we might more crassly call reading literally. The difference between surface and depth is not at all clear, and, reading closely, one might miss the complexity of what seems self-evident. Surface similarities matter, in other words. Especially in Hollywood.

28. Benjamin, "L Dream House, Museum, Spa," 410.

29. Fizgerald, *The Love of the Last Tycoon*, 25.

30. The comparison is, of course, made through simile, which Northrup Frye treats as a "displaced" and degraded metaphor. Frye, *Anatomy of Criticism*, see esp. 71–130. As Derrida has noted in "White Mythology," simile is the absent presence in classical rhetorical theory.

31. And yet what undergirds both descriptions is not their hallucinatory or dreamlike qualities but a confusing relationship between conception, representation, and material fact. In Hollywood, in other words, the present becomes a synecdoche for presence. Never mind the question of surface or depth.

32. I thank my student Eric Lindstrom for pointing this out (in a different context) in class one day. Drawing on Noël Burch, Mark Garrett Cooper contrasts what he sees as early cinema's presupposition of a "viewer 'external' to the world of the story" with Hollywood filmmaking's attempt to identify the spectator's "point of view with that of the camera, thereby effacing its own powers of narration and moving the viewer 'inside' a diegetic space." Cooper, "Narrative Spaces," 153.

33. See Benjamin, "The Work of Art in the Age of Mechanical Reproduction," in *Illuminations*, 217–51.

34. Celluloid was the first synthetic plastic, produced by treating cellulose nitrate (cotton dipped in nitric acid and sulfuric acid) with camphor and alcohol. Weschler, "Sublime Decay," 45.

35. "Federal Chemist Warns Against Improper Storage of Films," 22. Cited in Slide, *Nitrate Won't Wait*, 11.

36. Slide, *Nitrate Won't Wait*, 13. See also Weschler, "Sublime Decay," 45.

37. Weschler, "Sublime Decay," 42–47.

38. Usai, in *The Death of Cinema*, references his section XLIV "The Unseen": "Relatively few moving images can be seen in the course of a lifetime, a tiny fraction of those actually made. Given an average lifespan of seventy-five years, the time spent viewing them rarely exceeds one hundred thousand hours, little more than a decade. Those who live in communities where moving images are made and experienced on a regular basis sometimes have an urge to watch as many of them as possible [XXXIV]. This urge is often replaced by other impulses such as boredom, selectivity, or flat refusal. The death of cinema is primarily a mental phenomenon that will occur whether or not the factors mentioned in [IV] actually take place, and will be sanctioned by the natural tendency to forget the experience of pleasure. The search for its repetition, as represented by the practices referred to in [XXVII], is also typical of humans," (93). And so it goes. . . .

39. Ibid., 18–19.

40. Doane, *The Emergence of Cinematic Time*, esp. 206–32.

41. Harry Brand, Publicity Director, 20th Century-Fox Hollywood, "Set Designing," June 8, 1940. In Sets Designing (Art Dept.), Academy Library General Collection Clip Files. Courtesy of MHL.

42. Doane, *Emergence of Cinematic Time*, 8.

43. Ibid., 9–20.

44. Mark Garett Cooper argues that the driving force of film narrative lies in the manipulation of space. Using the Hollywood romance as a paradigmatic example, he argues that "the coherent, unified space we have been calling 'the diegesis' is less a precondition of Hollywood's favorite narrative than its goal." Transhistorically and "through myriad iterations," he writes, Hollywood narrative "presents and resolves a spatial problem." Cooper persuasively overthrows the privileged position of the shot in theorizations of film narrative. His reading falters, however, in its unself-conscious collapse between space and place. If "events take place" in film, it is not solely because film narrative is motivated by spatial problems, but because of a difficulty of reconciling space with place. Implicitly, Cooper equates place with objects, what he calls "production units" or shots, and space with action or operations, what he calls "reception units." When he argues that "Hollywood filmmaking works less to 'contain' spatial excess than to classify, transform and arrange the potentially infinite spaces it evokes—to narrate space," Cooper posits a narrative model that sounds a good deal like that of Michel de Certeau, who argues that stories "carry out a labor that constantly transforms places into spaces or spaces into places." Such a narrative model relies both on an opposition between space and place and a breakdown of that opposition. While we can see the kiss at the end of the romance narrative as an attempt to reconcile space and place (thinking two things in one place), we can also see continual attempts to thwart this reconciliation. See Cooper, "Narrative Spaces," 149–51; and de Certeau, "Spatial Stories," in *The Practice of Everyday Life*, 118.

45. Balázs, *Theory of Film*, 54–55.

46. Ibid., 58.

47. "Sound has no frame," notes Michel Chion; therefore it changes the nature of spatial relations, of the inside to the outside and of the opposition between them. Not surprisingly, much of the critical work on film sound is preoccupied with space and spatial relations. See especially Chion, *The Voice in Cinema*, 22–23; Doane, "The Voice in the Cinema: The Articulation of the Body and Space," 33–50; and Balázs, *Theory of the Film*, 194–241.

48. Heisner, *Hollywood Art*, 11, 22–23.

49. Cobb and Willems, *The Brown Derby Restaurant*, 12.

50. Hopkins, "From 'Then to Now,'" 8. Quoted in Heisner, *Hollywood Art*, 39. In a 1964 article, Serge Krizman, the production designer for the TV series "The Fugitive," creator of the Yugoslav Pavilion at the New York World's Fair, and designer of Louis B. Mayer's office and the glass-walled house for the "The Cabinet of Dr. Caligari," observed that, "Modern architecture and home decoration can never repay the debt they owe to motion pictures. We in the industry influence today's designers more than they know." See, "Design Ideas In Movies," in . . . "Sets Files," *General Collection*, MHL.

51. Beverly Heisner points out that most American architects who worked in the film industry had been trained in Beaux Arts style, which aspired to "absolute recall of period styles"; therefore, some of what has come to constitute Los Angeles's pastiche of styles—the pathetic period reproductions that West, for one, satirizes—might be said to have developed out of a kind of downsized architectural traditionalism. So too perhaps could this be said to have impacted Hollywood cinema's increasing romance with realism, which really was an aspiration for diegetic cohesion more than an eschewal of fantasy. After all, some of Hollywood's most influential art directors, such as MGM's Cedric Gibbons and RKO's Van Nest Polgase, and the independents Richard Day and William Cameron Menzies, found inspiration in the clean lines of modernist functionalism and design by Le Corbusier and the German Bauhaus architects. Heisner cites a *Theatre Arts Monthly* article that credits Gibbons, whose sleek Art Deco designs came to constitute the MGM style, with introducing film audiences to "the modernistic settings now so much in vogue." Other art directors, such as Warner Brothers' Anton Grot and Hans Dreier, drew haunting images that were influenced by the European Expressionists. See Heisner, *Hollywood Art*, 38–39.

52. Today, with the advent of digital landscapes, place making is going through another radical transformation.

53. Cited in Heisner, *Hollywood Art*, 111. From Haver, *David O. Selznick's Hollywood*, 319–21.

54. Goldner and Turner, *The Making of King Kong*, 159.

55. For more on understandings of the production of abstract space, see Lefebvre, *The Production of Space*; Casey, *The Fate of Place*; and Rose, *Feminism and Geography*.

56. Fitzgerald, *The Love of the Last Tycoon*, 69–70.

57. McCoy, *I Should Have Stayed Home*, 5.

58. Reprint of letter to MGM, August 8, 1938. In the Hal Roach Collection, box 2, file 69. Included in "Production Materials" for *Merrily We Live*. Courtesy of the Performing Arts Archive and the Warner Brothers Archives at the University of Southern California Cinema-Television Library (USC). Mrs. L____'s name has been erased for matters of privacy.

59. Reprint of letter from MGM, September 2, 1938. Ibid. Courtesy of USC.

60. See Derrida, "Signature, Event, Context."

61. See Freud's "A Note upon 'The Mystic Writing Pad,'" and Derrida's reading, "Freud and the Scene of Writing."

62. Schwartz, "Cinematic Spectatorship before the Apparatus: The Public Taste for Reality in *Fin-de-Siècle* Paris," 311. See also Schwartz, *Spectacular Realities*.

63. See Bruno, *Streetwalking on a Ruined Map*, 59–72. See also Michelle E. Bloom's summary of Bruno's work in *Waxworks*, 19–20.

64. In *Waxworks*, Bloom compares the cultural significance of wax spectacles to modern refigurings of the Pygmalion myth, in which the wax figure serves as a sign for a remaking of the subject. See esp., 130.

65. Ibid., 139.

66. Buckle, *The Mind and the Film*, 39.

67. For more on "suturing" in film, see Lisa Cartwright, *Screening the Body: Tracing Medicine's Visual Culture*.

68. See Doane, *The Emergence of Cinematic Time*.

69. Langley, Ryerson, and Woolf, *The Wizard of Oz*, 50–51.

70. Rushdie, *The Wizard of Oz*, 30.

71. Over the years, *The Wizard of Oz* has been read as an allegory for populism (see Littlefield, "The Wizard of Oz"); for money (see Rockoff, "The 'Wizard of Oz' as a Monetary Allegory," and Dighe, ed., *The Historian's Wizard of Oz*); for consumerism (see Culver, "What Manikins Want"); as a "secular myth of America" (see Nathanson, *Over the Rainbow*); and as a parable on mass culture (see Kim, "Strategic Credulity"), among other issues. It serves both as an advertising vehicle for MGM—and as a parody of it. (Consider the campy scene when Bert Lahr as the "Cowardly" Lion sings, "If I were the King of the Forest.")

72. See Rushdie, *The Wizard of Oz*, 30–31.

73. From Langley et al., *The Wizard of Oz*, 51. The history laid out here privileges the role of editing in cinematic history and is subject to some dispute. See, most recently, Cooper's critique of this version of cinema history in *Love Rules*, 66–68.

74. Langley et al., *The Wizard of Oz*, 52. Technicolor is not without its problems in the film. True, the Wicked Witch, with her black habillé and green-tinged face, harkens back to a time when Rudolph Valentino donned greenish face makeup in a kind of minstrelsy that made his olive-toned skin appear white on screen, suggesting that her death alludes to the demise of black-and-white cinema. Then again, it is the witch who is responsible for Oz's most dramatic color effects.

75. Rushdie, *The Wizard of Oz*, 33.

76. Certainly, the film can be read as a comment on the Hollywood-on-Hollywood film genre. Dorothy's trek through Oz simulates the narrative arc of the ingénue's quest from country girl (in Kansas) to Hollywood star (in the Emerald City) that is performed in most films of the Hollywood-on-Hollywood genre. But it does so to comment on the fallacy of apparent spatial reconciliation in Hollywood narrative.

77. Langley et al., *The Wizard of Oz*, 118–19, 126–27.

78. Doane argues that cinema serves as modernity's most potent metaphor for the irreversibility of time. See *The Emergence of Cinematic Time*, 112–13.

79. These are played by the former silent film stars Buster Keaton, Anna Q. Nilsson, and H. B. Warner.

80. Cited by Chion, *The Voice in Cinema*, 12. The arrival of sound was critiqued by both the Right and the Left. Bardèche and Brasillach, who published *Histoire du cinéma* in 1935, became vocal pro-Vichy collaborators during World War II.

81. For "Ever since the telephone...," see Chion, ibid., 46. Brackett is quoted in Meyers, "Introduction" to Sunset Boulevard, ix.

82. All memos in this series are in the Ron Haver Gift Collection, U-74, Box 1, folder "General Correspondence-GWTW," Special Collections, MHL, and are reproduced courtesy of the Margaret Herrick Library, the Academy of Motion Pictures. The first memo is excerpted from a longer one.

83. Refers to Ray Klune, the cinematographer.

84. DeMille, *Hollywood Saga*, 17.

85. As is often recounted, during the first screening of the film, confused spectators ran from the theater, fearing that the train would jut out of the screen and into their seats.

86. Bachelard, *The Psychoanalyis of Fire*, 1. Originally published in French as *La Pychoanalyse du Feu* (Paris: Librarie Gallimard, 1938).

87. Ibid., 16.

88. Following the publication of *The Psychoanalysis of Fire*, Bachelard wrote philosophical investigations of other elements: air, water, and earth.

89. Ibid., 10.

90. Ibid., 11.

91. I refer to Siegfried Kracauer's *Theory of Film*, esp. 163–66. Kracauer identifies two inseparable dreamlike movements in film spectatorship, "trance-like immersion in a shot" and "daydream-

ing which increasingly disengages itself from the imagery occasioning it."

92. In 1929, a wildfire destroyed thirteen homes on the Malibu beachfront that had been newly built and leased to such Hollywood luminaries as Jack Warner, Clara Bow, Dolores Del Rio, and Barbara Stanwyck. Davis, *Ecology of Fear*, 104. Davis cites an article in the *Los Angeles Examiner*, October 27, 1929.

93. Davis, *Ecology of Fear*, 95–147.

94. "Fire Razed Film Landmark," *Hollywood Reporter*, May 18, 1967, in the Set Designing File, General Collection, MHL.

95. Davis, *Ecology of Fear*, 105.

96. Margaret Hamilton, who played the Wicked Witch of the East in *The Wizard of Oz*, got badly burned during the shooting of her exit from Munchkinland and couldn't work for six weeks. When she returned, she refused to work near fire again. The producers gawked, but she is reported to have said, "I'm not suing you because I know enough about this business to know I won't work again if I do sue. But I won't go near fire again." Her stunt double, Betty Danko, did and ended up spending eleven days in the hospital. Harmetz, *The Making of the Wizard of Oz*, 272–79.

97. Cited in Doane, *The Emergence of Cinematic Time*, 188.

98. Ibid.

99. Cooper, *Love Rules*, 68.

100. Bataille, "Socratic College," in *The Unfinished System of Knowledge*, 6. Bataille's editor, Stuart Kendall, makes the following remark: Bataille "most likely delivered this lecture at his Paris apartment . . . during the spring of 1942. The title was added by the Gallimard editors. The date given in the *Œuvres completes*, for this text, spring 1943, is most likely incorrect. The text appears in Georges Bataille, *Œuvres completes* 6:279–91 (281)."

101. Bataille's editor does not explain the notation of the crossed-out passage.

102. Bataille, *The Unfinished System of Nonknowledge*, 5.

103. Heisner, *Hollywood Art*, 108–10, 223–25. See also Vertrees, *Selznick's Vision*, 69–115.

104. A memo of November 20, 1938, from Selznick to Ginsberg reads, "I feel that it [the fire scene] will be the equivalent of the Chariot Race in *Ben Hur* [1924] and that it is our one chance, particularly since we are in color, to give them a sensational stunt." Cited in Vertrees, *Selznick's Vision*, 74.

105. This film was itself "remade," when it was reissued in 1931 with a synchronized music and sound effects score. And the King Kong set was reused at least twice before being incinerated: for the Bela Lugosi serial *The Return of Chandu*, filmed at Pathé in 1934, and in RKO's 1935 motion picture of Rider Haggard's *She*. Goldner and Turner, *The Making of King Kong*, 207.

106. "An Oral History with Robert F. Boyle," 51–52, interviewed by George Turner between May 29, 1992, and August 26 1992 (with follow-up May 18, 1998). Oral History Program, Margaret Herrick Library, Academy of Motion Picture Arts and Sciences, Beverly Hills, Calif., copyright 1998 Academy Foundation, MHL. Boyle was trained as an architect at USC and worked as an illustrator, draftsman, and assistant art director in the Paramount art department, headed by Hans Dreier, between 1934 and 1939. He later worked as art director for a serial at Universal, for the Alfred Hitchcock films *Shadow of a Doubt*, *North by Northwest*, *The Birds*, and *Marnie*, and for other films, including *The Thomas Crowne Affair*, *Fiddler on the Roof*, *The Shootist*, and *In Cold Blood*.

107. This procedure of "making the same with a difference" is akin to "Reno-vation" described earlier in the book. See also Phillips, "Waiting for Returns," quoted in n. 125, below.

108. This is hearsay. An anecdote relayed to me in July 2000 by Ned Comstock, the director of Special Collections, Film and Television Library, USC.

109. Chisholm, "Missing Persons and Bodies of Evidence," 125.

110. Ibid., 142.

111. Rushdie, *The Wizard of Oz*, 46.

112. Lesley Stern alludes to Paul Willeman's reading of the film *Pursued* using the psychoanalytic theorist Serge Leclaire's comments about the pleasures of smoking cigars, that "it would be possible to substitute film for tobacco" because of "that slight giddiness which springs from the *not quite the same* in which we recognize *the same* tobacco." Willeman, "The Fugitive Subject," 65. Cited in Stern, "Burial," 20, 227.

113. The distinction between style and art or aesthetics, in Adorno's terms, is not really the point here. There is no pretense, even in the case of some American avant-garde filmmaking (consider the Florey example), that any modern artistic production is possible outside the sphere of capital.

114. The lot where Mack Sennett filmed his Keystone Cops films plays a cameo in the film—it's where the filming of the slapstick sequences were made. In addition to Chaplin, the film includes cameos by Douglas Fairbanks, William S. Hart, Elinor Glyn, and several other silent film actors.

115. A subtler inside joke is the casting of Billy Haines as Davies's lover, in one of his last roles before he left acting for interior decoration in the wake of the Hayes crackdown. Haines was one of the most flamboyant and least closeted gay men in Hollywood. He became one of the most influential decorators in Los Angeles after he retired from acting.

116. Fitzgerald, *The Love of the Last Tycoon*, 108.

117. Ibid., 64.

118. Ibid., 26.

119. Ibid., 26–27.

120. Ibid., 27.

121. Chion, *The Voice in Cinema*, 132–33.

122. Michael North argues that "dubbing" is a constitutive feature of modernism, and he uses as examples two Hollywood narratives, *The Jazz Singer* and *Singin' in the Rain* to make his argument. See North, *The Dialect of Modernism*, 4–11.

123. Rushdie, *The Wizard of Oz*, 46.

124. The film eventually became *What Price Hollywood?* with Constance Bennett. From *Film Daily*, April 20, 1932. In Scrapbook 1, George Cukor Collection, MHL.

125. I draw here on a lecture by Adam Phillips entitled "Waiting for Returns: Freud's New Love," given at the Modernist Studies Association in 2003. In a brilliant reading of Freudian repetition, Phillips argues that the new is "impossible and unbearable" for the modern individual, for the modern individual is bound by a resistance to the past as "incestuous," and a resistance to the new as "insufficiently incestuous." Can the modern individual find new love, he says Freud asks, and if so, what would be new about it? Phillips surmises finally that "the same things and the same things done up in a different fashion become the modernist problem and the modernist solution." Kathleen is and is not Minna, and her similarity with a difference (but not too much difference) from Minna is what enables Stahr to fall in love with her. He falls in love with her *after* her voice reveals that she is not identical. Minna, of course, is herself a repetition and substitution for, presumably, Stahr's first love, his mother.

126. F. Scott Fitzgerald, *The Love of the Last Tycoon*, 93–94.

127. Wallace Thurman to William Jourdan Rapp. Typed letter, signed, June 1, 1929, p. 2. Yale Collection of American Literature, Beinecke Rare Book and Manuscript Library.

128. "Allen Parkinson, 83," *New York Times*, October 2, 2002.

129. For the publication, research, and reception history of the Motion Picture and Youth Research series financed by the Payne Fund, see Jowett, Jarvie, and Fuller, *Children and the Movies*.

130. Black, *Hollywood Censored*, 152.

131. See ibid., 151–55. The "noodle soup" remark comes from Black, who cites an article by Kaspar Monahan in the *Pittsburgh Press*, 154. See also, Jowett, Jarvie, and Fuller, *Children and the Movies*, and Kellogg, "Minds Made by the Movies."

132. See Jowett, Jarvie, and Fuller, *Children and the Movies*, 70.

133. Jowett, Jarvie, and Fuller note that this was one of the first commentaries on the effects of film spectatorship on children. They surmise that Addams's "attitude toward the 'House of Dreams' is a mixture of naive amusement at the popularity of the movies and a fear of the powerful influence the entertainment seemed to have on its audience." In a more ambivalent way, she, like most of the Payne researchers, "saw in the movies a source of neurosis, delinquency, sexual license, antisocial behavior, bad health and even 'attempted murder'" and "was concerned that the ubiquity and popularity of the movies would cause children to forgo other recreational activities of a more wholesome character." See ibid., 24–25. See also Addams, *The Spirit of Youth and City Streets*.

134. The term has been used by many to describe Hollywood since the 1920s or before. A 1927 documentary about the so-called movie colony was titled, for instance, *The Hollywood Dream Factory And How it Grew* (Blackhawk Films 1927). A 1972 documentary was called *Hollywood: The Dream Factory.*

135. West, *Day of the Locust*, 132. (*Day of the Locust* was first published in 1933.)

136. Kracauer, *Theory of Film*, 163. He cites Lebovici, "Psychoanalyse et cinema," 54.

137. Barry, *Let's Go to the Movies*, 30–31.

138. Benjamin, "The Work of Art."

139. Metz, *The Imaginary Signifier*, 101.

140. Ibid., 102.

141. Ibid., 116–17.

142. See Benjamin, *The Arcades Project*, 389.

143. Renshaw et al., *Children's Sleep*, 208.

144. Walsh, *Yours for Sleep*, 157–58.

145. Marinetti, "The Founding Manifesto of Futurism 1909," 251.

146. Kracauer, *Theory of Film*, 163.

147. Avant-garde cinema arguably defines itself by pushing the limits of cinema's watchability—the successful film would be one that is difficult to watch, but that a viewer could not help but watch. The success of Studio-era Hollywood cinema relied on the ease of its watchability even when that desire was produced through and by resistance.

148. Bataille, "Pure Happiness," in *The Unfinished System of Nonknowledge*, 225.

149. Ibid.

150. West, *Day of the Locust*, 106.

151. Fitzgerald, *The Love of the Last Tycoon*, 102.

152. Ibid., 15.

153. Ibid., 109.

154. She has also just gotten a marriage proposal to be deferred until "after [they] have this picture done." Dos Passos, *The Big Money*, 422–423.

155. Ibid., 423.

156. West, *Day of the Locust*, 82.

157. Ibid., 102.

158. Bataille, "Pure Happiness," in *The Unfinished System of Nonknowledge*, 226.

159. This formulation is indebted to Anca Parvelescu's reading of Kate Chopin's *The Awakening* in "To Die Laughing and to Laugh at Dying."

160. Levinas uses horror to describe the "rustling of the "*there is*," which is outside of consciousness and therefore neither dream sleep nor wakefulness. See *Ethics and Infinity*, esp. 60–61. See also Guyer, "Wordsworthian Wakefulness," 106.

161. Levinas, *Ethics and Infinity*, 49. See also Alford, "Emmanuel Levinas and Iris Murdoch: Ethics as Exit?" 31.

162. "*On veille quand il n'y a plus rien à veiller. Le fair nu de las presence opprime: on est tenu à être.*" (One watches on [*veille*] when there is nothing to watch [*à veiller*] and despite the absence of any reason for remaining watchful [*de veiller*]. The bare face of presence is oppressive; one is held by being, held to be.) This point is made by Guyer in "Wordsworthian Wakefulness," 93–111. See Levinas, *Ethics and Infinity*, 49, and *Existence and Existents*, 66. Originally published as *De L'existence à l'existant* (Paris: Vrin, 1986), 109.

163. The phrase is Alford's in "Emmanuel Levinas and Iris Murdoch: Ethics as Exit?" 31.

164. Chion, *The Voice of Cinema*, 9.

165. Levinas, *Existence and Existents*, 57.

166. Ibid., 69.

167. See Lingis's introduction to *Existence and Existents*, xix.

168. Crary, *Suspensions of Perception*, 48–50.

169. Cooper, *Love Rules*, 80, and Tratner, "Working the Crowd."

170. McCoy, *They Shoot Horses Don't They?*, 8, 10.

171. Ibid., 36.

172. Ibid., 116–17.

173. Ibid., 117.

174. See Dennis Drabelle, "Ancient Egypt in the Pacific," 38–44.

AFTERWORD

1. In 1937, 158 adults and 64 children inhabited 51 sets of family quarters and so-called bachelor apartments.

2. Editorial in the *Philadelphia Inquirer*, November 29–December 1, 1937. Cited in Ward, "Alcatraz and Marion," 88.

3. Bechdolt, "Rock," 5.

4. Conway, "Twenty Months in Alcatraz," 31. The *American Mercury* called the prison "America's torture chamber." See Turano, "America's Torture-Chamber," 11–15.

5. Ward, "Alcatraz and Marion," 82.
6. Le Corbusier, *Towards a New Architecture*, 209.
7. Ward, "Alcatraz and Marion," 82–83.
8. Ibid., 83.
9. Ibid., 85–87.
10. Odier, *The Rock*, 116.
11. This desire leads to what Andrew Ross calls the "Alcatraz Effect" of postmodernity, in which we escape meaning by imagining that we cannot escape, knowing all the while that we already have. See Ross, "The Alcatraz Effect."
12. Baudrillard, "On Seduction," in *Selected Writings*, 159.
13. Foucault, *Discipline and Punish*, 298.
14. From the "History of Pentagon" on the present-day Pentagon Website: http://www.defenselink.mil/pubs/pentagon/about.html.
15. "Army's Giant Five-by-Five," 34.
16. From Franklin Delano Roosevelt's June 28, 1934, fireside chat. See Buhite and Levy, eds., *FDR's Fireside Chats* and APP. See also the introduction to this book.
17. "City within a Pentagon," 112.
18. Pringle, "My Thirty Days in the Pentagon," 27.
19. "Pentagon," in *Time*. See also Rose, "My Life in Pentagonia," and Shalett, "Mammouth Cave." The discourse is quite similar even today. The Pentagon Website proclaims, "Approximately 23,000 employees, both military and civilian, contribute to the planning and execution of the defense of our country. These people arrive daily from Washington, D.C., and its suburbs over approximately 30 miles of access highways, including express bus lanes and one of the newest subway systems in our country. They ride past 200 acres of lawn to park approximately 8,770 cars in 16 parking lots; climb 131 stairways or ride 19 escalators to reach offices that occupy 3,705,793 square feet. While in the building, they tell time by 4,200 clocks, drink from 691 water fountains, utilize 284 rest rooms, consume 4,500 cups of coffee, 1,700 pints of milk and 6,800 soft drinks prepared or served by a restaurant staff of 230 persons and dispensed in 1 dining room, 2 cafeterias, 6 snack bars, and an outdoor snack bar. The restaurant service is a privately run civilian operation under contract to the Pentagon.

Over 200,000 telephone calls are made daily through phones connected by 100,000 miles of telephone cable. The Defense Post Office handles about 1,200,000 pieces of mail monthly. Various libraries support our personnel in research and completion of their work. The Army Library alone provides 300,000 publications and 1,700 periodicals in various languages." See "History of Pentagon" on the present-day Pentagon Website: http://www.defenselink.mil/pubs/pentagon/about.html.

20. "City within a Pentagon," 112.
21. Pringle, "My Thirty Days in the Pentagon," 27.
22. Lauterbach, "Pentagon Puzzle," 175.
23. "City within a Pentagon," 112.
24. "Race between Claustrophobia and Agoraphobia," 64.
25. "Army's Giant Five-by-Five," 108.
26. Koolhaas, *S, M, L, XL*, 496.
27. Ibid., 501.
28. Ibid., 515.
29. Pringle, "My Thirty Days at the Pentagon," 27.
30. Ibid.
31. The *Oxford English Dictionary* charts the first use of "classified" as "secret for reasons of national security and forbidden to be disclosed except to specific persons" to 1944.
32. See Taussig, *Defacement*, from which the title of this section comes, and Sedgwick, *Epistemology of the Closet*, esp., 4–7, 77–80.
33. See http://www.asile.org/citoyens/numero13/pentagone/erreurs_en.htm.
34. Deleuze and Guattari, *A Thousand Plateaus*, 286–90.
35. See Markoff, "Pentagon Plans a Computer System that Would Peek at Personal Data of Americans," A 10.
36. See Newman, "Ideas and Trends," and Bumiller, "Bush Pushes Volunteerism."
37. See, for instance, Risen and Lichtblaw, "Bush Lets U.S. Spy on Callers without Courts."

Works Cited

"Abating the Garbage Nuisance." *Literary Digest* 98:4 (July 28, 1928): 18–19.

Adams, Paul C., Steven D. Hoelscher, and Karen E. Till. *Textures of Place: Exploring Humanist Geographies*. Minneapolis: University of Minnesota Press, 2001.

Addams, Jane. *The Spirit of Youth and City Streets*. New York: Macmillan, 1909.

Adorno, Theodor. *Kant's* Critique of Pure Reason. Edited by Rolf Tiedemann. Translated by Rodney Livingstone. Stanford: Stanford University Press, 2001.

"Aged Key Wester Used 'Body' to Gratify Sex Passion." *Miami Life* 15:6 (November 2, 1940).

Aglietta, Michel. *A Theory of Capitalist Regulation: The U.S. Experience*. London: NLB, 1979.

Alford, C. Fred. "Emmanuel Levinas and Iris Murdoch: Ethics as Exit?" *Philosophy and Literature* 26.1 (2002): 24–42.

Allen, Frederick Lewis. *Since Yesterday: The 1930s in America. September 3, 1929–September 3, 1939*. 1939. Reprint, New York: Harper and Row, 1968.

"Allen Parkinson, 83, Developer of Sleep-Eze and Wax Movieland," *New York Times* (October 2, 2002).

Altieri, Charles. "Taking Lyrics Literally: Teaching Poetry in a Prose Culture." *New Literary History* 32 (2001): 259–81.

Anderson, Benedict. *Imagined Communities: Reflections on the Origin and Spread of Nationalism*. London: Verso, 1991.

Anderson, Jervis. *This Was Harlem: 1900–1950*. 1982. Reprint, New York: Noonday Press, 1993.

Anderson, Paul Allen. *Deep River: Music and Memory in Harlem Renaissance Thought*. Durham: Duke University Press, 1991.

Anderson, Sherwood. "So This Is Reno." *Nevada Newsletter* (April 5, 1924): 23.

"Army's Giant Five-by-Five." *Popular Mechanics* 79 (March 1943): 8–13.

Arnold, William. *Harlem Women*. New York: Original Novels, 1952.

Ashton, Jennifer. "Modernism's 'New' Literalism." *Modernism/Modernity* 10:2 (April 2003): 381–90.

Attali, Jacques. *Noise: The Political Economy of Music*. Translated by Brian Massumi. 1985. Reprint, Minneapolis: University of Minnesota Press, 1999.

Atwood, Albert W. "Out of the Scrap Heap." *Saturday Evening Post* 209 (May 29, 1937): 8–9, 95–98.

Bachelard, Gaston. *The Psychoanalyis of Fire*. Translated by Alan C. M. Ross. Boston: Beacon Press, 1964. Originally published in French as La *Pychoanalyse du Feu*. Paris: Librarie Gallimard, 1938.

Badger, Anthony J. *The New Deal: The Depression Years, 1933–1940*. New York: Hill and Wang, 1989.

Baker, Houston A. *Modernism and the Harlem Renaissance*. Chicago: University of Chicago Press, 1987.

Bakhtin, Mikhail. *Rabelais and His World*. Translated by Hélène Iswolsky. Bloomington: Indiana University Press, 1984.

Balázs, Béla. *Theory of Film: Character and Growth of a New Art*. Translated by Edith Bone. New York: Dover Publications, 1970.

Balderrama, Francisco, and Raymond Rodriguez. *Decade of Betrayal: Mexican Repatriation in the 1930s*. Albuquerque: University of New Mexico Press, 1995.

Baldwin, Faith. *Temporary Address: Reno*. New York: P. F. Collier & Son, 1940.

Ballou, Harold. "Key West," In *Cayo Hueso* (August 1939).

Banta, Martha. *Taylored Lives: Narrative Productions in the Age of Taylor, Veblen, and Ford.* Chicago: University of Chicago Press, 1993.

Barnard, Rita. *The Great Depression and the Culture of Abundance.* Cambridge: Cambridge University Press, 1995.

Barnett, James Harwood. *Divorce and the American Divorce Novel 1858–1937: A Study in Literary Reflections of Social Influences.* Ph.D. dissertation, University of Pennsylvania, 1939.

Barrett, James R. "Americanization from the Bottom University Press: Immigration and the Remaking of the Working Class in the United States, 1880–1930." In *Discovering America: Essays on the Search for an Identity*, edited by David Thelen and Frederick E. Howe. Urbana: University of Illinois Press, 1994.

Barry, Dan, and Amy Waldman. "A Nation Challenged: The Landfill; At Landfill, Tons of Debris, Slivers of Solace." *New York Times* (October 21, 2001).

Barry, Iris. *Let's Go to the Movies.* London: Payson and Clarke, Ltd., 1926.

Barthel, Diane. *Historic Preservation: Collective Memory and Historical Identity.* New Brunswick: Rutgers University Press, 1996.

Barthes, Roland. "The Reality Effect." In *The Rustle of Language.* Translated by Richard Howard. Berkeley: University of California Press, 1986.

Bascom, Lionel, ed. *A Renaissance in Harlem: Lost Essays of the WPA, by Ralph Ellison, Dorothy West, and Other Voices of a Generation.* New York: Amistad, 1999.

Basso, Hamilton. "The Riot in Harlem." *New Republic*, April 3, 1935.

Bataille, Georges. *Œuvres completes.* Volume 6. Paris: Gallimard, 1970.

———. "Human Face." *October* 36 (Spring 1986).

———. *The Unfinished System of Nonknowledge.* Translated by Michelle Kendall and Stuart Kendall. Minneapolis: University of Minnesota Press, 2001.

———. *Visions of Excess: Selected Writings, 1927–1939.* Translated by Allen Stoekl. Minneapolis: University of Minnesota Press, 1985.

Baudrillard, Jean. *Selected Writings*, edited by Mark Poster. Stanford: Stanford University Press, 1988.

Bechdolt, Frederick. "Rock." *Saturday Evening Post* 208 (November 2, 1935): 5–7.

Benítez-Rojo, Antonio. *The Repeating Island: The Caribbean and the Postmodern Perspective.* Translated by James E. Maraniss. Durham: Duke University Press, 1992.

Benjamin, Walter. *Gesammelte Schriften.* Volume 6. Edited by Rolf Tiedemann and Hermann Schweppenhäuser. Frankfurt: Suhrkamp Verlag, 1972–89.

———. "In Almost Every Example We Have of Materialist Literary History." *Selected Writings.* Volume 2. Edited by Michael W. Jennings. Translated by Rodney Livingstone. Cambridge, Mass.: Harvard University Press, 1999.

———. *Illuminations: Essays and Reflections.* Edited by Hannah Arendt. Translated by Harry Zohn. New York: Schocken Books, 1969.

———. *Reflections: Essays, Aphorisms, Autobiographical Writings.* Edited by Peter Demetz. Translated by Edmund Jephcott. New York: Schocken Books, 1978.

———. *The Arcades Project.* Translated by Howard Eiland and Kevin McLaughlin. Edited by Rolf Tiedemann. Cambridge, Mass.: Harvard University Press, 1999.

Bennett, Gwendolyn. "The Harlem Community Art Center." New York: Federal Arts Project. http://newdeal.feri.org/art/art08.htm.

Bergson, Henri. *Matter and Memory.* Translated by Nancy Margaret Paul, and W. Scott Palmer. New York: Zone Books, 1988. Originally published in French as *Matière et Mémoire* by Presses Universitaires de France in 1896.

Berlant, Lauren. *The Anatomy of National Fantasy: Hawthorne, Utopia, and Everyday Life.* Chicago: University of Chicago Press, 1991.

Berman, Marshall. *All That Is Solid Melts Into Air: The Experience of Modernity.* New York: Penguin Books, 1988.

Bernard, Emily, ed. *Remember Me to Harlem: The Letters of Langston Hughes and Carl Van Vechten.* New York: Alfred Knopf, 2001.

Bethel, Rod. *A Halloween Love Story.* Key West: Rod's Books, 1988.

Bishop, Elizabeth. *The Collected Prose.* Edited by Robert Giroux. New York: Noonday Press, 1984.

———. *The Complete Poems: 1927–1979.* New York: Noonday Press, 1979.

———. *Edgar Allan Poe and the Juke-Box: Uncollected Poems, Drafts, and Fragments.* Edited by Alice Quinn. New York: Farrar, Straus and Gioux, 2006,

Black, Gregory D. *Hollywood Censored: Morality Codes, Catholics, and the Movies.* Cambridge: Cambridge University Press, 1994.

Blake, Nelson Manfred. *The Road to Reno: A History of Divorce in the United States.* New York: Macmillan, 1962.

Blanchot, Maurice. *The Writing of the Disaster.* Translated by Ann Smock. Lincoln: University of Nebraska Press, (1980) 1995.

Bloch, Marc. "Rayocide: 67 paragraphs on the death of Ray Johnson." *Lightworks Magazine.* 1995. http://www.panmodern.com/ray johnson/rayocide.html

Bloom, Michelle E. *Waxworks: A Cultural Obsession.* Minneapolis: University of Minnesota Press, 2003.

Bontemps, Arna, ed. *The Harlem Renaissance Remembered.* New York: Dodd, Mead and Company, 1972.

Boone, Joseph Allen. *Libidinal Currents: Sexuality and the Shaping of Modernism.* Chicago: University of Chicago Press, 1998.

Boyer, M. Christine. *The City of Collective Memory: Its Historical Imagery and Architectural Entertainments.* Cambridge, Mass.: MIT Press, 1996.

Brathwaite, Edward Kamau. *The History of the Voice: The Development of National Language in Anglophone Caribbean Poetry.* London: New Beacon Books, 1984.

Brown, Bill. *A Sense of Things: The Object Matter of American Literature.* Chicago: University of Chicago Press, 2003.

———. "The Secret Life of Things (Virginia Woolf and the Matter of Modernism)." *Modernism/Modernity* 6.2 (1999): 1–28.

Browne, Jefferson B. *Key West: The Old and the New.* Gainesville: University of Florida Press, 1973.

Browser, Aubrey. "A Negro Documentarian," *New York Amsterdam News* (August 13, 1939).

Bruno, Giuliana. *Streetwalking on a Ruined Map: Cultural Theory and the City Films of Elvira Notari.* Princeton: Princeton University Press, 1993.

Buckle, Gerard Fort. *The Mind and the Film: A Treatise on Psychological Factors in the Film.* New York: Routlege, 1926.

Buck-Morss, Susan. *The Dialectics of Seeing: Walter Benjamin and the Arcades Project.* Cambridge, Mass.: MIT Press, 1991.

Buhite, Russel D. and David W. Levy, eds. *FDR's Fireside Chats.* New York: Penguin, 1992.

"Building a park on a garbage dump, Portland, Ore." *American City* 37 (August 1927): 175.

Bumiller, Elisabeth. "Bush Pushes Volunteerism, but a Senate Seat Shares the Agenda." *New York Times* (April 9, 2002).

Burchfield, Charles, and Ralph Steiner. "Vanishing Backyards." *Fortune* 1:4 (May, 1930): 77–81.

Burg, B. R. *Sodomy and the Pirate Tradition: English Sea Rovers in the Seventeenth-Century Caribbean.* 1983. Reprint, New York: New York University Press, 1995.

Burns, Ken, and Geoffrey C. Ward. *Jazz: A History of America's Music.* New York: Knopf, 2000.

Butler, Judith. "Imitation and Gender Insubordination." In *Inside/Out: Lesbian Theories, Gay Theories.* Edited by Diana Fuss. New York: Routledge, 1991.

———. *Bodies that Matter: On the Discursive Limits of Sex.* New York: Routledge, 1993.

———. *Gender Trouble: Feminism and the Subversion of Identity.* New York: Routledge, 1990.

Cahen, Alfred. *Statistical Analysis of American Divorce.* New York: Columbia University Press, 1932.

Calhoon, Claudia Marie. "Tuberculosis, Race, and the Delivery of Health Care in Harlem, 1922–1939." *Radical History Review*, Issue 80 (Spring 2001): 104.

Calkins, Earnest Elmo. "The Beauty of the New Business Tool." *Atlantic Monthly* 140 (1927): 145.

Campbell, Hazel V. "Part of the Pack: Another View of Night Life in Harlem." In *Harlem's Glory: Black Women Writing, 1900–1950.*

Editeed by Lorraine E. Roses and Ruth E. Randolph. Cambridge, Mass.: Harvard University Press, 1996, 341–52.

Carman, Dorothy Walworth. *Reno Fever*. New York: Ray Long and Richard R. Smith, 1932.

Cartright, Lisa. *Screening the Body: Tracing Medicine's Visual Culture*. Minneapolis: University of Minnesota Press, 1995.

Caruth, Cathy. *Unclaimed Experience: Trauma, Narrative, and History*. Baltimore: Johns Hopkins University Press, 1996.

Casarino, Cesare. *Modernity at Sea: Melville, Marx, Conrad in Crisis*. Minneapolis: University of Minnesota Press, 2002.

Case, Mabel H. *The Singing Years*. New York: Vantage Press, 1953.

Casey, Edward S. *The Fate of Place: A Philosophical History*. Berkeley: University of California Press, 1997.

Cavell, Stanley. *Pursuits of Happiness: The Hollywood Comedy of Remarriage*. Cambridge, Mass.: Harvard University Press, 1981.

Cavendish, Henry. "Key West Fears Its Most Serious Economic Blow if F.E.C. Extension Is Abandoned." *Miami Herald*, October 5, 1935.

Century Dictionary and Cyclopedia, The. New York: Century Company, 1911.

Chauncey, George. *Gay New York: Gender, Urban Culture, and the Making of the Gay Male World, 1890–1940*. New York: Basic Books, 1995.

Cheng, Ann. *The Melancholy of Race*. New York: Oxford, 2001.

Chion, Michel. *The Voice in Cinema*. Edited and translated by Claudia Gorbman. New York: Columbia University Press, 1999.

Chisholm, Ann. "Missing Persons and Bodies of Evidence." *Camera Obscura* 43, vol. 15, no 1. (2000): 125.

"City within a City." *The Lion's Roar* 1:1 (1941–42): 2–3.

"City within a Pentagon." *Reader's Digest* 42 (January 1943): 112.

Clendening, Logan. "Breakfastless Children and Tuberculosis Youth." *Ladies Home Journal* 46 (November 1929): 121.

Clifford, James, and George Marcus, eds. *Writing Culture: The Poetics and Politics of Ethnography*. Berkeley: University of California Press, 1986.

Cobb, Michael L. "Insolent Racing, Rough Narrative: The Harlem Renaissance's Impolite Queers." *Callaloo* 23.1 (Winter 2000): 328–51.

Cobb, Sally Wright, and Mark Willems. *The Brown Derby Restaurant: A Hollywood Legend*. New York: Rizzoli, 1996.

Coleman, Anita Scott. "Unfinished Masterpieces." In *The Crisis Reader*, edited by Sondra Kathryn Wilson. New York: Modern Library, 1999.

Complete Report of Mayor LaGuardia's Commission on the Harlem Riot of March 19, 1935. New York: Arno Press, 1969.

Conway, Bryan. "Twenty Months in Alcatraz." *Saturday Evening Post* 210 (February 19, 1938): 8–9.

Cooper, Mark Garett. "Narrative Spaces." *Screen* 43:2 (Summer 2002): 139–57.

———. *Love Rules: Silent Hollywood and the Rise of the Managerial Class*. Minneapolis: University of Minnesota Press, 2003.

Cosgrove, Denis. *Social Formation and Symbolic Landscape*. Madison: University of Wisconsin Press, 1998.

Cousins, Norman. "Will Women Lose their Jobs?" *Current History and Forum* 41 (September 1939): 14.

Cowdery, Mae. "Lai-Li." In *Harlem's Glory: Black Women Writing, 1900–1950*, edited by Lorraine Elena Roses and Ruth Elizabeth Randolph. Cambridge, Mass.: Harvard University Press, 1996.

———. *We Lift Our Voices and Other Poems*. Philadelphia: Alpress, 1936.

Crane, Hart. *The Complete Poems of Hart Crane*, edited by Marc Simon. New York: Liveright, 2001.

Crary, Jonathan. *Suspensions of Perception: Attention, Spectacle, and Modern Culture*. Cambridge, Mass.: MIT Press, 1999.

———. *Techniques of the Observer: On Vision and Modernity in the Nineteenth Century*. Cambridge, Mass.: MIT Press, 1990.

Cresswell, Tim. *In Place/Out of Place: Geography, Ideology, and Transgression*. Minneapolis: University of Minnesota Press, 1996.

Crouse, Joan M. *The Homeless Transient in the*

Great Depression: New York State 1929–1941. Albany: State University of New York Press, 1986.

Cullen, Countee. "Ghosts." In *The Black Christ and Other Poems.* New York: Harper, 1929. Reprinted in *My Soul's High Song: The Collected Writings of Countee Cullen.* Edited by Gerald Early. New York: Anchor Books, 1991.

Culler, Jonathan. *On Deconstruction: Theory and Criticism after Structuralism.* Ithaca: Cornell University Press, 1982.

Culver, Stuart. "What Manikins Want: *The Wonderful World of Oz* and The Art of Decorating Dry Goods Windows," *Representations* 21 (winter 1988): 97–11.

Cunard, Nancy, ed. *Negro Anthology.* 1934. Reprint, New York: Negro Universities Press, 1969.

Danius, Sara. *The Senses of Modernism: Technology, Perception, and Aesthetics.* Ithaca: Cornell University Press, 2002.

Darden, Douglas. "The Architecture of Exhaustion." *Architecture and Urbanism* 214 (July 1988): 13–22.

Davis, Angela. *Blues Legacies and Black Feminism: Gertrude "Ma" Rainey, Bessie Smith, and Billie Holiday.* New York: Pantheon Books, 1998.

Davis, Elmer. "New World Symphony: With a Few Sour Notes." *Harper's Magazine* 170 (May 1935): 64.

Davis, Mike. *City of Quartz: Excavating the Future in Los Angeles.* New York: Vintage, 1992.

———. *Ecology of Fear: Los Angeles and the Imagination of Disaster.* New York: Vintage, 1999.

De Certeau, Michel. *The Practice of Everyday Life.* Translated by Steven Rendall. Berkeley: University of California Press, 1984.

De Certeau, Michel, Luce Girard, and Pierre Mayol. *The Practice of Everyday Life. Volume 2: Living and Cooking.* Translated by Timothy J. Tomasik. Minneapolis: University of Minnesota Press, 1998.

De Jongh, James. *Vicious Modernism: Black Harlem and the Literary Imagination.* Cambridge: Cambridge University Press, 1990.

Deleuze, Gilles. *Bergsonism.* Translated by Hugh Tomlinson and Barbara Habberjam. New York: Zone Books, 1991.

Deleuze, Gilles, and Félix Guattari. *A Thousand Plateaus: Capitalism and Schizophrenia.* Translated by Brian Massumi. Minneapolis: University of Minnesota Press, 1987.

DeMille, William Cecil B. *Hollywood Saga.* New York: E. P. Dutton, 1939.

Derrida, Jacques. "Freud and the Scene of Writing." In *Writing and Difference.* Chicago: University of Chicago Press, 1978.

———. "Signature, Event, Context." In *Margins of Philosophy.* Chicago: University of Chicago Press, 1982.

———. "White Mythology: Metaphor in the Text of Philosophy." *New Literary History* 6:1 (1974): 5–74.

———. *Cinders.* Translated by Ned Lukacher. Lincoln: University of Nebraska Press, 1987.

Descartes, René. *Discourse on Method and Meditations on First Philosophy.* Translated by Donald A. Cress. Indianapolis: Hackett, 1998.

"Design Ideas In Movies." *Los Angeles Herald Examiner* (September 13, 1964).

Dewan, Shaila. "From 9/11 Rubble, Unclaimed Mementos." *New York Times* (December 3, 2004).

Dewitt, Bernard C. "New Building First of Its Kind in All World." *Miami Daily News* (September 2, 1934).

Dickie, Margaret. "Race and Class in Elizabeth Bishop's Poetry." *Yearbook of English Studies* 24 (1994): 44–58.

Dighe, Ranjit S., ed. *The Historian's Wizard of Oz: Reading L. Frank Baum's Classic as a Political and Monetary Allegory.* Westport, Conn.: Praeger, 2002.

DiSantis, David J. "Wrong Turn on Radiology's Road to Progress." *Radiographics* 11 (1991): 1121–38.

Doane, Mary Ann. "The Voice in the Cinema: The Articulation of the Body and Space." *Yale French Studies* no. 60 (1980): 33–50.

———. *The Emergence of Cinematic Time: Modernity, Contingency, the Archive.* Cambridge, Mass.: Harvard University Press, 2002.

Dos Passos, John. *The Big Money.* New York: Penguin, 1969.

———. *The Garbage Man.* New York: Harper, 1926.

Douglas, Ann. *Terrible Honesty: Mongrel Manhattan in the 1920s*. New York: Farrar, Straus and Giroux, 1995.

Douglas, John W. "Unique Passion for Collecting Facts about the Negro." *Afro-American* (June 7, 1930).

Douglas, Mary. *Purity and Danger: An Analysis of the Concepts of Pollution and Taboo*. 1966. Reprint, London, New York: Routledge, 1995.

Drabelle, Dennis. "Ancient Egypt in the Pacific." *Preservation* 48:4 (August 1996): 38–45.

Du Bois, W. E. B. "The Browsing Reader." *The Crisis* (May 1928).

———. "The Health of Black Folk." *The Crisis* (February 1933).

———. *The Health and Physique of the Negro American. Report of a Social Study Made under the Direction of Atlanta University; Together with the Proceedings of the Eleventh Conference for the Study of Negro Problems, Held at Atlanta University, on May the 29th, 1906*. Atlanta: Atlanta University Press, 1906.

———. *The Souls of Black Folk*, edited by Henry Louis Gates and Terri Hume Oliver. New York: Norton, 1999.

Duncan, James. *The City as Text: The Politics of Landscape Interpretation in the Kandayan Kingdom*. Cambridge: Cambridge University Press, 1990.

Duncan, James and Nancy Duncan. *Landscapes of Privilege: The Politics of the Aesthetic in an American Suburb*. London: Routledge, 2003.

Duncan, James, Nuala Johnson, and Richard Schein, eds. *A Companion to Cultural Geography*. Oxford: Blackwell, 2004.

Dydo, Ulla E., ed. *A Stein Reader*. Evanston, Ill.: Northwestern University Press, 1993.

Early, Gerald, ed. *My Soul's High Song: The Collected Works of Countee Cullen*. New York: Anchor Books, 1991.

Early, Gerald., ed. *Speech and Power*. Volume 1. New York: Ecco, 1992.

Edelman, Lee. *Homographesis: Essays in Gay Literary and Cultural Theory*. New York: Routledge, 1994.

Edensor, Tim. *Industrial Ruins: Space, Aesthetics and Materiality*. London: Berg, 2005.

Ellison, Ralph. *Invisible Man*. New York: Vintage, 1990.

———. *Shadow and Act*. New York: Random House, 1994.

Entrikin, J. Nicholas. *The Betweenness of Place: Toward a Geography of Modernity*. Baltimore: Johns Hopkins University Press, 1991.

Erkkila, Betsy. "Elizabeth Bishop, Modernism, and the Left." *American Literary History* 8:2 (summer 1996): 284–310.

Ewen, Stewart. *All Consuming Images: The Politics of Style in Contemporary Culture*. New York: Basic Books, 1988.

Faber, Harold. "Body of Collyer is Found Near Where Brother Died." *New York Times* (April 9, 1947).

Fanon, Frantz. *Black Skin, White Masks*. Translated by Charles Markham. 1969. Reprint, New York: Evergreen-Grove Press, 1967. Translation of *Peau Noire, Masques Blancs*. Paris: Editions de Seuil, 1952.

Fearing, Kenneth. *Complete Poems*, edited by Robert M. Riley. Orono, Maine: National Poetry Foundation, 1994.

"Federal Chemist Warns Against Improper Storage of Films." *Motion Picture News* (December 28, 1929).

Felski, Rita. *The Gender of Modernity*. Cambridge, Mass.: Harvard University Press, 1995.

Fine, Richard. *West of Eden: Writers in Hollywood 1928–1940*. Washington: Smithsonian, 1993. Originally published as *Hollywood and the Profession of Authorship, 1928–1940*. UMI Research Press, 1985.

"Fire Razed Film Landmark." *Hollywood Reporter* (May 18, 1967).

Fisher, Rudolph. *Joy and Pain*. London: X Press, 1996.

———. *The Conjure-Man Dies: A Mystery Tale of Dark Harlem*. Ann Arbor: University of Michigan Press, 1995.

Fitzgerald, F. Scott. *The Love of the Last Tycoon*, edited by Matthew J. Bruccoli. 1941. Cambridge: Cambridge University Press, 1993.

Fogelon, Robert, and Richard E. Rubenstein, eds. *The Complete Report of Mayor La Guardia's Commission on the Harlem Riot of March, 19,*

1935. New York: Arno Press and *The New York Times*, 1969.

Foucault, Michel. "Of Other Spaces." *Diacritics* 16 (Spring 1986): 22–27.

———. "Questions of Geography." In *Power/Knowledge: Selected Interviews and Other Writings, 1972–1977*, edited by Colin Gordon. Translated by Colin Gordon et al. New York: Pantheon Books, 1980.

———. *Discipline and Punish: The Birth of the Prison*. Translated by Alan Sheridan. New York: Vintage, 1979.

———. *The Order of Things: An Archeology of the Human Sciences*. New York: Vintage Books, 1994.

Fountain, Gary, and Peter Brazeau. *Remembering Elizabeth Bishop: An Oral Biography*. Amherst: University of Massachusetts Press, 1994.

Freud, Sigmund. "A Note Upon 'The Mystic Writing Pad.'" (1925). *The Standard Edition of the Complete Psychological Works of Sigmund Freud* (S.E.) 19:227–32. London: Hogarth, 1953.

———. "Mourning and Melancholia." (1915, 1917). S.E. 14:239.

Fried, Michael. *Art and Objecthood: Essays and Reviews*. Chicago: University of Chicago Press, 1998.

Frye, Northrop. *Anatomy of Criticism: Four Essays*. 1957. Reprint, Princeton: Princeton University Press, 2000.

Gallagher, Catherine. *Nobody's Story: The Vanishing Acts of Women Writers in the Marketplace 1670–1820*. Berkeley: University of California Press, 1994.

"Gas Company Seizes Meters of 'Hermits.'" *New York Times* (April 5, 1939).

Georgetta, Clel Evan. *Nevada: The Silver State*. Carson City: Western States Historical Society, 1969.

"George Wingfield and Nevada's Peculiar Institutions." *Halcyon* 14 (1922).

Gibbons, Cedric. "The Art Director." In *Behind the Screen: How Films Are Made*, edited by Stephen Watts. New York: Dodge, 1938.

Giddens, Anthony. *The Consequences of Modernity*. Stanford: Stanford University Press, 1990.

Gikandi, Simon. *Writing in Limbo: Modernism and Caribbean Literature*. Ithaca: Cornell University Press, 1992.

Giles, Paul. *Hart Crane: The Contexts of The Bridge*. Cambridge: Cambridge University Press, 1986.

Giroux, Robert. ed. *One Art: Elizabeth Bishop Letters*. New York: Noonday Press, 1995.

Goeser, Caroline. "The Case of Ebony and Topaz: Racial and Sexual Hybridity in Harlem Renaissance Illustrations." *American Periodicals* 15:1 (2005).

Goldensohn, Lorrie. *Elizabeth Bishop: A Biography of Poetry*. New York: Columbia University Press, 1990.

Goldner, Orville, and George E. Turner, eds. *The Making of King Kong: The Story Behind a Film Classic*. Cranbury, N.J.: A. S. Barnes, 1975.

Gordon, Avery. *Ghostly Matters: Haunting and the Sociological Imagination*. Minneapolis: University of Minnesota Press, 1997.

Gramsci, Antonio. *Selections from the Prison Notebooks*, edited by Quintin Hoare and Geoffrey Nowell Smith. New York: International Publishers, 1971.

Greenberg, Cheryl. *Or Does It Explode? Black Harlem in the Great Depression*. New York: Oxford University Press, 1991.

Greenberg, Judith. "The Echo of Trauma and the Trauma of Echo." *American Imago* 55.3 (1998): 319–47.

Griffith, Jeannette. "Dug-outs and Settle-ins." *The Survey* 67 (January 1932): 381–83.

Grosz, Elizabeth. *Space, Time, and Perversion*. New York: Routledge, 1995.

Grove, Allen W. "Röntgen's Ghosts: Photography, X-Rays, and the Victorian Imagination." *Literature and Medicine* 16:2 (1997): 141–73.

Guillén, Nicolás. *Obra Poética 1920–1958*. Volume 1. Havana: Instituto Cubano del Libro, 1972.

Gumby, L. S. Alexander. "The Gumby Scrapbook Collection of Negroana. *Columbia Library World* 5:1 (January 1951).

Guyer, Sara. "Wordsworthian Wakefulness." *Yale Journal of Criticism* 16:1 (2003): 93–111.

Hacking, Ian. *Rewriting the Soul: Multiple Personality and the Sciences of Memory*. Princeton: Princeton University Press, 1995.

Halbwachs, Maurice. *On Collective Memory*. Chicago: University of Chicago Press, 1992.

Hamlin, John. *Whirlpool of Reno*. New York: Dial Press, 1931.

Harding, U. E. *Roads to Reno*. Grand Rapids, Mich.: Zondervan Publications, 1943.

Harmetz, Aljean. *The Making of the Wizard of Oz: Movie Magic and Studio Power in the Prime of MGM—and the Miracle of Production #1060*. New York: Knopf, 1977.

Harmon, W. W. "Garbage Park, Oakland, a Successful Experiment in Esthetics." *American City* 36 (June 1927): 787–90.

Harris, Leonard. "The Harlem Renaissance and Philosophy." In *A Companion to African-American Philosophy*, edited by Tommy L. Lott, and John Press Pittman. Malden, Mass., and Oxford: Blackwell, 2003.

Harrison, Ben. *Undying Love: A Key West "Love Story."* Key West: Les Editions Duval, 1993.

Hartman, Saidiya V. *Scenes of Subjection: Terror, Slavery, and Self-Making in Nineteenth-Century America*. New York: Oxford University Press, 1997.

Harvey, David. *The Condition of Postmodernity: An Enquiry into the Origins of Cultural Change*. Cambridge: Blackwell, 1990.

Haule, John Ryan. "From Somnambulism to the Archetypes: The French Roots of Jung's Split with Freud." *Psychoanalytic Review* 71 (1984): 635–59.

———. "Pierre Janet and Dissociation: The First Transference Theory and Its Origins in Hypnosis." *American Journal of Clinical Hypnosis* 29.2 (October 1986): 86–94.

Haver, Ron. *David O. Selznick's Hollywood*. New York: Alfred A. Knopf, 1980.

Hawthorne, Hildegarde. *Williamsburg: Old and New*. New York: Appleton-Century, 1941.

Hayden, Delores. *The Power of Place: Urban Landscapes as Public History*. Cambridge, Mass.: MIT Press, 1995.

Hays, Arthur Garfield. "When Is a Divorce Not a Divorce?" *Vanity Fair* (August 1931): 34–35, 74.

Hegel, Georg Wilhelm. *Lectures on the Philosophy of World History*, edited by D. Forbes. Translated by H. B. Nisbet. Cambridge: Cambridge University Press, 2002.

Hegger Lewis, Grace. *Half a Loaf*. New York: Horace Liveright, 1931.

Heinze, Andrew R. "*Schizophrenia Americana*: Aliens, Alienists and the 'Personality Shift' of Twentieth-Century Culture." *American Quarterly* 55.2 (June 2003): 227–56.

Heisner, Beverly. "Cedric Gibbons." *Theatre Arts Monthly* (October 1937): 784.

———. *Hollywood Art: Art Direction in the Days of the Great Studios*. Jefferson, N.C.: McFarland, 1990.

Helbling, Mark. *The Harlem Renaissance: The One and the Many*. Westport, Conn.: Greenwood Press, 1999.

Hemingway, Ernest. *To Have and Have Not*. New York: Charles Scribner's Sons, 1970.

Herbst, Josephine. *The Starched Blue Sky of Spain*. New York: Harper Collins, 1991.

Holcomb, Gary E. *Claude McKay, Code Name Sasha: Queer Black Marxism and the Harlem Renaissance*. Gainesville: University Press of Florida, 2007.

Honey, Maureen, ed. *Shadowed Dreams: Women's Poetry of the Harlem Renaissance*. 1989. Reprint, New Brunswick: Rutgers University Press, 1999.

Hoover, Herbert. "Annual Message to the Congress on the State of the Union," December 2, 1930. From the American Presidency Project (APP). (Http://www.presidency.ucsb.edu.)

———. "Message on National Thrift Week." January 16, 1932. (APP)

———. "Statement on the Hoarding of Currency." February 3, 1932. APP.

———. "Statement on the Hoarding of Currency." February 16, 1932. APP.

Hopkins, George James. "From 'Then to Now.'" *Production Design* 2:5 (1952): 8.

Horkeimer, Max, and Theodor Adorno. *Dialectic of Enlightenment*. New York: Continuum, 1993.

Hoy, Sullen. *Chasing Dirt: The American Pursuit of Cleanliness*. New York: Oxford University Press, 1996.

Huggins, Nathan Irvin, ed. *Voices from the Harlem Renaissance*. New York: Oxford University Press, 1995.

Hughes, Langston. *The Collected Poems of Langston Hughes, edited by Arnold Rampersad. New York: Vintage, 1995.

———. "Death Chant," In *Shakespeare in Harlem*. New York: Knopf, 1942.

———. "My Early Days in Harlem." In *Harlem: A Community in Transition*, edited by John Henrick Clarke. New York: Vintage, 1969, 62–64.

———. "The Negro Artist and the Racial Mountain." *The Nation* 122.3181 (June 1926): 392–94.

———. "The Twenties: Harlem and Its Negritude." *African Forum* 1.4 (Spring 1966): 11–20.

———. *The Big Sea*. 1940. Reprint, New York: Hill and Wang, 1993.

Hughes, Rupert. *No One Man*. New York: Harper, 1931.

Hurston, Zora Neale. *Dust Tracks on a Road*. 1942. Reprint, New York: Harper Perennial, 1995.

Huyssen, Andreas. *After the Great Divide: Modernism, Mass Culture, Postmodernism*. Bloomington: Indiana University Press, 1986.

"Immortal Kisses Were His Goal." *American Weekly* (1940).

Irigaray, Luce. "Place, Interval: A Reading of Aristotle, *Physics IV*." In *An Ethics of Sexual Difference*. Translated by C. Burke and G. C. Gill. Ithaca: Cornell University Press, 1993.

———. *Speculum of the Other Woman*. Translated by Gillian C. Gill. Ithaca: Cornell University Press, 1985.

———. *This Sex Which Is Not One*. Translated by Catherine Porter. Ithaca: Cornell University Press, 1985.

Jackson, Stanley W. *Melancholia and Depression: From Hippocratic to Modern Times*. New Haven: Yale University Press, 1986.

James, William. *The Principles of Psychology*. Volume 2. New York: Henry Holt, 1899.

Janet, Pierre. "L'influence somnambulique et la besoin de direction." In *Névroses et idées fixes*. Volume 1. Paris: Alcan, 1925.

———. *Les medications psychologiques*. 3 volumes. Paris: Felix Alcan, 1984. Reprint, Paris: Societý.

———. *Psychological Healing*. 2 volumes. New York: Macmillan, 1925.

Johnsen, Julia E., ed. *Selected Articles on Marriage and Divorce*. New York: H. W. Wilson, 1925.

Johnson, Barbara. *A World of Difference: Essays in the Contemporary Rhetoric of Reading*. Baltimore: Johns Hopkins University Press, 2006.

Johnson, James Weldon. *Black Manhattan*. 1930. Reprint, New York: Da Capo Press, 1991.

———, ed. *The Book of American Negro Poetry*. New York: Harcourt, Brace, 1922.

Johnson, Kirk. "Dumping Ends at Fresh Kills, Symbol of Throw-Away Era." *New York Times* (March 18, 2001).

Johnson, Latifa. *Sheila Goes to Reno*. New York: Vantage Press, 1952.

Johnston, R. J., Derek Gregory, Geraldine Pratt, and Michael Watts, eds. *The Dictionary of Human Geography*. 4th edition. Oxford: Blackwell, 2000.

Jowett, Garth S., Ian C. Jarvie, and Kathryn H. Fuller. *Children and the Movies: Media Influence and the Payne Fund Controversy*. Cambridge: Cambridge University Press, 1996.

Kalaidjian, Walter. *American Culture Between the Wars: Revisionary Modernism and Postmodern Critique*. New York: Columbia University Press, 1993.

Kaplan, Amy. "Romancing the Empire: The Embodiment of Masculinity in the Popular Historical Novel of the 1890s." *American Literary History* 2:4 (winter 1990): 659–90.

Kaplan, Carla, ed. *Zora Neale Hurston: A Life in Letters*. New York: Anchor Books, 2002.

Keith, Michael, and Steve Pile. *Place and the Politics of Identity*. London: Routledge, 1993.

Kelley, Robin D. *Hammer and Hoe: Alabama Communists during the Great Depression*. Chapel Hill: University of North Carolina Press, 1990.

Kellogg, Arthur. "Minds Made by the Movies." *Survey Graphic* 22.5 (May 1933). 245–50, 287, 290.

Kelly, Tina. "A Nation Challenged: The Relics, At Landfill, Buckets Full of Memories." *New York Times* (January 15, 2002).

Kennedy, John B. "So This Is Harlem?" *Collier's* (October 28, 1933).

Kent, Richard J. "Keynes's Lectures at the New

School for Social Research." *History of Political Economy* 36:1 (spring 2004): 195–206.

Kessler-Harris, Alice. *Out to Work: A History of Wage-Earning Women in the United States*. Oxford: Oxford University Press, 1982.

Kevles, Bettyann Holtzmann. *Naked to the Bone: Medical Imaging in the Twentieth Century*. New Brunswick, N.J.: Rutgers University Press, 1997.

Keynes, John Maynard. "An Open Letter to President Roosevelt: Our Recovery Plan Assayed." *New York Times* (December 31, 1933).

———. "Mr. Robertson on 'Saving and Hoarding.'" *The Economic Journal* 43:172 (December, 1933): 699–712.

Kittler, Friedrich A. *Discourse Networks 1800/1900*. Translated by Michael Metteer with Chris Cullens. Stanford: Stanford University Press, 1990.

Klein, Melanie. "A Contribution to the Psychogenesis of Manic Depressive States" (1935). In *Love, Guilt, and Reparation and Other Works, 1921–1945*. London: Vintage, 1998. 262–89.

Klinkenborg, Verlyn. "The Other Graveyard." *New York Times* (October 21, 2001).

Kim, Helen M. "Strategic Credulity: Oz as Mass Cultural Parable." *Cultural Critique* 33 (spring 1996): 212–33.

Knadler, Stephen. "Sweetback Style: Wallace Thurman and a Queer Harlem Renaissance." *Modern Fiction Studies* 48:4 (2002): 899–936.

Koolhaas, Rem, and Bruce Mau. *S, M, L, XL*. Cologne: Taschen, 1998.

Kornweibel, Theodore. *"Seeing Red": Federal Campaigns against Black Militancy, 1919–1925*. Bloomington: Indiana University Press, 1998.

Kostenbaum, Wayne. *Double Talk: The Erotics of Male Literary Collaboration*. New York: Routledge, 1989.

Koster, Donald Nelson. *The Theme of Divorce in American Drama, 1871–1939*. Ph.D. dissertation. University of Pennsylvania, 1942.

Kozarski, Richard, ed. *Hollywood Directors, 1914–1940*. New York: Oxford University Press, 1976.

Kracauer, Siegfried. *Theory of Film: The Redemption of Physical Reality*. New York: Oxford University Press, 1960.

Krasner, David. *A Beautiful Pageant: African American Theater, Drama, and Performance in the Harlem Renaissance, 1910–1927*. New York: Palgrave, 2002.

Kristeva, Julia. *Black Sun: Depression and Melancholia*. Translated by Leon S. Roudiez. New York: Columbia University Press, 1989.

———. *Desire in Language: A Semiotic Approach to Literature and Art*, edited by Leon S. Roudiez. New York: Columbia University Press, 1980.

———. *Powers of Horror: An Essay on Abjection*. New York: Columbia University Press, 1982.

———. *Strangers to Ourselves*. Translated by Leon S. Roudiez. New York: Columbia University Press, 1991.

———. "Women's Time." Translated by Alice Jardine and Harry Blake. In *The Kristeva Reader*, edited by Toril Moi. New York: Columbia University Press, 1986.

Kroker, Arthur, and David Cook. *The Postmodern Scene: Excremental Culture and Hyper-Aesthetics*. New York: St. Martin's Press, 1991.

Kutzinksi, Vera M. *Sugar's Secrets: Race and the Erotics of Cuban Nationalism*. Charlottesville: University of Virginia Press, 1993.

Laird, Holly A. *Women Coauthors*. Urbana: University of Illinois Press, 2000.

Langley, Noel, Florence Ryerson, and Edgar Allen Woolf. *The Wizard of Oz: The Screenplay*. 1938. Reprint, New York: Delta (Bantam Doubleday Dell), 1966.

Langum, David J. *Crossing Over the Line: Legislating Morality and the Mann Act*. Chicago: University of Chicago Press, 1994.

Lauterbach, R. E. "Pentagon Puzzle." *Life* 14 (May 24, 1943): 11–13.

Law and Contemporary Problems. Special Issue. School of Law, Duke University. 11:3 (June 1935).

Lebovici, Serge. "Psychoanalyse et cinéma." *Revue internationale de filmologie* 2:5 (1949): 49–57.

Le Corbusier (Charles-Edouard Jeanneret). *Towards a New Architecture*. New York: Dover Publications, 1986.

Lee, Danny. "Neighborhood Report: Staten Island

Up Close; At Fresh Kills Landfill, Garbage Out, Grand Plans In." *New York Times* (December 9, 2001).

Lee, Felicia R. "Plucking 9/11 Objects from History's Dustbin." *New York Times* (May 30, 2005).

Lefebvre, Henri. *The Production of Space*. Translated by Donald Nicholson-Smith. Oxford: Blackwell, 1991.

Lentricchia, Frank. *Ariel and the Police: Michel Foucault, William James, Wallace Stevens*. Madison: University of Wisconsin Press, 1988.

"Letter from a Richmond Wife in Reno." *Richmond Times Dispatch* (April 6, 1930): 44–45 (NHS).

Levinas, Emmanuel. *De L'existence à l'existant*. Paris: Vrin, 1986.

———. *Ethics and Infinity: Conversations with Philippe Nemo*. Translated by Richard Cohen. Pittsburgh: Duquesne University Press, 1985.

———. *Existence and Existents*. Translated by Alphonso Lingis. The Hague: Martinus Nijhoff, 1975.

Lévi-Strauss, Claude. *Elementary Structures of Kinship*. Boston: Beacon Press, 1969.

Lewis, Oscar. *Sagebrush Casinos: The Story of Legal Gambling in Nevada*. Garden City, N.Y.: Doubleday, 1953.

Lewis, Wyndham. "Space and Time." In *Time and Western Man*. 1927. Edited by Paul Edwards. Santa Rosa, Calif.: Black Sparrow Press, 1993.

Ley, David. "Modernism, Post-Modernism, and the Struggle for Place." In *The Power of Place: Bringing Together Geographical and Sociological Imaginations*, edited by J. A. Agnre and J. S. Duncan. Boston: Unwin Hyman, 1989.

Lidz, Franz. *Ghosty Men*. New York: Bloomsbury, 2003.

Lillard, Richard. *Desert Challenge: An Interpretation of Nevada*. New York: Alfred A. Knopf, 1942.

Limerick, Patricia Nelson. *The Legacy of Conquest: The Unbroken Past of the American West*. New York: W. W. Norton, 1987.

Littlefield, Henry M. "*The Wizard of Oz*: Parable on Populism." *American Quarterly* 16:1 (spring 1964): 47–58.

Locke, Alain, ed. *The New Negro*. 1925. Reprint New York: Atheneum, 1968.

———. "Art or Propaganda?" *Harlem* 1 (November 1928): 12.

———. "Harlem: Dark Weather-vane." In *A Documentary History of the Negro People in the United States: From the New Deal to the End of World War II*. Volume 4, edited by Herbert Aptheker. 1974. Reprint, New York: Carol Publishers, 1992.

Lombardi, Marilyn May, ed. *Elizabeth Bishop: The Geography of Gender*. Charlottesville: University Press of Virginia, 1993.

———. *The Body and the Song: Elizabeth Bishop's Poetics*. Carbondale: Southern Illinois University Press, 1995.

London, Bette. *Writing Double: Women's Literary Partnerships*. Ithaca: Cornell University Press, 1999.

Longenbach, James. *Wallace Stevens: The Plain Sense of Things*. Oxford: Oxford University Press, 1991.

MacLeish, Archibald. *Collected Poems: 1917–1982*. Boston: Houghton Mifflin, 1985.

Marcus, Grail. *Lipstick Traces: A Secret History of the Twentieth Century*. Cambridge, Mass.: Harvard University Press, 1990.

Marinetti, Filippo Tommaso. "The Founding Manifesto of Futurism 1909." In *Modernism: An Anthology of Sources and Documents*, edited by Vassiliki Kolocotroni, Jane Goldman, and Olga Taxidou. Chicago: University of Chicago Press, 1998.

Markoff, John. "Pentagon Plans a Computer System that Would Peek at Personal Data of Americans." *New York Times* (November 9, 2002).

Marks, Carole, and Diana Edkins. *The Power of Pride: Stylemakers and Rulebreakers of the Harlem Renaissance*. New York: Crown, 1999.

Marx, Karl. *Capital. Volume I: A Critique of Political Economy*. Translated by Ben Fowkes. London: Penguin, 1992.

Marx, Karl, and Friedrich Engels. *The German Ideology*, edited by Robert M. Baird and Stuart E. Rosenbaum. New York: Prometheus Books, 1998.

Massey, Doreen. *Space, Place, and Gender*. Minneapolis: University of Minnesota Press, 1994.

Maxwell, William J. *New Negro, Old Left: African-American Writing and Communism between the Wars*. New York: Columbia University Press, 1999.

May, Elaine Tyler. *Homeward Bound: American Families in the Cold War Era*. New York: Basic Books, 1988.

McCabe, Susan. *Elizabeth Bishop: Her Poetics of Loss*. University Park: Pennsylvania State University Press, 1994.

McCarthy, Mary. *The Company She Keeps*. New York: Harcourt Brace Jovanovich, 1970.

McCoy, Horace. *I Should Have Stayed Home*. 1938. Reprint, New York: Midnight Classics, 1996.

———. *They Shoot Horses Don't They?* 1935. Reprint, London: Midnight Classics, 1995.

McElvaine, Robert S. *The Great Depression: America, 1929–1941*. New York: Times Books, 1993.

McKay, Claude. *A Long Way from Home*. New York: Arno Press, 1937.

———. *Harlem: Negro Metropolis*. New York: E. P. Dutton, 1940.

Melosi, Martin. *Garbage in the Cities: Refuse, Reform, and the Environment, 1880–1890*. College Station: Texas A&M University Press, 1982.

Mencken, H. L. *The Philosophy of Friedrich Nietzsche*. 1908. Tucson: Sharp Press, 2003.

Merod, Jim. "The Question of Miles Davis." *Boundary 2* 28.2 (Summer 2001): 57–103.

Metz, Christian. *The Imaginary Signifier: Psychoanalysis and Cinema*. Translated by Celia Britton, Annwyl Williams, Ben Brewster, and Alfred Guzzetti. Bloomington: Indiana University Press, 1982.

Meyers, Jeffrey. *Sunset Boulevard: The Complete Screenplay*. Berkeley: University of California Press, 1999.

Meyers, Jeffrey, ed. *Hemingway: The Critical Heritage*. London: Routledge and Kegan Paul, 1982.

Michel, M. Scott. *House in Harlem*. Winnipeg: Harlequin Books, 1946.

Miller, J. Hillis. *Topographies*. Stanford: Stanford University Press, 1995.

Miller, Max. *Reno*. New York: Dodd, Mead, 1941.

Mitchell, Don. *Cultural Geography: A Critical Introduction*. Oxford and Malden, Mass.: Blackwell, 2000.

———. "The Lure of the Local: Landscape Studies at the End of a Troubled Century." *Progress in Human Geography* 25 (June 2001): 269–81.

Mitchell, Loften. "Harlem Reconsidered." *Freedomways* 4 (fall 1964): 473–75.

Mitchell, Verner D., ed. *This Waiting for Love: Helene Johnson, Poet of the Harlem Renaissance*. Amherst: University of Massachusetts Press, 2000.

Mitchell, Verner D., and Cynthia Davis, eds. *Dorothy West: Where the Wild Grape Grows: Selected Writings, 1930–1950*. Amherst: University of Massachusetts Press, 2005.

Mitchell, W. J. T. "Holy Landscape: Israel, Palestine, and the American Wilderness." *Critical Inquiry* 26 (winter 2000): 193–223.

Mizruchi, Susan. "Neighbors, Strangers, Corpses: Death and Sympathy in the Early Writings of W. E. B. Du Bois." In W. E. B. Du Bois, *The Souls of Black Folk: A Norton Critical Edition*, edited by Henry Louis Gates Jr. and Terri Hume Oliver. New York: Norton, 1999.

Moon, Bucklin. *The Darker Brother*. 1943. Reprint, New York: Bantam, 1949.

Morris, Lloyd. *Not So Long Ago*. New York: Random House, 1949.

Mowitt, John. *Percussion: Drumming, Beating, Striking*. Durham: Duke University Press, 2002.

Muller, John P., and William J. Richardson, eds. *The Purloined Poe: Lacan, Derrida, and Psychoanalytic Reading*. Baltimore: Johns Hopkins University Press, 1988.

Murphy, George, ed. *The Key West Reader: The Best of Key West's Writers: 1830–1990*. Key West: Tortugas, 1989.

Murray, Albert. *Stomping the Blues*. New York: Da Capo, 1976.

———. *The Blue Devils of Nada: A Contemporary American Approach to Aesthetic Statement*. New York: Vintage, 1996.

Murtagh, William J. *Keeping Time: The History and Theory of Preservation in America*. Pittstown, N.J.: Main Street Press, 1988.

Naison, Mark. *Communists in Harlem During the Depression*. Urbana-Champaign: University of Illinois Press, 2004

Nash, Roderick. *The Nervous Generation: American Thought, 1917–1930*. Chicago: Rand McNally, 1970.

Nathanson, Paul. *Over the Rainbow: The Wizard of Oz as a Secular Myth of America*. Albany: SUNY Press, 1991.

Nelson, Cary. *Repression and Recovery: Modern American Poetry and the Politics of Cultural Memory*. Madison: University of Wisconsin Press, 1989.

Nesbett, Peter T., and Michelle Dubois, eds. *Jacob Lawrence: Paintings, Drawings, and Murals (1935–1999): A Catalogue Raisonné*. Seattle: University of Washington Press, 2000.

"Nevada Dude Ranch Association." Pamphlet. Chamber of Commerce. Reno, n.d. (NHS).

Newman, Andy. "Ideas and Trends: Look Out; Citizen Snoops Wanted (Call Toll-Free)." *New York Times* (July 21, 2002).

Newman, Robert, ed. *Centuries' Ends, Narrative Means*. Stanford: Stanford University Press, 1996.

Nichols, Charles H., ed. *Arna Bontemps–Langston Hughes Letters, 1925–1967*. New York: Dodd, Mead, 1980.

Nietzsche, Friedrich. *On the Advantage and Disadvantage of History for Life*. Translated by Peter Preuss. Indianapolis: Hackett, 1980.

Nora, Pierre, ed. *Realms of Memory: The Construction of the French Past, Volume I*. Translated by Arthur Goldhammer. New York: Columbia University Press, 1996.

Norris, Kathleen. *Second Hand Wife*. New York: Triangle Books, 1931, 1932.

North, Michael. *The Dialect of Modernism: Race, Language, and Twentieth-Century Literature*. Oxford: Oxford University Press, 1998.

Nugent, Richard Bruce. "On Alexander Gumby." In *The Portable Harlem Renaissance Reader*, edited by David Levering Lewis. New York: Viking, 1994.

Odier, Pierre. *The Rock: A History of Alcatraz—The Fort. The Prison*. Eagle Rock, Calif.: L'Image Odier, 1997.

Oestreich, Alain E. "Radiographic History Exhibit. 1934: Fateful Year in the History of African-Americans in Radiology." *RadioGraphics* 15:4 (July 1995): 1013–20.

Orvell, Miles. *The Real Thing: Imitation and Authenticity in American Culture, 1880–1940*. Chapel Hill: University of North Carolina Press, 1989.

Osofsky, Gilbert. *Harlem: The Making of a Ghetto: Negro New York, 1890–1930*. 1966. Reprint, Chicago: Elephant Paperbacks, 1996.

Ott, Katherine. *Fevered Lives: Tuberculosis in American Culture Since 1870*. Cambridge, Mass.: Harvard University Press, 1996.

Page, Barbara. "Recording a Life: Elizabeth Bishop's Letters to Ilse and Kit Barker." In *Elizabeth Bishop: The Geography of Gender*, edited by Marilyn May Lombardi. Charlottesville: University Press of Virginia, 1993.

Palmer, Robert. *Deep Blues*. New York: Penguin, 1981.

Parmer, Charles. *After Divorce?* New York: A. L. Burt, 1932.

Parvulescu, Anca. "To Die Laughing and To Laugh at Dying: Revisiting *The Awakening*." *New Literary History* 36:3 (2005): 477–95.

"Passion in the Desert." *Fortune* 9 (April 1934): 100–107.

Pastoureau, Michel. *Blue: The History of a Color*. Translated by Markus I. Cruse. Princeton: Princeton University Press, 2001. Originally published as *Bleu: Histoire d'une coleur*. Paris: Editions du Seuil, 2000.

Patton, Ventria K., and Maureen Honey, eds. *Double-Take: A Revisionist Harlem Renaissance Anthology*. Rutgers: Rutgers University Press, 2001.

Pechinski, Mary. "The Landscape of Memory." In *Drawing Building Text*, edited by Andrea Kahn. New York: Princeton Architectural Press, 1991.

Pellegrini, Ann. *Performance Anxieties: Staging Psychoanalysis, Staging Race*. New York: Routledge, 1997.

"Pentagon." *Time* 41 (February 22, 1943): 60.

Pérez, Louis A. *Cuba: Between Reform and Revolution*. New York: Oxford University Press, 1988.

Perloff, Majorie. *The Poetics of Indeterminacy:*

Rimbaud to Cage. Evanston, Ill.: Northwestern University Press, 1999.

———. *21st-Century Modernism: The "New" Poetics*. Malden, Mass.: Blackwell, 2002.

Perry, Margaret, ed. "The Brief Life and Art of Rudolph Fisher." In *The Short Fiction of Rudolph Fisher*. New York: Greenwood Press, 1987.

Phillips, Adam. "Waiting for Returns: Freud's New Love." Plenary Address, Modernist Studies Association, Birmingham, England. September 27, 2003.

Phillips, Cabell. *From the Crash to the Blitz, 1929–1939*. New York: Macmillan, 1969.

Pile, Steve. *Real Cities: Modernity, Space and the Phantasmagorias of City Life*. London: Sage, 2005.

Pile, Steve, and Michael Keith. *Geographies of Resistance*. London: Routledge, 1997.

Powell, Jr., Adam Clayton. "Harlem Declares Its Rent Too High." *New York Post* (March 28, 1935).

———. "Harlem Demands Jobs for Starving." *New York Post* (March 29, 1935).

Pringle, Henry F. "My Thirty Days in the Pentagon." *Saturday Evening Post* 216 (October 16, 1943): 26–27.

Putnam, Nina Wilcox. "South from Miami." *Collier's* 100 (December 18, 1937): 74.

Rabaté, Jean-Michel. *The Ghosts of Modernity*. Gainesville: University of Florida Press, 1996.

Rabinbach, Anson. *The Human Motor: Energy, Fatigue, and the Origins of Modernity*. Berkeley: University of California Press, 1992.

Rabinowitz, Paula. "Pulping Ann Petry: The Case of *Country Place*." Paper delivered at the 2003 Modernist Studies Association conference in Birmingham, England, September 27, 2003.

———. *Black and White and Noir*. New York: Columbia University Press, 2002.

———. *Labor and Desire: Women's Revolutionary Fiction in Depression America*. Chapel Hill: University of North Carolina Press, 1991.

"Race between Claustrophobia and Agoraphobia for Those Pent up in Washington's *Pentagon*." *Newsweek* 21 (February 15, 1943): 64.

Rampersad, Arnold, ed. *The Collected Poems of Langston Hughes*. New York: Knopf, 1994.

———. "Slavery and the Literary Imagination: Du Bois' *The Souls of Black Folk*." In *Slavery and the Literary Imagination*, edited by Deborah McDowell and Arnold Rampersad. Baltimore: Johns Hopkins University Press, 1989.

Ratner, Sidney, and Jules Altman, eds. *John Dewey and Arthur F. Bentley: A Philosophical Correspondence, 1932–1951*. New Brunswick, N.J.: Rutgers University Press, 1964.

Rediker, Marcus. *Between the Devil and the Deep Blue Sea*. Cambridge: Cambridge University Press, 1987.

Relph, Edward. *Place and Placelessness*. London: Pion, 1976.

"Reno: Bother over Brothels." *Newsweek* 32.9 (August 30, 1948).

Renshaw, Samuel, Vernon L. Miller, and Dorothy P. Marquis. *Children's Sleep: A Series of Studies on the Influence of Motion Pictures; Normal Age, Sex, and Seasonal Variations in Motility; Experimental Insomnia; the Effects of Coffee; and the Visual Flicker Limens of Children*. New York: Macmillan, 1933.

"Rethinking Garbage." Editorial. *New York Times* (March 2, 2002).

Riley, Glenda. "Sara Bard Field, Charles Erskine Scott Wood, and the Phenomenon of Migratory Divorce." *California History* 69:4 (fall 1990): 251–59.

———. *Divorce: An American Tradition*. New York: Oxford University Press, 1991.

Risen, James, and Eric Lichtblau. "Bush Lets U.S. Spy on Callers Without Courts." *New York Times* (December 16, 2005).

Roach, Joe. *Cities of the Dead: Circum-Atlantic Preference*. New York: Columbia University Press, 1996.

Rockoff, Hugh. "The 'Wizard of Oz' as a Monetary Allegory." *Journal of Political Economy* 98:4 (August 1990): 739–60.

Rogin, Michael. "Two Declarations of Independence: The Contaminated Origins of American National Culture." In *Blackface, White Noise: Jewish Immigrants in the Hollywood Melting Pot*. Berkeley: University of California Press, 1996.

Ronald, Ann. "Reno: Myth, Mystique, or Madness?" In *East of Eden, West of Zion: Essays on Nevada*, edited by Wilbur Shepperson. Reno: University of Nevada Press, 1989. 134–48.

Roosevelt, Franklin D. "The Forgotten Man." Radio address, April 7, 1932. APP.

Roosevelt, Theodore. "The Strenuous Life." In *The Call of the Wild (1900–1916)*, edited by Roderick Nash. New York: George Braziller, 1970.

Rose, Carl. "My Life in Pentagonia." *New York Times Magazine* (May 7, 1944): 18–19.

Rose, Gillian. *Feminism and Geography: The Limits of Geographical Knowledge*. Cambridge: Polity, 1993.

Rosenbaum, Susan. "Elizabeth Bishop and the Miniature Museum." *Journal of Modern Literature* 28:2 (2005): 61–99.

———. *Professing Sincerity: Modern Lyric Poetry, Commercial Culture, and the Crisis in Reading*. Charlottesville: University of Virginia Press, 2007.

Ross, Andrew. "The Alcatraz Effect." *SubStance* 13.1.42 (1983): 71–84.

Roth, Martin. "Griffith's Walls." Unpublished manuscript. May 2003.

Rowlinson, Matthew. "Reading *Capital* with Little Nell." *Yale Journal of Criticism* 9 (1996): 347–80.

Rubin, Gayle. "The Traffic in Women." In *Toward an Anthropology of Women*, edited by Rayna Reiter. New York: Monthly Review Press, 1975.

Rule, Jane. *Desert of the Heart*. 1964. Reprint, Chicago: Talon Books, 1991.

Rushdie, Salman. *The Wizard of Oz*. London: British Film Institute, 1992.

Ryan, Con. "The City that Sex Built." *True Detective* 39:1 (November 1936): 12–17, 79–82.

Sack, Robert David. *Place, Modernity and the Consumer's World: A Relational Framework for Geographic Analysis*. Baltimore: Johns Hopkins University Press, 1992.

Saper, Craig J. "A Networked Introduction to Assemblings." *Postmodern Culture* 7:3 (May 1997).

Scandura, Jani, and Michael Thurston, eds. *Modernism, Inc.: Body, Memory, Capital*. New York: New York University Press, 2001.

Scanlon, John. *On Garbage*. London: Reaktion, 2005.

Schmidt, Dietmar. "Refuse Archeology: Virchow—Schliemann—Freud." *Perspectives on Science* 9:1 (2001): 210–32.

Schmitt, Peter J. *Back to Nature: The Arcadian Myth in Urban America*. New York: Oxford University Press, 1969.

Schrager, Cynthia D. "Both Sides of the Veil: Race, Science, and Mysticism in W. E. B. Du Bois." *American Quarterly* 48:4 (1996): 551–86.

Schuyler, George. *Black No More*. Boston: Northeastern University Press, 1989.

Schwartz, Vanessa R. "Cinematic Spectatorship before the Apparatus: The Public Taste for Reality in *Fin-de-Siècle* Paris." In *Cinema and the Invention of Modern Life*, edited by Leo Charney and Vanessa R. Schwartz. Berkeley: University of California Press, 1995.

———. *Spectacular Realities: Early Mass Culture in Fin-de-Siècle Paris*. Berkeley and Los Angeles: University of California Press, 1998.

Schwarz, A. B. Christa. *Gay Voices of the Harlem Renaissance*. Bloomington: Indian University Press, 2003.

Sedgwick, Eve Kosofsky. *Epistemology of the Closet*. Berkeley and Los Angeles: University of California Press, 1990.

Seltzer, Mark. *Bodies and Machines*. London: Routledge, 1992.

Shalett, Sidney M. "Mammouth Cave, Washington, D.C." *New York Times Magazine* (June 27, 1943): 8–9.

Shanks, Michael, David Platt, and William Rathje. "The Perfume of Garbage: Modernity and the Archaeological." *Modernism/Modernity* 11:1 (2004): 61–83.

Sherrard-Johnson, Cherene. *Portraits of the New Negro Woman: Visual and Literary Culture in the Harlem Renaissance*. New Brunswick, N.J.: Rutgers University Press, 2007.

Shiach, Morag. "Modernity, Labor and the Typewriter." In *Modernist Sexualities*, edited by Hugh Stevens and Caroline Howlett. Manchester: Manchester University Press, 2000.

Siemerling, Winfried. "W.E.B. Du Bois, Hegel, and the Staging of Alterity." *Callaloo* 24.1 (winter 2001): 325–33.

Sims, Marian. *Call it Freedom*. Philadelphia: Lippincott, 1937.

Singh, Amritjit, and Daniel M. Scott, eds. *The Collected Writings of Wallace Thurman: A Harlem Renaissance Reader*. New Brunswick, N.J.: Rutgers University Press, 2003.

Sklar, Robert. *Movie-Made America: A Cultural History of American Movies*. New York: Vintage, 1994.

Slide, Anthony. *Nitrate Won't Wait: A History of Film Preservation in the United States*. Jefferson, N.C.: McFarland, 1992.

Smith, Catherine Capshaw. *Children's Literature of the Harlem Renaissance*. New Brunswick, N.J.: Rutgers University Press, 2006.

Smith, Neil. "New City, New Frontier: The Lower East Side as Wild, Wild West." In *Variations on a Theme Park: The New American City and the End of Public Space*, edited by Michael Sorkin. New York: Hill and Wang, 1992.

Smith, Terry. *Making the Modern: Art and Design in America*. Chicago: University of Chicago Press, 1993.

Smith, Tom Q. "The Man Who Loved a Corpse." *True Story* 8:44 (January 1941): 4–7, 90–92.

Sontag, Susan. *AIDS and Its Metaphors*. New York: Doubleday, 1988.

———. *Illness as Metaphor*. New York: Doubleday, 1977.

———. *Under the Sign of Saturn*. New York: Anchor Books, 1991.

Spackman, Barbara. "Marfarka and Son: Marinetti's Homophobic Economics." *Modernism/Modernity* 1:3 (1994): 89–107.

Spillers, Hortense J. "'All the Things You Could Be by Now, If Sigmund Freud's Wife Was Your Mother': Psychoanalysis and Race." In *Female Subjects in Black and White: Race, Psychoanalysis, Feminism*, edited by Elizabeth Abel, Barbara Christian, and Helene Moglen. Berkeley and Los Angeles: University of California Press, 1997.

———. *Black, White, and in Color: Essays on American Literature and Culture*. Chicago: University of Chicago Press, 2003.

Spivak, Gayatri Chakravorty. "Harlem." *Social Text* 22:4 (2004): 136.

Sprengnether, Madelon. "Reading Freud's Life." *American Imago* 52:1 (1995): 9–54.

Stallybrass, Peter, and Allon White. *The Politics and Poetics of Transgression*. Ithaca: Cornell University Press, 1986.

Staples, Brent. "Manhattan's African Dead: Colonial New York, from the Grave." *New York Times* (May 22, 1995).

Stern, Lesley. "Burial." In *The Smoking Book*. Chicago: University of Chicago Press, 1999.

Stevens, John D. "Social Utility of Sensational News: Murder and Divorce in the 1920s." *Journalism Quarterly* 62:1 (spring 1985): 53–58.

Stevens, Wallace. *The Collected Poems*. New York: Vintage Books, 1982.

Stewart, Susan. *On Longing: Narratives of the Miniature, the Gigantic, the Souvenir, the Collection*. Durham: Duke University Press, 1993.

Stone, Julius. "Remaking a City." *Tampa Morning Tribune* (January 7, 1935).

Sundquist, Eric. *To Wake the Nations: Race in the Making of American Literature*. Cambridge, Mass.: Harvard University Press, 1993.

Susman, Warren I. *Culture as History: The Transformation of American Society in the Twentieth Century*. New York: Pantheon Books, 1984.

"Tarzan Fact and Fiction." In *The Lion's Roar* 1:10 (1941–42).

Tate, Claudia. *Psychoanalysis and Black Novels: Desire and the Protocols of Race*. New York: Oxford University Press, 1998.

Taussig, Michael. *Defacement: Public Secrecy and the Labor of the Negative*. Stanford: Stanford University Press, 1999.

Taylor, George R. *The Turner Thesis: Concerning the Role of the Frontier in American History*. Lexington, Mass.: Heath, 1972.

Terada, Rei. *Feeling in Theory: Emotion after the "Death of the Subject."* Cambridge, Mass.: Harvard University Press, 2001.

Terkel, Studs. *Hard Times: An Oral History of the Great Depression*. New York: New Press, 2000.

Thompson, Lawrence, ed. *Selected Letters of Robert Frost*. New York: Holt, Rinehart and Winston, 1964.

Thompson, Michael. *Rubbish Theory: The*

Creation and Destruction of Value. Oxford: Oxford University Press, 1979.

Thurman, Wallace. *Infants of the Spring*. Boston: Northeastern University Press, 1992.

Till, Karen E. *The New Berlin: Memory, Politics, Place*. Minneapolis: University of Minnesota Press, 2005.

Todd, Ellen Wiley. "Art, the 'New Woman,' and Consumer Culture: Kenneth Hayes Miller and Reginald Marsh on Fourteenth Street, 1920–40." In *Gender and American History since 1890*, edited by Barbara Melosh. London: Routledge, 1993.

Tolson, Melvin B. *The Harlem Group of Negro Writers*. Westport, Conn.: Greenwood Press, 2001.

Tratner, Michael. "Working the Crowd: Movies and Mass Politics." *Criticism* 45.1 (2003): 53–73.

Tschumi, Bernard. *Architecture and Disjunction*. Cambridge, Mass.: MIT Press, 1996.

Tuan, Yi-Fu. *Space and Place: The Perspective of Experience*. Minneapolis: University of Minnesota Press, 1977.

Turano, Anthony M. "America's Torture: Chamber." *American Mercury* 45 (September 1938): 11–15.

Turnbull, Andrew, ed. *The Letters of F. Scott Fitzgerald*. New York: Scribners, 1963.

Turner, Frederick Jackson. "The Significance of the Frontier in American History." 1893. In *The Turner Thesis: Concerning the Role of the Frontier in American History*, edited by George E. Taylor. Lexington, Mass.: Heath, 1972.

U.S. Chamber of Commerce, Bureau of the Census. *Historical Statistics of the United States, Colonial Times to 1970*. Series B-166, Volume. 1. Washington, D.C.: Government Printing Office, 1975.

Urry, John. *Consuming Places*. London: Routledge, 1995.

Usai, Paolo Cherchi. *The Death of Cinema: History, Cultural Memory and the Digital Dark Age*. London: British Film Institute, 2001.

van Notten, Eleonore. *Wallace Thurman's Harlem Renaissance*. Amsterdam and Atlanta: Editions Rodopi B.V., 1994.

Van Vechten, Carl. *Nigger Heaven*. New York: Knopf, 1926.

Venturi, Robert, Denise Scott Brown, and Steven Izenour. *Learning from Las Vegas: The Forgotten Symbolism of Architectural Form*, 1973. Reprint, Cambridge, Mass.: MIT Press, 1993.

Vertrees, Alan David. *Selznick's Vision: Gone With the Wind and Hollywood Filmmaking*. Austin: University of Texas Press, 1997.

Vidler, Anthony. *The Architectural Uncanny: Essays in the Modern Unhomely*. Cambridge, Mass.: MIT Press, 1994.

Vismann Cornelia. "The Love of Ruins." *Perspectives on Science* 9:2 (2001): 196–209.

Von Cosel, Karl Tanzler. "The Secret of Elena's Tomb." *Fantastic Adventures* 9:5 (September 1947): 8–77.

Wajcman, Judy. *Feminism Confronts Technology*. University Park: Pennsylvania State University Press, 1991.

Wald, Allen M. *Writing from the Left: New Essays on Radical Culture and Politics*. New York: Verso, 1994.

Wall, Cheryl A. *Women of the Harlem Renaissance*. Bloomington: Indiana University Press, 1995.

Walsh, William S. *Yours for Sleep*. New York: E. P. Dutton, 1920.

Ward, David A. "Alcatraz and Marion: Confinement in Super Maximum Custody." In *Escaping Prison Myths: Selected Topics in the History of Federal Corrections*, edited by John W. Roberts. Washington, D.C.: American University Press, 1994.

Weber, Brom. *The Letters of Hart Crane, 1916–1932*. New York: Hermitage House, 1942.

Weber, Devra. *Dark Sweat, White Gold: California Farm Workers, Cotton, and the New Deal*. Berkeley: University of California Press, 1944.

Wells, Sharon. *Forgotten Legacy: Blacks in Nineteenth-Century Key West*. Key West: Historic Florida Keys Preservation Board, 1991.

Wells, Susan. "Discursive Mobility and Double Consciousness in S. Weir Mitchell and W. E. B. Du Bois." *Philosophy and Rhetoric* 35:2 (2002): 120–37.

Weschler, Lawrence. "Sublime Decay." *New York Times Magazine* (December 22, 2002): 42–47.

West, Dorothy. *The Richer, the Poorer*. New York: Doubleday, 1995.

West, Mae. *The Constant Sinner*. 1937. Reprint, London: Virago, 1995.

West, Nathanael. *Miss Lonelyhearts and Day of the Locust*. New York: New Directions, 1969.

Wheeler, Lesley. "Review of Verner D. Mitchell's (ed.) *This Waiting for Love: Helene Johnson, Poet of the Harlem Renaissance*." *African American Review* 36:2 (2002): 340–42.

White, William, ed. *By-Line: Ernest Hemingway: Selected Articles and Dispatches of Four Decades*. New York: Charles Scribner's Sons, 1967.

Wigley, Mark. "Prosthetic Theory: The Disciplining of Architecture." *Assemblage* 15 (August 1991): 8–9.

———. *Derrida's Haunt: The Architecture of Deconstruction*. Cambridge, Mass.: MIT Press, 1993.

Wilcox Putnam, Nina. "South from Miami." *Collier's* 100 (December 18, 1937): 34.

Willeman, Paule. "The Fugitive Subject." In *Raoul Walsh*, edited by Phil Hardy. Edinburgh: Edinburgh Film Festival, 1974.

Williams, Dino, and Alexa Williams. *Hollywoodland: Established 1923*. Los Angeles: Papavasilopoulos Press, 1992.

Williams, Monte. "Harlem Journal: Gay White Pioneers, on New Ground." *New York Times* (November 19, 2000).

Williams, Tennessee. "Homage to Key West." In *Where I Live: Selected Essays*, edited by Christine R. Day and Bob Woods. New York: New Directions, 1978.

Wintz, Cary D., ed. *The Harlem Renaissance, 1920–1940, Analysis and Assessment*. New York: Garland Publishing, 1996.

Wirth, Thomas H., ed. *Gay Rebel of the Harlem Renaissance: Selections from the Work of Richard Bruce Nugent*. Durham: Duke University Press, 2002.

———. *Fire!!* 1926. Reprint, Elizabeth, N.J.: Fire Press, 1982.

Wittgenstein, Ludwig. *Bermerkungen Über Die Farben / Remarks on Colour*, edited by G. E. M. Anscombe. Translated by Linda L. McAlister and Margarete Schättle. 1951. Reprint, Berkeley: University of California, 1978.

Wollen, Peter. "Cinema/Americanism/the Robot." In *Modernity and Mass Culture*, edited by James Naremore and Patrick Brantlinger. Bloomington: Indiana University Press, 1991.

WPA Guide to California, The. The Federal Writers' Project Guide to 1930s California. Written and compiled by the Federal Writers' Project of the Works Progress Administration for the State of California. 1939. Reprint, New York: Pantheon, 1984.

WPA Guide to New York City, The. The Federal Writers' Project Guide to New York. Reprint, New York: New Press, 1992.

Wright, Louis T. "Factors Controlling Negro Health." *The Crisis* (September 1935): 283.

Yaeger, Patricia. "Ghosts and Shattered Bodies: What Does It Mean to Still Be Haunted by Southern Literature?" *South Central Review* 22:1 (spring 2005): 87–108.

Young, James O. *Black Writers of the Thirties*. Baton Rouge: Louisiana State University Press, 1973.

Zanjani, Sally Springmeyer. *The Unspiked Rail: Memoir of a Nevada Rebel*. Reno: University of Nevada Press, 1981.

Ziarek, Ewa. "The Uncanny Style of Kristeva's Critique of Nationalism." *Postmodern Culture* 5:2 (1995).

Zwarg, Christina. "Du Bois on Trauma: Psychoanalysis and the Would-be Black Savant." *Cultural Critique* 51 (spring 2001): 1–39.

Index

Page numbers in bold refer to illustrations.

abject geography, 108–12, 265n106
Addams, Jane, 226, 282n133
addiction, 121. *See also* alcoholism; consumption
Adler, Alfred, 177
Adorno, Theodore, 231–32, 255n19, 264n82, 271n107, 282n113
Adventures of Robin Hood, The, 200
aesthetics, 8–9, 86, 109, 153, 239, 267n4, 270n81, 273n128, 282n113; in cinema, 204, 226; Crane's aesthetic, 88; Du Bois and, 271n90; of salvaging, 92–96, 98, 266n145; Thurman's blue-pencil practice, 138–40. *See also* High Modernism; salvage
affect, 5; excess feeling and, 175; place and, 12, 21
After Divorce? (Parmer), 43, 48–49
"After the Storm" (Hemingway), 262n59
Alcatraz, **234**, **236**, 236–38, **237**, 241–42, 283n1, 284n11. *See also* prison
alcoholism, 173, 195, 247n17, 263n77
Ali Baba Goes to Town, 227
Allee, William, 2
Allen, Frederick Lewis, 78
allegory 3, 12, 29, 56, 82–84; as "history in miniature," 80; *The Wizard of Oz* as, 280n71
Alston, Charles, 129
American Culture between the Wars (Kalaidjian), 8
Americanism. *See* Fordism; Gramsci, Antonio; progressive modernity
Americanization, 41, 56–57, 81. *See also* imperialism
amputation, 116–21, 266n136. *See also* dismemberment; prosthesis
anal eroticism. *See* sexuality
analytic psychology, 28, 150, 212–13, 271n96, 271n103
Anatomy of Criticism (Frye), 277n30
Anderson, Benedict, 266n131

Anderson, Paul Allen, 149
Anderson, Sherwood, 33
androgyny, 64, 80, 89, 90–92. *See also* gender
Arcades Project, The (Benjamin), **16–17**, 23, 228
architectural theory, 7, 114, 250n31, 256n28, 263n67
architecture, 9, 200–201, 239, 249n28, 250n31, 251n43, 279nn50–51, 281n106
archives, 3, 8–9, 75–76, 136, 162, 183, 198; James Weldon Johnson Collection at Yale, 134–35, 141, 167; Margaret Herrick Library of the Academy of Motion Pictures, 189; Nevada Historical Society, 41, 61; Special Collections of Columbia University, 157, 167–68, 268n28. *See also* Gumby Scrapbooks; Harlem
Arens, Egmont, 19
Arno, Peter, **13**
Ashton, Jennifer, 25, 252n68
Asian Americans, 168, 250n30
associationist psychology, 28
authenticity, 14, 21, 191–93, **192**, 209–10

Babson, Al, 227
Babylon set of *Intolerance*, **190**, 194, 200, 276n9
Bachelard, Gaston, 24, 212–13, 215–16, 280n88
Bahama Village, **102**
Baker, Douglas A., 57–59
Baker, Houston A., Jr., 8, 133
Baker v. Baker transcript, **58**
Bakhtin, Mikhail, 265n112
Balázs, Béla, 195, 199
Baldwin, Faith, 34, 46, 257n64
Ballou, Harold, 116
Bardèche, Maurice, 208
Barnard, Rita, 77
Barnard, W. E., 62
Barnes, Djuna, 262n50
Barry, Iris, 227
Barrymore, John, 198

Bartlett, George, 41, 45
Bataille, Georges, 115, 215–16, 229, 281n100
Bates, Sanford, 238
Batista, Fulgencio, 81
Baudelaire, Charles-Pierre, 13, **113**, 143, 160, 273n128
Baudrillard, Jean, 238
Baum, Frank, 206
Bearden, Romare, 125, 267n4
Benítez-Rojo, Antonio, 79, 95, 100
Benjamin, Walter, 23, 27–29; *The Arcades Project*, **16–17**, 23, 228; on collecting vs. hoarding, 163–65, 172; on "dream city," 195; on echo, 146–47; on façade, 194–95; on film spectatorship, 195, 227–28, 277n27; impact of dissociationism on, 27–28; on refuse, 7, 23, 84; on slowing down, standstill, and idling, 11, 23, 34–35, 247n12, 249n25, 252n60, 255n16; on spatial disorientation, 194–95; on states of consciousness, 228, 231–32; on storm of progress, 84; on teleological accounts of history, 247n8; theory of place of, 5, 11, 194–95, 249n24
Bennett, Gwendolyn, 129, 134, 136
Benstock, Shari, 8
Bentley, Arthur F., 87
Bergson, Henri: *durée* of, 5, 249n23; impact of dissociationism on, 27–28; linking of space and time of, 5, 249n24; primitivism in, 270n78
Berlant, Lauren, 248n18
"Berlin Chronicle, A" (Benjamin), 146–47
Berman, Marshall, 84
Betweenness of Place, The (Entrikin), 248n20
Bigger, Earl Derr, 34
Big Money, The (Dos Passos), 230, 283n154
"Bigness" (Koolhaas), 240–41
Big Sea, The (Hughes), 131, 134, 140, 147, 151, 180
bi-polar disorder, 145, 247n17. *See also* depression; dissociationism; melancholia
Bishop, Elizabeth, 8, 25–27, 85, 262n60, 262n61, 276n3; aesthetic salvaging of, 94–95, 96, 100–101, 263n77, 264n79, 264n90; embrace of loose ends of, 27; on graft and dismemberment, 118–21; "Grandmother's Glass Eye," 112, **113**; on Hemingway, 92; on Key West's cartographic presence, 114; on Marianne Moore, 92; "Mercedes Hospital," 96, **97**; physical descriptions of Key West of, 76, 261n39; on racial politics in Key West, 110–11, 264n90; on Valdes's painting, 263n73
Black Arts era of 1966, 131
Blackmail, 223
Black No More (Schuyler), 179–80
Black Renaissance. *See* Harlem
Black Skin, White Masks (Fanon), 268n29
Black Thunder (Bontemps), 132
Blanchot, Maurice, 269n55
Bloch, Marc, 160
Blodget, Walton, 76
Bloom, Michelle E., 204, 279n54
Bloomberg, Michael, 3
blues, the, 125, 153, 247n11, 271n107
body, the, 3, 22; amputation and dismemberment of, 116–21, 266n136; decay and reanimation of, in Key West, 76–78, 98–101, 103–7, 264n82; disease in Harlem, 127–29, 173–85, **174**, 267n10; FERA's sterilization of, 74–75; in Hollywood, 188, 212–17. *See also* women
Body and the Song, The (Lombardi), 263n77
bones. *See* body, the
Bontemps, Arna, 132, **132**, 135
Boone, Joseph A., 8, 142, 146, 147, 270n81
borders and boundaries. *See* place, places; space
Borrows, John W., 57
Bowles, Grace Bulmer, 101
Boyle, Kay, 33
Boyle, Robert, 220, 281n106
Brackett, Charles, 208
Brasillach, Robert, 208
Breakfast in Hollywood, 277n10
Breen, Joe, 225
Breuer, Josef, 28
bridges, highways, and railroad links: Divorcée Special train to Reno, **33**, 34–35, 37, **65**, 254n3; in Key West, 72, 82–84, **83**, 112–14, **120**, 265n121; in Reno, 255n25
Brokaw, Clare. *See* Luce, Clare Boothe
Brosnan, Peter, 233
Brown, Bill, 24, 264n79
Brown Derby restaurant, 189, 200, **216**, 216–17, 229
Bruce, Richard. *See* Nugent, Richard Bruce
Bruno, Giuliana, 204
Buckle, Gerard Fort, 204

304 INDEX

Buck-Morss, Susan, 34–35, 50, 255n16
Buñuel, Luis, 227
Burch, Noël, 215, 278n32
Burg, B. R., 79
Bush, George W., administration, 5, 244–45
Butler, Dorothy, 57–59, 69
Butler, Judith, 67

"Cabaret Girl Dies on Welfare Island" (Hughes), 181
Cabot, Eveillo, 96–98
Cage, John, 266n136
Cahen, Alfred, 42
Calhoon, Claudia Marie, 176
Caliban (Shakespeare character), 110–11
Calkins, Earnest Elmo, 19
Campbell, Hazel, 171
cancer, 173–76
capitalism, 3, 5, 14, 19, 165–67, 175, 184, 228, 255n16; Du Bois on, 274n163; failure of, 12; imperialism and, 35
Capone, Al, 237
Caribbean: aesthetic of salvage of, 8–9, 92–101, 263nn75–77; piracy in, 78–80, 260n23, 261n25. *See also* Cuba; salvage
Carlston, Erin G., 8
Carman, Dorothy Walworth, 44
Carey, Jim, 217
Carteles magazine, **82**
cartoons: about divorce, **44**, 49, 51; by Galbraith, **33**; of Reno, **33**
Casablanca, 200
Casarino, Cesare, 261n25, 276n2
Casel, Von, **104**
Casey, Edward S., 248n20, 260n154
Catholic Legion of Decency, 225
Cavell, Stanley, 34
Cayo Hueso, 78, **79**. *See also* Key West
Century Film Company, 214
Certeau, Michel de, 106, 189, 278n44
Céspedes, Carlos Manuel, 81
Chacon, José, 96
Chaney, Lon, 214
Chaplin, Charlie, 222, 254n5, 282n114
Chase, 180, **181**
Chasing Dirt: The American Pursuit of Cleanliness (Hoy), 18

Children and the Movies (Jowett, Jarvie, and Fuller), 226
Chion, Michel, 208, 223, 231, 279n47
Chisholm, Ann, 221
cigar manufacturing, 76
cinders, 136–38, 148. *See also* Derrida, Jacques; fire; refuse
cinema. *See* film; Hollywood(land); sets, set design
City of Wax, 199, 203–4
classified (term), 241, 284n31
cleanups and renovations: body doubles and stand-ins in, 215, 217–24, **222**, 282nn114–15, 122, 125; of Collyer brothers' hoard, 155, 162–68, **164**, 273n135, 273n141; of Colonial Williamsburg, 14; of Key West by FERA, **70**, 72–75, **73**, 105–6; moral, 74–75, 80–81, 116; Reno-vation, 9, 45–46, 51–54, 258n90, 259nn150–51; repetition with a difference in, 9, 45–46, 146–47, 221–22, 258n90, 259nn150–51, 270n84, 281n107; of White House, 11–14, 249n28, 250n29
Clifford, James, 264n82
Clinton, Bill, 130
Coleman, Anita Scott, 173
collages, 96, **97**, 155, 157, 160, 163, 166–67, **167**, 172. *See also* scrapbooks and assemblings of Harlem
collecting. *See* hoarding; salvage; scrapbooks and assemblings of Harlem; souvenirs
Collyer, Homer, 155, 162–68, **164**
Collyer, Langley, 155, 162–68, **164**
Collyer Brothers Park, 163, **164**, 273n135
Colonial Williamsburg, 14, 20, 21, 55, 252n49
Color Struck (Hurston), 144, 269n66
Columbia University, Special Collections, 157, 167–68, 268n28. *See also* Gumby Scrapbooks
commodity, 50, 52; fetish and, 23–24, 105, 166; Key West as commodity, 78; re-commodification and, 53–54, 69; sexual economy of, 259n141
Communism, 170–71. *See also* Marx, Karl; Marxist geography
Company She Keeps, The (McCarthy), 59–60, 258n112
Conches, 85, 121, 261n36, 266n147. *See also* Key West

INDEX 305

Condition of Postmodernity, The (Harvey), 248n20
Conjure-Man Dies, The (Fisher), 148, 180–81, 270n89
conjuring. *See* Harlem; haunting; spectrality
conspiracy theories, 244
Consuming Places (Urry), 256n30
consumption, 76–78; addiction and, 121; as cure in Reno, 62–63, 66–67, **67**, 259n152; as eating, 114–16; gendering of, 256n 33, 259nn150–52; during Great Depression, 77–78, 165–67; in Harlem, 149, 160, 171–72; places of, 39–41, 256nn30–31; overconsumption and, 173; reading as, 147, 173; shifts in personality and, 271n96; underconsumption and, 76. *See also* tuberculosis
"Consumptive, The" (Hughes), 181, 275n206
Cook, David, 116
Cooper, Mark Garrett, 215, 232, 278n32, 278n44
"Cootchie" (Bishop), 100–101
"Cordelia the Crude" (Thurman), 140–41, 143–44, 181
corpses, 26, 98–101, 148, 163, 185, 266n145; disinterment of, 103; of Elena Milagro Hoyos, 103–8; in set decoration, 209–210. *See also* death
Cosgrove, Denis, 249n21
Cousins, Norman, 42–43
Cowdery, Mae, 270n81
Cowley, Peggy, 89
Crane, Hart, 8, 76, 247n17, 262n61, 265n119; on fluidity of Key West, 88–89, 92, 261–62nn48–49; gender ambiguity of, 269n70; on hurricanes, 112; salvage aesthetics of, 98
Crane, Louise, 101, 263n73
Crary, Jonathan, 232
Cruise, Tom, 189
crypts, 90, 104, 107, 184–85
C Street, Virginia City, **55**, 55–56
Cuba, **81**; revolutions in, 80–81, **82**, 98–99, 264n80; U.S. imperialism and, 81, 99–100
Cukor, George, 193, 223
Cullen, Countee, 134, 151, 157
Culler, Jonathan, 117
cultural geography, 7, 248n20
Cunard, Nancy, 160–61, 268n27
cures for divorce, 62–69, 259n141, 144, 151–52. *See also* divorce; Reno
Curler, B. F., 57–59

Danius, Sara, 179
Danko, Betty, 281n96
Darden, Douglas, 86, 263n67
Davies, Marion, 222, 282n115
Davis, Angela, 271n107
Davis, Elmer, 80
Davis, John, 136
Davis, Stuart, 125, 267n4
Day of the Locust, The (West), 188, 191, 212, 229, 230
Dean, Jimmy, 85
Dean-Lopez Funeral Home, 85, 104, **106**
Dear Lovely Death (Hughes), 181
death, 3, 22, 266n145, 278n38; decay and reanimation in Key West and, 72, **73**, 76–78, 98–101, 103–7, 118, 264n82; decomposition of flesh and, 74–75, 106, 108; disease and, in Harlem, 127–29, 162, 173–85, **174**, 267n10; in Hollywood, 188, 195–98, 212–17, 229, 233; "living dead" and, 207–8; metaphor of, 24; sterilization of, by FERA, 74–75, 114. *See also* corpses; graveyards; haunting; spectrality
"Death Chant" (Hughes), 181
Death of Cinema, The (Usai), 197–98, 278n38
"Death Writes a Book" (Chase), 180–81, **181**
Decasia: The State of Decay (Morrison), 196–97
decay. *See* death
Decker Canyon fire, 214
De Jongh, James, 149, 271n91
Delaney, Francis, 103
Deleuze, Gilles, 27, 28, 244, 249n22
DeLongchamps, Frederic, 39, 62
DeMille, Cecil B., 9, 212, 217, 233
depression, 4, 26, 179; as concept, 133–34, 247n11, 247n12, 247n13, 247n17, 248n19, 268n24. *See also* Great Depression; melancholia
depressive modernity, 3, 4–5, 7, 11, 247n8; oldness of newness and, 138
Derrida, Jacques, 117, 252n62; on cinders, 136–38; hauntology of, 250n31; on simile, 277n30; on supplements, 221
desire. *See* consumption; sexuality
Descartes, René, 203, 250n31
Desert Hearts (Rule), 259n144
Dewey, John, 76, 87
Dialect of Modernism, The (North), 8
Diaz, Norberto, 107–8
Dickie, Margaret, 264n90

dirt. *See* refuse
dismemberment, 82, 114–21, 266n136. *See also* amputation; memory; prosthesis
Disneyland, 21, 55, 193, 277n11
disorder. *See* Harlem; hoarding
disposal. *See* refuse
dissociationism: in Harlem writings, 136–53, 270n78; Janet's model of, 27–28, 253n82; in psychological theory, 150, 271n96, 271n103
dissolve, 204–8, 213, 227, 280n73, 280n76
divorce, 9, 32–69; *Baker v. Baker* transcript and, **58**; blurring of class boundaries by, 48–49; cartoons and jokes about, **44**, 49, 51; of celebrities, 32, 254n5, 254n11; costs of, 32–33, 254n10; fictional portrayals of, 33–35, **34**, 51–54, **53**, 66–67, **67**, 254n12, 255n14, 259n152; Fordist approach to, 43–46, **44**, 49–51, **60**, 60–61, 256nn41–42; imprisonment metaphors of, 60–61; jargon of, 37, 255nn25–26; legal regulation of, 57, 61, 253n2, 258n105, 258n106, 259n119, 259n144; liminal state of, 59–61, 258n112; modernity and, 35–36; motherhood and children in, 53–54; New Woman and, 66–69, 259n151; postcards of, **36**, **52**, **63**, **65**; prostitution and, 45–51, **47**; queering impact of, 64–66, 259n141, 259n144; railroad quests of, **33**, 34–35, **65**, 254n3; Reno-vation and remarriage, 9, 45–46, 51–54, **52**, **63**, 258n90, 259nn150–51; spatial implications of, 49–51; statistics on, 32, 42–44, 254n6, 256n33; trope of "the cure" for, 62–69, 259nn141, 144, 151–52. *See also* Reno; *Women, The*
Divorcée Special train to Reno, 34–35, 37, **65**
Doane, Mary Ann, 198, 199, 215, 230, 280n76
domesticity, 42, 54, 256n35
Dorothy. *See Wizard of Oz, The*
Dos Passos, John, 18, 76, 230, 283n154
double-consciousness, 149–50, 175. *See also* Du Bois, W. E. B
doubles. *See* repetition with a difference
Double Talk (Koestenbaum), 161
Douglas, Aaron, 125, 136
Douglas, Ann, 8, 247n17
Douglas, John W., 157
Douglas, Mary, 251n36
Douglass, Frederick, 124
Downtown Gallery, The, and Jacob Lawrence's exhibits, 124, **124**, **126**, 266n1

dream states, 193, 213, 225–33, 253n82, 280n91, 282n133, 283nn147, 160, 162
Droysen, Johann Gustav, 22
Du Bois, Burghardt, 174–75, **175**
Du Bois, Nina Gomer, **175**
Du Bois, W. E. B.: on aesthetics, 271n90; on consumption, 171–72, 274n163; dissociationism and, 149–50, 174–75, **175**; on *Fire!!*, 270n72, 271n90; historicist project of, 149–50, 158, 271n90, 98; racial uplift message of, 144; on scrapbooks, 158–59; on tuberculosis, 176
dude ranches, 48, 51, 56, 64, 254n10. *See also* divorce
Duke, Arthur M., 72
dump encampments, 12, 19–20, 251n42
dumps. *See* refuse
Duncan, James, 249n21
durée, 5, 249n23
Dust Tracks on a Road (Hurston), 134

East Harlem Health Center, 177
Ebony and Topaz (Johnson), 158–59
echo, 146–47, 270n84
economics of trash: consumption debates of the 1930s and, 77–78; hoarding, 165–67; progressive obsolescence, 19, 52–53; in Reno divorce industry, 32–35, 43–46, 49–51, **60**, 253n2, 254n8. *See also* hoarding; New Deal; refuse
Edgecombe Sanitarium, 177
Edison, Thomas, 212
Edwin Boomer (character), 25–27
ego formation, 26n2, 108–9, 179, 269n70; Fanon on, 268n29
Eisenstein, Serge, 227
"Elevator Boy" (Hughes), 143–44
Eliot, T. S., 18, 32, 183–84, 254n4, 273n128, 275n214
Ellison, Ralph, 131, 276n1
Entrikin, J. Nicholas, 248n20
Ewen, Stuart, 19, 53

Fanon, Frantz, 179, 268n29
"Farewell to Florida" (Stevens), 89–90
Fate of Place, The (Casey), 248n20, 260n154
Federal Economy Act of 1932, 42–43
Federal Emergency Relief Administration (FERA), 4–5, 9; ban on gambling by, 74;

Federal Emergency Relief Administration (FERA), *continued*
cleanup training programs of, 74; Key West cleanup by, **70**, 72–75, **77**, **79**, 86, 110, 116, 260n4, 265n112; photo of dead relief worker of, **109**; racist policies of, 109–12, 265n109, 265n112; sterilization approach of, 74–75, 80–81, 116

Federal Writer's Project, 131, 134

Felski, Rita, 8, 259n149

femininity. *See* gender; women

feminist geography, 248n20. *See also* geography

Fernandez, Ramón, 262n52

fetish. *See* commodity

Fevered Lives (Ott), 177

film: acetate, 206; analogies of, to wax, 204, 213, 224–25; celluloid, 196, 278n34; chemical self-destruction of, 196–98, 278n38; cinematic dissolve in, 204–8, 227; close-up in, 199; disorientation and illusion in, 193, 194–96, 277n22, 277n27, 277n30, 278nn31–32; Hollywood's production of itself in, 199–200, 280n76; Lawrence's paintings as, 267n4; as medium of representation, 199; sound in, 200, 203–4, 279n47; spectatorship of, 214–17, 225–33, 282n133, 283n147, 283n160, 283n162; Technicolor in, 280; threats of fire to, 213–14. *See also* Hollywood(land); scale; sets, set design

filth, 216, 251n36. *See also* refuse

fire, 184, 194–98, 212–17, 281n92, 281n105; analogies of, to wax, 213; at film studios, 214, **214**; in *Gone With the Wind*, 217–20, **219**, 281n104; as refuse removal, 21; smoke and smoking in, 215–16; watching of, 212–13; in *The Wizard of Oz*, 214, 215, 281n96

Fire!! magazine, 136–48, **137**, 172, 268n34; Hughes's "Elevator Boy" in, 143–44; press release for, **137**; queer writing by Nugent in, 142–43, 270n72; Thurman's dissociative editorial aesthetic in, 136–41, 270n78, 270n84, 271n103; tropes of walking in, 141–44; on Van Vechten's view of Harlem, 149

Fisher, Rudolph, 8, 132, 148, 173–76, 180–81

Fiske University questionnaire, 158–59, **160**

Fitzgerald, F. Scott, 195, 223–24, 229

"Flame Heart" (McKay), 267n12

Florey, Robert, 191, 193

"Florida" (Bishop), 100

"The Florida East Coast Railroad, Dawn" (Bishop), 261n39

fluidity, 87–95, 262nn50–54, 262n61, 263nn66–67

food waste, 22–23

Forbes, Kermit "Shine," 103

Ford, Clara Bryant (Mrs. Henry Ford), 18

Ford, Harrison, 189

Ford, Henry, 42

Ford, Leslie, 34

Fordism, 9, 11, 41, 259n150; on Alcatraz, 237; domestic applications of, 42, 54, 256n35; gender in, 42; Gramsci on, 45–46, 50, 256n35, 257n56; Hollywood(land) as "Dream Factory" and, 226, 283n134; New Industrial Wives and, 45–46, 51–54, 66, 258n90; progressive obsolescence and, 19, 52–53; in Reno divorce industry, 43–46, 49–51, 60–61, 256nn41–42; in Reno prostitution industry, 46–49, 60–61, 257nn59–61; in Reno-vation and remarriage, 51–54, 258n90, 259nn150–51; repetition with a difference in, 221–22; sexual and spatial implications of, 45–46, 49–51, 256n30. *See also* mass production

forgetting. *See* memory; refuse

Forgotten Man, the, 14, **15**, 20, 250n30, 251n42

Foucault, Michel, 250n31; on heterotopias, 261n25, 276n2; on prisons, 61, 238; on spatial metaphors, 12, 250n31

Frank, Waldo, 33

Frankenberg, Lloyd, 76

Fresh Kills, Staten Island, 2–3

Freud, Sigmund, 25, 28, 150, 171, 180, 224, 231, 282n125

Fried, Michael, 25, 252n68

Frost, Robert, 72, 76

Frye, Northrup, 277n30

"Full Moon, Key West" (Bishop), 94–95

Galbraith cartoon, **33**

Gallagher, Catherine, 263nn66–67

gambling, 35, 61–62, 96, 257n76; banning of, 74 254n8

garbage, 18–20, 72, 168–69, 177. *See also* refuse

Garbage in the Cities (Melosi), 18

"Garbage Man, The" (Dos Passos), 18

Garbage Park, Sausalito, California, 18, 20
Garvey, Marcus, 131, **133**
gay men, 89, 143, 161–62; gentrification and, 154–55. *See also* gender; masculinity; queer constructions; sexuality
Gay Metropolis, The (Kaiser), 154
Gelhorn, Martha, 90–92
gender, 21; blues and, 271n107; of Cuban *mestizaje*, 100–101; divorce and, 64–69, **65**, 254n5, 260n154; fluidity of, 88–90, 92–93, 100, 262nn50–54, 262n61; of Fordism, 42; of Hemingway's house, 92; of mass culture, 256n33; of New Woman who shops, 66–69, 259n151; of place, 56–57, 69, 91–92, 248n20; in Stevens's works, 262nn52–54; Turner's masculinized frontier and, 56–57; of United States, 106, 265n104. *See also* androgyny; masculinity; queer constructions; sexuality
Gender of Modernity, The (Felski), 8
Gentleman Jigger (Nugent), 134, 151–53, **152**
geography, 7, 248n20, 249n21; of abjection and drift in Key West, 108–12, 265n106; of places of memory, 134, 136–38, 268n25, 269nn44–45. *See also* place, places; site; space
Georgetta, Clel, 44, 51
ghostwriting, 140, 148, **181**, 184, 275n214. *See also* haunting, spectrality
Gidden, Anthony, 250n29
Gikandi, Simon, 95, 263n70
Gilbert, John, 188
Giles, Paul, 88
Gilligan's Island, 217
Girard, Luce, 189
Giuliani, Rudolph, 2
God Sends Sunday (Bontemps), 132
Gone With the Wind, **201**, 208–12, 214, 217–20, **219**, 281n104
Gordon, Avery, 184
Gordon, Richard, 110
Gramsci, Antonio, 249n28; on Fordist sexuality, 45–46, 50, 256n35, 257n56; on New Industrial Wives, 45–46, 51, 66; Wollen's analysis of, 42
"Grandmother's Glass Eye" (Bishop), 112, **113**
Grauman's Chinese Theater, 189, 196, **196**, 277n10
Grau San Martín, Ramón, 81
graveyards, 104, 184–85, 188; Key West as "civic grave" and, 72. *See also* crypts

Great Depression, 4–6, 21; blurring of economics and psychology of, 4–5, 134, 247n17, 248n19, 268n24; dump encampments during, 19–20; economic consumption debates during, 77–78; Federal Writer's Project and, 131, 134; FERA's sterilization of death and decay of, 74–75; Forgotten Man archetype of, 14, **15**, 20, 250n30, 251n42; in Harlem, 132–34, 136–38, 168–72, **170**; hoarding policies of, 165–67, 273n139, 273n141; migration and Americanization during, 57; origins of the throw-away economy in, 19; role of place in discourse of, 6, 12; scrap collection during, 19–20; set-design work during, 200–201; shattering of progressive narratives by, 14; suicide rates during, 4–5, 247n16; trash discourse in, 18–19; tuberculosis during, 173–79; visceral emptiness of, 78, 260n17; women's employment during, 42–43. *See also* Fordism; New Deal
Great Train Robbery, The, 212, 280n85
Greenberg, Cheryl Lynn, 169
Greenberg, Judith, 146
"Gregorio Valdes" (Bishop), 263n73
Griffith, D. W., 188, **190**, 194, 200, 276n9
Griffith, Jeannette, 19–20
Grinch, The, 217
Grove, Allen W., 179, 180
Guattari, Félix, 244
Guillén, Nicolás, 99–100
Gumby, L. S. Alexander, 134, 155–68, 172; collection goals of, 157–58; homosexuality of, 158, 159, 161, 273n128; tuberculosis of, 158, 176
Gumby Book Studio, **156**, 157, 158, 160, **160**
Gumby Scrapbooks, 134, 155–68, **156**, **181**, 268n28; Collyer brothers in, 162–68, **164**; Fiske University questionnaire in, 158–59, **160**; organization of, 157–58; revisions of, 158–59; riot of 1935 in, 168–72, **170**
Guyer, Sara, 231, 283n162

Haines, Billy, 282n115
Half a Loaf (Lewis), 35, 43, 44, 48, 59–60, 63–64
Hall, Walter L., 200
Halpert, Edith, **124**, 266n1
Hamilton, Margaret, 281n96
Hamlin, John, 35–36
Harding, U. E., 54, 57

Harlem, 9, 21, 121, 123–85, 266n147; author's quest in, 129–31, 148, 162; Collyer brothers' hoard in, 155, 162–68, **164**, 273n135, 273n141; the Depression in, 132–34, 136–38, 269n42; disease and death in, 127–29, 173–85, **174**, **178**, **181**, **182**, 274n176; Du Bois's concept of double consciousness in, 149–50; health care in, 173–74, **174**, 177; historicist project of, 149–50, 158–59, 270n72, 271nn90–91, 94; Hollywood and, 131; individualist project of, 144–51, 159, 269n70, 271n96; jazz inspiration in, 124–27; Lawrence's paintings of, **124**, 124–29, **126**, **128**; living and working conditions of, 168–72, 176–77, 274nn150–51; "Luxurious Condos" in, **154**; Malcolm X Boulevard in, 129, **130**, **185**; map of, **122**; memoirs of Renaissance of, 131–34, 267nn12–13, 268n20; Nugent's stories of, 141–48; queer culture in, 129–30, 136, 142–48, 154, 158, 159, 161, 166–67, **167**, 269n70; real estate in, 129–31, 154, **154**; riots in, 125, 135, 155, 168–72, **170**, 268n33, 271n91, 274n157, 274n163; street scenes of, **130**, **142**, **185**; 306 Group of artists in, 129; uplift narratives of, 144; Van Vechten's portrayals of, 131–35, 141, 149, 157, 163, 166–67, **167**; women writers in, 132, 268n20, 273n131. *See also* archives; *Fire!!* magazine; Gumby Scrapbooks; scrapbooks and assemblings of Harlem; Thurman, Wallace

Harlem: A Melodrama of Negro Life in Harlem (Rapp and Thurman), 131, 140–41, 144, 153, 224, 268n34, 272n108

Harlem Community Art Center, **128**, 129

"Harlem" exhibit (Lawrence), **124**, 124–29, **128**, 267nn3–6, 9–10

"Harlem/Good Morning, Daddy" (Hughes), **139**

Harlem Hospital, 177

Harlem journal, 270n72

Harlem magazine, 136

Harlem (McKay), 269n42

Harlem Renaissance in Black and White, The (Hutchinson), 8

Harlem Renaissance Remembered, The (Bontemps), 132

Harlow, Jean, **196**

Harris, Leonard, 271n90

Harry Morgan (character), 98–99, 118–21, 260n23

Harvey, David, 6, 248n20

Haule, John Ryan, 28

haunting, 23, 107–8, 162, 183–84, 196, 207–8, 249n26, 250n31, 265n105, 272n123. *See also* spectrality; ghostwriting

Havana, postcard of, **81**

Hawthorne, Hildegarde, 14

Hayes, William H., 225, 276n7

Hayes Code, 225

health. *See* cures for divorce; dismemberment

Hearst, William Randolph, 222

Hegel, Georg Wilhelm Friedrich, 149–50, 247n8, 271n98

Heidegger, Martin, 24

Heinze, Andrew R., 149, 271n96

Heisner, Beverly, 193, 279n51

Hemingway, Ernest, 8, 76, 247n17, 266n145; on FERA's goals in Key West, 77, **109**, 109–10, 111, 116–21, 265n109; on graft and dismemberment, 116–21, 266n136; presence of, in Key West, 90–92, **91**, 103; "Who Murdered the Vets?," 109–10. See also *To Have and Have Not*

Hemingway Collection, **109**

Herbert, George, 111

Herbst, Josephine, 76

High Modernism, 7–8, 19, 193

highways. *See* bridges, highways, and railroad links

historic preservation: authenticity in, 14, 21; of Colonial Williamsburg, 14, 20, 21, 252n49; of dumps, 20; sanitization aspects of, 14; of Virginia City, Nevada, 55–56; of White House, 11–14, 249n28, 250n29

history and death, 3, 278n38

history of trash, 18–20. *See also* refuse

Hitchcock, Alfred, 217, 223

hoarding, 162–68, 172; Benjamin on, 163–65, 172; by Collyer brothers, 155, 162–68, **164**, 273n135, 273n141; Hoover's policies on, 165–66, 273n139; Keynes on, 273n141. *See also* scrapbooks and assemblings of Harlem

Hoffman, William, 76, **79**

Hollywood(land), 9, 187–233; architecture in, 9; author's quest of, 194, 217; Babylon set in, 188, **190**; beehive images of, 199; body doubles and stand-ins in, 215, 217–24, **222**, 282nn114–15, 122, 125; Brown Derby restaurant in, 189, 200, **216**, 216–17, 229; cemeteries in, 188; documentation and archives in, 189; as "Dream Factory," 226, 283n134; fire and smoke in, 21,

212–17, **214**, **219**, 281nn92, 96, 104; Grauman's Chinese Theater in, 196, **196**, 277n10; housing in, **188**, **190**, 191, 202; impact of sound on, 200, 208; Kodak Theatre in, **190**; map of, **186**; movie extras in, 232–33, 282n124; Movieland Wax Museum in, 224–25; racism in, 198, 224; Reno in, 194; sitelessness of place in, 188–93, 202, 276nn1–2, 276n5; sleep, dreams, and insomnia in, 193, 213, 225–33, 280n91, 282n133, 283n147, 283n160, 283n162; street scene in, **229**; studios as places in, 189–91; wax metaphors of, 203–8, **205**, 213, 224–25, 279n54. *See also* film; sets, set design
Hollywood Production Code, 225
Hollywood Speaks, 277n10
"Homage to Key West" (Williams), 114–16, 121, 266n123
home and domesticity, 42, 54, 256n35; *chez soi*, 231
homosexuality. *See* queer constructions
Honey, Maureen, 183, 275n210
Hoover, Herbert, 251n42; on citizen self-reliance, 78; on hoarding, 165–66, 273n139
Hoover, J. Edgar, 236, 250n30
Hoovervilles, 12, 251n42
Hopkins, George James, 200
"House Machine" (Le Corbusier), 54
Hoy, Suellen, 18
Hoyos, Elena Milagro, 103–7, **106**
Hughes, Langston, **122**, **132**, 159; on end of Harlem, 131, 134; *Fire!!* magazine and, 136; memoir of Harlem by, 131, 134, 140, 147, 151, 180; nighttime walk of, with Nugent, 141–44; Nugent on, 141–42; on Thurman, 140, 147, 173, 181, 275n206; Thurman on, 138; Thurman's editing of, **139**, 150–51; travels of, 76, 131, **147**, 268n30; in Yale's Harlem collection, 135, 141
Hughes, Rupert, 57
Hull, Elizabeth, 182–83, 275n209
humanistic geography, 248n20
Hunchback of Notre Dame, 214
"Hundreds are receiving free instruction" poster (Rothstein), **128**
"Hurricane" (Crane), 112
"Hurricane" (MacLeish), 265n119
hurricane (1935), 72–75, 82–84, **83**, 108–12, **109**
Hurst, Fannie, 134
Hurston, Zora Neale, 134, 159, **182**, 275n207, 276n218; *Color Struck*, 144, 269n66; death of, 181–82, 184, 275n207; in *Fire!!* magazine, 136; *Mule Bone* rewrite by, 150; on Southern folk, 172; on Thurman, 141
Hutchinson, George, 8
hypermaterialism, 25–27
hypnotism, 145, 148, 150, 153

"Idea of Order at Key West, The" (Stevens), 89–90, 119–20, 262n52, 266n145
"I'm Down in the Dumps" (song), 4, 247n12
Immigration and Naturalization Service (INS), 5
immigration roundups, 5
imperialism, 41; frontier and, 56–57; of United States in Caribbean, 81, 112, 116
Ince, Thomas, 222
incineration. *See* cinders; fire
Infants of the Spring (Thurman), 134, 144–45, 151
insomnia, 225–33
International Style, 6
"In the Dumps—a profitable pastime," **15**
Intolerance (Griffith), **190**, 194, 200, 276n9
Invisible Man, The (Wells), 179
Iraq invasion and occupation (2003–), 5
Irigaray, Luce, 52
I Should Have Stayed Home (McCoy), 202

Jackman, Harold, 151
Jackson, Hughlings, 177
James, C. L. R., 33
James, William, 150
Jameson, Fredric, 6
Janet, Pierre, 27–28, 145, 150, 253n82
Jansen, Richard, 76
jazz, 42, 124–27, 267n4
Jim Crow laws, 250n30
Johnsen, Julia, 63
Johnson, Abigail, 183–84, **184**
Johnson, Avery, 76
Johnson, Barbara, 252n62
Johnson, Charles, 144, 149, 158–59
Johnson, Helene, 132, **147**, 182–84, **184**, 275nn206, 210–14
Johnson, James Weldon, 132, 134, 144; papers of, at Yale, 134–35, 141, 167
Johnson, Latifa, 54
Johnson, Ray, 159–60, **161**, 272n126
Joyce, James, 13, 23
Jung, Carl, 28

Jungletown (MacIver), **102**
junk, 19, 163. *See also* refuse

Kaiser, Charles, 154
Kalaidjian, Walter, 8
Kaplan, Amy, 81
Kazin, Alfred, 93
Keith, Michael, 7, 248n20
Kelly, Machine Gun, 237
Kennedy, Stetson, 76, 107–8
Kessler-Harris, Alice, 42–43
Kevles, Bettyann Holtzmann, 180, 275n193, 275n198
Keynes, John Maynard, 165, 273n141
Key West, 9, 21, 91–121; abandoned cigar factory in, **75**; Anglo-Afro-Cuban population of, 72, 74, 80, 95–96, 99–101, 116–17, 261n36, 263nn73–76; allegories of dismemberment and prosthetics in, 112–21, **113**, **119**, 266nn123, 126, 131, 136, 145; aquarium in, 86–87, **87**, 261n45; artists' colony of, 76–77, 92, 95–96, 262n61, 263nn73–77; author's quest in, 84–85, 90–92, 96–98, 101–3, 121; bridges, highways, and railroad links to, 72, 82–84, **83**, 112–14, **120**, 265n121; consumption in, 76–78; death, decay, and reanimation narratives of, 76–78, **97**, 98–101, 103–7, **104**, **106**, **109**, 264n82; FERA's cleanup and reconstruction of, 72–75, **73**, **79**, 80–84, 86, 110, 116, 260n4, 265n112; FERA's sterilization of, 74–75, **75**, 80–81, 116; gambling ban in, 74; geography of abjection and drift of, 108–12, 265n106; Hemingway in, 90–92, **91**; hurricane of 1935 in, 72–75, 82–84, **83**, **94**, 108–12, **109**; Isleno, ghost of, 107–8, 265n105; "New Birth" of, **73**; physical space of, 85–87; piracy myths of, 78–80, 260n23, 261n25; poetry, films, and stories of, 88–90, 92–93, 95–96; prostitution in, 101–3, **102**; queer culture in, 90–92, 262nn60–61; racial instability of, 94–96, 100–101, 263nn69–70; racism narratives of, 109–12; role of Cuba in, 80–81, 99–100; salvaged aesthetics of, 92–101, 263nn75–77, 264nn79, 93; salvage history of, 78–84; secession of the Conch Republic and, 121, 266n147; spatial fluidity of, 87–95, 263nn66–67; tourism in, **70**, **73**, 74, 77, 78, **84**, 86, **87**, 90–92, 105, 107, 261n45; Von Cosel's corpse-doll of, 103–7, **104**, **106**, 265n101. *See also* salvage
"Key West: An Island Sheaf" (Crane), 88–89, 261–62n48, 262n49
"Key West" (Bishop), 265n111
Key West Scrapbooks (Peirce), **91**, 93, **113**
Key West Tropical Aquarium, 86–87, **87**, 261n45
King, Rodney, 213
King Kong, 201–2, 217, **218**, 281n105
King of Kings, 217, **218**, 281n105
Klein, Melanie, 26n2
Klune, Ray, 201
Knadler, Stephen, 269n70
Kodak Theatre, **190**
Koestenbaum, Wayne, 161, 273n131
Koolhaas, Rem, 240–41
Kracauer, Siegfried, 213, 227, 228, 231–32, 280n91
Kristeva, Julia, 26, 108–9, 263n76, 265n106
Krizman, Serge, 279n50
Kroker, Arthur, 116
Kronenberger, Louis, 92
Kubelka, Peter, 277n22
Ku Klux Klan, 107–8, 111, 265n105

Labor and Desire (Rabinowitz), 7–8, 258n112
labor movements, 79, 110, 117, 249n30, 251n42, 261n25, 265nn109–10
Lacan, Jacques, 13, 23–24, 251n36, 252n62. *See also* symbolic order
LaGuardia, Fiorello, 171, 274nn150–51, 157
"Lai-Li" (Cowdery), 270n81
landscape, 249n21. *See also* place, places; site; space
Last Tycoon, The, 229–30
Las Vegas, 36, 193, 256n30, 277n11
"Late Air" (Bishop), 265n94
Lawrence, Jacob, 124–29; death imagery of, 127–29, 267n10; "Harlem" series of, **124**, 124–29, **128**, 267nn3–6, 9–10; influence of jazz and blues on, 124–27, 267n4; "The Life of John Brown" series, **126**; *The Migration of the Negro* series, 124–25, 266nn1–2, 267n7
Lebovici, Serge, 227
Le Corbusier (Jeanneret), 54, 237
Lefebvre, Henri, 6, 267n11
Lenox Lounge, Harlem, **130**
lesbianism. *See* queer constructions; sexuality

Let's Go to the Movies (Barry), 227
Levinas, Emmanuel, 230–32, 283n160, 283n162
Lewis, Grace Hegger, 33, 35, 44
Lewis, Sinclair, 33, 35
Lewis, Theophilus, 174
Lewis, Wyndham, 249n24
Libidinal Currents (Boone), 8
Life and Death of 9413: A Hollywood Extra (Florey), 191
Life of an American Fireman (Edison and Porter), 212, 214–15
"Life of John Brown, The" series (Lawrence), **126**
Light Is Calling (Morrison), 197
Lillard, Richard G., 32, 37, 47–48, 50, 52
Lincoln Highway, 39
Lind, Jenny, 55
literal, the: figurative language and, 144, 153, 252n62; letter and, 12–13, 23–25; literalist art object and, 25, 252n68; literality of the abject and, 109; New Literalism and, 252n68; representation and, 24
literal reading, 23–27, 88, 252n62, 252n68, 277n27
literary modernism, 7
literary montage, 1
litter, 23–24, 163, 182. *See also* refuse
Locke, Alain, 136, 271n90; on end of Harlem, 132; on *Fire!!*, 270n72; on Harlem riot of 1935, 171; historicist project of, 158–59, 271n90; racial uplift message of, 144
Lombardi, Marilyn May, 263n77
Long Way from Home, A (McKay), 134
Looking Glass, The, 138
looting, 172. *See also* consumption
Los Angeles. *See* Hollywood(land); sets, set design
Love of the Last Tycoon, The (Fitzgerald), 188, 195, 223–24, 229
Love of Zero, The (Florey), 193
L'Overture, Toussaint, 124
"Love Song of J. Alfred Prufrock, The" (Eliot), 183–84, 275n214
Luce, Clare Boothe, 8, 33, 34, 41–42
lynching, 107–8, 159
Lyotard, Jean-François, 8–9

Macaulay Company, 138, 275n195
Machado, Gerardo, 80–81
MacIver, Loren, 76, 93–94, **94**, **102**
MacLeish, Archibald, 76, 265n119
Magic Mountain, The (Mann), 179
Making the Modern (Smith), 43, 49–50
Malcolm X Boulevard (Harlem), 129, **130**, **185**
"Male X" (Thurman), 177–79, **178**, 275n187
Manderley set, 201
manic-depressive symptoms, 247n17. *See also* depression
"Manifesto of Futurism" (Marinetti), 229
Mann, Thomas, 179
Mann Act of 1910, 61, 259n119, 259n144
Mapes Hotel, demolition of, **68**
maps: of Harlem, **122**; of Hollywood, **186**; of Reno, **30**
Marcus Garvey clubs, **133**
Margaret Herrick Library of the Academy of Motion Pictures, 189
Marinetti, Filippo, 229
Marlow, Brian, 193
Marshman, D. M., 208
Martí, José, 100, 263n69
Marx, Karl, 34–35, 166
Marxist geography, 248n20
masculinity, 56–57, 63–65, 268n29; remasculinization and, 89. *See also* gender; sexuality
Massey, Doreen, 7
mass production, 32, 39, 67, 176, 221, 237, 251n33. *See also* Fordism; commodity; consumption
Matter and Memory (Bergson), 5, 28, 249n23, 270n78
Mayol, Pierre, 189
McCabe, Susan, 85, 263n77
McCarthy, Mary, 8, 33, 59–60, 258n112
McCoy, Horace, 202, 232–33
McFadden (publisher), 138
McKay, Claude, 134, 136, 171, 267n12, 269n42
Meditations on First Philosophy (Descartes), 203
melancholia, 4, 247n12, 268n24; melancholic cinema and, 207–8; mourning and, 166–67. *See also* depression
Melosi, Martin, 18
memory, 203–4, 270n78; Benjamin on, 146–47; dissociationist model of, 27–28, 145–46, 253n82, 270n78; forgetting and, 23, 109, 114; forgotten city and, 82, 120; nation formation and, 266n131; places of, 3, 21, 134, 136–38,

memory: places, of, *continued*
　268n25, 269nn44–45; "object-memory" and, 272n123; Proust's *mémoire involuntaire* and, 155; re-memberment and, 108–19; re-membrance and, 133–34; repetition in, 43, 146–47, 221–22, 270n84; in scrapbooks, 155–57, 272nn123–24, 126
Mencken, H. L., 145, 270n74
Menzies, William Cameron, 193
"Mercedes Hospital" (Bishop), 96, **97**
Mesmerist, The (Morrison), 197, **197**
Messenger, The, 138
mestizaje of Caribbean, 94–95, 99–101, 263nn69–70
mestizo poetics, 95, 111–12
metaphor, 59–61, 116, 155, 199, 203, 249n21, 277n30; dead, 24
method of refuse, 22–27; dissociationist logic of, 28–29, 253n82; Droysen's theory of remains and, 22; literal reading and, 23–27, 252n62; littoral reading and, 25–27; passivity as, 269n55; Virchow's refuse archeology and, 22–23, 252n53, 252n56
metonymy, 5, 115
metric films, 277n22
Metz, Christian, 228
Meyer, Adolf, 177
MGM "French Street" set, **220**
Michaels, Walter Benn, 8
"Migration of the Negro, The" (Lawrence series), 124–25, **126**, 266nn1–2, 267n7
Miller, Arthur, 33
Miller, Edward J., 237
Miller, J. Hillis, 119–20
Miller, Max, 35
Mills, Florence, 131, 267n13
miniature, 199–202, 208, 210, 217; Bishop's writing as, 118, 263n73; "New Deal in miniature," 79–80; "small discarded objects," 35. *See also* scale
Mind and the Film, The (Buckle), 204
Mitchell, Loften, 143
Mitchell, W. J. T., 116
Modernism and the Harlem Renaissance (Baker), 8
modernism of 1930s, 7–9
modernity. *See* depressive modernity; progressive modernity

Modernity at Sea (Casarino), 261n25
montage, 1
Moore, Marianne, 92, 111, 114
Moore, Owen, 32
moral cleanups, 74–75, 80–81, 116
Morgan, W. Townsend, 76
Morris, Lloyd, 254n5
Morris, Vivian, 131, 172, 274n165
Morrison, Bill, 196–97, **197**
Motion Picture Research Council, 225–26
Motion Pictures Producers and Distributors Association, 276n7
Motley, Archibald, 129
movement. *See* space
Movieland Wax Museum, 224–25
movies. *See* film; Hollywood(land); sets, set design
"Mrs. Massie on way to Reno" photograph, **47**
Mule Bone (Hughes and Hurston), 150
multiple personality disorder, 28
Murray, Albert, 153
Museum of Modern Art (MOMA), 263n73
music, 124–27, 153, 267n4, 271n107
My Man Godfrey, **15**, 20
Mystery of the Wax Museum, The, 204, **205**, 213
myth, 79, 183, 237, 271n91, 279n64

NAACP, 144
narrative, 47–48, 51, 127, 271n107, 254n12, 261n25, 267n2; in cinema, 201, 204–6, 212, 214–15, 221–24, 278n32, 278n44; gender and, 67–68, 115; queering of, 143. *See also* place, places
national imaginary, 14. *See also* place, places; symbolic order
Negro anthology (Cunard), 160–61, 268n27
"Negro Digs Up His Past, The" (Schomburg), 149
"Negro Literature" review, 138
Negro Renaissance. *See* Harlem
"Negros Burial Ground, The," 184–85
Nelson, Alice Dunbar, 134
Nelson, Baby Face, 237
Nelson, Cary, 8
Nevada, 55–57, 253n2, 254n8, 257n60. *See also* Reno
Nevada Transcontinental Exposition, 39
New Deal, 6, 9, 12, 236–42, 250n30; allegory of, 109–10; constructed homogeneity of, 109–12,

116; ideological foundations of, 72, 80; Key West project of, 72–75, 109–12, 116; microcosm of, 9; prison reform of, 236–38; Second New Deal, 11–14, 239; Tennessee Valley Authority and, 12. *See also* Federal Emergency Relief Administration
New Industrial Wives, 9, 45–46, 51–54, 66, 258n90
Newman, Charles W., 158, 160
New Negro anthology (Locke), 136
New Negro Renaissance. *See* Harlem
New Victory Highway, 39
New Woman who shops, 66–69, 259n151
New World A-Coming (Ottley), 134
New York City, 184–85. *See also* Harlem
"New York Correspondence School" (Johnson), 159–60, **161**, 272n126
New Yorker, The, unpublished cover of, **13**
New York Intellectuals, The (Wald), 7
"New York's Harlem has it's Housing Problems" photograph, **142**
Nietzsche, Friedrich, 145, 149, 269n45, 270n74
Nigger Heaven (Van Vechten), 132, 167
9/11 terrorist attacks, 2–3, 5, 243–44
1930s modernism, 7–9
Nipomo Dunes, 233, **233**
No One Man (Hughes), 57
Norse, Harold, 273n128
North, Michael, 8, 269n66
"Northern—Key West, A" (Bishop), 110–11
Not So Long Ago (Morris), 254n5
Nugent, Richard Bruce, 134, 136, 159, 168; dissociative voice of, in *Fire!!*, 141–48; hoarding of, 172; recordings of, 183, 271n106; Thurman's alleged plagiarism of, 151–53; Thurman's editing of, 151–53, **152**

"O Carib Isle!" (Crane), 98
"O Florida, Venereal Soil" (Stevens), 99
Olson, Charles, 76
Onassis, Jacqueline Kennedy, 183
O'Neil, Eugene, 33
"On Ethnographic Allegory" (Clifford), 264n82
One Way To Heaven (Cullen), 134
"On Harlem" (Nugent), 134
"on the nature of experience (or what i might have said)," 26
Opportunity journal, 174, 181

Opposite Sex, The, 258n90
Orvell, Miles, 20n7
Osborne, Peter, 6
Ott, Katherine, 177
Ottley, Roi, 134, 135
"Our America" (Martí), 263n69
Our America (Michaels), 8
Our Movie Made Children (Payne studies), 225–26, 228
Overseas Highway to Key West, 112–14, **120**, 266n147
Overseas Railroad to Key West, 72, **83**, 112

Page, Barbara, 118–19
Paine, Thomas, 249n28
Palés Matos, Luis, 111–12
Palmer, Robert, 271n107
Paramount Studios, 188, 214
Parkinson, Allen, 224–25
Parmer, Charles, 43–44
patriarchy 42, 44, 51–52, 81
Payne Fund studies, 225–26, 228, 282n133
Peirce, Waldo, 76, **91**, 93, **119**
Pellegrini, Ann, 268n29
Pentagon, The, **239**, 239–43; courtyard hot-dog stands of, **242**, 242–43; 9/11 terrorist attack on, 243–44; restricted access and secrecy in, 241–45, 284n31; size of, 239–41, 284n19; Total Information Awareness surveillance system of, 244–45; wasteland site of, 239, **243**
Pepper, Peggy, 222
Perkins, Maxwell, 140
performative, the, 68–69
Perloff, Marjorie, 25, 252n68
Pfieffer, Pauline, 90–92
Phillips, Adam, 224, 282n125
Phillips, Cabell, 260n17
philosophical history of place, 248n20
Pickford, Mary, 32, 193, 254n5
Pile, Steve, 7, 248n20
piracy, 78–80, 260n23, 261n25
Piute Pete, 48
place, places, 5–11, 248n20, 249n21, 249n26, 279n52; in aesthetics of everyday life, 8–9; in Benjamin's theory of standstill, 5, 11, 249n25; in Bergson's *durée*, 5, 249n23; in cinematic dissolve, 204–6; of consumption, 39–41, 256n31; in Depression discourse, 12;

INDEX **315**

place, places, *continued*
Derrida on, 136–38; displacement and emplacement and, 89, 124; flicker-effect of, 193; gendered constructions of, 64–69, **65**, 260n154; heterotopias, 276n2; inside and outside in, 194–96; Lacan on, 13; in Lawrence's Harlem paintings, **124**, 125–27, **126**, **128**, 267n11; Levinas's "there is" (*il y a*) and, 193, 231–32; matter of, 251n36; of memory, 134, 136–38, 268n25, 269nn44–45; in modernist constructs of space, 6; in movie sets, 199–202, 278n44; in opposition to space, 202; in postmodern spatiality, 6–7; production through imitation of, 67–69; reading of, 199–202; in relation to time, 205–6; in salvage aesthetics of Key West, 92–101; sitelessness of Hollywood and, 188–93, 276nn1–2, 5; space-time links in, 249n24; as translation of *lieu*, 137; Urry's construction of, 256n30. *See also* site; space
Place and the Politics of Identity (Keith), 248n20
plan of work for *Down in the Dumps*, 6–10
Platt, David, 21, 23
Platt Amendment of 1903, 81
"Plena de menéalo" (Palés Matos), 111–12
Poe, Edgar Allan, 13, 23–24, 251n36, 252n62
Poindexter, John M., 244–45
Pool Parlor (Lawrence), 267n10
Porter, Edwin S., 212
Porter, Katherine Anne, 33
postcards: of divorce, **36**, **52**, **63**, **65**; of Havana, **81**; of Reno and Reno Arch, **38**, **65**
Postmodern Condition, The (Lyotard), 8–9
postmodern spatiality, 6–7
Powell, Adam Clayton, Jr., 169, 274nn154–55
Powell, William, **15**, 20
primitivism, 167–68, 191, 193; in Bergson, 270n78
Principles of Psychology, The (James), 150
Pringle, Henry, 241
prison, 235–45; Alcatraz, **234**, **236**, 236–38, **237**, 241–42, 283n1, 284n11; classification of inmates in, 237–38; divorce metaphors of, 60–61; Gramsci's notebooks in, 257n56; as metaphor for prostitution, 59–61; New Deal reforms of, 236; Pentagon as, 241–43; secrecy surrounding, 238; tourism of, **234**, 238, 284n11
production. *See* Fordism; mass production
Production Code Administration (PCA), 225
progressive history, 21, 247n8, 266n2, 269n45

progressive modernity, 3, 5, 12–14, **15–16**, 34, 109, 248n18; concept of Renaissance and, 133; divorce rates in, 42–44, 256n33; employment of women in, 42–43; Fordism in, 9, 41, 42, 43–51, 60–61; of frontier America, 41, 56–57; in Reno, 35–41, 256n28, 256n30; specter of depression in, 5; speed metaphors of, 34–35, 255n16. *See also* depressive modernity
progressive obsolescence, 19, 52–53, 64
Progressivism, New Deal, 72
prosthesis, 114–21, 266n123; grafts and, 117, 266n135. *See also* amputation; body, the
prostitution: banality of, 47–48, 257n65; in *Fire!!*, 143–44; imprisonment metaphor of, 60–61; industrial version of, in Reno, 46–51, **47**, 59–60, 257nn59–61; in Key West, 101–3; Marxist commodification of, 50; streetwalking as, 60, 144
Proust, Marcel, 155
Psycho, 217
Psychoanalysis of Fire, The (Bachelard), 212–13
puns, 37, 88–89, 261n48
"Pure Happiness" (Bataille), 229
"Purloined Letter, The" (Poe), 13, 23–24, 251n36, 252n62
Putnam, Nina Wilcox, 75

queer constructions: in Eliot's objective correlative, 273n128; in Harlem culture, 129–30, 136, 142–48, 154, 158, 159, 161, 166–67, **167**, 269n70, 270n72; in Key West, 90–92, 262nn60–61; of pirate culture, 79; of Reno cure, 64–66, 259n141, 259n144
Quijano, Leo, 198

Rabaté, Jean-Michel, 141
Rabinowitz, Paula, 7–8, 258n112
racism: in Caribbean *mestizaje*, 94–95, 99–101, 184, 250n30, 263nn69–70; in FERA's revival of Key West, 109–12, 265n109, 265n112; of Jim Crow laws, 250n30; slavery and, 248n19. *See also* Harlem
radiology, 173, **174**, 179–80, 275n193, 275n198
Raffetto, Fiore, 57
railroads: Alcatraz Express, 237; in cinema history, 280n85; Divorcée Special train to Reno, **33**, 34–35, 37, **65**, 254n3; to Key West, 72, **83**, 110, 261n31

Rampersad, Arnold, 150

Rapp, William Jourdan, 131, 140–41, 144, 153, 224, 268n34

Rathje, William L., 21, 23

reading literally, 23–27, 252n62

Real Thing, The (Orvell), 20n7

Rebecca, 201, 221

Rediker, Marcus, 79

Refiguring Modernism (Scott), 8

refuse, 7, 12–14, 21–27, 250n33, 251n36; Bataille on, 216; Benjamin on, 7; in Collyer brothers' hoard, 155, 162–68, **164**, 273n139, 273n141; as commodity, 19–20, 255n19; conservation and recycling of, 20n4; etymology of terms for, 252n56; in Harlem, 168–69; history of trash and, 18–20, 251n36; insignificance of, 13–14; instability of, 12–13; Lacan on, 13, 23–24, 251n36; municipal house-cleaning movement and, 18; as object of inquiry, 22, 252nn53, 56, 58; realism in, 191; remains vs., 22–23; in Reno divorce culture, 35, 255n19; rubbish theory and, 250n33; in salvage economy of Key West, 72–74, 78–84; sanitary landfills and, 18; throwaway economy and, 19, 52–53; World War I veterans and, **109**, 109–10; writing and, 27, 75–76, 159, 162, 173, 182–83. *See also* archives; economics of trash; hoarding; junk; method of refuse; salvage; trash

refuse archeology, 22–23, 252n53, 252n56, 252n58

Relph, Edward, 248n20

remains, 184–85; place and, 137; as remnants (*überreste*), 22–23; trace as, 143, 204. *See also* cinders; corpses; death; refuse

Renaissance, Harlem. *See* Harlem

Reno, 32–69; author's quest in, 36–37, 41–42, 55–56, 57–59, **58**, 61–62, 69, 260n157; blurring of class boundaries in, 48–49; cartoons of, **33**; "cure factory" of, 62–69, 259nn141, 144, 151; divorce industry of, 9, 21, 32–35, 43–46, **44**, 49–51, **60**, 62–69, 253n2, 254n8; divorce jargon of, 37, 255nn25–26; frontier process of, 56–57; gender production in, 64–69, 256n33; imprisonment metaphors of, 60–61; landmarks of, **38**, **40**, **68**; map of, **30**; migration through, 57, 59–61, 258n106; pamphlets on, 54; progressive modernity in, 35–41, 256n28, 256n30, 256n31, 260n157; prostitution in, 46–49, **47**, 59–60, 257nn59–61; railroad quests to, **33**, 34–35, **65**, 254n3; Reno-vation in, 9, 45–46, 51–54, 258n90, 259nn150–51; residency requirement in, 32–33, 253n2; "Richmond Wife" exposé of, 59, 63; spatial production in, 256n30; as wasteland, 32. *See also* divorce

Reno Arch, postcards and drawings of, **38**

Reno Divorce Racket, The, **60**, 61

Reno Fever (Carmen), 44, 48, 53, 54, 60, 63, 64–66, 69

renovations. *See* cleanups and renovations; Reno repetition with a difference, 210–11; in blues and jazz, 125, 271n107; body doubles and stand-ins in, 215, 217–24, **222**, 282nn114–15, 122, 125; in film spectatorship, 278n38; Freud and, 282n125; in memory and *déjà vu*, 146–47, 175, 270n84, 281n112; in Reno-vation and remarriage, 9, 45–46, 258n90, 259nn150–51; in standing-set use, 221–22, 281n105, 281n107

Repression and Recovery (Nelson), 8

reproduction, 53, 56; copies and, 105, 107, 115, 172; homoerotic collaborations and, 161–62

research methods, 9–10

Revolutionary Imagination, The (Wald), 7

"Richmond wife" exposé, 59, 63

Riding, Laura, 262n50

riots. *See* Harlem

Rivera, Lino, 169–71

Riverside Hotel, Reno, 39, **40**

Riviera set, Hollywood, **192**

Rockefeller, John D., 14, 21, 252n49

Rockefeller, Laura Celestia Spelman (Mrs. John D. Rockefeller), 18

Roosevelt, Franklin D.: administration of, **13**, 250n30; on Forgotten Man, 14, 251n42; on hoarding, 165–66, 273n141; memorial to, **xx**; on Pentagon, 239; White House renovations by, 11–14, 249n28, 250n29. *See also* Great Depression; New Deal

Roosevelt, Theodore, 62

Rosenbaum, Susan, 263n73

Ross, Andrew, 241–42, 284n11

Roth, Martin, 194, 276n9

Rothstein, Arthur, **75**

Rothstein, Jerome Henry, **128**

Rowlinson, Matthew, 166

rubbish. *See* refuse

Rubbish Theory (Thompson), 250n33

Rubin, Gayle, 52

ruins, 74–75, 189
Rule, Jane, 259n144
Rushdie, Salman, 206–7, 221, 223, 232
Ryan, Con, 48

Sack, Robert David, 256n31
salvage, 9, 21, 78–84, 91–121; Benjamin's storms and wreckage of progress and, 84; Bishop's writing and, 263n77, 264n79; Caribbean aesthetic of, 8–9, 92–101, 264n82, 263nn75–77; death, decay, and reanimation in, 98–101, 103–7, 264n82; dis-membering and prosthetics allegories in, 112–21, **119**, 266nn123, 126, 131, 136, 145; ethnography, 264n82; FERA's cleanup and renovation of Key West and, **70**, 72–75, **73**, 105–6; practice of wrecking and, 78, 112; racial legacies in, 100–101. See also Key West; piracy
San Francisco Ferry Terminal, **234**
Sauer, Martha, 101
Savage, Augusta, 129
scale, 199–202, 248n20, 255n16. See also "Bigness"; miniature
Scheeline, H. H., 62
Schmidt, Dietmar, 12–13, 22, 251n36, 252nn53, 56, 58
Schoenberg, Arnold, 125
Schomburg, Arthur, 134, 135, 149, 158, 168
Schuyler, George, 169, 179–80
Schwartz, Delmore, 92
Schwartz, Vanessa R., 204
Scorcese, Martin, 189
Scott, Bonnie Kime, 8
scrapbooks and assemblings of Harlem, **133**, 134, 155–68; Cunard's anthology Negro and, 268n27; Fanon's theory and, 268n29; Johnson's "New York Correspondence School" and, 159–60, **161**, 272n126; memory in, 155–57, 272nn123–24, 126; Nugent's collection, 172; Van Vechten's collages, 157, 163, 166–67, **167**, 172. See also Gumby Scrapbooks
"Sea and Its Shore, The" (Bishop), 25–27, 264n79, 276n3
Second New Deal, 11–14, 251n43
secrecy, 37, 117, 238, 241–45, 284n31
"Secret Life of Things, The" (Brown), 264n79
Sedgwick, Eve, 243

Seifert, Charles, 124
Selected Articles on Marriage and Divorce (Johnsen), 63
self-publishing, 140
Selznick, David O., 201, 208–12, 217, 281n104
"Seminar on *The Purloined Letter*" (Lacan), 251n36
Sense of Things, A (Brown), 24
September 11, 2001, terrorist attacks, 2–3, 5, 243–44
series, 208–12; distinctions from theme and, 124–29; of Lawrence's paintings, 124–29, 266–67nn1–7; serial categorization and, 25; serial film and, 220, 281n105; serial music and, 125; seriality of collection and, 157
sets, set design, 9, 199–202, **218–20**, **226**, **233**; architects as designers of, 200–201, 279nn50–51, 281n106; cinematic dissolve of, 204–8, 227; color in, 206, 280n74; Cooper's narrative model of, 278n44; creation for destruction in, 198, 217–20; digital landscapes in, 279n52; in Disneyland, 193; disorientation and illusion in, 194–96, 277n27, 277n30, 278nn31–32; fire and smoke in, 212–17, **214**, **219**, 281n96, 281n104; in *Gone With the Wind*, **201**, 208–12, **219**; impact of sound on, 200, 208, 279n47; impact on American design of, 200, 202–3, 279nn50–51; location of *Intolerance* sets, **190**, 194, 200, 276n9; manipulation of scale in, 199–202, **201**; of Nipomo Dunes, 233, **233**; place making in, 199–202, 278n44; realism in, 191–93, **192**, 208–12, 279n51; Reno Stockade as, 47; spatial and temporal disorientation in, 194–96; special effects in, **197**, 200–202; standing, **220**, 220–21, 281n105, 281n112, 282n113; substitutability in, 215, 217–24, **222**; of Tarzan, 191–93. See also Hollywood(land)
Seven Mile Bridge, Key West, 114, **120**
sexuality: anal eroticism and, 166; anxiety about women's, 45, 50, 54, 256n33; bisexuality and, 89; collaboration and homoeroticism and, 160–62; Fordist, 50, 63; lesbian desire, 64–66, 118–19, 270n81; necrophilia and, 104; queer, 63–67, 166–67, 269n70, 270n72; sex appeal and, 43; sexual dissatisfaction and, 48. See also gender; queer constructions
Shadowed Dreams (Honey), 183, 275n210

Shakespeare in Harlem (Hughes), 181
Shanks, Michael, 21, 23
Sheila Goes to Reno (Johnson), 54
Sheldon, Roy, 19
Shew, William D., 45
Showers, Pearl, 135
Show People, 222, 280n76, 282n115
Shuffle Along (Miller and Lyle), 267n13
Simmel, Georg, 231–32
Since Yesterday (Allen), 78
site, 29, 47, 116, 136–38; narrative and, 47; translation of *lieu* as, 137. *See also* place, places
Sklar, Robert, 276n9
slavery, 61, 99–100, 138, 146, 248n19; trope of slave suicide and, 276n214
Smith, Adam, 165
Smith, Bessie, 4, 135, 247n12, 275n214
Smith, Neil, 7
Smith, Terry, 43, 49–50
"Smoke, Lilies, and Jade" (Nugent), 142–43, 147
smoke and smoking, 215–16, 281n112
social geography, 248n20
"Social Utility of Sensational News" (Stevens), 254n5
Soja, Edward, 7
somnambulism, 253n82
Sontag, Susan, 80, 175
Souls of Black Folk, The (Du Bois), 150
Southernmost Point, The (Key West), **84**
souvenirs, 103; collections and, 155–57. *See also* Harlem; hoarding; scrapbooks and assemblings of Harlem
space: of abject, 108–12, 265n106; as commodity, 220; fluidity of Key West and, 87–95, 263nn66–67; inside out and outside in and, 194–98; in performance of social power, 12, 250n31; postmodern spatiality and, 6–7; principle of drift in Key West and, 86; regulation of, 46, 49, 257n60; spatial boundaries and, 46; spatial implications of divorce and, 49–51; spatial metaphor and, 12, 14; spatial modernism and, 6; spatial movement and, 34, 59, 61, 88, 127, 193, 245, 272n123; spatial reconciliation and, 280n76; time and, 5, 46, 194–95, 204, 214–15, 278n44; universal, 5. *See also* place, places; scale; temporality
Spackman, Barbara, 166

Spaniards Landing at Cayo Hueso (mural), **79**
Spanish-Cuban-American War, 81
spectrality, 136–40, 146, 179–81, 196–98, 249n26, 275n214. *See also* ghostwriting; haunting; X rays
spectatorship, 196–98, 213–17, 225–33, 280n85, 280n91, 282n133, 283nn147, 160, 162
Spirit of Youth and City Streets, The (Addams), 226, 282n133
Spivak, Gayatri, 127
stand-ins. *See* repetition with a difference
standstill, 5, 11, 23, 27, 247n12, 249n25, 252n60
Staples, Brent, 185
Star Is Born, A, 195–96, 277n10, 280n76
Stern, Lesley, 221, 281n112
Stevens, John D., 254n5
Stevens, Wallace, 8, 27, 76; modernism of, 27; resistance of ambiguity of Key West by, 89–90, 99, 119–20, 262nn52–54, 263n75, 266n145
Stewart, Harry, 257n60
Stewart, Susan, 155–57
Stockade, the (Reno), 46–48, **47**, 50–51, 257n60
Stone, Julius, 72–74, 76–77, 96–98
Strangers to Ourselves (Kristeva), 263n76
Strater, Mike, 76
"Strenuous Life" of Teddy Roosevelt, 62, 63
strolling, 143
"Struggle to Live, The" (Woodward and Woodward), 199
"Studio" (MacIver), 93–94, **94**
suicide, 4, 26, 195–96, 247n16, 276n214
Sullivan, Noel, 135, 268n30
Sumner, William Graham, 251n42
Sunset Boulevard, 207–8
Survey Graphic, 19–20
Susman, Warren, 149, 260n4, 271n96
symbolic order, 12, 24, 199, 207; Depression and, 21; the Real and, 28; reality and, 21

Taussig, Michael, 243
Taylor, William Desmond, 188, 276n7
Taylorization. *See* Fordism
Technicolor, 206, 280n74
Temporary Address: Reno (Baldwin), 46, 48, 257n64
Ten Commandments, The (film), 9, 217, 233, **233**

temporality, 5, 136, 159, 193, 204–6; "archive as stored time" and, 198; irreversibility of time and, 204–5, 230, 247n12, 280n78; materiality and, 278n31; time-space relationship and, 5, 46, 194–95, 204, 214–15, 252n49; transience and, 250n33; wasting time and, 35
Tennessee Valley Authority, 12
Terrible Honesty (Douglas), 8
Terrorism Information and Prevention System, 244–45
Thalberg, Irving, 223–24
20th Century Fox studios, 214
Theory of Film (Balázs), 195
"Theory" (Stevens), 90
They Shoot Horses Don't They?, 232–33
Thinking Fascism (Carlston), 8
This is Harlem (Lawrence), 127–29, **128**
Thompson, Louise, 140–41, 181
Thompson, Michael, 12, 250n33
Thornton, Mildred, 135
Thurman, Wallace, 131, 132, **147**, 159, **178**; aliases of, 140; alleged plagiarism of, 151–53; autobiography of, 134, 144–45, 148, 151; dissociative aesthetic of, 136–53, **139**, **152**, 269n55, 270n78, 270n84, 271n103; editorial experience of, 138, 173, 275n195; *Harlem* play of, 131, 140–41, 144, 153, 268n34, 272n108; Hughes and, 138, 140, 173; illness and death of, 173–81, **177**, **178**, 275n187; individualism of, 144–45, 269n70; marriage and divorce of, 140–41, 181; on movie version of *Harlem*, 224; political philosophy of, 145, 147–48, 270n74; on Van Vechten's view of Harlem, 149; West on, 138
Till, Karen E., 249n26, 268n25
"Time after Time" (Johnson), 183–84, 275n214
Todd, Ellen Wiley, 66
To Have and Have Not (Hemingway), 103, 262n51; critical response to, 92–93; death and dismemberment in, 98–99, 116–21, 266n136, 266n145; FERA in Key West and, 77, 110, 265n109; piracy tropes in, 260n23
Tolson, Melvin, 136
Tombstones (Lawrence), 267n10
Toomer, Jean, 157
Total Information Awareness surveillance system, 244–45
tourism: in Harlem, 129–31; in Hollywood, 188; in Key West, 72–74, **73**, **77**, 86, 120, 266n147; in Reno, 36, 67–68; in Virginia City, 55–56; tourist attractions and, 55, 86–87, 188
trash, 35, 148; brief history of, 18–20; trash pickers and, 2, 25. *See also* refuse
Tratner, Michael, 232
True Story, The, 138–40
Truman, Harry S, 166
Truth about Hollywood, The, 223, 282n124
Tschumi, Bernard, 74–75
Tuan, Yi-Fu, 248n20
tuberculosis, 76, 103, 158, 173–81, **178**, 274n176; libidinal energies and, 177; race and, 176–77; Sontag on, 76, 175
Tubman, Harriet, 124
Turner, Frederick Jackson, 56–57
Twain, Mark, 55
Twin Towers, 2–3, 5

UCLA film archives, 189
unbuilding, 256n28
"Unfinished Masterpieces" (Coleman), 173
United States: gendered constructions of, 106, 265n104; imperialism of, and Cuba, 80–81, 99–100
Universal Studios, 214, 217
Untitled (f.x. profumo) by Ray Johnson, **161**
Urban League, 144, 174
Urry, John, 256n30
U.S. Route 1, 112–14
Usai, Paolo Cherchi, 197–98, 278n38
USA trilogy (Dos Passos), 230, 283n154

vacant lots, 19, 69, 163, 273n135
Valdes, Gregorio, 263n73
Valentino, Rudolph, 188
Van Deusen, Robert O., 86
Van Gogh, Vincent, 115, 266n126
van Notten, Eleonore, 270n74
Van Vechten, Carl: archival work of, on Harlem, 131, 135, 141; *Nigger Heaven*, 132, 149, 167; scrapbook collages of, 134, 157, 163, 166–67, **167**, 172
Vasquez, Raul, 96–98, 264n80
Vicious Modernism (De Jongh), 149
Vidor, King, 222
Vincent Sanitarium, 177

Virchow, Rudolph, 22–23, 252n56
Virginia City, Nevada, 55–56
Vismann, Cornelia, 22
Von Cosel, Carl Tanzler, 103–7, **104**, **106**, 265n101

Wajcman, Judy, 54
Wald, Alan M., 7
Walker, A'Leila, 131
Walker, Jan, 244–45
Walsh, William S., 228
Warner Brothers Studio, 214, 217
Washington, Booker T., 150
wasteland, 4, 18, 32, 254n4. *See also* place, places
"Wasteland, The" (Eliot), 254n4
waste products, 32 35, 216, 250n33; consumption and, 39; wasting time and, 35. *See also* refuse
wax: analogies of cinematic dissolve with, 204–8, 213; as metaphor for Hollywood, 203–8, 279n54; museums, 204, **205**, 224–25; in myth, 279n64
Wedding, The (West), 183
We Lift Our Voices (Cowdery), 270n81
Welles, Orson, 33
Welles, Sumner, 81
Wells, H. G., 179
Weschler, Lawrence, 196
West, Dorothy, 136, 138, **147**, 183
West, Nathanael, 9, 207–8, 212, 227
West Cure, 62–63
"West Indies, Ltd" (Guillén), 99–100
Weyl, Carl Jules, 200
What Price Hollywood?, 277n10, 280n76, 282n124
Wheeler, Leslie, 275n214
Wheeler, Lyle, **201**
Whirlpool of Reno, The (Hamlin), 35–36, 51, 54
White House renovations, 11–14, 249n28, 250n29
white slavery, 61
"Who Murdered the Vets?" (Hemingway), 109–10
Wigley, Mark, 114, 256n28
Wilder, Billy, 208
Williams, Tennessee, 76, 114–16, 121, 262n61, 266n123
Williams, William Carlos, 24
Williamsburg, Virginia, 14, 20, 21, 252n49
Wilson, Edmund, 78

Wingfield, George, 39
Wirth, Thomas H., 151, 172, 271n106
Wizard of Oz, The, 280n71; color in, 206, 280n4; disorienting dissolves in, 206–7, 280n73, 280n76; dream states in, **226**, 227, 232; fire and smoke in, 214, 215, 281n96; stand-ins in, 221
Wollen, Peter, 42
women: decay and reanimation of, 76–78, 98–101, 103–7, 264n82; employment of, 42–43; housework and scientific management and, 54; motherhood and children and, 53–54; writers in Harlem and, 132, 268n20, 273n131. *See also* divorce; gender; sexuality
Women, The, 34, **34**; consumption as cure in, 66–67, **67**, 259n152; Fordist Reno-vation and remarriage in, 51–52, 256n42; motherhood and children in, **53**, 53–54; musical remake of, 258n90; sound stage set of, 194
Women of the Left Bank (Benstock), 8
Woodson, Carter G., 149, 158, 271n94
Woodward, Stacey and Horace, 199
"The Work of Art in the Age of Mechanical Reproduction" (Benjamin), 195, 277n27
Works Progress Administration (WPA): Key West project of, 72–75; tourist guidebooks of, 12, 188; writing of, on Harlem, 134. *See also* Federal Emergency Relief Administration
World Fair of 1933, 224
World Tomorrow, The, 138
World Trade Center, 2–3, 5, 243
World War I: divorce rates after, 42; veterans of, **109**, 109–10
wreckage of progress. *See* Benjamin, Walter; progressive modernity; salvage
Wright, Louis T., 176–77
Wright, Richard, 131
Writing from the Left (Wald), 7
"Writing of Harlem, The" (Thurman and Rapp), 153, 272n108

X rays, 173, 179–80, 275n193, 275n198; in Harlem clinic, **174**

Yaeger, Patricia, 159, 272nn123–24
Yale University, James Weldon Johnson Collection of, 134–35, 141, 167

JANI SCANDURA is associate professor in the English Department and the co-founder of the Space and Place Research Collective at the University of Minnesota. She is coeditor of *Modernism, Inc: Body, Memory, Capital* (2001).

Library of Congress
Cataloging-in-Publication Data
Scandura, Jani.
Down in the dumps : place, modernity, American Depression / Jani Scandura.
p. cm.
Includes bibliographical references and index.
ISBN 978-0-8223-3654-9 (cloth : alk. paper)
ISBN 978-0-8223-3666-2 (pbk. : alk. paper)
1. United States—Civilization—1918–1945.
2. United States—Civilization—1945– 3. National characteristics, American. 4. Depressions—1929—United States. 5. Depression, Mental—Social aspects—United States. 6. Memory—Social aspects—United States. 7. Reno (Nev.)—History—20th century—Sources. 8. Key West (Fla.)—History—20th century—Sources.
9. Harlem (New York, N.Y.) —History—20th century—Sources. 10. Hollywood (Los Angeles, Calif.) —History—20th century—Sources.
I. Title.
E169.S352 2007
973.91—dc22   2007026683